OpenGL ES 3.0 Cookbook

Over 90 ready-to-serve, real-time rendering recipes on Android and iOS platforms using OpenGL ES 3.0 and GL shading language 3.0 to solve day-to-day modern 3D graphics challenges

Parminder Singh

PUBLISHING

BIRMINGHAM - MUMBAI

OpenGL ES 3.0 Cookbook

First published: May 2015

Production reference: 1270515

Published by Packt Publishing Ltd.
Livery Place
35 Livery Street
Birmingham B3 2PB, UK.

ISBN 978-1-84969-552-7

www.packtpub.com

Credits

Author
Parminder Singh

Reviewers
Tomasz Adam Dzieniak
Brian Gatt
Alin Loghin
Abhinav Singhal

Commissioning Editor
Erol Staveley

Acquisition Editors
James Jones
Purav Motiwalla

Content Development Editor
Athira Laji

Technical Editor
Shashank Desai

Copy Editors
Relin Hedly
Karuna Narayanan

Project Coordinator
Harshal Ved

Proofreaders
Stephen Copestake
Safis Editing

Indexer
Monica Ajmera Mehta

Graphics
Disha Haria

Production Coordinators
Nilesh R. Mohite
Alwin Roy

Cover Work
Alwin Roy

About the Author

Parminder Singh is a senior 3D graphics engineer at Continental Automotive, Singapore. He also works as a part-time freelancer. In 2006, Parminder obtained his CSE degree from Punjab Technical University.

He is a strong believer of design simplicity. In his opinion, this is a key factor that plays an important role in building scalable and manageable products. With this philosophy and as a passionate 3D architect, he has worked in the fields of network simulations, geomodeling, navigation, automotive, and infotainment systems. His research interests include GPU-based real-time rendering, geospatial terrain rendering, screen-spaced techniques, real-time dynamic shadows, scientific visualization, scene graphs, and anti-aliasing techniques.

He is an OpenGL ES trainer and a member of the Khronos Group. Parminder loves to take up challenges related to real-time rendering. His current research and work includes futuristic implementation for next-generation graphics in the automobile domain in order to create stunning data, user interface, and visualization effects (merging 2D and 3D concepts). His hobbies include cooking, traveling, sharing knowledge, and exploring the possibilities of applied physics and mathematics.

Feel free to reach Parminder at https://www.linkedin.com/in/parmindersingh18.

Acknowledgments

First and foremost, I would like to thank my wife, Gurpreet, for her love, encouragement, and extreme patience during the book writing process, which mostly occurred on vacations, weekends, and overnights. I dedicate this book to my parents and brother; without their support, this book wouldn't have been possible.

I wish to extend my special thanks to Amit Dubey for his guidance and directions, which always proved helpful. I would like to express my gratitude to Vijay Sharma. I learned ways to handle complex problems with a simple approach from him. I am highly grateful to Saurav Bhattacharya, Mohit Sindwani, and Tarun Nigam for being highly supportive during the course of this book. I am also very thankful to Dr. Ulrich Kabatek for providing me flexible timings, which helped me finalize this title.

I acknowledge the contribution of the entire Packt Publishing team and external reviewers. Their constant feedback and constructive comments have helped me take this book to another level. I am grateful to James Jones and Harshal Ved for their support on this title. A big thanks to Shashank Desai, whose coordination helped us meet the deadlines on time. I would also like to thank Athira Laji who has done a remarkable job over the year to bring the best out of this title. Her constant motivation, tracking deliverables, self-correction, and review comments has contributed a lot to this title.

I would like to express my gratitude to Shraddha Parganiha, Neeraj Sahu, and my close friends, Nidhi Pasricha, Jitendra Verma, and Rubina Hasrat, for their help and support during the time when I needed them the most.

Last but not least, I would like to say thanks to the "Gang of four"—Abhinav Singhal, Nisha Dawar, Smitha Nair, and myself—for all the happy moments we shared together. Cheers!

About the Reviewers

Tomasz Adam Dzieniak has been coding since 1998 (for 16 years), which equals two-third of his life. He has mastered languages such as C++11, C#, Java, HLSL, JavaScript, and Python. Currently, he is working towards improving his skills in Ruby and Swift programming languages.

In 2013, he got his bachelor's of science degree in applied informatics at the Nicolaus Copernicus University, faculty of physics, astronomy, and applied informatics. He holds the position of senior developer and software architect, working with technologies based on C++, Java, and Python languages.

In his spare time, he works with autonomous systems, crashing more and more drones. Also, he works on a few independent projects, such as mobile games (dedicated to Android and iOS platforms) and business platforms (client-server solutions) on demand. After all the coding stuff, he reads books and goes jogging.

Brian Gatt is a software developer who holds a bachelor's degree in computer science and artificial intelligence from the University of Malta. He also holds a master's degree in computer games and entertainment from Goldsmiths, the University of London. From the time he was introduced to OpenGL ES at the university level, he developed an interest in graphics programming. He likes to keep himself updated with the latest graphics that APIs have to offer, native C++ programming, and game development techniques.

Alin Loghin is a video programmer with a passion for computer graphics and has been in the field for almost 3 years now. He's also a freelancer 3D artist and has combined this modeling/texturing along with its technical side (post processing via HLSL) in the modding scene to become the lead artist for the Europa Barbarorum series.

He currently works for Telenav as a senior C++ engineer, focusing on the rendering side (OpenGL ES1, ES2, and GLSL) for a navigation library, which is used by TripAdvisor, Bosch, and other mobile or automotive clients.

He was mainly responsible for making the switch to ES2 from ES1, performance, and visual improvements on various platforms, such as iOS and Android. He has also worked on porting the library for the tile server project used to render hundreds of tiles per second.

Abhinav Singhal is a software developer who holds a master's degree in computer science from the University of Southern California. He has mainly worked in the networking domain for nearly 6 years with a focus on C and C++. Apart from his job, he reads a lot on topics pertaining to philosophy and cognitive processes to better understand how people think and react, which helps him to design software in a better way.

www.PacktPub.com

Support files, eBooks, discount offers, and more

For support files and downloads related to your book, please visit www.PacktPub.com.

Did you know that Packt offers eBook versions of every book published, with PDF and ePub files available? You can upgrade to the eBook version at www.PacktPub.com and as a print book customer, you are entitled to a discount on the eBook copy. Get in touch with us at service@packtpub.com for more details.

At www.PacktPub.com, you can also read a collection of free technical articles, sign up for a range of free newsletters and receive exclusive discounts and offers on Packt books and eBooks.

https://www2.packtpub.com/books/subscription/packtlib

Do you need instant solutions to your IT questions? PacktLib is Packt's online digital book library. Here, you can search, access, and read Packt's entire library of books.

Why subscribe?

- ▸ Fully searchable across every book published by Packt
- ▸ Copy and paste, print, and bookmark content
- ▸ On demand and accessible via a web browser

Free access for Packt account holders

If you have an account with Packt at www.PacktPub.com, you can use this to access PacktLib today and view 9 entirely free books. Simply use your login credentials for immediate access.

Table of Contents

Preface

OpenGL ES 3.0 is a royalty free, hardware-accelerated graphics rendering application programming interface for embedded systems. It is used for visualizing 2D and 3D graphics with the modern programmable graphics pipeline. "Write once, use anywhere" is truly the power behind OpenGL ES, which has made it an embedded industry standard. OpenGL ES 3.0 is a cross-platform graphics library and opens its gates to many other cutting-edge technologies, such as parallel processing libraries (OpenCL) and digital image processing (OpenCV) that works in conjunction with many other open community solutions.

The main strength of this book is that it covers development of real-time rendering graphics and visualization development using OpenGL ES 3.0 from scratch. It lets the user know how to define the framework for the OpenGL ES 3.0 application. These are some of the techniques that make this book entirely different from other books available on the market. The idea behind this book is to give you an in-depth knowledge of this new version of graphics API and use it to implement computer graphics fundamentals and advance concepts from scratch using Android and iOS as embedded platforms. This book covers a lot of ground, from basic concepts of modern 3D graphics to advanced real-time rendering techniques using OpenGL ES 3.0.

What this book covers

Chapter 1, *OpenGL ES 3.0 on Android/iOS*, takes you through the process of how to develop the Android and iOS OpenGL ES 3.0 application. This chapter shows you how to load and compile a shader program apart from the process to program shaders in GL shading language 3.0.

Chapter 2, *OpenGL ES 3.0 Essentials*, provides you with a detailed description of the basic concepts that are required to understand 3D graphics and implement them using OpenGL ES 3.0. We will build prototypes using the GLPI framework and implement touch events and scene with model, view, and projection analogy.

Chapter 3, New Features of OpenGL ES 3.0, helps you understand the various new features introduced in OpenGL ES 3.0 and GL shading language 3.0. This chapter tells you how to manage variable attributes with qualifiers and render multiple objects with geometry instancing and primitives with primitive restart.

Chapter 4, Working with Meshes, teaches you how to create simple meshes using Blender, which is an open source 3D modeling tool. In addition, this chapter covers various aspects of the 3D mesh model that will be helpful to render them in 3D graphics. This chapter also teaches how to use the created mesh model in OpenGL ES 3.0 applications.

Chapter 5, Light and Materials, introduces the concepts of light and materials in 3D graphics. It also covers some important common illumination techniques, such as Phong and Gouraud shading, which will help you implement realistic looking lighting models in computer graphics.

Chapter 6, Working with Shaders, gives you an in-depth understanding on the shaders programming technique. It discusses various techniques that can be implemented using the vertex and fragment shader, revealing their capabilities. This chapter helps you play with fragments by programing them using procedural shaders.

Chapter 7, Textures and Mapping Techniques, sheds some light on textures, which is a very interesting part of the 3D computer graphics study. Texturing is a technique in which the surface of a 3D mesh model is painted with static images. This chapter is all about image texturing and explains its various applications in the field of 3D computer graphics. This chapter covers ample techniques on mapping, such as environment, bump, displacement mapping, and so on.

Chapter 8, Font Rendering, provides a detailed description on how to build the font engine and render different languages with Harfbuzz and text on Head Up Display (HUD).

Chapter 9, Postscreen Processing and Image Effects, unfolds the endless possibilities of scene-based effects and image-based effects, which are widely used in the field of data visualization and after effects. This includes applications such as edge detection, image blurring, real-time glow, emboss effect, and so on.

Chapter 10, Scene Management with Scene Graphs, introduces a scene graph paradigm that allows you to program and manage complex scenes efficiently. This chapter will help you create a small architecture that allows you to manage multiple scenes. Each scene consists of multiple lights, cameras, and models.

Chapter 11, Anti-aliasing Techniques, tells you how to implement fast approximate anti-aliasing (FXAA), adaptive anti-aliasing, and anti-aliased circle geometry.

Chapter 12, Real-time Shadows and Particle System, shows you how to implement shadows using shadow mapping and improve it with percentile closer filtering and variance shadow mapping technique. It also discusses the basics of particle rendering. This chapter teaches you the transform feedback with sync objects and fence, which help you implement high-performance, GPU-driven, and real-time graphics applications.

Appendix, Supplementary Information on OpenGL ES 3.0, covers all the basic requirements that we need to develop OpenGL ES 3.0 applications on the iOS and Android platforms. This chapter teaches you two ways of Android application development with Android ADT and Android Studio. This also provides you a simple overview of OpenGL ES 3.0 architectures. This overview also helps you understand the technical jargon of various computer graphics terminology.

What you need for this book

OpenGL ES 3.0 is platform-independent; therefore, you can use any platform machines, such as Windows, Linux, or Mac, for your application development.

Who this book is for

If you are new to OpenGL ES or have some experience in 3D graphics, then this book will be extremely helpful in raising your expertise level from a novice to professional. The book implements more than 90 recipes to solve everyday challenges, helping you transition from a beginner to a professional.

Sections

This book contains the following sections:

Getting ready

This section tells us what to expect in the recipe, and describes how to set up any software or any preliminary settings needed for the recipe.

How to do it...

This section characterizes the steps to be followed for "cooking" the recipe.

How it works...

This section usually consists of a brief and detailed explanation of what happened in the previous section.

There's more...

It consists of additional information about the recipe in order to make the reader more anxious about the recipe.

See also

This section may contain references to the recipe.

Conventions

In this book, you will find a number of styles of text that distinguish between different kinds of information. Here are some examples of these styles, and an explanation of their meaning.

Code words in text, database table names, folder names, filenames, file extensions, pathnames, dummy URLs, user input, and Twitter handles are shown as follows: "Create a vertex shader file called `SimpleTextureVertex.glsl`."

A block of code is set as follows:

```
glTexImage2D ( target, 0, GL_RGBA,  memData.width,
memData.height,0,GL_RGBA,GL_UNSIGNED_BYTE,memData.bitsraw);
```

New terms and **important words** are shown in bold. Words that you see on the screen, in menus or dialog boxes for example, appear in the text like this: "Provide a path to include the header files for the Harfbuzz project using **Build Settings | Search Paths | Header Search Paths**."

 Warnings or important notes appear in a box like this.

 Tips and tricks appear like this.

Reader feedback

Feedback from our readers is always welcome. Let us know what you think about this book—what you liked or may have disliked. Reader feedback is important for us to develop titles that you really get the most out of.

To send us general feedback, simply send an e-mail to `feedback@packtpub.com`, and mention the book title via the subject of your message.

If there is a topic that you have expertise in and you are interested in either writing or contributing to a book, see our author guide on `www.packtpub.com/authors`.

Customer support

Now that you are the proud owner of a Packt book, we have a number of things to help you to get the most from your purchase.

Downloading the example code

You can download the example code files for all Packt books you have purchased from your account at http://www.packtpub.com. If you purchased this book elsewhere, you can visit http://www.packtpub.com/support and register to have the files e-mailed directly to you.

Downloading the color images of this book

We also provide you a PDF file that has color images of the screenshots/diagrams used in this book. The color images will help you better understand the changes in the output. You can download this file from https://www.packtpub.com/sites/default/files/downloads/5527OT_ColoredImages.pdf.

Errata

Although we have taken every care to ensure the accuracy of our content, mistakes do happen. If you find a mistake in one of our books—maybe a mistake in the text or the code—we would be grateful if you could report this to us. By doing so, you can save other readers from frustration and help us improve subsequent versions of this book. If you find any errata, please report them by visiting http://www.packtpub.com/submit-errata, selecting your book, clicking on the **Errata Submission Form** link, and entering the details of your errata. Once your errata are verified, your submission will be accepted and the errata will be uploaded to our website or added to any list of existing errata under the Errata section of that title.

To view the previously submitted errata, go to https://www.packtpub.com/books/content/support and enter the name of the book in the search field. The required information will appear under the **Errata** section.

Piracy

Piracy of copyright material on the Internet is an ongoing problem across all media. At Packt, we take the protection of our copyright and licenses very seriously. If you come across any illegal copies of our works, in any form, on the Internet, please provide us with the location address or website name immediately so that we can pursue a remedy.

Please contact us at copyright@packtpub.com with a link to the suspected pirated material.

We appreciate your help in protecting our authors, and our ability to bring you valuable content.

Questions

You can contact us at questions@packtpub.com if you are having a problem with any aspect of the book, and we will do our best to address it.

1
OpenGL ES 3.0 on Android/iOS

In this chapter, we will cover the following recipes:

- ▶ Programming shaders in OpenGL ES shading language 3.0
- ▶ Loading and compiling a shader program
- ▶ Linking a shader program
- ▶ Checking errors in OpenGL ES 3.0
- ▶ Using the per-vertex attribute to send data to a shader
- ▶ Using uniform variables to send data to a shader
- ▶ Programming OpenGL ES 3.0 Hello World Triangle
- ▶ Using JNI on Android to communicate with C/C++
- ▶ Developing an Android OpenGL ES 3.0 application
- ▶ Developing an iOS OpenGL ES 3.0 application

Introduction

OpenGL ES 3.0 stands for Open Graphics Library for embedded systems version 3.0. It is a set of standard API specifications established by the Khronos Group. The Khronos Group is an association of members and organizations that are focused on producing open standards for royalty-free APIs. OpenGL ES 3.0 specifications were publicly released in August 2012. These specifications are backward compatible with OpenGL ES 2.0, which is a well-known de facto standard for embedded systems to render 2D and 3D graphics. Embedded operating systems such as Android, iOS, BlackBerry, Bada, Windows, and many others support OpenGL ES.

OpenGL ES 3D APIs are the stripped-down version of OpenGL, which is a cross-platform standard 3D API on a desktop environment for Linux, various flavors of UNIX, Mac OS, and Windows. This stripped-down version is mainly focused on providing the capabilities of 3D graphics as per embedded system requirements such as low-power consumption, limited processing capabilities, and small memory footprints.

The OpenGL ES 2.0/3.0 graphics library is shading-language compliant, unlike its predecessor 1.1. The major difference between OpenGL ES 1.1 and OpenGL ES 2.0/3.0 is the graphics pipeline architecture. The graphics pipeline framework for the former is known as a fixed function pipeline, and for the latter, it is a programmable pipeline. These frameworks are explained in the following table:

OpenGL ES version	Architecture pipeline type	Need shader
1.1	Fixed function pipeline	No
2.0 and 3.0	Programmable pipeline	Yes

A pipeline is a set of events that occur in a predefined fixed sequence, from the moment input data is given to the graphic engine to the output generated data for rendering the frame. A frame refers to an image produced as an output on the screen by the graphics engine.

Each frame in a fixed function pipeline architecture is generated by a fixed set of algorithms, calculations, and sequences of events. You can only specify what you want, but not how it will be calculated. For example, if you are interested in applying some light shading on your solid sphere model, then you will need to specify the light position, its intensity, material properties, and other similar attributes. The fixed pipeline uses these inputs and takes care of all the physics and mathematics required to generate the light shading. Therefore, you don't need to worry, as the how factor is fully abstracted. The good side of the fixed function pipeline is that it is very easy to understand and quick to program.

In contrast, with the programmable pipeline architecture, you not only need to specify what you want to achieve, but you also need to mention how to implement it. This pipeline also provides extraordinary capabilities through shaders. Shaders are the special programs that control your scene's geometry and shading appearance. For example, in order to achieve the same light-shading effect on solid sphere, you must know the basics of physics and mathematics in order to program the light-shading techniques. Since you are programming the behavior of light shading, you can fully control it. This opens up endless possibilities to create infinite shading effects. Shaders are super fast. They execute rendering in parallel-processing mode using **Graphics Processing Unit** (**GPU**).

Now, the question is if fixed function pipeline is doing all the light physics and mathematical abstraction, then why do we need to understand it for programmable pipelines? The reason is with fixed pipeline, we can only do finite graphics capabilities, and it cannot be used to produce realistic graphics effectively. However, the programmable pipeline opens endless possibilities and opportunities to produce state-of-art graphics rendering.

This chapter will provide OpenGL ES 3.0 development on Android and iOS. We will begin this chapter by understanding the basic programming of the OpenGL ES 3.0 with the help of a simple example to render a triangle on the screen. You will learn how to set up and create your first application on both platforms step by step.

Understanding EGL: The OpenGL ES APIs require the EGL as a prerequisite before they can effectively be used on the hardware devices. The EGL provides an interface between the OpenGL ES APIs and the underlying native windowing system. Different OS vendors have their own ways to manage the creation of drawing surfaces, communication with hardware devices, and other configurations to manage the rendering context. EGL provides an abstraction, how the underlying system needs to be implemented in a platform-independent way. The platform vendor's SDK provides an implementation of EGL through their own framework. These can be directly used in the application to accomplish the development task quickly. For example, the iOS provides EGL through the EAGL (`EAGLContext`) class in conjunction with `GLkit` to create `GLSurface`. On the Android platform, the `GLView` class provides interfaces for EGL through `GLView.EGLContextFactory` and `GLView.EGLConfigChooser`.

The EGL provides two important things to OpenGL ES APIs:

▶ **Rendering context**: This stores the data structure and important OpenGL ES states that are essentially required for rendering purpose

▶ **Drawing surface**: This provides the drawing surface to render primitives

The following screenshot shows the programmable pipeline architecture of OpenGL ES 3.0:

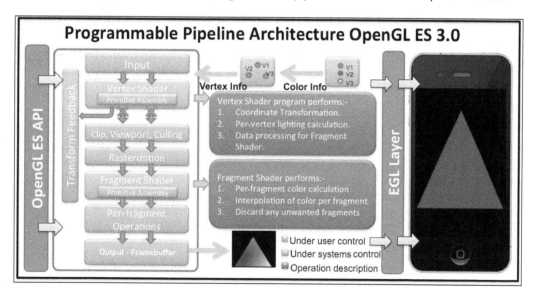

EGL works on top of the native windowing system, such as WGL (Windows), GLX, or X-Windows (Linux), or Mac OS X's Quartz. With EGL specifications, cross-platform development becomes easier.

EGL provides the following responsibilities:

- Checking the available configuration to create rendering context of the device windowing system

- Creating the OpenGL rendering surface for drawing

- Compatibility and interfacing with other graphics APIs such as OpenVG, OpenAL, and so on

- Managing resources such as texture mapping

 You can refer to the following link for more information on EGL `http://www.khronos.org/egl`.

Programming shaders in OpenGL ES shading language 3.0

OpenGL ES shading language 3.0 (also called as GLSL) is a C-like language that allows us to writes shaders for programmable processors in the OpenGL ES processing pipeline. Shaders are the small programs that run on the GPU in parallel. Without these programs, it is impossible to write OpenGL ES 3.0 programs.

OpenGL ES 3.0 supports two type of shaders: vertex shader and fragment shader. Each shader has specific responsibilities. For example, the vertex shader is used to process geometric vertices; however, the fragment shader processes the pixels or fragment color information. More specially, the vertex shader processes the vertex information by applying 2D/3D transformation. The output of the vertex shader goes to the rasterizer where the fragments are produced. The fragments are processed by the fragment shader, which is responsible for coloring them.

The order of execution of the shaders is fixed; the vertex shader is always executed first, followed by the fragment shader. Each shader can share its processed data with the next stage in the pipeline. The GLSL facilitates user-defined variables such as C language; these variables are used for input and output purposes. There are also inbuilt variables that track the states in the shaders to make decisions while processing data in these shaders. For example, the fragment shader provides a state where the incoming fragment can be tested to see if it belongs to the front face or back face of a polygon.

Getting ready

There are two types of processors in the OpenGL ES 3.0 processing pipeline to execute vertex shader and fragment shader executables; it is called programmable processing unit:

- **Vertex processor**: The vertex processor is a programmable unit that operates on the incoming vertices and related data. It uses the vertex shader executable and run it on the vertex processor. The vertex shader needs to be programmed, compiled, and linked first in order to generate an executable, which can then be run on the vertex processor.

- **Fragment processor**: This is another programmable unit in the OpenGL ES pipeline that operates on fragments and related data. The fragment processor uses the fragment shader executable to process fragment or pixel data. The fragment processor is responsible for calculating colors of the fragment. They cannot change the position of the fragments. They also cannot access neighboring fragments. However, they can discard the pixels. The computed color values from this shader are used to update the framebuffer memory and texture memory.

How to do it...

Here are the sample codes for vertex and fragment shaders:

1. Program the following vertex shader and store it into the `vertexShader` character type array variable:

```
#version 300 es
in vec4     VertexPosition;
in vec4     VertexColor;
uniform float  RadianAngle;

out vec4     TriangleColor;
mat2 rotation = mat2(cos(RadianAngle),sin(RadianAngle),
                     -sin(RadianAngle),cos(RadianAngle));
void main() {
  gl_Position = mat4(rotation)*VertexPosition;
  TriangleColor = VertexColor;
}
```

2. Program the following fragment shader and store it into another character array type variable called `fragmentShader`:

```
#version 300 es
precision mediump float;
in vec4    TriangleColor;
out vec4   FragColor;
void main() {
   FragColor = TriangleColor;
};
```

How it works...

Like most of the languages, the shader program also starts its control from the `main()` function. In both shader programs, the first line, `#version 300 es`, specifies the GLES shading language version number, which is 3.0 in the present case. The vertex shader receives a per-vertex input variable `VertexPosition`. The data type of this variable is `vec4`, which is one of the inbuilt data types provided by OpenGL ES Shading Language. The `in` keyword in the beginning of the variable specifies that it is an incoming variable and it receives some data outside the scope of our current shader program. Similarly, the `out` keyword specifies that the variable is used to send some data value to the next stage of the shader. Similarly, the color information data is received in `VertexColor`. This color information is passed to `TriangleColor`, which sends this information to the fragment shader, and is the next stage of the processing pipeline.

The `RadianAngle` is a uniform type of variable that contains the rotation angle. This angle is used to calculate rotation matrix into `rotation`. Refer to following *See also* section to get reference for the `per-vertex` attribute and `uniform` variables.

The input values received by `VertexPosition` are multiplied using the rotation matrix, which will rotate the geometry of our triangle. This value is assigned to `gl_Position`. The `gl_Position` is an inbuilt variable of the vertex shader. This variable is supposed to write the vertex position in the homogeneous form. This value can be used by any of the fixed functionality stages, such as primitive assembly, rasterization, culling, and so on. Refer to the *The fixed function and programmable pipeline architecture* recipe in *Appendix, Supplementary Information on OpenGL ES 3.0,* for more information on the fixed stages.

In the fragment shader, the precision keyword specifies the default precision of all floating types (and aggregates, such as `mat4` and `vec4`) to be `mediump`. The acceptable values of such declared types need to fall within the range specified by the declared precision. OpenGL ES Shading Language supports three types of the precision: `lowp`, `mediump` and `highp`. Specifying the precision in the fragment shader is compulsory. However, for vertex, if the precision is not specified, it is consider to be highest (`highp`).

`FragColor` is an `out` variable, which sends the calculated color values for each fragment to the next stage. It accepts the value in the RGBA color format.

There's more...

As mentioned there are three types of precision qualifiers, the following table describes these:

Qualifier	Description
highp	These variables provide the maximum range and precision. But they can cause operations to run more slowly on some implementations; generally, vertices have high precision.
lowp	These variables may typically be used to store high dynamic range colors and low precision geometry.
mediump	These variables may typically be used to store 8-bit color values.

The range and precision of these precision qualifiers are shown here:

Qualifier	Floating Point Range	Floating Point Magnitude Range	Floating Point Precision	Integer Range	
				Signed	Unsigned
highp	As IEEE-754 $(-2^{126}, 2^{127})$	As IEEE-754 $0.0, (2^{-126}, 2^{127})$	As IEEE 754 relative: 2^{-24}	$[-2^{31}, 2^{31}-1]$	$[0, 2^{32}-1]$
mediump (minimum requirements)	$(-2^{14}, 2^{14})$	$(2^{-14}, 2^{14})$	Relative: 2^{-10}	$[-2^{15}, 2^{15}-1]$	$[0, 2^{16}-1]$
lowp (minimum requirements)	$(-2, 2)$	$(2^{-8}, 2)$	Absolute: 2^{-8} / 2^{-9} signed/unsigned	$[-2^8, 2^8-1]$	$[0, 2^9-1]$

The preceding image is taken from page 48 of https://www.khronos.org/registry/gles/specs/3.0/GLSL_ES_Specification_3.00.3.pdf.

See also

▸ *Loading and compiling a shader program*

▸ *Using the per-vertex attribute to send data to a shader*

▸ *Using uniform variables to send data to a shader*

Loading and compiling a shader program

The shader program created in the previous recipe needs to be loaded and compiled into a binary form. This recipe will be helpful in understanding the procedure of loading and compiling a shader program.

Getting ready

Compiling and linking a shader is necessary so that these programs are understandable and executable by the underlying graphics hardware/platform (that is, the vertex and fragment processors).

The following figure provides an overview of the complete process of creating a shader executable. The different number labels help us understand the order of flow in the build process. Each stage within the build process is marked with the respective OpenGL ES APIs responsible for it.

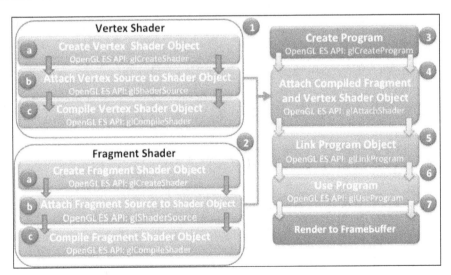

How to do it...

In order to load and compile the shader source, use the following steps:

1. Create a `NativeTemplate.h/NativeTemplate.cpp` and define a function named `loadAndCompileShader` in it. Use the following code, and proceed to the next step for detailed information about this function:

```
GLuint loadAndCompileShader(GLenum shaderType, const char*
sourceCode) {
      // Create the shader
    GLuint shader = glCreateShader(shaderType);
    if ( shader ) {
        // Pass the shader source code
        glShaderSource(shader, 1, &sourceCode, NULL);

        // Compile the shader source code
        glCompileShader(shader);

        // Check the status of compilation
        GLint compiled = 0;
        glGetShaderiv(shader,GL_COMPILE_STATUS,&compiled);
        if (!compiled) {

          // Get the info log for compilation failure
          GLint infoLen = 0;
          glGetShaderiv(shader,GL_INFO_LOG_LENGTH, &infoLen);
          if (infoLen) {
             char* buf = (char*) malloc(infoLen);
             if (buf) {
                glGetShaderInfoLog(shader, infoLen, NULL, buf);
                printf("Could not compile shader %s:" buf);
                free(buf);
             }

        // Delete the shader program
            glDeleteShader(shader);
            shader = 0;
          }
       }
    }
    return shader;
}
```

This function is responsible for loading and compiling a shader source. The argument `shaderType` accepts the type of shader that needs to be loaded and compiled; it can be `GL_VERTEX_SHADER` or `GL_FRAGMENT_SHADER`. The `sourceCode` specifies the source program of the corresponding shader.

2. Create an empty shader object using the `glCreateShader` OpenGL ES 3.0 API. This shader object is responsible for loading the vertex or fragment source code depending on the specified `shaderType` parameter:

   ❑ **Syntax:**

   ```
   GLuint glCreateShader(  Glenum shaderType);
   ```

   This API returns a non-zero value if the object is successfully created. This value is used as a handle to reference this object. On failure, this function returns 0. The `shaderType` argument specifies the type of the shader to be created. It must be either `GL_VERTEX_SHADER` or `GL_FRAGMENT_SHADER`:

   ```
   // Create the shader object
   GLuint shader = glCreateShader(shaderType);
   ```

    Unlike in C++, where object creation is transparent, in OpenGL ES, the objects are created behind the curtains. You can access, use, and delete the objects as and when required. All the objects are identified by a unique identifier, which can be used for programming purposes.

   The created empty shader object (`shader`) needs to be bound first with the shader source in order to compile it. This binding is performed by using the `glShaderSource` API:

   ```
   // Load the shader source code
   glShaderSource(shader, 1, &sourceCode, NULL);
   ```

   The API sets the shader code string in the shader object, `shader`. The source string is simply copied in the shader object; it is not parsed or scanned.

   ❑ **Syntax:**

   ```
   void glShaderSource(GLuint shader, GLsizei count, const
   GLchar * const *string, const GLint *length);
   ```

Variable	Description
shader	This is the handle of the shader object whose source code needs to bind
count	This is the number of elements in the string and length arrays

Variable	Description
string	This specifies the array of pointers to strings containing source code that needs to be loaded
length	This specifies the array of string lengths

The count specifies the number of strings in the array. If the length array is NULL, this means that all the strings are null terminated. If the values inside in this array are non-zero, it specifies the length of the corresponding string. Any value less than 0 is assumed it to be a null-terminated string.

3. Compile the shader using the glCompileShader API. It accepts a shader object handle shader:

   ```
   glCompileShader(shader);      // Compile the shader
   ```

   ❑ **Syntax**:

   ```
   void glCompileShader (GLuint shader);
   ```

Variable	Description
shader	This is the handle of the shader object that needs to be compiled

4. The compilation status of the shader is stored as a state of the shader object. This state can be retrieved using the glGetShaderiv OpenGL ES API:

   ```
   GLint compiled = 0;      // Check compilation status
   glGetShaderiv(shader, GL_COMPILE_STATUS, &compiled);
   ```

   The glGetShaderiv API accepts the handle of the shader and GL_COMPILE_STATUS as an argument to check the status of the compilation. It retrieves the status in params. The params returns GL_TRUE if the last compilation was successful. Otherwise, it returns GL_FALSE.

   ❑ **Syntax**:

   ```
   void glGetShaderiv(GLuint shader, GLenum pname, GLint
   *params);
   ```

Variable	Description
shader	This is the handle of the shader object whose compilation status needs to be checked.
pname	This specifies the object's state parameter. The symbolic names accepted are GL_SHADER_TYPE, GL_DELETE_STATUS, GL_COMPILE_STATUS, GL_INFO_LOG_LENGTH, and GL_SHADER_SOURCE_LENGTH.

Variable	Description
params	This returns the requested object parameter state.

In the case of compilation failure, the glGetShaderiv API can also be used to retrieve the information log from the OpenGL ES state machine by passing GL_INFO_LOG_LENGTH as the parameter. The infoLen returns the length of the information log. If the returned value is 0, it means there is no information log. If the infoLen value is greater than 0, then the information log message can be retrieved using glGetShaderInfoLog:

```
if (!compiled) {        // Handle Errors
    GLint infoLen = 0; // Check error string length
    glGetShaderiv(shader, GL_INFO_LOG_LENGTH,
    &infoLen);
    . . . . .
}
```

5. Use glGetShaderInfoLog to get the error report:

   ❑ **Syntax:**

   ```
   void glGetShaderInfoLog(GLuint shader, GLsizei maxLength,
   GLsizei*length, GLchar* infoLog);
   ```

Variable	Description
shader	This is the handle of the shader object whose information log is required
maxLength	This is the size of the character buffer to store the returned information log
length	This is the length of the string returned by the information length
infoLog	This specifies array of characters

6. The shader is deleted if the shader source cannot be compiled. Delete the shader object using the glDeleteShader API.

   ❑ **Syntax:**

   ```
   void glDeleteShader(GLuint shader);
   ```

Variable	Description
shader	This is the handle of the shader object that needs to be deleted

7. Return the shader object ID if the shader is compiled successfully:

```
return shader; // Return the shader object ID
```

How it works...

The `loadAndCompileShader` function first creates an empty shader object. This empty object is referenced by the `shader` variable. This object is bound with the source code of the corresponding shader. The source code is compiled through a shader object using the `glCompileShader` API. If the compilation is successful, the shader object handle is returned successfully. Otherwise, the shader object returns 0 and needs to be deleted explicitly using `glDeleteShader`. The status of the compilation can be checked using `glGetShaderiv` with `GL_COMPILE_STATUS`.

There's more...

In order to differentiate among various versions of OpenGL ES and GL Shading Language, it is useful to get this information from the current driver of your device. This will be helpful to make the program robust and manageable by avoiding errors caused by version upgrade or application being installed on older versions of OpenGL ES and GLSL. The other vital information can be queried from the current driver, such as the vendor, renderer, and available extensions supported by the device driver. This information can be queried using the `glGetString` API. This API accepts a symbolic constant and returns the queried system metrics in the string form. The `printGLString` wrapper function in our program helps in printing device metrics:

```
static void printGLString(const char *name, GLenum s) {
    printf("GL %s = %s\n", name, (const char *) glGetString(s));
}
// Print the OpenGL ES system metrics
void printOpenGLESInfo(){
    printGLString("Version",      GL_VERSION);
    printGLString("Vendor",      GL_VENDOR);
    printGLString("Renderer",      GL_RENDERER);
    printGLString("Extensions",      GL_EXTENSIONS);
    printGLString("GLSL version",   GL_SHADING_LANGUAGE_VERSION);
}
```

See also

▶ *Linking a shader program*

Linking a shader program

Linking is a process of aggregating a set (vertex and fragment) of shaders into one program that maps to the entirety of the programmable phases of the OpenGL ES 3.0 graphics pipeline. The shaders are compiled using shader objects, as we created in the previous recipe. These objects are used to create special objects called program objects to link it to the OpenGL ES 3.0 pipeline. In this recipe, you will understand the shader linking process.

How to do it...

The following instructions provides a step-by-step procedure to link as shader:

1. Create a new function, `linkShader`, in `NativeTemplate.cpp`.This will be the wrapper function to link a shader program to the OpenGL ES 3.0 pipeline. Follow these steps to understand this program in detail:

```
GLuint linkShader(GLuint vertShaderID,GLuint fragShaderID){
    if (!vertShaderID || !fragShaderID){ // Fails! return
  return 0;
}

    // Create an empty program object
    GLuint program = glCreateProgram();
    if (program) {
    // Attach vertex and fragment shader to it
       glAttachShader(program, vertShaderID);
       glAttachShader(program, fragShaderID);

    // Link the program
glLinkProgram(program);
        GLint linkStatus = GL_FALSE;
        glGetProgramiv(program, GL_LINK_STATUS, &linkStatus);

        if (linkStatus != GL_TRUE) {
            GLint bufLength = 0;
            glGetProgramiv(program, GL_INFO_LOG_LENGTH,
            &bufLength);
            if (bufLength) {
                char* buf = (char*) malloc(bufLength);
    if(buf) { glGetProgramInfoLog(program,bufLength,NULL,buf);
            printf("Could not link program:\n%s\n", buf);
```

```
            free(buf);
          }
        }
        glDeleteProgram(program);
        program = 0;
      }
    }
    return program;
  }
```

2. Create a program object with `glCreateProgram`. This API creates an empty program object using which the shader objects will be linked:

```
GLuint program = glCreateProgram(); //Create shader program
```

   ❑ **Syntax**:

```
      GLint glCreateProgram( void);
```

3. Attach shader objects to the program object using the `glAttachShader` API. It is necessary to attach the shaders to the program object in order to create the program executable:

```
// Attach the vertex and fragment shader
glAttachShader(program, vertShaderID);
glAttachShader(program, fragShaderID);
```

   Here is the syntax of the `glAttachShader` API:

   ❑ **Syntax**:

```
      void glAttachShader(GLuint program, GLuint shader);
```

Variable	Description
program	This specifies the program object to which the shader object (shader) will be attached
shader	This specifies the program object that is to be attached

4. The shader must be linked to the program in order to create the program executable. The linking process is performed using `glLinkProgram`. This API links the program object, specified by the `program` identifier, which must contain the attached vertex and fragment shaders objects:

```
glLinkProgram(program); // Link the shader program
```

5. The status of the link operation can be checked using `glGetShaderiv`. This API accepts program and `GL_LINK_STATUS` as arguments. This will return `GL_TRUE` if the last link on program was successful; otherwise, it will return `GL_FALSE`.

    ❑ **Syntax:**

    ```
    void glGetProgramiv(GLuint program, GLenum pname, GLint
    *params);
    ```

Variable	Description
`program`	This specifies the program object to be queried
`pname`	This specifies symbolic state parameters
`params`	This returns the requested program object parameter state

If link status is returned `GL_FALSE`, the program object must release its allocated memory using `glDeleteProgram`. This API undoes all the effects of `glCreateProgram`. It also invalidates the handle with which it was associated.

    ❑ **Syntax:**

    ```
    void glDeleteProgram(Glint program);
    ```

Variable	Description
`program`	This specifies the handle of program that needs to be deleted

How it works...

The `linkShader` wrapper function links the shader. It accepts two parameters: `vertShaderID` and `fragShaderID`. They are identifiers of the compiled shader objects. The `createProgram` function creates a program object. It is another OpenGL ES object to which shader objects are attached using `glAttachShader`. The shader objects can be detached from the program object if they are no longer in need. The program object is responsible for creating the executable program that runs on the programmable processor. A program in OpenGL ES is an executable in the OpenGL ES 3.0 pipeline that runs on the vertex and fragment processors.

The program object is linked using `glLinkShader`. If the linking fails, the program object must be deleted using `glDeleteProgram`. When a program object is deleted it automatically detached the shader objects associated with it. The shader objects need to be deleted explicitly. If a program object is requested for deletion, it will only be deleted until it's not being used by some other rendering context in the current OpenGL ES state.

If the program's object link successfully, then one or more executable will be created, depending on the number of shaders attached with the program. The executable can be used at runtime with the help of the `glUseProgram` API. It makes the executable a part of the current OpenGL ES state.

See also

▸ *Checking errors in OpenGL ES 3.0*

Checking errors in OpenGL ES 3.0

While programming, it is very common to get unexpected results or errors in the programmed source code. It's important to make sure that the program does not generate any error. In such a case, you would like to handle the error gracefully. This section will guide us to track errors in the OpenGL ES 3.0 and GL shading language.

How to do it...

OpenGL ES 3.0 allows us to check the error using a simple routine called `getGlError`. The following wrapper function prints all the error messages occurred in the programming:

```
static void checkGlError(const char* op) {
    for(GLint error = glGetError(); error; error= glGetError()){
        printf("after %s() glError (0x%x)\n", op, error);
    }
}
```

The `getGlError` returns an error code. The following table describes these errors:

Syntax:

```
GLenum glGetError(void);
```

Error code	Description
GL_NO_ERROR	This indicates if no error found
GL_INVALID_ENUM	This indicates if the GLenum argument is out of range
GL_INVALID_VALUE	This indicates if the numeric argument is out of range
GL_INVALID_OPERATION	This indicates if the operation illegal in current state
GL_STACK_OVERFLOW	This indicates if the command would cause a stack overflow
GL_STACK_UNDERFLOW	This indicates if the command would cause a stack underflow
GL_OUT_OF_MEMORY	This indicates if there is not enough memory left to execute the command

Here are few examples of code that produce OpenGL ES errors:

```
// Gives a GL_INVALID_ENUM error
glEnable(GL_TRIANGLES);

// Gives a GL_INVALID_VALUE
// when attribID >= GL_MAX_VERTEX_ATTRIBS
glEnableVertexAttribArray(attribID);
```

How it works...

When OpenGL ES detects an error, it records the error into an error flag. Each error has a unique numeric code and symbolic name. OpenGL ES does not track each time an error has occurred. Due to performance reasons, detecting errors may degrade the rendering performance therefore, the error flag is not set until the `glGetError` routine is called. If there is no error detected, this routine will always return `GL_NO_ERRORS`. In distributed environment, there may be several error flags, therefore, it is advisable to call the `glGetError` routine in the loop, as this routine can record multiple error flags.

Using the per-vertex attribute to send data to a shader

The per-vertex attribute in the shader programming helps receive data in the vertex shader from OpenGL ES program for each unique vertex attribute. The received data value is not shared among the vertices. The vertex coordinates, normal coordinates, texture coordinates, color information, and so on are the example of per-vertex attributes. The per-vertex attributes are meant for vertex shaders only, they cannot be directly available to the fragment shader. Instead, they are shared via the vertex shader through out variables.

Typically, the shaders are executed on the GPU that allows parallel processing of several vertices at the same time using multicore processors. In order to process the vertex information in the vertex shader, we need some mechanism that sends the data residing on the client side (CPU) to the shader on the server side (GPU). This recipe will be helpful to understand the use of per-vertex attributes to communicate with shaders.

Getting ready

The vertex shader in the *Programming shaders in GL shading language 3.0* recipe contains two per-vertex attributes named `VertexPosition` and `VertexColor`:

```
// Incoming vertex info from program to vertex shader
in vec4   VertexPosition;
in vec4   VertexColor;
```

The `VertexPosition` contains the 3D coordinates of the triangle that defines the shape of the object that we intend to draw on the screen. The `VertexColor` contains the color information on each vertex of this geometry.

In the vertex shader, a non-negative attribute location ID uniquely identifies each vertex attribute. This attribute location is assigned at the compile time if not specified in the vertex shader program. For more information on specifying the ID, refer to the *See also* section of this recipe.

Basically, the logic of sending data to their shader is very simple. It's a two-step process:

- **Query attribute**: Query the vertex attribute location ID from the shader.
- **Attach data to the attribute**: Attach this ID to the data. This will create a bridge between the data and the per-vertex attribute specified using the ID. The OpenGL ES processing pipeline takes care of sending data.

How to do it...

Follow this procedure to send data to a shader using the per-vertex attribute:

1. Declare two global variables in `NativeTemplate.cpp` to store the queried attribute location IDs of `VertexPosition` and `VertexColor`:

    ```
    GLuint positionAttribHandle;
    GLuint colorAttribHandle;
    ```

2. Query the vertex attribute location using the `glGetAttribLocation` API:

    ```
    positionAttribHandle = glGetAttribLocation
    (programID, "VertexPosition");
    colorAttribHandle    = glGetAttribLocation
    (programID, "VertexColor");
    ```

    This API provides a convenient way to query an attribute location from a shader. The return value must be greater than or equals to `0` in order to ensure that attribute with given name exists.

    ❑ **Syntax**:

    ```
    GLint glGetAttribLocation(GLuint program, const GLchar
    *name);
    ```

Variable	Description
program	This is the handle of a successfully linked OpenGL program
name	This is the name of the vertex attribute in the shader source program

3. Send the data to the shader using the `glVertexAttribPointer` OpenGL ES API:

    ```
    // Send data to shader using queried attrib location
    glVertexAttribPointer(positionAttribHandle, 2, GL_FLOAT,
            GL_FALSE, 0, gTriangleVertices);
    glVertexAttribPointer(colorAttribHandle, 3, GL_FLOAT,
            GL_FALSE, 0, gTriangleColors);
    ```

    The data associated with geometry is passed in the form of an array using the generic vertex attribute with the help of the `glVertexAttribPointer` API.

    □ **Syntax:**

    ```
    void glVertexAttribPointer(GLuint index, GLint size, GLenum
    type,  GLboolean normalized, GLsizei stride, const GLvoid *
    pointer);
    ```

Variable	Description
`index`	This is the index of the generic vertex attribute.
`size`	This specifies the number of components per generic vertex attribute. The number must be 1, 2, 3,or 4. The initial value is 4.
`type`	This is the data type of each component in the array containing geometry info.
`normalized`	This specifies whether any fixed-point data values should be normalized (GL_TRUE) or converted directly as fixed-point values (GL_FALSE) when they are accessed.
`stride`	This is used for consecutive generic attribute; it specifies the offset between them.
`pointer`	These are pointers to the first attribute of the array data.

4. The generic vertex attributes in the shaders must be enabled by using the `glEnableVertexAttribArray` OpenGL ES API:

    ```
    // Enable vertex position attribute
    glEnableVertexAttribArray(positionAttribHandle);
    glEnableVertexAttribArray(colorAttribHandle);
    ```

    It's important to enable the attribute location. This allows us to access data on the shader side. By default, the vertex attributes are disabled.

    □ **Syntax:**

    ```
    void glEnableVertexAttribArray(GLuint index);
    ```

Variable	Description
`index`	This is the index of the generic vertex attribute to be enabled

5. Similarly, the attribute can be disabled using `glDisableVertexAttribArray`. This API has the same syntax as that of `glEnableVertexAttribArray`.

6. Store the incoming per-vertex attribute color `VertexColor` into the outgoing attribute `TriangleColor` in order to send it to the next stage (fragment shader):

```
in vec4 VertexColor; // Incoming data from CPU
. . .
out vec4 TriangleColor; // Outgoing to next stage
void main() {
    . . .
    TriangleColor = VertexColor;
}
```

7. Receive the color information from the vertex shader and set the fragment color:

```
in vec4    TriangleColor; // Incoming from vertex shader
out vec4    FragColor;     // The fragment color
void main() {
    FragColor = TriangleColor;
};
```

How it works...

The per-vertex attribute variables `VertexPosition` and `VertexColor` defined in the vertex shader are the lifelines of the vertex shader. These lifelines constantly provide the data information form the client side (OpenGL ES program or CPU) to server side (GPU). Each per-vertex attribute has a unique attribute location available in the shader that can be queried using `glGetAttribLocation`. The per-vertex queried attribute locations are stored in `positionAttribHandle`; `colorAttribHandle` must be bound with the data using attribute location with `glVertexAttribPointer`. This API establishes a logical connection between client and server side. Now, the data is ready to flow from our data structures to the shader. The last important thing is the enabling of the attribute on the shader side for optimization purposes. By default, all the attribute are disabled. Therefore, even if the data is supplied for the client side, it is not visible at the server side. The `glEnableVertexAttribArray` API allows us to enable the per-vertex attributes on the shader side.

See also

▶ Refer to the *Managing variable attributes with qualifiers* recipe in *Chapter 3, New Features of OpenGL ES 3.0*

Using uniform variables to send data to a shader

The uniform variables contain the data values that are global. They are shared by all vertices and fragments in the vertex and fragment shaders. Generally, some information that is not specific to the per-vertex is treated in the form of uniform variables. The uniform variable could exist in both the vertex and fragment shaders.

Getting ready

The vertex shader we programmed in the *Programming shaders in OpenGL ES shading language 3.0 recipe* contains a uniform variable `RadianAngle`. This variable is used to rotate the rendered triangle:

```
// Uniform variable for rotating triangle
uniform float  RadianAngle;
```

This variable will be updated on the client side (CPU) and send to the shader at server side (GPU) using special OpenGL ES 3.0 APIs. Similar to per-vertex attributes for uniform variables, we need to query and bind data in order to make it available in the shader.

How to do it...

Follow these steps to send data to a shader using uniform variables:

1. Declare a global variable in `NativeTemplate.cpp` to store the queried attribute location IDs of `radianAngle`:

   ```
   GLuint radianAngle;
   ```

2. Query the uniform variable location using the `glGetUniformLocation` API:

   ```
   radianAngle=glGetUniformLocation(programID, "RadianAngle");
   ```

   This API will return a value greater than or equal to 0 to ensure that a uniform variable with the given name exists.

   □ **Syntax:**

   ```
   GLint glGetUniformLocation(GLuint program,const GLchar
   *name)
   ```

Variable	Description
program	This is the handle of a successfully linked OpenGL ES program
name	This is the name of the uniform variable in the shader source program

3. Send the updated radian value to the shader using the `glUniform1f` API:

```
float degree = 0; // Global degree variable
float radian;     // Global radian variable

// Update angle and convert it into radian
radian = degree++/57.2957795;
// Send updated data in the vertex shader uniform
glUniform1f(radianAngle, radian);
```

There are many variants of the `glUniform` API.

❑ **Syntax:**

```
void glUniform1f(GLint location, GLfloat v0);
```

Variable	Description
location	This is the index of the uniform variable in the shader
v0	This is the data value of type float that needs to be sent

 For more information on other variants, refer to OpenGL ES 3.0 Reference Pages at `http://www.khronos.org/opengles/sdk/docs/man3/`.

4. Use a general form of 2D rotation to apply on the entire incoming vertex coordinates:

```
. . . .
uniform float  RadianAngle;
mat2 rotation = mat2(cos(RadianAngle),sin(RadianAngle),
                 -sin(RadianAngle),cos(RadianAngle));
void main() {
  gl_Position = mat4(rotation)*VertexPosition;
  . . . . .
}
```

How it works...

The uniform variable `RadianAngle` defined in the vertex shader is used to apply rotation transformation on the incoming per-vertex attribute `VertexPosition`. On the client side, this uniform variable is queried using `glGetUniformLocation`. This API returns the index of the uniform variable and stores it in `radianAngle`. This index will be used to bind the updated data information that is stored the radian with the `glUniform1f` OpenGL ES 3.0 API. Finally, the updated data reaches the vertex shader executable, where the general form of the Euler rotation is calculated:

```
mat2 rotation = mat2(cos(RadianAngle),sin(RadianAngle),
            -sin(RadianAngle),cos(RadianAngle));
```

The rotation transformation is calculated in the form of 2 x 2 matrix rotation, which is later promoted to a 4 x 4 matrix when multiplied by `VertexPosition`. The resultant vertices cause to rotate the triangle in a 2D space.

See also

- ▶ Refer to the *Grouping uniforms and creating buffer objects* recipe in *Chapter 3, New Features of OpenGL ES 3.0*

Programming OpenGL ES 3.0 Hello World Triangle

This recipe basically comprises of all the knowledge we gathered from our previous recipes in this chapter. The output of this recipe will be a `NativeTemplate.h/cpp` file that contains OpenGL ES 3.0 code, which demonstrates a rotating colored triangle. The output of this recipe is not executable on its own. It needs a host application that provides the necessary OpenGL ES 3.0 prerequisites to render this program on a device screen. Therefore, this recipe will be used later by the following two recipes, which will provide the host environment for OpenGL ES 3.0 in Android and iOS:

- ▶ Developing Android OpenGL ES 3.0 application
- ▶ Developing iOS OpenGL ES 3.0 application

This recipe will provide all the necessary prerequisites that are required to set up OpenGL ES, rendering and querying necessary attributes from shaders to render our OpenGL ES 3.0 "Hello World Triangle" program. In this program, we will render a simple colored triangle on the screen.

Getting ready

OpenGL ES requires a physical size (pixels) to define a 2D rendering surface called a viewport. This is used to define the OpenGL ES Framebuffer size.

A buffer in OpenGL ES is a 2D array in the memory that represents pixels in the viewport region. OpenGL ES has three types of buffers: color buffer, depth buffer, and stencil buffer. These buffers are collectively known as a framebuffer. All the drawings commands effect the information in the framebuffer.

The life cycle of this recipe is broadly divided into three states:

- **Initialization**: Shaders are compiled and linked to create program objects
- **Resizing**: This state defines the viewport size of rendering surface
- **Rendering**: This state uses the shader program object to render geometry on screen

In our recipe, these states are represented by the GraphicsInit(), GraphicsResize(), and GraphicsRender() functions.

How to do it...

Follow these steps to program this recipe:

1. Use the NativeTemplate.cpp file and create a createProgramExec function. This is a high-level function to load, compile, and link a shader program. This function will return the program object ID after successful execution:

```
GLuint createProgramExec(const char* vertexSource, const
                                char* fragmentSource) {
GLuint vsID = loadAndCompileShader(GL_VERTEX_SHADER,
vertexSource);
GLuint fsID = loadAndCompileShader(GL_FRAGMENT_SHADER,
fragmentSource);
    return linkShader(vsID, fsID);
}
```

Visit the loading and compiling a shader program and linking a shader program recipes for more information on the working of loadAndCompileShader and linkShader.

2. Use `NativeTemplate.cpp`, create a function `GraphicsInit` and create the shader program object by calling `createProgramExec`:

```
GLuint programID; // Global shader program handler
bool GraphicsInit(){

// Print GLES3.0 system metrics
printOpenGLESInfo();

// Create program object and cache the ID
programID = createProgramExec(vertexShader,
fragmentShader);
    if (!programID) { // Failure !!! return
        printf("Could not create program."); return false;
    }
    checkGlError("GraphicsInit"); // Check for errors
}
```

3. Create a new function `GraphicsResize`. This will set the viewport region:

```
// Set viewing window dimensions
bool GraphicsResize( int width, int height ){
    glViewport(0, 0, width, height);
}
```

The viewport determines the portion of the OpenGL ES surface window on which the rendering of the primitives will be performed. The viewport in OpenGL ES is set using the `glViewPort` API.

□ **Syntax:**

```
void glViewport( GLint x, GLint y, GLsizei width, GLsizei
height);
```

Variable	Description
x, y	These represent lower-left rectangle for viewport specified in pixels
width, height	This specifies the width and height of the viewport in pixels

4. Create the `gTriangleVertices` global variable that contains the vertices of the triangle:

```
GLfloat gTriangleVertices[] = {
{ 0.0f,  0.5f}, // Vertex 0
{-0.5f, -0.5f}, // Vertex 1
{ 0.5f, -0.5f}  // Vertex 2
}; // Triangle vertices
```

5. Create the `GraphicsRender` renderer function. This function is responsible for rendering the scene. Add the following code in it and perform the following steps to understand this function:

```
bool GraphicsRender(){
    // Which buffer to clear? - color buffer
    glClear( GL_COLOR_BUFFER_BIT );

    // Clear color with black color
    glClearColor(0.0f, 0.0f, 0.0f, 1.0f);

    // Use shader program and apply
    glUseProgram( programID );
    radian = degree++/57.2957795;

// Query and send the uniform variable.
radianAngle = glGetUniformLocation(programID, "RadianAngle");
    glUniform1f(radianAngle, radian);

    // Query 'VertexPosition' from vertex shader
    positionAttribHandle = glGetAttribLocation
                             (programID, "VertexPosition");
    colorAttribHandle    = glGetAttribLocation
                             (programID, "VertexColor");

    // Send data to shader using queried attribute
    glVertexAttribPointer(positionAttribHandle, 2,
            GL_FLOAT, GL_FALSE, 0, gTriangleVertices);
    glVertexAttribPointer(colorAttribHandle, 3,
            GL_FLOAT, GL_FALSE, 0, gTriangleColors);

    // Enable vertex position attribute
    glEnableVertexAttribArray(positionAttribHandle);
```

```
glEnableVertexAttribArray(colorAttribHandle);

// Draw 3 triangle vertices from 0th index
glDrawArrays(GL_TRIANGLES, 0, 3);
}
```

6. Choose the appropriate buffer from the framebuffer (color, depth, and stencil) that we want to clear each time the frame is rendered using the `glClear` API. In our recipe, we want to clear color buffer. The `glClear` API can be used to select the buffers that needs to be cleared. This API accepts a bitwise `OR` argument mask that can be used to set any combination of buffers.

   ❑ **Syntax:**

   ```
   void glClear( GLbitfield mask )
   ```

Variable	Description
mask	Bitwise `OR` masks, each mask points to a specific buffer. These masks are GL_COLOR_BUFFER_BIT, GL_DEPTH_BUFFER_BIT, and GL_STENCIL_BUFFER_BIT.

   The possible value mask could be a bitwise or of GL_COLOR_BUFFER_BIT (color buffer), GL_DEPTH_BUFFER_BIT (depth buffer) and GL_STENCIL_BUFFER_BIT (stencil buffer).

   ```
   glClear(GL_COLOR_BUFFER_BIT | GL_DEPTH_BUFFER_BIT)
   ```

7. Clear the color buffer with black color using the `glClearColor` API. This buffer is responsible for storing color information of the scene. It accepts the argument as RGBA space that ranges between 0.0 and 1.0.

8. Use a shader program and set as the current rendering state using the `glUseProgram` API. The `glUseProgram` API installs the program object specified by the program as the current rendering state. The program's executable for the vertex shader runs on the programmable vertex processor. Similarly, the fragment shader executable runs on the programmable fragment processor.

   ❑ **Syntax:**

   ```
   void glUseProgram(GLuint program);
   ```

Variable	Description
program	This specifies the handle (ID) of the shader program.

9. Query the `VertexPosition` generic vertex attribute location ID from the vertex shader into `positionAttribHandle` using `glGetAttribLocation`. This location will be used to send triangle vertex data that is stored in `gTriangleVertices` to the shader using `glVertexAttribPointer`. Follow the same instruction in order to get the handle of `VertexColor` into `colorAttributeHandle`:

```
// Query attribute location & send data using them
positionAttribHandle = glGetAttribLocation
                          (programID, "VertexPosition");
colorAttribHandle = glGetAttribLocation
                          (programID, "VertexColor");
glVertexAttribPointer(positionAttribHandle, 2, GL_FLOAT,
GL_FALSE, 0, gTriangleVertices);
glVertexAttribPointer(colorAttribHandle, 3, GL_FLOAT,
                          GL_FALSE, 0, gTriangleColors);
```

10. Enable the generic vertex attribute location using `positionAttribHandle` before the rendering call and render the triangle geometry. Similarly, for the per-vertex color information, use `colorAttribHandle`:

```
glEnableVertexAttribArray(positionAttribHandle);
glDrawArrays(GL_TRIANGLES, 0, 3);
```

How it works...

When the application starts, the control begins with `GraphicsInit`, where the system metrics are printed out to make sure that the device supports OpenGL ES 3.0. The OpenGL ES programmable pipeline requires vertex shader and fragment shader program executables in the rendering pipeline. The program object contains one or more executables after attaching the compiled shader objects and linking them to program. In the `createProgramExec` function the vertex and fragment shaders are compiled and linked, in order to generate the program object.

The `GraphicsResize` function generates the viewport of the given dimension. This is used internally by OpenGL ES 3.0 to maintain the framebuffer. In our current application, it is used to manage color buffer. Refer to the *There's more ...* section for more information on other available buffers in OpenGL ES 3.0.

Finally, the rendering of the scene is performed by `GraphicsRender`, this function clears the color buffer with black background and renders the triangle on the screen. It uses a shader object program and sets it as the current rendering state using the `glUseProgram` API.

Each time a frame is rendered, data is sent from the client side (CPU) to the shader executable on the server side (GPU) using `glVertexAttribPointer`. This function uses the queried generic vertex attribute to bind the data with OpenGL ES pipeline.

There's more...

There are other buffers also available in OpenGL ES 3.0:

- ▶ **Depth buffer**: This is used to prevent background pixels from rendering if there is a closer pixel available. The rule of prevention of the pixels can be controlled using special depth rules provided by OpenGL ES 3.0. For more information on this, refer to *Chapter 2, OpenGL ES 3.0 Essentials*.

- ▶ **Stencil buffer**: The stencil buffer stores the per-pixel information and is used to limit the area of rendering.

The OpenGL ES API allows us to control each buffer separately. These buffers can be enabled and disabled as per the requirement of the rendering. The OpenGL ES can use any of these buffers (including color buffer) directly to act differently. These buffers can be set via preset values by using OpenGL ES APIs, such as `glClearColor`, `glClearDepthf`, and `glClearStencil`.

 You can refer to `http://www.khronos.org/opengles/sdk/docs/man3/` for more information on `glClearDepthf`, `glClearStencilAPI` and all other APIs. The same link can be used to explore OpenGL ES 3.0 official API specifications.

See also

- ▶ Refer to the *Depth testing in OpenGL ES 3.0* recipe in *Chapter 2, OpenGL ES 3.0 Essentials*
- ▶ *Developing an Android OpenGL ES 3.0 application*
- ▶ *Developing an iOS OpenGL ES 3.0 application*

Using JNI on Android to communicate with C/C++

Android applications are typically developed in Java. However, at times, there could be requirements for the development of C/C++ code or for reusing an existing C/C++ library in Android. For example, if you are looking to develop for cross-platform deployment, then there is no better option than choosing C/C++ as the development language. The code in this book is written in C/C++ to meet cross-platform requirements. This recipe will provide a demo to communicate with C/C++ code from an Android Java application. You will learn how to call the C/C++ method from Java using **Java Native Interface (JNI)**.

Getting ready

JNI creates a bridge between Java and native code via JNI interfaces. The Android NDK provides all the necessary tools such as libraries, source files, and compilers to help in building native code. It is believed that the development of the native code is faster, compared to Java code. Therefore, native development is better for memory management, performance, and cross-platform development.

In our first recipe, you will learn to program C/C++ code in the Android Java application. In this recipe, we will create a UI `TextView` control in the Android framework and display its contents as a string message sent from the C/C++ code. Java communicates with C/C++ through static/shared libraries, the NDK uses JNI and provides a means to develop these libraries under a Java environment.

As a prerequisite for NDK development, you must add Android NDK into the PATH environment variable, so that the NDK APIs are directly accessible from the command-line terminal.

How to do it...

Follow these steps to create an Android application with JNI support:

1. Create a New Android application project by going to **New | Android Application Project**.

2. Set **Application Name** as `HelloNativeDev`, **Project Name** as `CookbookNativeDev`, and **Package Name** as `com.cookbookgles`. You can provide the names as per your choice—there is no restriction:

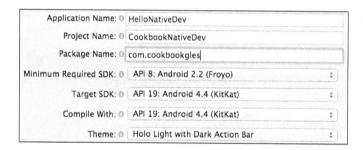

3. Accept the default settings and click on **Next** until the **Create Activity** page appears. Select **Blank Activity** from the given options and click on **Next**.

4. On the last **Blank Activity** page, change **Activity Name** to NativeDevActivity, and click on **Finish**. This will create the project solution, as shown here:

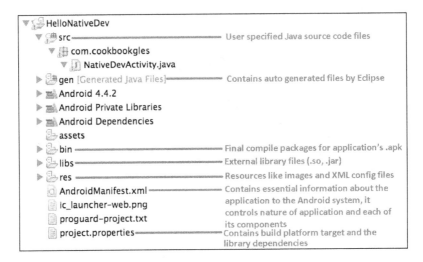

The project solution contains various files and folders in it. Each of these has a specific role and responsibility, which is shown in the preceding image.

5. Go to src | com.cookbookgles | NativeDevActivity.java and replace the code with the following code snippet. Compile and execute the program. This will generate the necessary classes, which will be used by JNI:

```
package com.cookbookgles;

import android.os.Bundle;
import android.widget.TextView;
import android.app.Activity;

public class NativeDevActivity extends Activity {

    static {
      //Comment #1
      // "jniNativeDev.dll" in Windows.
      System.loadLibrary("jniNativeDev");
    }

      //Comment #2
      // Native method that returns a Java String
```

```
// to be displayed on the TextView
public native String getMessage();

@Override
public void onCreate(Bundle savedInstanceState) {
    super.onCreate(savedInstanceState);

    //Comment #3
    // Create a TextView widget.
    TextView textView = new TextView(this);

    //Comment #4
    // Retrieve the text from native method
    // getMessage() and set as text to be displayed
    textView.setText(getMessage());
    setContentView(textView);
    }
}
```

6. Add a new folder named JNI in the project solution. This folder will contain all the C/C++ files. Create another new folder include inside JNI. This will be used for header files. Add HelloCookbookJNI.h and HelloCookbookJNI.c under include and JNI folders, respectively. Add the following code:

   ❏ HelloCookbookJNI.h:

   ```
   #ifndef _Included_com_cookbook_JNIActivity
   #define _Included_com_cookbook_JNIActivity
   #include <jni.h>

   JNIEXPORT jstring JNICALL Java_com_cookbookgles_
   NativeDevActivity_getMessage(JNIEnv *, jobject);

   #endif
   ```

   ❏ HelloCookbookJNI.c:

   ```
   #include "include/HelloCookbookJNI.h"

   JNIEXPORT jstring JNICALL Java_com_cookbookgles_
   NativeDevActivity_getMessage(JNIEnv *env, jobject thisObj){
       return (*env)->NewStringUTF(env,
                   "Hello from Cookbook native code.");
   }
   ```

The JNI function syntax is as follows:

```
JNIEXPORT <return type> JNICALL <static function name>
(JNIEnv *, jobject);
```

The function name under JNI contains the complete hierarchical path of the location where it is defined in the project. The rules are as follows:

- The function name should be prefixed by `Java_`

- Starting from the package name (`com.cookbookgles`), each hierarchical folder and filename must be concatenated

- Each concatenation must contain an underscore (_) between two consecutive names

For example:

```
com.cookbookgles -> NativeDevActivity.java -> getMessage()
```

The name of the function will be defined as follows:

```
Java_com_cookbookgles_NativeDevActivity_getMessage
```

The full signature and name are given here:

```
JNIEXPORT jstring JNICALL
Java_com_cookbookgles_NativeDevActivity_getMessage
(JNIEnv *, jobject);
```

This process can be automated using the javah tool. For more information, refer to the *There more ... section*):

7. Add `Android.mk` under JNI. Add the following code:

```
// Android.mk
LOCAL_PATH := $(call my-dir)

include $(CLEAR_VARS)

LOCAL_MODULE    := JNINativeDev
LOCAL_SRC_FILES := HelloCookbookJNI.c

include $(BUILD_SHARED_LIBRARY)
```

The native code build process uses `Android.mk` for compilation of files. This makefile instructs the NDK compiler list of all the files that need to be compiled. It also maintains the order of files in which they need to be compiled.

- ❏ `LOCAL_PATH` is a predefined variable. It sets the path of the build system to the path of the current working directory. In other words, it is used to locate source files in the development tree It is specified with the current directory path using `$(call my-dir)`.

- ❏ The `include $(CLEAR_VARS)` helps the build system to remove any previous existing variables. It makes sure that no system or local variables are used from other modules. Such a multiple declaration of the same variable across different makefiles can confuse the build system. This command cleans all the local predefined variables, such as `LOCAL_PATH`, `LOCAL_MODULE`, and `LOCAL_SRC_FILES`.

- ❏ `LOCAL_MODULE` is a system variable that contains the name of the library exported by JNI. On successful compilation of the native code, JNI will generate a library with the name specified in `LOCAL_MODULE`. In the current recipe, it is `JNINativeDev.so`. `LOCAL_SRC_FILE` helps the JNI compiler understand which files need to undergo compilation.

- ❏ `include $(BUILD_SHARED_LIBRARY)` helps the compiler build the library into a dynamic form (for example, `.dll` on Windows or `.so` on Linux). These libraries can also be built into static form using `include $(BUILD_STATIC_LIBRARY)`. This recipe uses the shared library.

8. Open a command-line terminal. Go to the current `JNI` folder path and execute `ndk-build`. This command, with the help of `Android.mk`, compiles the source files and generates the shared library called `JNINativeDev.so` in the `CookbookNativeDev\libs\armeabi` folder path:

9. Inside `NativeDevActivity.java`, you need to load the library before using it:

   `System.loadLibrary("jniNativeDev");`

---

10. Connect your physical Android device to the system and execute the Android project with *Ctrl + F11*. This will display the following output on the screen. You can access the first example in the sample code folder `simpleJNI`:

 All of the recipes in this book use the Android device as a target. You can also make use of Android emulators. The primary reason to avoid the use of emulation here is the spotty support available for Android emulator and slower performance.

How it works...

The regular Java code needs to know how to call the native C code. This is done by declaring functions in Java files where each function's signature is prefixed with a `native` keyword. The definition of these functions is defined in C/C++ source files. These functions need to redeclare in the header files, which must be located in the `JNI` folder. These declarations are in a special syntax rule that the `ndk` build understands. The functions are finally made available to Java in the form of shared or static libraries. You need to call this shared/static library within the Java code to use these exported functions.

There's more...

In this recipe, you learned the convention to produce the JNI function's native method signatures. While working on large projects, sometimes, it is cumbersome to make such changes as the code could be significantly large. Additionally, the chances of human errors are also substantially high.

Alternately, the **javah tool** can be used to automate this process. It generates the C header and source files that are needed to implement native methods. It reads a Java class file and creates a C-language header file in the current working directory. The generated header and source files are used by C programs to reference an object's instance variables from the native source code. A detailed description of the usage of this tool is beyond the scope of this book. However, I highly recommend that you refer to the *See also* section for more information on this.

See also

▸ You can learn JNI programming (JNI specification) in detail from `http://docs.oracle.com/javase/7/docs/technotes/guides/jni/spec/jniTOC.html`

▸ The javah tool reference is available at `http://docs.oracle.com/javase/7/docs/technotes/tools/windows/javah.html`

Developing an Android OpenGL ES 3.0 application

This recipe uses the NDK and JNI knowledge from the previous recipe to develop our first Android OpenGL ES 3.0 application. We will use our source code for `NativeTemplate.h/NativeTemplate.cpp` that we programmed in the *Programming OpenGL ES 3.0 Hello World Triangle* recipe. This recipe uses the Android framework to provide the necessary services to host the OpenGL ES program in it.

Getting ready

For our first Android OpenGL ES 3.0 recipe, we advise you to locate the sample `AndroidHelloWorldTriangle` recipe with this chapter. It will be helpful to import the contents to quickly build the application. To import recipes, refer to the *Opening a sample project in Android ADT and iOS* recipe in *Appendix, Supplementary Information on OpenGL ES 3.0*.

How to do it...

Here is the step-by-step procedure to program our first OpenGL ES 3.0 application in Android:

1. Create a blank activity project by going to **New | Android Project**. Provide a proper name for the application and project. For example, specify **Application Name** as `AndroidBlueTriangle`, **Project Name** as `AndroidBlueTriangle`, and specify **Package Name** as `cookbookgles`. The package name in Java is equivalent to the namespace concept in C/C++.

2. On the last page, specify **Activity Name** as `GLESActivity`, **Layout Name** as `activity_gles`, and **Navigation Type** as `None`.

3. In **Package Explorer**, browse to `AndroidBlueTriangle | src | cookbook.gles`. Here, you will find our `GLESActivity` class. Under the same package called `cookbook.gles`, add two new classes called `GLESView` and `GLESNativeLib`. In order to add a new class, right-click on the `cookbookgles` package in the package explorer and go to **New | Class**.

4. Use the sample recipe `AndroidBlueTriangle` and copy/paste the contents of `GLESActivity.java`, `GLESView.java`, and `GLESNativeLib.java` to the respective files of your project. In the next section, you will better understand these files and the classes contained in them.

5. Add a new folder called JNI under this project. Inside this folder, create `Android.mk`, `Application.mk`, `NativeTemplate.h`, and `NativeTemplate.cpp`. The `android.mk` native code makefile is used by the JNI, as discussed in the previous recipe. Use `HelloWorldAndroid` to copy the contents of these two files from source to their respective files.

6. For OpenGL ES 3.0, `Android.mk` must contain the `-lEGL` and `-lGLESv3` flags in order to link with the EGL and OpenGL ES 3.0 libraries. Also, as we target Android devices running Android version 18 (Jelly Bean), the `Applicaton.mk` must contain the `APP_PLATFORM:=android-18` platform.

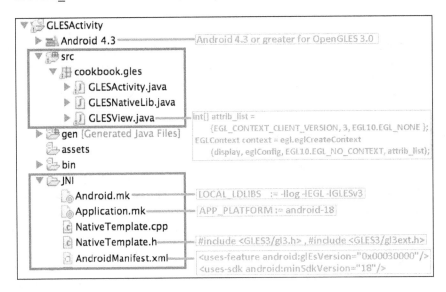

7. Open the command-line terminal and run `ndk-build` inside the `jni` folder. Under Eclipse, refresh **Package Explorer** so that the library created by `ndk-build` is updated in
the project. Here is the rendering output upon execution:

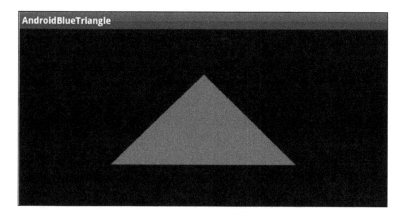

How it works...

The first Android recipe for OpenGL ES 3.0 contains two OpenGL ES classes:

- `GLESActivity` is an extended version of Activity. Activity is an application component that allows various types of views on the screen. Each activity has a window region, within which various type of views are rendered. For our requirements, we need a surface where we can render OpenGL ES. Therefore, the `GLESActivity` class is using `GLESView` for viewing purpose.

- `GLESView` is our custom class that is extended from `GLSurfaceView`. It provides a surface for OpenGL ES rendering. It helps OpenGL ES know about various events, such as the status of activity, whether it is in active or sleep mode, whether it has changed its dimensions, and so on. `GLSurfaceView` provides some important class interfaces. Among them, the three most important ones are as follows:

    - `GLSurfaceView.EGLConfigChooser`: This class is responsible for choosing the correct EGL configuration, as per our requirements. Basically, an EGL is an interface between the OpenGL ES APIs and the rendering context. In order to use the correct rendering context, we should know the EGL configuration that suits our requirements. In this recipe, we have extended `ConfigChooser` from `GLSurfaceView.EGLconfigChooser`.

- ❏ `GLSurfaceView.EGLContextFactory`: The rendering context is very much dependent on the device hardware configuration. OpenGL ES APIs do not know or care about creating the rendering context. Your local SDK provider is responsible for providing an interface to create it and attach it to your local application system. In Android, it is accomplished with the `EGLContextFactory` class. This requires EGL configuration. We have already seen how the `EGLConfigChooser` class gave us the correct EGL configuration, as per our requirement. You need to use this configuration to create your custom `ContextFactory`, which is the extended version of `GLSurfaceView.EGLContextFactory` in our recipe.

  To create OpenGL ES 3.0 context, use the `eglCreateContext` function. This function accepts an attribute list where the second item belongs to the OpenGL ES version, which must be 3.0. See the sample code give here for OpenGL ES 3.0 support:

  ```
  private static double glVersion = 3.0;
  int[] attrib_list = {EGL_CONTEXT_CLIENT_VERSION, (int)
  glVersion, EGL10.EGL_NONE };
  EGLContext context = egl.eglCreateContext(display,
  eglConfig, EGL10.EGL_NO_CONTEXT,  attrib_list);
  ```

- ❏ `GLSurfaceView.Renderer`: This provides the interface to manage OpenGL ES calls to render a frame. It calls the render function in loop.

- ▶ `NativeTemplate.cpp`: This is the native code file that contains OpenGL ES commands responsible for rendering the blue triangle on screen.

When the Android OpenGL ES framework launches an activity, it first checks the available EGL configurations on device and chooses the one best suited to our requirements. This configuration is used to create OpenGL ES rendering context. Finally, rendering is performed by `GLSurfaceRenderer`, where it calls the native OpenGL ES code with the help of the `GLESNativeLib` class.

The OpenGL ES rendering source is coded in `NativeTemplate.cpp`, which is exposed to the Android framework via the `libglNative.so` static library. This library is compiled from the NDK using the `ndk-build` command and is automatically stored under the folder `AndroidBlueTriangle | libs | armeabi | libglNative.so`.

 After compilation of an NDK build, the library generated is prefixed with `lib`. If the name mentioned in `Android.mk` is already prefixed with `lib`, then this prefixing is discarded.

There's more...

You can explore more about the official Android OpenGL ES and its framework classes at `http://developer.android.com/reference/android/opengl/package-summary.html`.

See also

- ▸ Refer to the *Software requirements for OpenGL ES 3.0 – Android ADT* recipe in *Appendix, Supplementary Information on OpenGL ES 3.0*

- ▸ *Using JNI on Android to communicate with C/C++*

Developing an iOS OpenGL ES 3.0 application

Development of OpenGL ES applications on iOS is much simpler compared to Android. The iOS 7 SDK, Xcode 5.0, and later versions support OpenGL ES 3.0. Using App Wizard in Xcode 5.0, the OpenGL ES 3.0 applications can be developed effortlessly.

Getting ready

Make sure that you should have iOS 7 support in your Xcode IDE. For more information, refer to the *Software requirements for OpenGL ES 3.0 – Android ADT* recipe in *Appendix, Supplementary Information on OpenGL ES 3.0*. It's advisable to import the sample recipe `iOSHelloWorldTriangle` in the Xcode. This will be helpful in understanding the theory quickly.

How to do it...

Here are the step-by-step descriptions of the first iOS OpenGL ES 3.0 application:

 The development of an OpenGL ES 3.0 application uses Xcode App Wizard.

1. Open Xcode, go to **File** | **New** | **Project**, select **OpenGL Game**, and then click on **Next**.

2. Give **Product Name**, **Organization Name**, and **Company Identifier** as per your choice. For example, we are using `iOSBlueTriangle`, `macbook`, and `Cookbook`, respectively. Go to the **Next** page, select the location, and create project.

3. Delete `ViewController.m` from the project navigator. Instead, we will use our own file. Go to **File | Add Files** to `iOSBlueTriangle`. Now, locate the source code provided with this book and open the `HelloWorldiOS` folder. Select `ViewController.mm`, `NativeTemplate.cpp`, and `NativeTemplate.h`, and add these into the project. Feel free to explore these added files. Build (*command + B*) and execute (*command + R*) the project.

4. The development of OpenGL ES in Xcode makes sure that the correct version of OpenGL ES is used. It is automatically resolved by the Xcode build system using **Deployment Target**. If the deployment target is iOS 7, then OpenGL ES 3.0 libraries are used; otherwise, OpenGL ES 2.0 libraries are used. If the code in source files uses fixed function pipeline programming APIs, then it is understood that OpenGL ES 1.1 is used. For our current recipe, make sure you have set **Deployment Target** to **7.0**:

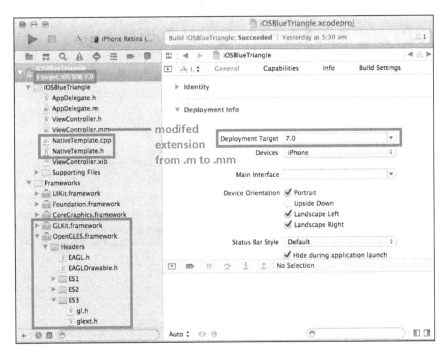

The program handles reference counting by itself. Therefore, it is advised that you disable the **automatic reference count** (**ARC**) to build the program. Otherwise, the compilation may fail. Follow these steps to disable the ARC:

▶ Click on you project in the organizer on the left-hand side

▶ Select your target in the next column

▶ Select the **Build Settings** tab at the top

▶ Scroll down to **Objective-C Automatic Reference Counting** (it may be listed as `CLANG_ENABLE_OBJC_ARC` under the **User-Defined** settings group) and set it to **NO**

How it works...

The Xcode provides an app wizard to the build the applications for iOS 7.0. The OpenGL ES development uses GLKit, which was introduced in iOS 5.0. The GLKit is an OpenGL ES development framework in objective C/C++. It is used to develop 3D graphics applications for programmable pipeline architecture. Since we are developing a portable application that works across platforms, this kit might not be fully helpful for us (GLKit is in Objective C/C++) in that direction. We will create our custom graphics development framework, which will be helpful for portable applications across Android and iOS. We will use GLKit to build the bridge between our graphics development framework kit and iOS. We will introduce this framework in *Chapter 2, OpenGL ES 3.0 Essentials*.

The app wizard creates two classes for us, `AppDelegate` and `ViewController`. These classes are described here:

- `AppDelegate`: This class is inherited from `UIResponder<UIApplicationDelegate>`, which defines the interfaces for a `UIobject` that respond to touch and motion events. `UIApplication` and `UIView` are also derived from `UIResponder`. In iOS, the `UIApplication` class provides a centralized point of control to the underlying OS to coordinate with applications. Each `UIApplication` must implement some methods for `UIApplicationDelegate`, which provides the information on the key event happening with in an application. For example, such key events could be application launching, termination, memory status, and state transition.

- `ViewController`: GLKit provides a standard `View` and `Controller` analogy, through `GLKitView` and `GLKitController`. `ViewController` is derived from `GLKitController`. Both classes work together to accomplish the rendering job. `GLKitView` manages the frame buffer object for the application. It takes the responsibility of rendering a draw command into the framebuffer when it is updated. However, `GLKitController` provides the necessary interfaces to control the pace of frames and their rendering loop:

```
//AppDelegate.h
#import <UIKit/UIKit.h>

@class ViewController;
@interface AppDelegate : UIResponder
<UIApplicationDelegate>
@property (strong, nonatomic) UIWindow *window;
@property (strong, nonatomic) ViewController
*viewController;
@end
```

When iOS launches an application, it creates an instance of `UIResponder`, which basically creates the application object. This application object is a service for the application to provide a physical space in the screen window. This windowing is provided by the object of `UIWindow`, which will be created during the construction of `UIApplication`. This window object contains the desired view to display something on screen. In our case, this view should be some OpenGL rendering surface, which is provided by `GLKitController` to display. When the class object of `GLKitController` is created, it automatically creates the view associated with it. This helps the application to provide the necessary OpenGL rendering surface:

```
// AppDelegate.m
- (BOOL)application:(UIApplication *)application
didFinishLaunchingWithOptions:(NSDictionary *)launchOptions
{
self.window = [[[UIWindow alloc] initWithFrame:[[UIScreen
mainScreen]  bounds]] autorelease];
// Override point for customization after application launch.
self.viewController = [[[ViewController alloc]
initWithNibName:@"ViewController" bundle:nil] autorelease];
self.window.rootViewController = self.viewController;
[self.window makeKeyAndVisible];
return YES;
}
```

The `didFinishLaunchingWithOptions` interface from `UIApplicationDelete` informs the event status of the application that it has completed loading. Within this event, we created the window and set the `ViewController`.

When a subclass from `GLKitController` is extended, it's very important that we override the `viewDidLoad` and `viewDidUnload` methods:

```
//  ViewController.mm
- (void)viewDidLoad
{
  [super viewDidLoad];

  self.context = [[[EAGLContext alloc]
  initWithAPI:kEAGLRenderingAPIOpenGLES3] autorelease];
  if (!self.context) {
    NSLog(@"Failed to create ES context");
  }

  GLKView *view = (GLKView *)self.view;
  view.context = self.context;
```

```
    view.drawableDepthFormat = GLKViewDrawableDepthFormat24;

    [self setupGL];
}
```

The `viewDidLoad` method helps create the rendering context and set up all its drawable properties for an appropriate configuration. To create an OpenGL ES 3.0 render context, we use `initWithAPI`. It accepts `kEAGLRenderingAPIOpenGLES3` as an argument. This argument makes sure that the rendering context is meant for OpenGL ES 3.0 version.

We can modify the rendering context properties to configure the format of the drawable frame buffer object, such as `drawableColorFormat`, `drawableDepthFormat`, `drawableStencilFormat` and `drawableMultisample`.

This method is also a good place for initialization and other resource allocations. The last line is calling the setupGL `function [self setupGL]` in the objective C++ language syntax. Therefore, it is equivalent to this `setupGL()` in C++:

```
//  ViewController.mm
- (void)setupGL
{
    [EAGLContext setCurrentContext:self.context];
    GLint defaultFBO, defaultRBO;

    glGetIntegerv(GL_FRAMEBUFFER_BINDING &defaultFBO);
    glGetIntegerv(GL_RENDERBUFFER_BINDING, &defaultRBO);
    glBindFramebuffer( GL_FRAMEBUFFER, defaultFBO );
    glBindRenderbuffer( GL_RENDERBUFFER, defaultRBO );

    setupGraphics(self.view.bounds.size.width,
    self.view.bounds.size.height);

}
```

The setupGL function sets the current context with the one we created in `viewDidApplication`. This is very important to make the OpenGL ES APIs work. The `glBindFramebuffer` and `glBindRenderbuffer` APIs help the other APIs to know which target framebuffer to render on. In OpenGLES, the data is rendered in a rectangular array of information buffer container called a framebuffer. A framebuffer comprises many other helping buffers, such as color, depth, and stencil buffer, to accomplish rendering on the screen window. Sometimes, there could be cases where we may lose framebuffer or the render buffer. In such cases, it is advisable to bind these buffers with these two functions before you call any OpenGL ES3.0 API.

In order to render our application, we must override the `drawRect` method:

```
//  ViewController.mm
- (void)glkView:(GLKView *)view drawInRect:(CGRect)rect
{
    renderFrame();
}
```

The `renderFrame` function contains all the necessary code to render blue triangle.

See also

▸ Refer to the *The fixed function and programmable pipeline architecture* recipe in *Appendix, Supplementary Information on OpenGL ES 3.0*

▸ Refer to the *Software requirements for OpenGL ES 3.0 – iOS* recipe in *Appendix, Supplementary Information on OpenGL ES 3.0*

▸ Refer to the *Building prototypes using the GLPI framework* recipe, *Chapter 2, OpenGL ES 3.0 Essentials*

2
OpenGL ES 3.0 Essentials

In this chapter, we will cover the following recipes:

- ▶ Building prototypes using the GLPI framework
- ▶ Implementing touch events
- ▶ Rendering primitives with vertex arrays
- ▶ Drawing APIs in OpenGL ES 3.0
- ▶ Efficient rendering with Vertex Buffer Object
- ▶ Transformations with the model, view, and projection analogies
- ▶ Understanding the projection system in GLPI
- ▶ Culling in OpenGL ES 3.0
- ▶ Depth testing in OpenGL ES 3.0

Introduction

This chapter will provide a detailed description of the basic concepts that are required to understand 3D graphics and implement them using OpenGL ES 3.0. In the beginning of this chapter, we will build a mini portable 3D engine that will be helpful in creating small prototype-based projects quickly. It manages the code effortlessly in the OpenGL ES 3.0 programmable pipeline. You will learn event handling to manage gestures on the screen surface under Android and iOS platforms. These will be helpful in implementing gesture-based applications.

As we move on, we will discuss the fundamental transformation in the 3D graphics with the help of the model, view, and projection analogy. At the core side, we will look at the different types of available primitives to render a given geometry in OpenGL ES 3.0 and discuss optimization techniques that could increase rendering performance using **Vertex Buffer Object** (**VBO**). As we approach the end, we will understand geometry culling. It controls the rendering of front or back faces of an object. The last recipe of the chapter will implement depth testing, which is a very important aspect of computational graphics.

Building prototypes using the GLPI framework

The GLPI is an OpenGL ES platform-independent framework. It is a mini 3D engine that is highly useful for developing prototype applications rapidly. It provides higher-level utility classes to render engines, shader compilations, 3D transformations, mesh management, buffer management, textures, and many more. The framework primarily supports Android and iOS platforms and is designed to be easily portable to other platforms such as WinCE, Blackberry, Bada, and so on. We will go through each module of this framework in detail in this chapter.

This framework provides dedicated modules for rapid development of the OpenGL ES 3.0 prototype applications. It comprises of three main modules, as shown in the following figure:

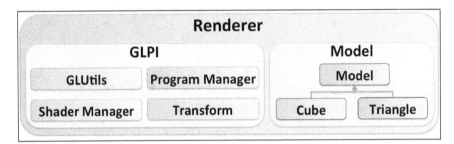

Let's look at each of them in detail:

 ▸ **GLPI module**: This module is the backbone of the GLPI framework. It contains the following classes inside it:

Class	Function
Program Manager	This class is responsible for creating the shader program from program objects. It maintains all the program objects in a single manageable piece that other modules can use as and when required.

Class	Function
Shader Manager	This class is responsible for generating the shader's object. It automates the processes of loading, compiling, and generating the shader object for the program manager.
Transform	This class provides high-level APIs for 3D transformation operations. It also provides wrapper functions to mimic fixed function pipeline APIs, such as transformation, model-view-projection matrices, push and pop matrix operation, and so on.
GLUtils	This class provides helper functions for the GLPI module.

▶ **Model module**: This module will help us create custom models for our application. A Model class essentially represents any type of geometric object that we are interested in rendering on the device screen. This class provides the model's initialization, state management, processing, and rendering routines. It also provides touch events handling within the model.

> The Model class of the renderer module represents any kind of 3D rendering object that we are interested to render on the screen. For example, if we are willing to render a triangle, then we should be creating a Triangle class that must be derived from the Model class and should be added to the Renderer class as a child member.

▶ **Renderer module**: This is the rendering engine's manager that acts as an interface between the underlying platform (such as Android or iOS) and our platform-independent graphics framework. It manages the entire graphics system rendering life cycle. In addition to this, the custom models created by us will also be managed by it.

How to do it...

In the previous chapter, we implemented the Hello World Triangle recipe for Android and iOS platforms. Now, you will learn to use the GLPI framework by reimplementing the same recipe in GLPI. You can refer to the source code of this recipe by locating GLPIFrameworkIntro in the sample code of this chapter. In the following steps, we will set up the GLPI framework for Android/iOS platforms and learn to use it.

Follow these instructions to set up GLPI for the Android platform:

1. Create the `Android.mk` makefile as. The makefile includes the path of the `zlib` makefile for compilation purpose. It is used to read/write compressed files. The `zlib` file is compiled as a shared library and included in the project. The additional libraries include `-lEGL -lGLESv3`, which provides support for EGL, and OpenGL ES 3.0 and `-llog`, which allow log information that would be helpful in debugging the application:

```
# Get the current local of the working directory
MY_CUR_LOCAL_PATH := $(call my-dir)

# Initialize variables to store relative directories
FRAMEWORK_DIR        = ../../../../GLPIFramework
SCENE_DIR            = ../../Scene
GLM_SRC_PATH         = $(FRAMEWORK_DIR)/glm
ZLIB_DIR             = $(FRAMEWORK_DIR)/zlib

# Clear the any garbage variable and include ZLIB
include $(CLEAR_VARS)
include $(MY_CUR_LOCAL_PATH)/../../../../GLPIFramework/zlib/
Android
.mk

LOCAL_PATH := $(MY_CUR_LOCAL_PATH)
include $(CLEAR_VARS)

# Name of the library
LOCAL_MODULE     :=   glNative

# Include the library and GLPI framework files
LOCAL_C_INCLUDES :=   $(GLM_SRC_PATH)/core \
                      $(GLM_SRC_PATH)/gtc \
                      $(GLM_SRC_PATH)/gtx \
                      $(GLM_SRC_PATH)/virtrev \
                      $(ZLIB_DIR) \
                      $(FRAMEWORK_DIR) \
                      $(SCENE_DIR)

# Specify the source files to compile
LOCAL_SRC_FILES :=    $(FRAMEWORK_DIR)/GLutils.cpp \
                      $(FRAMEWORK_DIR)/Cache.cpp \
                      $(FRAMEWORK_DIR)/ShaderManager.cpp \
                $(FRAMEWORK_DIR)/ProgramManager.cpp \
                $(FRAMEWORK_DIR)/Transform.cpp \
```

```
$(SCENE_DIR)/Model.cpp \
$(SCENE_DIR)/Renderer.cpp \
$(SCENE_DIR)/Triangle.cpp \
../../NativeTemplate.cpp

# include necessary libraries
LOCAL_SHARED_LIBRARIES    := zlib
LOCAL_LDLIBS              :=  -llog -lEGL -lGLESv3

# Build as shared library
include $(BUILD_SHARED_LIBRARY)
```

2. Create a new make-file `Application.mk` in the same directory and add STL, RTTI, and exception support to your project as shown in the following lines of code. For OpenGL ES 3.0, the Android platform API level must be 18 or greater:

```
APP_PLATFORM      := android-18
APP_STL           := gnustl_static
APP_CPPFLAGS      := -frtti -fexceptions
```

3. The chapters from now onwards contain two separate sections for Android and iOS development. These sections will be identified by folder names called Android and iOS. `NativeTemplate.h` and `NativeTemplate.cpp` (as described in the first chapter) are placed next to these folders. If we look at these files now, we will realize that they are much cleaner and contain lesser code than earlier. We have moved the code from these files to other files in the `Scene` folder:

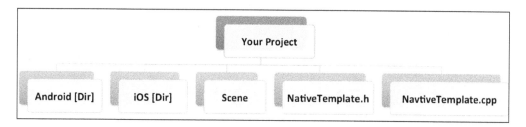

4. The `Scene` folder contains the `Model` and `Renderer` classes that take care of generating models and rendering them. Another class that is present in this folder is the `Triangle` class. It contains the code to render the blue triangle. Make sure that all classes are included in `Android.mk`:

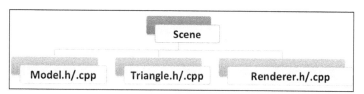

5. Create a new folder called `Shader` under the `assets` folder and create the shader files (`BlueTriangleVertex.glsl` and `BlueTriangleFragment.glsl`) inside this folder. Move the shader programs that were earlier present in `NativeTemplate.cpp` (in the form of a string) into the newly created `Shader` folder. From now on, we will manage our shader programs in this folder.

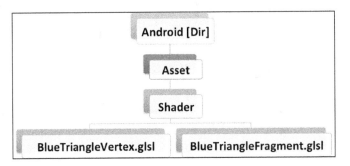

For iOS, the steps to set up the framework are relatively easy and are listed here:

1. Import (**Xcode** | **File** | **Add Files to <Project>**) all the GLPI framework contents into your project, except the `zlib` library. This library is only used for Android for file management. It is not required by iOS.

2. In the imported contents, go to the `glm` library and remove the `core` folder (this folder contains some sample programs that may cause errors in the existing project because of the presence of multiple `main()` entries).

3. Import the shader files by going to `Android | Asset | Shader` folder (`BlueTriangleVertex.glsl` and `BlueTriangleFragment.glsl`) into the current project.

4. Set the `"FILESYSTEM"` environment variable in `main.m`. This will provide the current path of the application in the device:

    ```
    setenv( "FILESYSTEM", argv[ 0 ], 1 );
    ```

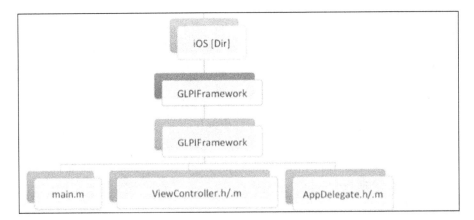

The use of the GLPI framework is very simple. We must follow this set of rules in order to render our 3D geometric models:

1. Create a new custom model class that is derived from the `Model` class. For example, we have created the `Triangle` class that was derived from the `Model` class in `Triangle.h`:

```
class Triangle : public Model{
private:
    // variables for holding attribute values
    GLuint positionAttribHandle,colorAttribHandle;
    GLuint radianAngle;

    float degree; // Rotation in degree form
    float radian; // Rotation in radian form

public:
    Triangle(Renderer* parent = 0); // Constructor
    ~Triangle();                    // Destructor

    void InitModel();  // Initialize the model here
    void Render();     // Perform the rendering
};
```

2. Open `constant.h` and edit enum `ModelType`. Add the enumeration of your choice to recognize the model type. For example, there are two enums added for `Triangle` and `Cube`. This enumeration will be helpful for the renderer to manage model objects:

```
enum ModelType{
    //! The Triangle Model identifier.
    TriangleType  = 0,
    CubeType      = 1
};
```

3. In the constructor of `Triangle`, define `ModelType`. Each model contains the renderer object as its parent. It also contains reference to `ProgramManager` and `Transform`:

```
Triangle::Triangle( Renderer* parent ){
    if (!parent) return;

    RenderHandler       = parent;
    ProgramManagerObj   = parent->RendererProgramManager();
    TransformObj        = parent->RendererTransform();
    modelType           = TriangleType;
    degree              = 0;
}
```

4. Create the `VERTEX_SHADER_PRG` and `FRAGMENT_SHADER_PRG` macros in `Triangle.cpp` to define the relative path of the shader files in the iOS and Android platforms. These macros provides a platform-independent way to access the shader source code files from the project solution:

```
#ifdef __APPLE__
#define VERTEX_SHADER_PRG "BlueTriangleVertex.glsl"
#define FRAGMENT_SHADER_PRG "BlueTriangleFragment.glsl"
#else
#define VERTEX_SHADER_PRG "shader/BlueTriangleVertex.glsl"
#define FRAGMENT_SHADER_PRG "shader/BlueTriangleFragment.glsl"
#endif
```

5. Override the `InitModel()` function. Here, we need to compile our shader and register it with `ProgramManager` for the future use. `ProgramManager` stores the compiled shaders in an optimal way to provide quick access to the queried attributes. Always provide a name to the shader (in our case, `Triangle`). `ProgramManager` uses it as a handle, which will be helpful to retrieve the shader from any type of model class:

```
void Triangle::InitModel(){
if(!(program = ProgramManagerObj->Program
  ( ( char* )"Triangle") )){
    program = ProgramManagerObj->ProgramInit
( ( char * )"Triangle" );
    ProgramManagerObj->AddProgram( program );
 }
 // Initialize Shader
 program->VertexShader   = ShaderManager::ShaderInit
            (VERTEX_SHADER_PRG, GL_VERTEX_SHADER);
 program->FragmentShader = ShaderManager::ShaderInit
            (FRAGMENT_SHADER_PRG, GL_FRAGMENT_SHADER);

 // Allocate the buffer memory for shader source
 CACHE *m = reserveCache( VERTEX_SHADER_PRG, true );
 if( m ) {
   if(!ShaderManager::ShaderCompile
     (program->VertexShader,(char*)m->buffer, 1)) exit(1);
      mclose( m );
 }

 m = reserveCache( FRAGMENT_SHADER_PRG, true );
 if( m ) {
   if(!ShaderManager::ShaderCompile
       (program->FragmentShader,(char*)m->buffer,1))exit(2);
```

```
            mclose( m );
    }
    // Link and Use the successfully compiled shader
    if(!ProgramManagerObj->ProgramLink(program,1)) exit(3);
    glUseProgram( program->ProgramID );
}
```

6. Override the `Render()` function. It is responsible for rendering the colored triangle on the screen surface. In this function, first, the shader program is used to query the respective attributes. These attributes are used to send the data to the shader. Each frame of the triangle is rotated by 1 degree and updated in the shader:

```
void Triangle::Render(){
    // Use the shader program for this render
    glUseProgram( program->ProgramID );

    radian = degree++/57.2957795;

    // Query and send the uniform variable.
    radianAngle = glGetUniformLocation
                (program->ProgramID, "RadianAngle");
    glUniform1f(radianAngle, radian);


    positionAttribHandle = ProgramManagerObj->
                    ProgramGetVertexAttribLocation
                    (program, (char*)"VertexPosition");
    colorAttribHandle = ProgramManagerObj->
                    ProgramGetVertexAttribLocation
                    (program, (char*)"VertexColor");

    // Send the data to the shader
    glVertexAttribPointer(positionAttribHandle, 2,
            GL_FLOAT, GL_FALSE, 0, gTriangleVertices);
    glVertexAttribPointer(colorAttribHandle, 3,
            GL_FLOAT, GL_FALSE, 0, gTriangleColors);

    // Enable the attribute and draw geometry
    glEnableVertexAttribArray(positionAttribHandle);
    glEnableVertexAttribArray(colorAttribHandle);
    glDrawArrays(GL_TRIANGLES, 0, 3);
}
```

7. Destroy the shaders when they are not required. For this recipe, we will use the destructor:

```
Triangle::~Triangle(){
   // Remove the shader in the destructor
   if (program = ProgramManagerObj->Program
                  ((char*) "Triangle"))
   {   ProgramManagerObj->RemoveProgram(program); }
}
```

The shader created in our class is publicly accessible to other models in our rendering engine. Therefore, it is completely up to us whether to destroy it or to keep it in the rendering engine.

8. Inside `Renderer.cpp`, add the `Triangle` model in `Renderer::createModels()` after the `clearModels()` function:

```
void Renderer::createModels(){
  clearModels();
  addModel(new Triangle(this )); //Add custom models here
}
```

The `clearModels()` ensures that there is no conflict in the rendering engine for the `Model` object and shaders. Therefore, it provides a clean approach to avoid any redundancy in OpenGL ES shaders.

9. Override the `Render()` function. This function is responsible for making the rendering model to appear on the screen.

How it works...

The `Renderer` class is the manager of the rendering system. Each custom model defined in the GLPI framework acts as a registered member of `Renderer` and is recognized by its unique model type. `Renderer` provides services to the registered components through utility and helper classes such as `Transform` and `ProgramManager` interfaces. The rendering engine iterates through the entire registered models to define their life cycles. It ensures that the initialization, rendering, and destruction of the models takes place at the right time and in the right order.

The `ProgramManager` is responsible for compiling the shader and caches it for later use. Transform plays a vital role in the geometric transformation operations. For example, it helps in placing models in the 3D space using rotation, translation, and scaling operations.

For more information on the internals of the 3D transformation, you can refer to *Understanding transformation in 3D graphics* in *Appendix, Supplementary Information on OpenGL ES 3.0*. This topic covers types of transformation, transformation matrix conventions, homogenous coordinates, and transformation operations such as translation, scaling, and rotation.

There's more...

Inside the `Renderer` class, the scene's projection can be adjusted using the `setUpProjection()` function. This function is responsible for setting the view clipping planes. The clipping plane can be defined in the form of frustum (perspective) or cuboid (orthographic) shape. We will discuss more about projections later in this chapter in the *Understanding the projection system in GLPI* recipe.

See also

▸ Refer to the *Developing an Android OpenGL ES 3.0 application* and *Developing an iOS OpenGL ES 3.0 application* recipes in *Chapter 1, OpenGL ES 3.0 on Android/iOS*

Implementing touch events

Today's smartphones are capable of interacting with applications through gestures. These gestures are made on the surface of the touch-sensitive device screen. When the device senses these gesture inputs, it reports the touch events to the corresponding application handler. The application handler receives these events and filters them out, according to the application's requirement. In this recipe, we will implement the touch events using OpenGL ES 3.0 on iOS and Android platforms. You will learn to receive the events and handle them in a platform-independent way.

Getting ready

The `GLSurfaceView` class in Android and `GLKViewController` in iOS provide the necessary APIs to implement touch events. These APIs report the nature of detected touch events, such as if the user has tapped or moved their figure on the device screen. These APIs are exposed to the GLPI framework through common touch event interfaces. These interfaces are responsible for reporting and propagating the touch events to the registered members. The base class of the registered member (`Model`) contains all the touch event interfaces that can be handled by the derived versions. Since these are the only interfaces, the registered members need to override them in order to use them according to their custom needs.

How to do it...

This section will provide a detailed description of how to set up and implement touch events on the Android and iOS platforms.

First, implement the common interfaces in the `NativeTemple` and `Renderer` classes that can receive the touch events in a common fashion, irrespective of the platform implementation.

1. Declare and define the touch event interface in the `Renderer` class. For example, the following code shows the tap event implementation:

   ```
   // Declaration
   void TouchEventDown(float x, float y);


   // Definition
   void Renderer::TouchEventDown( float x, float y ){
   for( int i=0; i<RenderMemData.models.size(); i++ ){
       RenderMemData.models.at(i)->TouchEventDown(x, y);
   }
   }
   ```

2. In `NativeTemple.h/.cpp`, call the renderer's touch events from the globally declared and defined wrapper functions:

   ```
   void TouchEventDown( float x, float y ) // Declaration
   void TouchEventDown( float x, float y ){ // Definition
       Renderer::Instance().TouchEventDown( x, y );
   }
   ```

3. On the Android platform, we need to define new JNI native methods in `NativeTemplate.h/.cpp` that can communication with the Android framework in order to retrieve the touch events. For this, define the following interface for tap events in the `GLESNativeLib` Java class:

   ```
   public static native void TouchEventStart(float x,float y);
   ```

4. In `NativeTemplate`, declare and define the JNI interface for the tap event declared earlier:

   ```
   // Declaration of Tap event
   JNIEXPORT void JNICALL
   Java_cookbook_gles_GLESNativeLib_TouchEventStart
                           (JNIEnv * env, jobject obj, float x,
   float y );


   // Definition of Tap event
   ```

```
JNIEXPORT void JNICALL
Java_cookbook_gles_GLESNativeLib_TouchEventStart
                              (JNIEnv * env, jobject obj, float x,
float y )
{
    TouchEventDown(x ,y);
      }
```

5. Repeat steps 1 to 4 to implement the move and release touch events.

6. Override `onTouchEvent()` of the `GLSurfaceView` class. This function provides
    various types of touch events. For example, the tap, move, single/multi touch, and so
    on are some of the important events. These events needs to be filtered in order that
    they can be used:

```
public boolean onTouchEvent( final MotionEvent e ){
  switch( event.getAction() ){
  case MotionEvent.ACTION_DOWN: // Tap event
  GLESNativeLib.TouchEventStart(e.getX(0),e.getY(0));
  break;

  case MotionEvent.ACTION_MOVE: // Move event
  GLESNativeLib.TouchEventMove (e.getX(0), e.getY(0));
  break;

  case MotionEvent.ACTION_UP: // Release event
  GLESNativeLib.TouchEventRelease(e.getX(0),e.getY(0));
  break;
  }
  return true;
}
```

7. On the iOS platform, the GLKit's `GLKViewController` class provides touch
    functions that need to be overridden in order that they can be used in our application.
    For example, have a look at the following code. It implements the tap, move, and
    release events similar to the Android case. Each of the definitions calls the global
    wrapper functions of `NativeTemplate.h/.cpp`:

```
- (void)touchesBegan:(NSSet*)touches withEvent:(UIEvent *)event{
    UITouch *touch; CGPoint pos;
    for( touch in touches ){
        pos = [ touch locationInView:self.view ];
        TouchEventDown( pos.x, pos.y ); //The global wrapper
    }
}

- (void)touchesMoved:(NSSet *)touches withEvent:(UIEvent *)event{
```

```
        UITouch *touch; CGPoint pos;
        for( touch in touches ){
            pos = [ touch locationInView:self.view ];
            TouchEventMove( pos.x, pos.y ); // The global wrapper
        }
    }

    - (void)touchesEnded:(NSSet*)touches
      withEvent:(UIEvent*)event{
      UITouch *touch; CGPoint pos;
      for( touch in touches ){
          pos = [ touch locationInView:self.view ];
          TouchEventRelease(pos.x,pos.y); // The global wrapper
      }
    }
```

How it works...

When an Android or iOS application receives the touch event from the device, it is the responsibility of `GLSurfaceView` and `GLKViewController` to convey these touch events to the external world. These classes report the touch events to the global wrapper function that is defined in the `NativeTemple`. This file provides higher level cross-platform functions for touch events such as tap, move, and release. These functions are internally interfaced with the corresponding touch event interfaces of the `Renderer` class. The `Renderer` class provides the interface to handle touch events in an abstracted way in which it works seamlessly on either platform. These functions or interfaces are called from the Android or iOS platform through `NativeTemplates` global methods and propagated to all the registered models. For instance, the following example shows the handling of the move event:

```
void Renderer::TouchEventMove( float x, float y ){
    for( int i=0; i<RenderMemData.models.size(); i++ ){
        // Handle the Touch events at model levels.
        RenderMemData.models.at(i)->TouchEventMove(x, y);
    }
}
```

See also

▶ *Depth testing in OpenGL ES 3.0*

Rendering primitives with vertex arrays

In OpenGL ES 3.0, the vertex array is a simplest mean to draw the objects in the 3D space. The objects are drawn with the help of vertices, which are arranged in a specific order guided by the rendering primitives. The rendering primitives represent how an individual or a set of vertices can assemble to draw a geometry. For example, four vertices can be represented by a point, line, or triangle, as shown here:

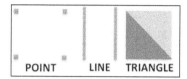

The vertex array is the way in which the geometric data, such as vertex coordinates, normal coordinates, color information, and texture coordinates, are specified in the form of arrays. In this recipe, you will learn to program a vertex array in the GLPI framework. In addition to this, we will also demonstrate various available rendering primitives in OpenGL ES 3.0.

How to do it...

Create a new class called `Primitive` derived from the `Model` class and follow this step-by-step procedure to implement the rendering primitive with the vertex array:

1. Create `PrimitiveVertex.glsl` and `PrimitiveFragment.glsl` and use the following code for the vertex and fragment shaders:

```
// Source code PrimitiveVertex.glsl
#version 300 es
in vec4 VertexPosition, VertexColor;
out vec4 VarColor;
uniform mat4 ModelViewProjectMatrix;

void main(){
   gl_Position = ModelViewProjectMatrix * VertexPosition;
   VarColor    = VertexColor;
}

// Source code PrimitiveFragment.glsl
#version 300 es
precision mediump float;

in vec4 VarColor;
```

```
out vec4 FragColor;
void main() {
   FragColor = vec4(VarColor.x,VarColor.y,VarColor.z,1.0);
}
```

2. Create a set of 10 vertices, as shown in the following figure. Then, store the information into the vertices array and assign colors to each vertex. The color information is stored in the form of RGB in the colors array.

(-1.0, 2.0)	(1.0, 2.0)	`const GLfloat vertices[] = {`	`GLfloat   colors[] ={`
		`      1.0f,   2.0f,`	`      0.0, 0.0, 1.0,`
		`     -1.0f,   2.0f,`	`      1.0, 0.0, 1.0,`
(-1.0, 1.0)	(1.0, 1.0)	`      1.0f,   1.0f,`	`      1.0, 1.0, 0.0,`
		`     -1.0f,   1.0f,`	`      0.0, 0.0, 1.0,`
(-1.0, 0.0)	(1.0, 0.0)	`      1.0f,   0.0f,`	`      1.0, 0.0, 1.0,`
		`     -1.0f,   0.0f,`	`      1.0, 1.0, 0.0,`
		`      1.0f,  -1.0f,`	`      0.0, 0.0, 1.0,`
(-1.0, -1.0)	(1.0, -1.0)	`     -1.0f,  -1.0f,`	`      1.0, 0.0, 1.0,`
		`      1.0f,  -2.0f,`	`      1.0, 1.0, 0.0,`
		`     -1.0f,  -2.0f`	`      1.0, 1.0, 0.0`
(-1.0, -2.0)	(1.0, -2.0)	`};`	`};`

3. In the `initModel` function, compile and link the vertex and fragment shaders. On successful creation of the shader program object, query the vertex attributes `VertexPosition` and `VertexColor` using a GLPI wrapper function called `ProgramGetVertexAttribLocation`. This function internally uses OpenGL ES 3.0 generic vertex attribute query APIs. Using the wrapper APIs decreases the chances of errors and increases the performance, as these queries are optimized:

```
void Primitives::InitModel(){
  // Shaders are compiled and linked successfully
  // Many line skipped, please refer to the code
  glUseProgram( program->ProgramID );
  attribVertex=ProgramManagerObj-
  >ProgramGetVertexAttribLocation
            (program, (char*)"VertexPosition");
  attribColor=ProgramManagerObj->ProgramGetVertexAttribLocation
            (program, (char*)"VertexColor");
}
```

`ProgramGetVertexAttribLocation` returns the generic attribute location ID. A negative value of the location ID specifies that no attribute with that name exists in the shader.

   ❑ **Syntax:**

```
char ProgramManager::ProgramGetVertexAttribLocation
                        (PROGRAM *program, char* name);
```

Variable	Description
program	This is the GLPI program object containing shader's information
name	This is the name of the attribute in the shader source program

4. Within the same `initModel` function, query the uniform using another wrapper API from the GLPI framework:

```
mvp = ProgramManagerObj->ProgramGetUniformLocation
                (program, (char*)"MODELVIEWPROJECTIONMATRIX");
```

`ProgramManager` in the GLPI framework provides a high-level wrapper function `ProgramGetUniformLocation` to query any uniform type variable from the shader program.

❑ **Syntax**:

```
GLint ProgramGetUniformLocation
                (PROGRAM *program, char* name);
```

Variable	Description
program	This is the GLPI program object containing shader's information
name	This is the name of the uniform object in the shader source program

5. Create a `RenderPrimitive` function and call it inside `Render`. Inside this function, send the uniform and per-vertex attribute data to the shader:

```
void RenderPrimitives(){
  glDisable(GL_CULL_FACE); // Disable the culling
  glLineWidth(10.0f);      // Set the line width

  glUniformMatrix4fv( mvp, 1, GL_FALSE, ( float * )
   TransformObj->TransformGetModelViewProjectionMatrix() );

  glVertexAttribPointer(attribVertex, 2, GL_FLOAT,
  GL_FALSE, 0, vertices);
  glVertexAttribPointer(attribColor, 3, GL_FLOAT,
  GL_FALSE, 0, colors);
  }
```

6. Enable the vertex and color-generic attributes and draw various primitives using switch case statements:

```
glEnableVertexAttribArray(attribVertex);
glEnableVertexAttribArray(attribColor);
glDrawArrays(primitive, 0, numberOfElement);
```

How it works...

This recipe has two arrays, vertices, and colors, which contains the vertex information and color information. There are 10 vertices, and each vertex stores an X, Y component. The color information also contains 10 different colors for each vertex. The color information is specified in the RGB color space in the range of 0.0 to 1.0.

The vertex shader contains two per-vertex attributes, `VertexPosition` and `VertexColor`. These attributes are uniquely recognized in the program via the attribute location. This location is queried using the `ProgramGetVertexAttribLocation` function. The queried attribute serves the purpose of binding vertex array information to the per-vertex attributes. The vertex attribute data is sent using `glVertexAttribPointer`.

Similarly, the uniform variable is also queried in the same fashion using a separate function called `ProgramGetUniformLocation`. The uniform variable is a 4 x 4 matrix of `ModelViewProjection`. Therefore, the data is sent to the shader using `glUniformMatrix4fv`. The `glLineWidth` function is meant for the `GL_LINE` variant primitives to define the width of the line as 10 pixels wide.

Finally, the OpenGL ES 3.0 primitives are rendered using `glDrawArrays`. Various primitive rendering can be seen in action by a simple tap on the screen. Upon tapping, the tap event will invoke the `TouchEventDown` function of the `Primitive` class, which is responsible for changing the current primitive type for rendering:

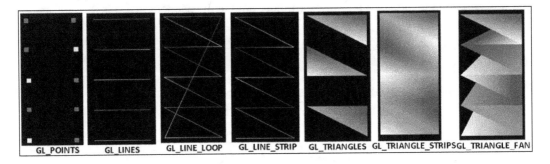

| GL_POINTS | GL_LINES | GL_LINE_LOOP | GL_LINE_STRIP | GL_TRIANGLES | GL_TRIANGLE_STRIP | GL_TRIANGLE_FAN |

In computer 3D graphics, the polygon shapes are rendered using the triangle primitives. Using `GL_TRIANGLE_STRIP`, as compared to `GL_TRIANGLES`, is preferred because the number of vertices needed to specify the shape of the triangle is lesser when compared to `GL_TRIANGLES`. In the latter case, more data has to be sent from the CPU to the GPU, as adjacent edges share common vertices. In the former case, the vertices are arranged in a special order in which duplicate vertices from the shared edges are avoided. Hence, it requires less data. It is true that `GL_TRIANGLE_STRIP` may be better in certain cases due to lesser data needed to be defined. However, this needs to be considered on a case-by-case basis, depending on the 3D model format.

There are plenty of tools available that can be used to convert the geometry information in the triangle-strip form. For example, nVIDIA's `NvTriStrip` library generates triangle strips from an arbitrary 3D geometry. For more information, visit `http://www.nvidia.com/object/nvtristrip_library.html`.

 For more information on the drawing APIs, refer to the *Drawing APIs in OpenGL ES 3.0* recipe. It demonstrates `glDrawArrays` and `glDrawElements`.

There's more...

This section will focus on the basic rendering primitives available in OpenGL ES 3.0. Primitives are the simplest shapes that can be used to generate any complex shape in 3D graphics. The OpenGL ES 3.0 primitives can be categorized into three basic types: point, line and triangle. The rest are variations of these.

The following table describes all the variant primitives of point, line, and triangle available in OpenGL ES 3.0:

Primitive types	Input vertex	Output shape	Description
GL_POINTS	V1 V2 V0 V3	V1 V2 V0 V3	A point on the screen that represents each vertex.
GL_LINES	V1 V2 V0 V3	V1 V2 V0 V3	Each pair of vertices is used to render a line between them. We can use the `glLineWidth()` API to control the width of the line rendering.
GL_LINE_LOOP	V1 V2 V0 V3	V1 V2 V0 V3	Each vertex makes a line between itself and the vertex preceding it. The last vertex always joins the first vertex to form a closed loop.
GL_LINE_STRIP	V1 V2 V0 V3	V1 V2 V0 V3	Each vertex makes a line between itself and the vertex preceding it.

Primitive types	Input vertex	Output shape	Description
GL_TRIANGLES			A set of three vertices is used to form a filled triangle.
GL_TRIANGLE_STRIP			Every vertex makes a triangle with the preceding two vertices.
GL_TRIANGLE_FAN			Every vertex makes a triangle with the first vertex and the vertex preceding it. This generates a fan-like pattern.

See also

▸ Refer to the *Using uniform variables to send data to a shader* and *Using per-vertex attribute to send data to a shader* recipes in *Chapter 1, OpenGL ES 3.0 on Android/iOS*

Drawing APIs in OpenGL ES 3.0

OpenGL ES 3.0 provides two types of rendering APIs: `glDrawArrays` and `glDrawElements`. These APIs allows us to render the geometric data on the screen in the form of primitives. In this recipe, you will learn how these APIs are used in programming and understand the difference between them.

This recipe will render a cube by using the two different rendering APIs mentioned earlier. The datasets used by these APIs are entirely different. Tap on the screen to see the difference between the two APIs.

Getting ready

The `glDrawArray` API reads the vertex information in the form of an array in sequential order, starting from the first index to total number of indexes specified by the count. The `glDrawArray` API renders primitives specified by the mode argument using vertex array data information.

Syntax:

```
void glDrawArrays( GLenum mode, GLint first, GLsizei count);
```

Variable	Description
mode	This specifies the type of OpenGL ES primitive that needs to be rendered
first	This is the start index of the data array
count	This denotes the total number of indices to be rendered

For example, a square can be rendered as a set of two triangles:

```
GLfloat   square[6][3] = {
    -1.0, -1.0, 1.0, /*Vertex0*/  1.0,-1.0, 1.0,  /*Vertex3*/
    -1.0,  1.0, 1.0, /*Vertex1*/  1.0, -1.0, 1.0, /*Vertex3*/
     1.0,  1.0, 1.0, /*Vertex2*/ -1.0,  1.0, 1.0, /*Vertex1*/
    };
glDrawArrays(GL_TRIANGLES, 0, 18);
```

In contrast, the `glDrawElement` API maps each vertex using an index similar to the one that accesses elements in an array using C++/Java. This method of rendering consumes less memory compared to `glDrawArray`, where each redundant vertex needs to be mentioned with its X, Y, and Z components. For example, take a case of regular cube geometry and calculate the memory saving offered by `glDrawElement`.

Syntax:

```
void glDrawElements( GLenum mode, GLsizei count, GLenum type,
const GLvoid * indices);
```

Variable	Description
mode	This specifies the primitive type as described in the preceding table
count	This specifies the number of elements to be rendered
type	This specifies the data type of indices
indices	This specifies the order of indices for vertex arrangement in an array form

For example, the same square can be represented as follows using this API:

```
GLfloat square[4][3] = {
    -1.0, -1.0, 1.0, /*Vertex0*/  -1.0,  1.0, 1.0, /*Vertex1*/
     1.0,  1.0, 1.0, /*Vertex2*/   1.0, -1.0, 1.0, /*Vertex3*/
    };
GLushort squareIndices[] = {0,3,1, 3,2,1};    // 6 indices
glDrawElements(GL_TRIANGLES, 6, GL_UNSIGNED_SHORT, squareIndices);
```

How to do it...

The following instructions will provide a step-by-step procedure to demonstrate the use of the `glDrawArrays` and `glDrawElements` APIs:

1. Create a `Cube` class derived from `Model`. There is no change required in the vertex and fragment shaders. `Shaders` from the previous recipe can be reused.

2. Define the vertex and color dataset for the `glDrawArray` API:

```
GLfloat vertexBuffer[][3] = {           GLfloat colorBufferData[][3] = {
  {-1,-1, 1}, { 1,-1, 1}, {-1, 1, 1}, // V0-V3-V1    {1,0,0}, {1,0,0}, {1,0,0},
  { 1,-1, 1}, { 1, 1, 1}, {-1, 1, 1}, // V3-V2-V1    {1,0,0}, {1,0,0}, {1,0,0},
  { 1,-1,-1}, {-1,-1,-1}, { 1, 1,-1}, // V7-V4-V6    {1,1,0}, {1,1,0}, {1,1,0},
  {-1,-1,-1}, {-1, 1,-1}, { 1, 1,-1}, // V4-V5-V6    {1,1,0}, {1,1,0}, {1,1,0},
  {-1,-1,-1}, {-1,-1, 1}, {-1, 1,-1}, // V4-V0-V5    {0,1,0}, {0,1,0}, {0,1,0},
  {-1,-1, 1}, {-1, 1, 1}, {-1, 1,-1}, // V0-V1-V5    {0,1,0}, {0,1,0}, {0,1,0},
  { 1,-1, 1}, { 1,-1,-1}, { 1, 1,-1}, // V3-V7-V2    {0,1,1}, {0,1,1}, {0,1,1},
  { 1,-1,-1}, { 1, 1,-1}, { 1, 1, 1}, // V7-V6-V2    {0,1,1}, {0,1,1}, {0,1,1},
  {-1, 1, 1}, { 1, 1, 1}, {-1, 1,-1}, // V1-V2-V5    {0,0,1}, {0,0,1}, {0,0,1},
  { 1, 1, 1}, { 1, 1,-1}, {-1, 1,-1}, // V2-V6-V5    {0,0,1}, {0,0,1}, {0,0,1},
  { 1,-1, 1}, {-1,-1, 1}, { 1,-1,-1}, // V3-V0-V7    {1,0,1}, {1,0,1}, {1,0,1},
  {-1,-1, 1}, {-1,-1,-1}, { 1,-1,-1}  // V0-V4-V7    {1,0,1}, {1,0,1}, {1,0,1}
};                                      };
```

3. Similarly, define the dataset for the `glDrawElement` API:

```
GLfloat cubeVerts[][3]=  GLfloat  cubeColors[][3]=  GLushort cubeIndices[]=
{                        {                          {   // 36 of indices
  -1, -1,  1 , // V0        { 0,  0,  0 }, //0          0,3,1, 3,2,1,
  -1,  1,  1 , // V1        { 0,  0,  1 }, //1          7,4,6, 4,5,6,
   1,  1,  1 , // V2        { 0,  1,  0 }, //2          4,0,5, 0,1,5,
   1, -1,  1 , // V3        { 0,  1,  1 }, //3          3,7,2, 7,6,2,
  -1, -1, -1 , // V4        { 1,  0,  0 }, //4          1,2,5, 2,6,5,
  -1,  1, -1 , // V5        { 1,  0,  1 }, //5          3,0,7, 0,4,7
   1,  1, -1 , // V6        { 1,  1,  0 }, //6       };
   1, -1, -1   // V7        { 1,  1,  1 }, //7
};                       };
```

4. In `InitModel`, compile and link the shaders. On successful compilation, query `ModelViewProjectionMatrix`, `VertexPosition`, `VertexColor` and store them into `MVP`, `attribVertex`, `attribColor`, respectively. Enable vertex and color-generic attributes:

```
void Cube::InitModel(){
  . . . . . // Load shaders
```

```
    glUseProgram( program->ProgramID );

    MVP = ProgramManagerObj->ProgramGetUniformLocation
              (program, (char*)"ModelViewProjectionMatrix");
    attribVertex=ProgramManagerObj-
>ProgramGetVertexAttribLocation
              (program, (char*)"VertexPosition");
    attribColor = ProgramManagerObj->ProgramGetVertexAttribLocation
              (program, (char*)"VertexColor");
    // Enable Vertex atrb
glEnableVertexAttribArray(attribVertex);
    // Enable Color atrb
glEnableVertexAttribArray(attribColor);
    }
```

5. Inside the render function, implement the following code to demonstrate both APIs in action:

```
    glUseProgram( program->ProgramID );
    TransformObj->TransformRotate(k++, 1.0, 1.0, 1.0);
    glUniformMatrix4fv( MVP, 1, GL_FALSE,(float*)TransformObj->

    if ( useDrawElementAPI ){ //Toggle the flag by tap event
glVertexAttribPointer(attribColor, 3, GL_FLOAT, GL_FALSE, 0,
cubeColors);
glVertexAttribPointer(attribVertex, 3, GL_FLOAT, GL_FALSE, 0,
cubeVerts);
glDrawElements(GL_TRIANGLES, 36, GL_UNSIGNED_SHORT, cubeIndices);
    }
    else{
        glVertexAttribPointer(attribColor, 3, GL_FLOAT,
        GL_FALSE, 0, colorBufferData);
        glVertexAttribPointer (attribVertex, 3, GL_FLOAT,
        GL_FALSE, 0, vertexBuffer);
        glDrawArrays(GL_TRIANGLES, 0, 36);
    }
```

How it works...

The `glDrawArray` rendering API uses vertex attributes, such as vertex coordinates, color information, and texture coordinate, in the form of a continuous data array in which the data reading cannot be skipped or hopped. The information is highly redundant, as the same vertices share among the different face are repeatedly written. In this recipe, `vertexBuffer` and `colorBufferData` store vertex coordinates and color information. This information is sent to the vertex shader using `attribVertex` and `attribColor`. Finally, the `glDrawArray` call is made with parameters specifying the type of primitive and index of the vertices that need to go for rendering (the start and end index).

In contrast, `glDrawElement` uses `cubeVert` and `cubeColors`, which contain the nonredundant vertex and color information. It uses an additional array that contains the indices of the vertex information. Using this array, the primitives are rendered by hopping around the vertex arrays. Unlike `glDrawArray`, which works on the continuous set of vertex data, `glDrawElement` can jump from one vertex to another using the index information provided to it in the last parameter.

There's more...

In OpenGL ES 3.0, the polygons are drawn as a set of triangles. Each of these triangles has two faces: a front face and back face. For example, the following image represents a square geometry with vertices v0, v1, v2, and v3. It is made up of two triangles. The order of vertex winding (clockwise or anticlockwise) is used by OpenGL ES 3.0 to determine whether the triangle is front facing or back facing. In this case, the vertices are winded in an anticlockwise direction. By default, OpenGL ES 3.0 considers the anticlockwise windings as front facing. This convention can be changed by setting `glFrontFace` (counter clockwise) as `GL_CW` or `GL_CCW` (counter clockwise).

The winding order is always specified from the user's visualization point of view. The OpenGL ES pipeline takes care of this winding and displays them correctly from the camera's point of view. For example, when we specify the vertices of a cube geometry, it should be in the counter-clockwise order as per the default convention. However, we know very well that the faces that are parallel to each other have opposite winding orders when viewed from the camera's point of view, as shown in the following figure. OpenGL ES automatically generates the correct winding order from the camera's point of view.

The front and back faces are used in geometry culling. For more information on geometry culling and front/back face definitions, refer to the *Culling in OpenGL ES 3.0* recipe later in this chapter.

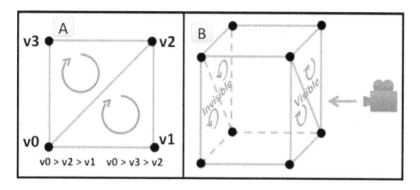

See also

▸ *Drawing APIs in OpenGL ES 3.0*

▸ *Culling in OpenGL ES 3.0*

Efficient rendering with Vertex Buffer Object

The vertex information comprises of geometric coordinates, color information, texture coordinates, and normal vectors. This information is stored in the form of an array and always resides in the local memory (RAM, which is accessible by the CPU) of the device. Each frame when rendering command is executed. This information is copied from the local memory and sent to the GPU. This vertex information is sent over the data bus, which has a slower speed compared to the GPU's processing speed. Additionally, the latency time on the local memory also adds a slight delay.

VBO is a faster way to render 3D objects. The VBO uses the full advantage of **Graphics Processor Unit** (**GPU**) and store the geometric data on GPU's memory instead of storing it on the local RAM memory. This helps OpenGL ES to avoid continuous sending of data from local memory to the GPU each time a draw call is made.

The implementation of the VBO can be divided into four steps:

1. Create a new buffer object using `glGenBuffers()`.
2. Bind this buffer object to pipeline with `glBindBuffer()`.
3. Allocate memory to store data using `glBufferData()`.
4. Store/modify the data into portions of the allocated buffer object with `glBufferSubData()`.

How to do it...

Follow this step-by-step procedure to implement the VBO recipe:

1. First, create a vertex buffer object using the `glGenBuffers` API. This API generates n number of vertex buffer objects, where each vertex buffer object is recognized by a unique name or handle returned by this API. This handle is an unsigned `int` ID that is used to perform various operations on the VBO.

   ❏ **Syntax:**

   ```
   void glGenBuffers(GLsizei n, GLuint* buffers);
   ```

Variable	Description
N	This is a number of buffer object names that need to be generated
buffers	This specifies an array that contains buffer objects on successful creation

2. Bind the created vertex buffer object IDs to the underlying pipeline with the `glBindBuffer` API.

   ❏ **Syntax:**

   ```
   void glBindBuffer(GLenum target, GLuint buffer);
   ```

Variable	Description
target	This specifies the symbolic constant target to which the buffer object name needs to be bound. It could accept GL_ARRAY_BUFFER, GL_ELEMENT_ARRAY_BUFFER, GL_UNIFORM_BUFFER, GL_TRANSFORM_FEEDBACK_BUFFER, and so on.
buffers	This is the name of the buffer object that we created using glGenBuffer.

3. Allocate and initialize the memory by specifying the size of the geometric arrays, such as vertex, color, normal, and so on, with `glBufferData`.

   ❏ **Syntax:**

   ```
   void glBufferData(GLenum target, GLsizeiptr size, const
   GLvoid * data, GLenum usage);
   ```

Variable	Description
target	This parameter is similar to what is defined in glBindBuffer, as described earlier.
size	The size of the buffer needs to be allocated in bytes.

Variable	Description
data	This is a pointer to the data array that contains geometry information. If this is NULL, then no data would be copied. The data can be copied later using the glBufferSubData API.
usage	This is the expected type of pattern used for data store.

4. The usage parameter provides hints to the OpenGL ES system about how the data is patterned, so that it can be handled intelligently and efficiently when it comes to storing or accessing the data. This parameter can accept one of the following types:

Types	Meaning
GL_STREAM_DRAW	This type of vertex buffer data is rendered for a small number of times and then discarded
GL_STATIC_DRAW	This is a type of buffer data that is rendered many times, and its contents never changes
GL_DYNAMIC_DRAW	This type of buffer data is rendered many times, and its content changes during rendering

5. The glBufferData creates the buffer data store for the current bound target with the required size. If the data parameter is initialized with NULL, then the buffer remains uninitialized. This VBO can be initialized later using the glBufferSubData API.

   ❑ **Syntax:**

   ```
   void glBufferSubData(GLenum target, GLintptr
   offset,GLsizeiptr size, const GLvoid * data);
   ```

Variable	Description
target	This parameter is similar to what is defined in the glBindBuffer as described earlier
offset	This is the index on the buffer store, specifying the start location from where the data will be written
size	This is the data size in bytes that needs to be filled in the buffer store, starting from the offset position
data	This is a pointer to the new data that will be copied into the data store

6. The following program implements the VBO with all the APIs discussed earlier:

```
float size = 24*sizeof(float);
glGenBuffers(1, &vId);

glBindBuffer(GL_ARRAY_BUFFER, vId );;
glBufferData(GL_ARRAY_BUFFER,size+size,0,GL_STATIC_DRAW);;
```

```
glBufferSubData(GL_ARRAY_BUFFER, 0, size, cubeVerts);
glBufferSubData(GL_ARRAY_BUFFER, size,size,cubeColors);

unsigned short indexSize = sizeof( unsigned short )*36;
glGenBuffers(1, &iId);
glBindBuffer(GL_ARRAY_BUFFER, iId);
glBufferData(GL_ARRAY_BUFFER, indexSize,0,GL_STATIC_DRAW);
glBufferSubData(GL_ARRAY_BUFFER,0,indexSize,cubeIndices);
/* Once the VBO created and used, reset the array and element
buffer array to its original state after use, this is done by
binding 0 to array and element buffer*/
glBindBuffer( GL_ARRAY_BUFFER, 0 );
glBindBuffer( GL_ELEMENT_ARRAY_BUFFER, 0 );
```

7. Finally, the rendering will be performed by binding the VBO and specifying the generic
    attribute data in terms of offset in the buffer object, as shown here:

```
// Specify VBO-ID for send attribute data
glBindBuffer( GL_ARRAY_BUFFER, vId );
glVertexAttribPointer
    (attribVertex, 3, GL_FLOAT, GL_FALSE, 0,
(void*)0);glVertexAttribPointer
    (attribColor, 3, GL_FLOAT, GL_FALSE, 0,(void*)size);

// Specify VBO for element index array
glBindBuffer( GL_ELEMENT_ARRAY_BUFFER, iId );
glDrawElements(GL_TRIANGLES,36,GL_UNSIGNED_SHORT,(void*)0);
glBindBuffer( GL_ARRAY_BUFFER, 0 );
glBindBuffer( GL_ELEMENT_ARRAY_BUFFER, 0 );
```

How it works...

The glGenBuffers API creates a number of vertex buffer objects specified by the
first parameter n. It returns the VBO ID (handle) array if the vertex buffer objects are
successfully created.

Once the VBO are created, they need to bind to the target with the glBindBuffer API.
Basically, the target tells the VBO what type of vertex data it can store. This data can be either
a vertex array or an index array data. The vertex array data contains vertex information, such
as position, color, texture coordinate, and so on. However, the index array contains the order
vertex index information. Therefore, the target could be specified as GL_ARRAY_BUFFER or
GL_ELEMENT_ARRAY_BUFFER.

The data size required to fill into the bound vertex buffer object is specified using `glBufferData`. We also need to specify the nature of data the VBO is going to store. The final `step` is to fill in the buffer object with data. We can use `glBufferSubData` to fill the vertex data. The VBO allows us to specify multiple arrays in the same buffer object. We can use offset and size one after the other. Make sure that you bind the buffer object to the current rendering state before rendering with the `glBindBuffer` API. The VBO can be deleted using `glDeleteBuffers` as per the program requirement.

 If an application uses multiple VBO, then it is advisable to bind the VBO to `0` after rendering of the model. This way, the original states remain preserved.

Transformations with the model, view, and projection analogies

To define a rendering scene in computer 3D graphics, model, view, and projection is the cleanest approach. It dissects a scene into these three logical concepts that helps us visualize the scene clearly before it appears on paper or in the form of a program. It will not be wrong to say that it is a modular approach to scene visualization.

Object: An object is a defined by a set of vertices in the 3D space. Each object has its own origin. For example, a cube contains eight vertices with respect to the origin at the center. The vertices used to define the object are called object coordinates:

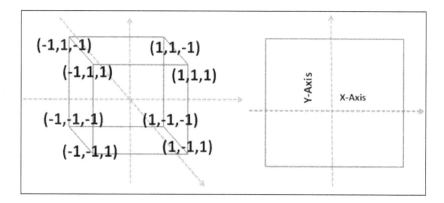

Model: Modeling in 3D graphics is a transformation process where an object is displaced to an arbitrary position in the 3D space. This 3D space is called world space (also known as model space). For example, we can use several instances of our cube object and place them in the 3D space so that they form the English alphabet **T**.

 Modeling is achievable by a 4 x 4 matrix called the Model Matrix. Programmatically, an identity matrix, which is multiplied by transformation matrices, contains scale, translation, and rotation information. The resultant is the Model Matrix.

Viewing: In simpler terms, we can say that the view is a position in the 3D space from which the model needs to be viewed. For example, in engineering drawing, there are three types of views: the top, front, and side views. These are produced by moving the camera in the *x*, *y*, and *z* axes and looking towards the origin of the viewing object. The viewing is a transformation that applies on the world coordinates to produce eye coordinates.

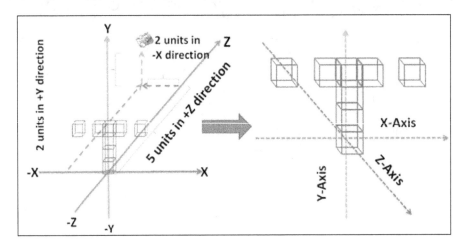

 Model-view analogy: The model and view concepts we discussed earlier are completely interchangeable. This means that we can do all the view transformations with model transformation and vice versa. For example, we can make the object scale by viewing it closer or placing it near the viewing location. Similarly, translation and rotation operations can also be performed on this object. Therefore, many books represent it as a model-view approach, so don't get confused with this term. Mathematically, model view is just another 4 x 4 matrix that is achieved by multiplying view matrix and the model matrix.

Projection: Projection transformation is the process where a scene is restricted by a clipping region in the form of a frustum or cuboidal. Both forms have six clipping planes that are helpful in restricting the objects, by clipping the objects present outside these clipping planes. This stage helps the graphics system increase the performance by considering only a finite set of objects within the frustum box. The following figure shows the role of frustum clipping planes. The result of the eye coordinates on projection system is clip coordinates:

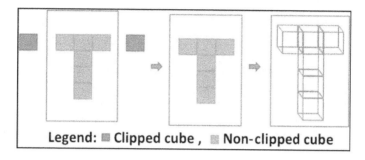

Legend: ■ Clipped cube , ▨ Non-clipped cube

Normalize view: The clip coordinates are used to create normalize device coordinates that shrink the clipped view to a unity range by dividing it by **W**, where W is the constant used to create homogenous coordinates.

Viewport transformation: This is the final transformation in which the normalize device coordinates are converted into screen coordinates system (that is, window coordinates):

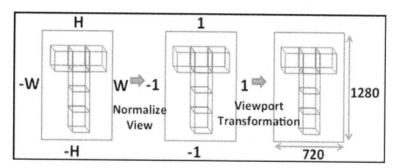

The preceding figure shows how the vertex processing takes place in 3D graphics that is transformed from object-coordinate system to appear onto the physical screen in the window-coordinate system.

Getting ready

The model-view-projection is purely a mathematical transformation concept. This is not a part of OpenGL ES 3.0; it's entirely up to an end user to implement these transformations in its own way. This book uses transformations through an open source `maths` library called `glm` and uses the 0.9.4 version of this library.

> **OpenGL Mathematics (GLM)** is a header only C++ mathematics library for graphics software based on the **OpenGL Shading Language (GLSL)** specification. You can download this library at `http://glm.g-truc.net`.
>
> The transformation-based function of the GLM library is wrapped under a higher-level class called `Transform` in the GLPI framework.

Overview of transformation:

Transformation is a process by which one coordinate space is converted to another coordinate space, for example, translation, rotation, and scaling. There are two types of transformations:

- **Geometric transformation**: This specifies when an object undergoes the transformation relative to the coordinate system.
- **Coordinate transformation**: This specifies when the coordinate system undergoes the transformation and the object remains still.

On the computer, these transformations are stored in the form of 4 x 4 transformation matrices. The transformation matrix used for 3D systems contain 16 elements in a continuous memory location. There are two ways in which multidimensional arrays can be represented in the memory.

- **Row Major**: The element in the memory location is stored row-wise
- **Column Major**: The element in the memory location is stored column-wise

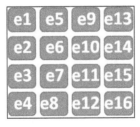

Logical representation of matrix in **Row Major (RM)** and **Column Major (CM)**:

Offset	0	1	2	3	4	5	6	7	8	9	10	11	12	13	14	15
RM	e1	e5	e9	e13	e2	e6	e10	e14	e3	e7	e11	e15	e4	e8	e12	e16
CM	e1	e2	e3	e4	e5	e6	e7	e8	e9	e10	e11	e12	e13	e14	e15	e16

In order to fix the pipeline OpenGL ES, the convention used for matrices is column major. Programmers have to abide by this convention. However, there is no restriction in the programmable pipeline to use either the row major or column major convention because all matrixes are managed by programmers themselves. It's advisable to stick to the column matrix representation as a convention to avoid any confusion.

Vertex representation in the matrix form: A vertex in 3D space is represented by three coordinates (x, y, and z). However, in reality, it's represented by four tuples(x, y, z, and w) instead of three. The forth tuple is called as homogeneous coordinate. In OpenGL ES, all three-dimensional coordinates and vectors use homogenous coordinates.

Homogenous coordinates: In homogenous coordinates, one set of coordinates can be represented by different types of coordinates. For example, for 1, 2, and 3, the various homogenous representations can be 5, 10, 15, and 5 or 4, 8, 12, and 4 because they can be simplified in a general form:

```
(a, b , c, w) => (a/w, b/w, c/w, w/w) => (a/w, b/w, c/w, 1)
```

Therefore, the preceding two coordinates can be deduced as 5/5, 10/5, 15/5, and 5/5 or 4/4, 8/4, 12/4, and 4/4. This is logically equal to 1, 2, 3, and 1.

The perspective division stage in the fixed/programmable pipeline uses the w component of clip coordinates to normalize them. For translation purposes, always use the w component as 1. Therefore, any 3D vertex (x, y, and z) is represented as (x, y, z, and 1).

How to do it...

Perform the following procedure to implement the model-view-projection paradigm with the help of various mathematical transformation operations:

 For more information on the internals of the 3D transformation, you can refer to the *There's more...* section in this recipe. This section covers transformation operations, such as translation, scaling, and rotation.

1. When a scene is rendered to the model-view-project information stored in the model, view, and projection matrices. In order to use any of these matrices, use the `TransformSetMatrixMode` function from the `Transform` class. This class allows you to set the relevant matrix as per the requirement of the application. This API accepts one parameter called mode, which tells the GLPI framework what kind of operation it is presently in; the accepted values of this parameter will be MODEL_MATRIX (modeling), VIEW_MATRIX (viewing), or PROJECTION_MATRIX (projection).

   ❑ **Syntax**:

   ```
   void Transform::TransformSetMatrixMode( unsigned int mode )
   ```

 You can manipulate these matrices in any arbitrary order before executing the drawing command. This book follows the convention of first processing the projection matrix, which is followed by view and model matrix operations.

   The projection information is computed in the `Renderer::setupProjection` function. For this, the projection matrix needs to be activated first. For more information on projection systems and the working logic under this function, refer to the *Understanding the projection system in GLPI* recipe. This function is responsible for defining the clipping planes for projection frustum; any object that stays in this frustum box will be visible:

   ```
   void Renderer::setUpProjection(){
       Transform*   TransformObj = &RenderMemData.TransformObj;

   //Set up the PROJECTION matrix.
       TransformObj->TransformSetMatrixMode( PROJECTION_MATRIX );
       TransformObj->TransformLoadIdentity();
   // Many lines skipped.
   // For more information refer to next recipe
   }
   ```

 Whenever the current matrix is switched, it may contain some garbage or old transformation values. These values can be cleaned by setting the matrix as an identity matrix. This can be done using the `TransformLoadIdentity()` function from the `Transform` class.

2. Activate the view matrix in the `Renderer::setupView` function. This function is responsible for viewing information. For example, in this recipe, the viewer is -2 and -15 units away from the origin (0.0f, 0.0f, and 0.0f):

   ```
   void Renderer::setUpView(){
       Transform*  TransformObj = &RenderMemData.TransformObj;
   ```

```
//Set up the VIEW matrix.
    TransformObj->TransformSetMatrixMode( VIEW_MATRIX );
    TransformObj->TransformLoadIdentity();

// The viewer is -2 and -15 units away on y and z axis
    TransformObj->TransformTranslate(0, -2, -15);
}
```

3. Now, we are good to go; the rendering where the modeling transformation is preserved. The model matrix is activated in the `Renderer::setupModel`. From now on, any modeling transformation is always applied to the model matrix because it's the most recent activated matrix:

```
void Renderer::setUpModel(){
    Transform*      = &R TransformObj enderMemData.TransformObj;
//Set up the MODEL matrix.
    TransformObj->TransformSetMatrixMode( MODEL_MATRIX );
    TransformObj->TransformLoadIdentity();
}
```

4. Render the drawing objects; the transformation applied to these objects will affect the model matrix.

   1. Create eight simple 3D cubes, such as C1, C2, C3, C4, C5, C6, C7, and C8 each with a dimension of 2 x 2 x 2 logical units (length x breadth x height). Note that units in OpenGL ES are logical.

   2. Keep the C1 at origin. Displace C2 by 2 units, C3 by 4 units, and C4 by 6 units along positive *y* axis.

   3. Displace C5 by 6 units in the positive *y* axis and 2 units in the negative *x* axis. Displace C6 by 6 units in the positive *y* axis and 2 units in the positive *x* axis.

   4. Displace C7 by 6 units in the positive *y* axis and 6 units in the negative *x* axis.

   5. Displace C8 by 6 units in the positive *y* axis and 6 units in the positive *x* axis:

```
void Cube::Render(){

    static float k = 0;
    Transform* TransformObj = MapRenderHandler->
RendererTransform();
    // Rotate the whole Geometry along Y-Axis
    TransformObj->TransformRotate(k++, 0, 1, 0);

    // Render C1 Box at Vertical 2 Units Up
    TransformObj->TransformPushMatrix();
    TransformObj->TransformTranslate( 0, 2, 0);
    RenderCubeVBO();
```

```
            TransformObj->TransformPopMatrix();

            // Render C2 Box at Vertical 4 Units Up
            TransformObj->TransformPushMatrix();
            TransformObj->TransformTranslate( 0, 4, 0);
            RenderCubeVBO();
            TransformObj->TransformPopMatrix();

            // Similarly, Render C3 to C8 boxes
        }
```

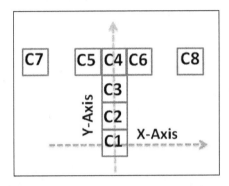

How it works...

A scene is a composition of model, view, and projection. Each of these has a specific responsibility. Model stores the modeling transformation that is applied to the rendering items, such as rotation or translation. The model matrix (MODEL_MATRIX) is activated in the setupModel function. From here on, any kind of model rendering transformation is applied to the model matrix. For example, in the present recipe, various transformations (such as rotation and translation) are applied to a simple 3D cube to render it to different spatial positions. When object coordinates of the cube geometry are applied to model transformations, it yields world coordinates. The selection of the required matrix (model, view, and projection) can be done using TransformSetMatrixMode.

The viewing transformation is the middle stage in the scene construction, which is responsible for setting up the view or camera in the 3D space. In other words, it tells you how a scene will be viewed in a 3D space. In the present recipe, the scene is viewed from a position 15 units away from the origin on the z axis and -2 units away from the y axis. The view transformation is carried out in the setupView function and it affects the view matrix (VIEW_MATRIX). The view matrix is applied to world coordinates in order to produce eye coordinates.

The projection system defines a view volume and keeps track of all objects that falls in it. Only these objects will be rendered. The viewing volume or the frustum consists of six clipping planes. These are constructed in the `setupProject` function. Here, the transformation is carried out on the projection matrix (`PROJECTION_MATRIX`). This projection matrix uses eye coordinates and converts them to clipping coordinates.

The following diagram shows the complete process of the vertex life cycle for transformation purposes:

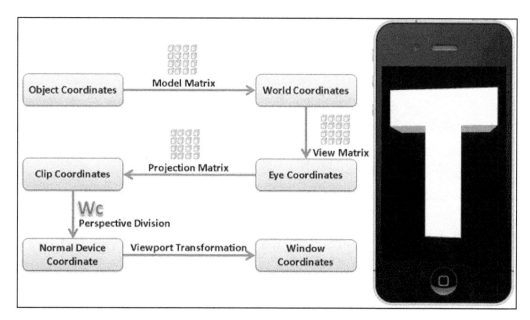

There's more...

Transformation operation: There are mainly three types of transformations that are majorly used. Each of these transformations is stored in the mathematical column major matrix form under the OpenGL ES convention. These transformations are represented by a 4 x 4 matrix.

> ▸ **Translation**: This translation operation occupies the 13th, 14th, and the 15th position in the 4 x 4 transformation matrix or in the row-column format, that is, [0, 3], [1, 3], and [2, 3]. The P vertex (Vx, Vy, and Vz) with T translation (Tx, Ty, and Tz) can be represented in a general form: $P' = T.P$.

> The `Transform` class provides the `TransformTranslate` API for the translation operation.

❑ **Syntax:**

```
void TransformTranslate(float Tx, float Ty, float Tz);
```

Variables	Description
Tx	This specifies the translation distance in a logical unit along the x axis
Ty	This specifies the translation distance in a logical unit along the y axis
Tz	This specifies the translation distance in a logical unit along the z axis

▸ **Scale**: Scale components along x, y, and z components in matrices are represented using diagonal elements. The P vertex (Vx, Vy, and Vz) scaled by the S factor (Sx, Sy, and Sz) can be generalized, as shown in the following figure:

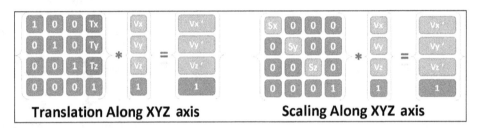

Translation Along XYZ axis   **Scaling Along XYZ axis**

 The `Transform` class provides the `TransformScale` API for the scale operation.

❑ **Syntax:**

```
void TransformScale(float Sx, float Sy, float Sz);
```

Sx	This denotes scaling along the *x* axis
Sy	This denotes scaling along the *y* axis
Sz	This denotes scaling along the *z* axis

▸ **Rotation**: This transformation along the x, y, and z axis through zero degree can be represented in the matrix form, as given in the following diagram:

Assume, $\cos(\theta) = C$ and $\sin(\theta) = S$.

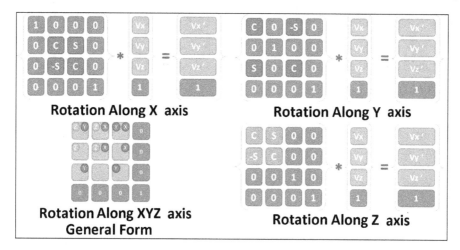

Rotation Along X axis   Rotation Along Y axis

Rotation Along XYZ axis
General Form   Rotation Along Z axis

 The `Transform` class provides the `TransformRotate` API for the rotation operation.

❑ **Syntax**:

```
void TransformRotate(float angle,float Rx,float
Ry,float Rz);
```

Variable	Description
angle	This indicates the degree of rotation
Rx	This indicates the degree of rotation along the x axis
Ry	This indicates the degree of rotation along the y axis
Rz	This indicates the degree of rotation along the z axis

See also

▸ *Understanding the projection system in GLPI* recipe in *Appendix, Supplementary Information on OpenGL ES 3.0*

Understanding the projection system in GLPI

In this recipe, we will understand two types of projection systems that are very commonly used in 3D graphics: perspective projection system and orthographic projection system:

> ▶ **Perspective projection system**: This type of projection system creates a view that is similar to how our eyes view the objects. This means that the objects that are near to us will appear bigger when compared to the far off objects. This type of projection system uses a frustum-clipping region, as shown on the left-hand side of the next figure.
>
> In the GLPI framework, the `Transform::TransformSetPerspective()` function can be used to create a perspective view.
>
> > ❑ **Syntax**:
> >
> > ```
> > void Transform::TransformSetPerspective( float fovy, float
> > aspect_ratio, float clip_start, float clip_end, float
> > screen_orientation )
> > ```
> >
> > | Variable | Description |
> > |---|---|
> > | `fov` | This defines the field of view |
> > | `aspect_ratio` | This is the rendering aspect ratio (width/height) |
> > | `clip_start` and `clip_end` | These are the near and far clipping planes |
> > | `screen_orientation` | These are the vertical or horizontal orientation for scene rendering |

> ▶ **Orthographic projection system**: This type of projection system is specially used in engineering applications where near and far objects always appear with the same dimensions. Therefore, the orthographic projection system retains the geometric dimensions. This projection system uses a clipping region in the cuboidal shape, as shown in the next figure.

The GLPI framework provides orthographic projection with the `TransformOrtho()` function. Any model rendered within this clipping plane range will be displayed on the screen, and the rest will be clipped out.

❑ **Syntax**:

```
void Transform::TransformOrtho( float left, float right,
float bottom,float top,float clip_start,float clip_end )
```

Variable	Description
`left` and `right`	These are the left and right range of the clipping planes
`bottom` and `top`	These are the bottom and top range of clipping planes
`clip_start` and `clip_end`	These are the near and far clipping planes

The following figure shows that the cubes nearer to the camera are appearing bigger compared to others placed at far distance. On the right-hand side, the projection generated by this is displayed. This projection clearly shows that irrespective of the distance of the cube from the camera, they all appear with same dimensions:

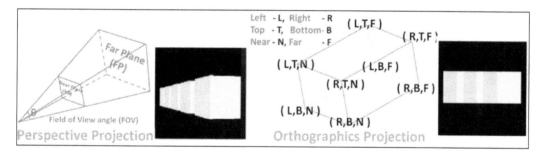

How to do it...

Here are the steps to implement the perspective and orthographic projection systems:

1. In order to apply a specific projection onto the scene, we will use the setup `Projection()` function in the `Renderer` class. This will be the first function that gets called before rendering each frame. It is very important to set the current matrix as the projection matrix using the `TransformSetMatrixMode (PROJECTION_MATRIX)` function. This will ensure that the projection matrix will be in current use. Now, the orthographic or perspective projection systems can be applied using the `TransformOrtho()` or `TransformSetPerspective()` function.

2. After setting the projection system, it is important to set the current matrix as VIEW_MATRIX in order to set the camera position in the 3D space. Finally, before rendering the object's models, set the current matrix as MODEL_MATRIX, using TransformSetMatrixMode.

> Whenever the current matrix is switched, it may contain some garbage or old transformation values. These values can be cleaned by setting the matrix as identity matrix. This can be done using the TransformLoadIdentity() function.

```
void Renderer::setUpProjection(){
  RenderMemData.isPerspective    = true;
  float span                     = 10.0;

  //Set up the projection matrix.
  TransformObj->TransformSetMatrixMode( PROJECTION_MATRIX );
  TransformObj->TransformLoadIdentity();


  //Set up the Perspective/Orthographic projection.
  if (RenderMemData.isPerspective){
    TransformObj->TransformSetPerspective(60.0f, 1, 1.0,
100,0);
  }
  else{
    TransformObj->TransformOrtho( -span,span,-
span,span,span,span);
  }

  // Set the camera 10 units away
  TransformObj->TransformSetMatrixMode( VIEW_MATRIX );
  TransformObj->TransformLoadIdentity();
  TransformObj->TransformTranslate(0.0f, 0.0f, -10.0f);

  // Make the scene ready to render models
  TransformObj->TransformSetMatrixMode( MODEL_MATRIX );
  TransformObj->TransformLoadIdentity();
}
```

How it works...

This recipe renders a few cubes arranged in a linear manner in the perspective and orthographic projection systems. The projection systems can be switched on by a single tap on the screen.

This recipe first defines a 3D space volume (frustum or cuboid) using the projection system with the projection matrix. This 3D space volume consists of six planes that are responsible for displaying the object contents that are falling under this volume. The objects outside of this 3D volume will be clipped off. The view matrix is responsible for setting the eye or camera in the 3D space. In our recipe, the camera is 10 units away from the origin. Finally, set the model matrix to render the objects in the 3D space.

Culling in OpenGL ES 3.0

Culling is an important technique in 3D graphics. It is used to discard the faces that are not visible to the user. In an enclosed geometry, the faces pointing towards the camera hide the faces behind it, either partially or completely. These faces can be easily avoided during rendering by the culling technique. This is an easier way to speed up the performance in OpenGL ES graphics. There are two types of faces:

▶ **Front face**: The face in an enclosed 3D object that points outward are considered to be the front face

▶ **Back face**: The face in an enclosed 3D object that points inside of these faces are considered as to be the back face

How to do it...

Culling can be enabled in OpenGL ES 3.0 using the `glenable` API with `GL_CULL_FACE` as state flag. By default, OpenGL ES 3.0 culls the back face. This can be changed using the `glCullFace` API. Tap on the screen to switch between the front and back culling modes. This recipe will display the outside faces of the cube when back face culling is set; otherwise, it displays the inside faces when front face culling is enabled:

Syntax:

```
void glCullFace(GLenum mode);
```

Variable	Description
`mode`	This is the mode argument parameter accepts symbolic constant `GL_FRONT` (front faces are discarded), `GL_BACK` (back faces are discarded), and `GL_FRONT_AND_BACK` (no facets are drawn)

Depending on the application requirement, culling can be applied during initialization of the graphics engine or before rendering the primitives:

```
void Cube::Render(){
   glEnable( GL_CULL_FACE  ); // Enable the culling
   if (toogle){
      glCullFace( GL_FRONT ); // Culls geometries front face
   }
   else{
      glCullFace ( GL_BACK ); // Culls geometries back face
   }
   . . . . . . .}
```

The following figure shows the back-face culling and front-face culling:

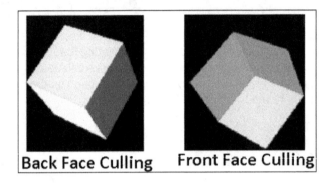

Back Face Culling   Front Face Culling

How it works...

Unlike human eyes, the computer recognizes the front face and back face of an object from the order of the vertices winding. There are two ways in which these vertices can be arranged: clockwise and anticlockwise. In the following figure, the rectangle is comprised of two triangles whose vertices are specified in a counterclockwise direction:

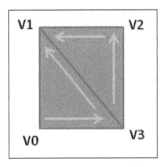

When culling is enabled using the `glEnable` API, then the order of arrangement of vertices in the array data defines the orientation of vertices in a face. This orientation plays an important role in defining the front and back faces. Using `glCullFaces` APIs, the OpenGL ES knows which all faces can be discarded. All the faces that satisfy culling rules are discarded. By convention, the default way of orientation is counterclockwise. We can change this using the `glFrontFace` API by specifying the argument as `GL_CCW` (counter clockwise) or `GL_CW` (clockwise).

Depth testing in OpenGL ES 3.0

Depth testing allows us to render the object in the order of distance from the viewer. Without depth testing the rendering of the objects is similar to the painter's algorithm on the device screen. It will render the object on first-come-first-draw basis. For example, if there are three different colored triangles rendered in the order of, say, red, green, and blue, then as per painter's algorithm, it draws red first, green second, and blue at last. The result will appear on the screen in an opposite order, with blue on the top, green in the middle, and red at the bottom. This type of rendering does not take the distance of the triangle objects from the camera into consideration. In real life, the object closer to the camera hides the objects behind them. In order to deal with such real-time scenarios, depth testing is used. It renders the objects based on the depth of the distance from the camera, instead of using the drawing order (painter's algorithm).

In depth testing, each fragment's depth is stored in a special buffer called depth buffer. Unlike the color buffer that stores the color information, the depth buffer stores depth information of the primitive's corresponding fragment from the camera view. The depth buffer's dimension is usually the same as the color buffer. The depth buffer stores the depth information as 16-, 24-, or 32-bit float values.

Apart from rendering the objects in the correct depth order, there are many other applications in which the depth buffer is used. One of the most common use of depth buffer is to produce real-time shadows with the shadow-mapping technique. For more information, refer to the *Creating shadows with shadow mapping* recipe in *Chapter 11, Anti-aliasing Techniques*.

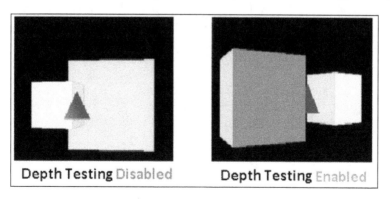

Depth Testing Disabled   **Depth Testing** Enabled

Getting ready

For this recipe, we will render three objects and apply depth testing in the toggle fashion (enable/disable) to see the effect of depth test in rendering the scene. In order to toggle the behavior, single tap on the screen.

How to do it...

In this recipe, the triangle object is in the center, and two cubes are revolving around the triangle object. The depth testing is disabled by default in OpenGL ES 3.0. It needs to be enabled by using the `glEnable` API with the `GL_DEPTH_TEST` as symbolic constant. Once depth testing is enabled, then behind the curtains, OpenGL ES creates a depth buffer. This depth buffer is used during the rendering of scenes to predict the correct order of the appearance of model objects. Make sure that you clear the depth buffer before rendering each frame with `glClear(GL_DEPTH_BUFFER_BIT)`:

```
void Cube::Render(){
   static float k,j,l = 0;
   if (toogle){
      glEnable( GL_DEPTH_TEST );
   }
   else{
      glDisable( GL_DEPTH_TEST );
   }

   // Rotate Both Cube Models
   TransformObj->TransformPushMatrix();
   TransformObj->TransformRotate(k=k+1, 0, 1, 0);

   // Render and Rotate Cube model
   TransformObj->TransformPushMatrix();
      TransformObj->TransformTranslate( 0, 0, -3);
      TransformObj->TransformRotate(j=j+4, 0, 1, 0);
      RenderCubeVBO();
   TransformObj->TransformPopMatrix();

   // Render and Rotate Second Cube model
   TransformObj->TransformPushMatrix();
      TransformObj->TransformTranslate( 0, 0, 3);
      TransformObj->TransformRotate(l=l-2, 0, 1, 0);
      RenderCubeVBO();
   TransformObj->TransformPopMatrix();
   TransformObj->TransformPopMatrix();
}
```

How it works...

The depth buffer is a kind of buffer that contains the depth information of all the fragments on the window screen. The depth buffer contains z (depth) values that range between 0.0 and 1.0. The depth buffer compares its content with z value of all the objects in the scene, as seen from the camera view. When the glClear(GL_DEPTH_BUFFER_BIT) function is called, it sets the z values of all fragments with the depth value as 1.0. Depth buffer with pixel value 0.0 is considered to be the closest to the camera position (at near plane), whereas a fragment value of 1.0 is considered to be the farthest (at far plane). When an object is rendered, the associated fragment depth is compared to the corresponding value already present in the depth buffer. This comparison is based on the glDepthFunction depth API.

 The depth test always passes if the depth test is disabled or no depth buffer exists.

The depth value can be controlled by the glDepthFunction API. This API specifies how the incoming depth values will be compared with the values already present in the depth buffer.

Syntax:

```
Void glDepthFunc(GLenum func);
```

Variable	Description
func	This indicates the condition under which the pixel will be drawn

The following table specifies the conditional checks that can be used to pass or fail the depth test. Here are the defined meanings of the symbolic constants:

Symbolic constant	Meaning
GL_NEVER	Never passes
GL_LESS	Passes if the incoming depth value is less than the stored value
GL_EQUAL	Passes if the incoming depth value is equal to the stored value
GL_LEQUAL	Passes if the incoming depth value is less than or equal to the stored value
GL_GREATER	Passes if the incoming depth value is greater than the stored value
GL_NOTEQUAL	Passes if the incoming depth value is not equal to the stored value
GL_GEQUAL	Passes if the incoming depth value is greater than or equal to the stored value
GL_ALWAYS	Always passes

There's more...

The z value of an object in the view space could be any value in between frustum's near and far planes. Therefore, we need some conversion formulas to produce z values in the range 0.0 and 1.0. The following image shows the mathematical formula to calculate the depth of an object inside the frustum using a linear transformation.

In reality, the linear transformation to calculate the z value is hardly used because it gives constant precision at all depths. However, we need more precision for items that are closer to the viewer's eyes and less precision that are farther. For this purpose, a nonlinear function is used that is proportional to 1/z to calculate the depth. Clearly in the second image, the nonlinear function produces an enormous precision at the near plane for the objects falling in the range [1, 20]. In contrast, the farther object has less precision that is fulfilling the ideal requirements:

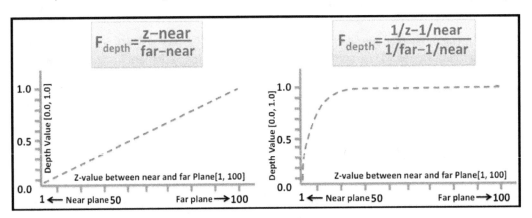

3
New Features of OpenGL ES 3.0

In this chapter, we will cover the following recipes:

- ▶ Managing variable attributes with qualifiers
- ▶ Grouping uniforms and creating buffer objects
- ▶ Managing VBO with Vertex Array Objects
- ▶ Reading and writing buffer objects with mapping
- ▶ Rendering multiple objects with geometry instancing
- ▶ Rendering multiple primitives with primitive restart

Introduction

OpenGL ES 3.0 was publicly released in August 2012. It brings the mobile 3D graphics to the next level. This release was focused to provide 3D-enriched features and enhanced the portability across diverse mobiles, embedded operating systems, and platforms. OpenGL ES 3.0 is fully backward compatible with OpenGL ES 2.0. This enables the applications to grow the graphics capabilities and visual features incrementally. OpenGL ES 3.0 also introduces a new version of **GL Shading Language** (**GLSL**) 3.0. The GLSL is used for programing shaders. The new shading language has also extended the capabilities in many directions, which you will learn in the next section.

This chapter will be helpful in understanding the new features introduced in OpenGL ES 3.0 and GL shading language 3.0. This book uses OpenGL ES 3.0 in conjunction with GLSL 3.0 for all its recipes.

The new features of OpenGL ES 3.0 can be broadly divided into the following five categories:

- **Geometry**: These features focus on the vertex attributes specifications, such as data storage, data transfer, attribute states, primitive assembly, and so on. They are explained as follows:

  - **Transform feedback**: This feature allows us to capture the vertex shader output to provide feedback to the GPU for next frame rendering. This way, it avoids CPU intervention and makes the rendering efficient.

  - **Occlusion query**: This enables fast hardware testing to check whether a pixel is going to appear on screen or whether it is occluded by another pixel. This kind of check is helpful in deciding whether to skip certain operations such as geometry processing because it's occluded.

  - **Geometry instancing**: This allows efficient rendering of an object multiple times without calling multiple render API's. This is very helpful in situations such as crowd simulation, trees rendering, and so on.

  - **Primitive restart**: This new feature allows us to render multiple disconnected primitives using a single drawing API call. The index array is used to pack multiple primitives (of the same type) in a single bundle. This array contains multiple disconnected primitives with a special marker that helps the GPU o render disconnected primitives in one go.

- **Textures**: There are many new features added into OpenGL ES 3.0 for textures. The features are described here:

  - **Depth textures and shadow comparison**: Depth textures allow the storing of the depth buffer information into a texture. This is helpful in rendering shadows using the **percentile closest filtering** (**PCF**) technique in which depth information is explicitly stored from the depth buffer to a texture using the render-to-texture technique. Later, this information is used to test incoming fragments for whether they are a part of shadow or not. OpenGL ES 3.0 allows this comparison test implicitly.

  - **Seamless cube maps**: The cubemap rendering is improved to remove artifacts from the boundary edges of the images. Now, the filtering techniques take adjacent faces texture data into account to produce seamless texture boundaries on the face edges. You can refer to the *Implementing Skybox with seamless cube mapping* recipe in *Chapter 7, Textures and Mapping Techniques*.

- ❑ **ETC2/EAC texture-compression formats**: Before OpenGL ES 3.0, there was no standard compression format officially supported by OpenGL ES. Developers relied on the specific compression formats provided by different vendors, such as PVRTC by Imagination Technologies, **Ericsson Texture Compression** (**ETC**) by Sony Ericsson, ATC by Qualcomm, and so on. Now, ETC2 and EAC texture-compression formats are integrally supported in OpenGL ES 3.0. Refer to the *Efficient rendering with ETC2 compressed texture* recipe in *Chapter 7, Textures and Mapping Techniques*.

- ❑ **Nonpower of two** (**NPOT**) texture: Now, textures with pixel dimensions of the nonpower of two texture are supported with full wrap mode and mipmapping. In earlier specifications of OpenGL ES, the textures had to be in the form of power of two (POT) dimensions. Therefore, external imaging tools were required to convert NPOT to POT format.

- ❑ **Texture swizzles**: The GLSL provides a level of abstraction in accessing the components of texture, R, G, B, and A, irrespective of the order in which they are stored physically.

- ❑ **Increased 2D texture dimension**: The dimension of 2D texture in OpenGL ES 3.0 is 2048, which is much more compared to OpenGL ES 2.0.

- ❑ **3D texture**: OpenGL ES 3.0 supports 3D texture targets. 3D textures are widely used in medical imaging.

- ❑ **Arrays of 2D texture**: This new features allows us to store multiple 2D textures in the form of an array. This is useful for animation purpose. Prior to this, texture sprites were used.

- ▸ **Shaders**: These are the special small programs that are used in modern computer graphics programming to control geometry and pixel color shading. The features on shaders are as follows:

  - ❑ **Program binaries**: The vertex and fragment shaders are compiled and stored in a binary format. This binary format needs to be linked to the program at run time in OpenGL ES 2.0. OpenGL ES 3.0 allows an optimization by storing this binary into an offline binary format that does not require linking at run time. This optimization helps load the application faster by avoiding runtime linking.

  - ❑ **Flat/smooth interpolators**: In OpenGL ES 2.0, all the interpolators perform linear interpolation across the primitives. With the help of GLSL 3.0, in OpenGL ES 3.0, the interpolation can be explicitly declared to have flat and smooth shading.

- **Buffer objects**: These allow us to store vertex data on the GPU memory. The new features have extended the capabilities of buffer objects to make them more efficient. Here are the new features:

  - **Uniform blocks**: This allows to group related uniform values into a single manageable group. This increases the readability of the shader program.

  - **Layout qualifiers**: The attributes defined in the vertex and fragment shaders can be directly bound to the user-defined locations. This way, the on-fly binding API calls are not required.

  - **Vertex Array Objects**: This feature provides an efficient way to bind vertex array data and respective attributes. **Vertex Array Objects (VAO)** are used to encapsulate the VBO. When a VAO API is called, it efficiently switches the states stored in VBO without calling several APIs. This reduces the overhead in the switching of vertex array states.

  - **Uniform buffer object**: This feature stores the uniform block in an efficient way as a buffer object. This uniform block object can be bound on fly time. This gives an opportunity to share the uniform data among multiple programs at once. Additionally, it allows us to set multiple uniform variables in one go.

  - **Subrange buffer mapping**: Unlike mapping the complete buffer from the GPU to the CPU side, this mechanism provides an efficient way to access a range of memory contents from the GPU memory space. Sometimes, the intention is to update only a small section of the buffer. Therefore, mapping the complete buffer is inefficient. In such situations, subrange buffer mapping reduces the time of marshaling from GPU to CPU to GPU.

  - **Buffer object copies**: This mechanism transfers the data of one buffer object to the other one without intervening the CPU.

  - **Sync object**: This provides a synchronized mechanism between the applications and GPU. In this way, the application can assure completion of OpenGL ES operations on the GPU side.

  - **Fencing**: This feature informs the GPU to wait for queuing up new OpenGL ES operations until the old operations are completely executed on the GPU.

- **Framebuffer**: The new features also include enhancements related to off-screen rendering for the framebuffer. Here are the new features:

  - **Multiple render target (MRT)**: This feature allows us to perform off-screen rendering simultaneously to several color buffers or textures at the same time. These textures can be used as input to other shaders or can be used on 3D models. MRTs are most commonly used to achieve deferred shading.

- ❑ **Multisample render buffer**: This feature enables the application to perform off-screen framebuffer rendering with multisample anti-aliasing. This improves the visual quality of the generated image and reduces the jagged-line effect that appears in the lines or sharp geometry edges drawn diagonally to the screen.

This chapter will focus on the new features of geometry and buffer objects. As we progress with the upcoming chapters, we will also introduce the new features of shaders, textures, and framebuffers.

 You can explore more about OpenGL ES 3.0 specifications and documentation on `http://www.khronos.org/registry/gles/specs/3.0/es_spec_3.0.3.pdf` and `http://www.khronos.org/opengles/sdk/docs/man3/`.

Managing variable attributes with qualifiers

GLSL 3.0 has introduced two new qualifiers: storage and layout. Let's take a look at them in detail:

- ▶ **Storage qualifier**: This is a special keyword that specifies the storage or the behavior of a global or local variable. It is used in shader programming. It enables the communication bridge between the application and shaders. It is also used to share information from one shader stage to another. For example, a 3D light illumination technique requires an object's geometry information in order to create realistic light shading. This geometry information is calculated in the vertex shader and passed to the fragment shader, where this input is used to color the fragments of the geometric primitives.

    There are six types of storage qualifiers available in GL SL 3.0. They are described in the following table:

Qualifier	Meaning
`const`	This is the value of variable does not alter compile time.
`in`	This is the copied input variable from the previous stage, which is linked to the current shader. If specified in a function argument, this is an input variable.
`centroid in`	This is the input type variable linked to the centroid interpolator.
`out`	This is the copied input variable from the previous stage, which is linked to the current shader. If specified in a function argument, this is an output variable.
`centroid out`	This is the output type variable that is linked to the centroid interpolator.
`uniform`	This is the value of the variables does not change across the primitives during the processing. The uniforms are shared across the shaders.

▶ **Layout qualifier**: This influences the properties of a variable, such as storage, location, memory alignment, and so on. This qualifier is widely used in declaring the location of the variable(s) in shaders. Each variable or generic attribute declared in the shader is stored in an allocated memory location on the GPU. This memory location is used to store data in the variables as a result of runtime calculation or input data from the previous stage of the shader. Unlike C/C++ pointers, the shading language uses a location ID to access the variable. A location is an ID (numeric value(s)) of a variable that is used to connect the variable present in the shading language to the application program.

Getting ready

The next table specifies the syntax for the storage and layout qualifiers. The storage qualifiers are mentioned before the data type of the variable. The most commonly used qualifiers are in and out. These storage qualifiers tell us whether the vertex attribute is an incoming or outgoing variable.

The layout qualifier assigns an ID or location to the vertex attribute so that run the binding and querying of the location can be avoided. The layout qualifier is always mentioned before the storage qualifier.

Qualifier	Syntax
Storage	`(storage qualifier) [Data type] [Variable Name]`
Layout	`layout (qualfier1, qualifier2 = value, . . .) [Storage qualifier]`

How to do it...

The variables in a shader are abstracted in the form of location IDs. Each variable or generic attribute is recognized using its location ID and used to bind the data in the OpenGL ES program. These location IDs/indexes can be defined using the `location` keyword in the layout qualifier.

In our first recipe, we will demonstrate the use of storage and layout qualifiers:

1. Create a vertex shader `LayoutVertex.glsl`, as shown here:

```
#version 300 es
layout(location = 0) in vec4 VertexPosition;
layout(location = 1) in vec4 VertexColor;
out vec4 Color;
uniform mat4 MODELVIEWPROJECTIONMATRIX;

// Function with two input and one output storage qualifier
```

```
void calculatePosition(in mat4 MVP, in vec4 vp, out vec4
position){
    position = MVP * vp;
}

void main()
{
    vec4 position;
    calculatePosition(MODELVIEWPROJECTIONMATRIX,
                        VertexPosition, position);
    gl_Position  = position;
    Color        = VertexColor;
}
```

2. Create the fragment shader `LayoutFragment.glsl` and modify it, as shown here:

```
#version 300 es
precision mediump float;
in vec4 Color; //in variable receive from shader
float blendFactor = 0.8;
layout(location = 0) out vec4 outColor;
// Function with input argument and output as return type
vec4 addBlend( in vec4 colorOpaque )
{
    return vec4(colorOpaque.x, colorOpaque.y,
colorOpaque.z, blendFactor);
}

void main() {
    outColor = addBlend( Color );
}
```

3. Reuse the *Efficient rendering with Vertex Buffer Object* recipe *Chapter 2, OpenGL ES 3.0 Essentials* and define the location index according to your choice in the application program, `Cube.cpp`. Make sure that the same index is specified in the shader program:

```
#define VERTEX_LOCATION 0
#define COLOR_LOCATION 1
```

4. Create the VBO and IBO in the constructor and enable the following attributes like:

```
glGenBuffers(1, &vId); // Create VBO and bind data
glGenBuffers(1, &iId); // Create IBO and bind data

// Enable the attribute locations
glEnableVertexAttribArray(VERTEX_LOCATION);
glEnableVertexAttribArray(COLOR_LOCATION);
```

5. Attach the VBO geometry data to the location ID. This will be used to send data from application to the GPU shader processor. Clearly, with the layout qualifier, the location query (glGetAttribLocation) for the vertex attribute can be avoided:

```
void Cube::RenderCube() {
    . . . . .
    glBindBuffer( GL_ARRAY_BUFFER, vId );
    glVertexAttribPointer(VERTEX_LOCATION, 3,
    GL_FLOAT, GL_FALSE, 0, (void*)0);
    glVertexAttribPointer(COLOR_LOCATION, 3, GL_FLOAT,
    GL_FALSE, 0, (void*)size);
    glBindBuffer( GL_ELEMENT_ARRAY_BUFFER, iId );
    glDrawElements(GL_TRIANGLES, 36,
    GL_UNSIGNED_SHORT, (void*)0);
    . . . . .
}
```

How it works...

The OpenGL ES program defines two index ID's in Cube.cpp, VERTEX_LOCATION and COLOR_LOCATION for vertex and color data, respectively. These indices will be used to define the attribute location in the shader program. The programmer must ensure that the layout location ID used in the shader program for the attribute must be same as the one used in the OpenGL ES program. This can be achieved by declaring the variable attributes using the layout qualifier. Prefixing the layout keyword in conjunction with the location qualifier allows the user-defined locations to attach with attribute variables. If some attribute variables are not specified by user-defined location indices, then the compiler would automatically generate and assign them.

In the shader program, VertexPosition and VertexColor are assigned to the same location indices, 0 and 1, respectively, what was defined in the OpenGL ES program. These two variable declarations are of the vec4 type, which is prefixed with the storage qualifier in. This gives information that these two variables are input to the vertex shader from the OpenGL ES program. The geometry data (vertex and color) is sent to the vertex shader by attaching the data to the location indexes of VertexPosition and VertexColor using the glVertexAttribPointer API in the RenderCube function. It should be noted that the generic attribute variables must be enabled before they are attached using the glEnableVertexAttribArray API. This recipe enables them in the Cube constructor.

When the vertex shader receives an input data for vertices in `VertexPosition` and transformation coordinates in the uniform `MODELVIEWPROJECTIONMATRIX`, it uses these two variables as an input argument to the `calculatePosition` function to calculate the transformed position of the incoming vertex. This calculated position returns to the main function as an output storage qualifier in the variable called position. The `calculatePosition` function is introduced in this recipe to demonstrate another possible use of storage qualifiers in the local scope of the shader program.

The `Color` variable uses the incoming value of `VertexColor` and passes it to the next stage in which the fragment shader consumes this value to assign the color to the fragments. In order to send data from the vertex shader to fragment shader, both shaders should use the same attribute variable name. The storage qualifier for the vertex shader must be defined as `out` since it is producing an output data for fragment shader. In contrast, the fragment shader must be specified with the `in` storage qualifier, as this receives the data from the previous stage. The fragment shader demonstrates another way of using return values from the shader programming functions.

There's more...

In the current recipe, you learned how to bind the location indices of the generic attribute variables in OpenGL ES from the shader program using layout qualifiers. As an alternative, the `glBindAttribLocation` API can also be used to explicitly bind the location index.

Syntax:

```
void glBindAttribLocation( GLuint program, GLuint index, const
GLchar *name );
```

Variable	Description
`program`	This is the program object handle
`index`	This is the index of the generic vertex attribute or variable
`name`	This is the vertex shader attribute variable that the index is to be bound

However, it is advisable to encourage layout qualifier as it does not produce the overhead of an API call for attaching the location index to shader program. The use of a layout location qualifier in the shader programing avoids the binding of attribute location at runtime in the OpenGL ES program.

See also

- ▶ Refer to the *Using the per-vertex attribute to send data to a shader* recipe in *Chapter 1, OpenGL ES 3.0 on Android/iOS*
- ▶ Refer to the *Efficient rendering with Vertex Buffer Object* recipe in *Chapter 2, OpenGL ES 3.0 Essentials*

Grouping uniforms and creating buffer objects

The interface block helps in grouping the uniform variables into one logical bunch. This is very useful in grouping the related variables in the shader programing. The interface block gives an opportunity to share the uniform data among multiple programs at once. This allows us to set multiple uniform variables in one go, which can be used many times.

A **Uniform Buffer Object** (**UBO**) is a buffer object for the interface blocks (containing uniform) similar to VBO, IBO, and so on. It stores the contents of the interface block in the GPU memory for quick data access at runtime. The UBO uses bind points that act as a mediator between the uniform block and uniform buffer. In this recipe, we will create a uniform block and learn how to program uniform buffer objects.

This recipe demonstrates the concept of interface block. In this recipe, we created an interface block to store transformation matrices. This block contain three uniforms. The interface block is stored as a buffer object using the UBO feature. This allows us to store the interface block as an OpenGL ES buffer object.

Getting ready

The syntax to create the uniform block is very simple. The following table shows the syntax and use test cases of the implementation:

Syntax	Individual uniforms	Uniform blocks
```uniform <block name>{ [Type] <variable name 1>; [Type] <variable name 2>; . . . };```	```uniform mat4 ModelMatrix; uniform mat4 ViewMatrix; uniform mat4 ProjectionMatrix;```	```uniform Transformation{ mat4 ModelMatrix; mat4 ViewMatrix; mat4 ProjectionMatrix; };```

How to do it...

Here is the step-by-step description that demonstrates the interface block and helps in programming the uniform block object:

1. Reuse the previous recipe, *Managing variable attributes with qualifiers*, and create the vertex shader (`UniformBlockVertex.glsl`) as shown here:

```
#version 300 es

layout (location = 0) in vec4 VertexPosition;
layout (location = 1) in vec4 VertexColor;

out vec4 Color;
// Uniform Block Declaration
uniform Transformation{
    mat4 ModelMatrix;
    mat4 ViewMatrix;
    mat4 ProjectionMatrix;
};

void main()
{
    gl_Position = ProjectionMatrix * ViewMatrix *
                ModelMatrix * VertexPosition;
    Color = VertexColor;
}
```

2. Create the fragment shader, (`UniformBlockFragment.glsl`), as follows:

```
#version 300 es
precision mediump float;
in vec4 Color;
layout (location = 0) out vec4 outColor;
void main() {
    outColor = vec4(Color.x, Color.y, Color.z, 1.0);
}
```

3. In the `Cube::InitModel()` function, compile the given shader(s) and create the program object. Make sure that the program is in use (`glUseProgram`) before the UBO creation is attempted. In this recipe, we created the UBO in a separate class member function `CreateUniformBufferObject`. Follow these steps to understand this function:

```
void Cube::CreateUniformBufferObject()
{
```

```
    // Get the index of the uniform block
    char blockIdx = glGetUniformBlockIndex
    (program->ProgramID, "Transformation");

    // Query uniform block size
    GLint blockSize;
    glGetActiveUniformBlockiv(program->ProgramID, blockIdx,
    GL_UNIFORM_BLOCK_DATA_SIZE, &blockSize);

    // Bind the block index to BindPoint
    GLint bindingPoint = 0;
    glUniformBlockBinding(program->ProgramID,
    blockIdx, bindingPoint);

    // Create Uniform Buffer Object(UBO) Handle
    glGenBuffers(1, &UBO);
    glBindBuffer(GL_UNIFORM_BUFFER, UBO);
    glBufferData(GL_UNIFORM_BUFFER, blockSize,
    0, GL_DYNAMIC_DRAW);

    // Bind the UBO handle to BindPoint
    glBindBufferBase(GL_UNIFORM_BUFFER, bindingPoint, UBO);
}
```

4. Query the index of the uniform block that is defined in the vertex shader using the `glGetUniformBlockIndex` API into `blockIdx`. This API accepts the program ID and the name of the uniform block whose block index needs to be queried.

5. Use `blockIdx` and query the block data size in the `blockSize` variable with the help of the `glGetActiveUniformBlockiv` API. Bind the uniform block index to binding point `bindingPoint` with `glUniformBlockBinding`.

6. Create the object handle for uniform buffer block and bind it to the symbolic constant `GL_UNIFORM_BUFFER`, and allocate the required memory specified by `blockSize`. Finally, bind the UBO with binding point by using `glBindBufferBase`.

7. In the render function, make use of buffer object memory mapping to modify the content of UBO:

```
void Cube::RenderCube()
{
    // Bind the UBO
    glBindBuffer( GL_UNIFORM_BUFFER, UBO );
    // Map the buffer block for MVP matrix
    glm::mat4* matrixBuf = (glm::mat4*)glMapBufferRange
    (GL_UNIFORM_BUFFER, 0, sizeof(glm::mat4)*(3),
```

```
GL_MAP_WRITE_BIT);
// Assign updated matrix
   matrixBuf[0] = *TransformObj->TransformGetModelMatrix();
   matrixBuf[1] = *TransformObj->TransformGetViewMatrix();
           matrixBuf[2]=*TransformObj->TransformGetProjectionMatr
ix();
// UnMap the buffer block
   glUnmapBuffer ( GL_UNIFORM_BUFFER );

// Draw Geometry using VBO..
. . . .
}
```

How it works...

The uniform block declaration in the vertex shader groups the model, view, and projection matrices into one logical block called **transformation**. When the shader program gets compiled, it assigns a unique ID/index to the block called block index. The user-defined location indexes are not permitted in uniform blocks. The following five steps are required to create a UBO:

1. Use the `glGetUniformBlockIndex` API to query the `Transformation` ID in the `blockIdx` variable.

2. In order to allocate the memory for the UBO, use the `glGetActiveUniformBlockiv` API to query the size of the `Transformation` uniform block in the `blockSize` variable.

3. Bind `blockIdx` (block index) to `bindingPoint` (binding point) using the `glUniformBlockBinding` API. UBO uses the concept of binding points to create a connection between the block index and the buffer object. Both must be bound to the binding point.

4. Unlike the buffer objects (VBO and IBO) are created in OpenGL ES, similarly create the uniform buffer object. The `glBindBuffer` and `glBufferData` APIs must use the `GL_UNIFORM_BUFFER` symbolic constant to ensure UBO buffer to the OpenGL ES state machine.

5. As mentioned in step 3, we need to attach the UBO with the respective binding point that is already attached to the block index. Use the `glBindBufferBase` API to bind UBO and `bindingPoint`.

The UBO can be used to set several values with the single UBO binding call. `RenderCube()` binds the UBO to set the uniform values for model, view, and projection matrices. The buffer object allows modifications to buffer elements using buffer-mapping techniques.

The OpenGL ES 3.0 release has introduced a new feature for range buffer mapping. This feature allows us to modify a subset of the buffer object. Unlike the old buffer-mapping technique, where the complete buffer needs to be mapped onto the CPU side, this technique appears to be much more efficient.

Use the `glMapBufferRange` API to map the UBO on the client side to modify the model, view, and projection matrices with updated values. Make sure that you unmap the buffer object after modification is completed by sing the `glUnmapBufferAPI`. Use the existing code for VBO rendering.

There's more...

The following figure describes the concept of binding point in UBOs. Each uniform block is identified with a unique index within the shader program. This index is attached to a binding point. Similarly, the UBO is also attached to the binding point and provides a mechanism to share the same data among different programs.

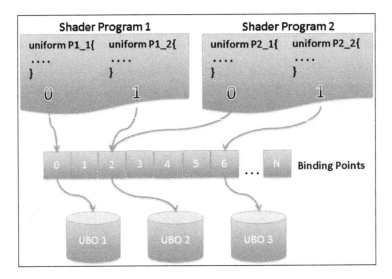

In the preceding figure, **P1_2** and **P2_1** are pointing to the same binding point. Therefore, both share the same data.

See also

▸ Refer to the *Efficient rendering with Vertex Buffer Object* recipe in *Chapter 2, OpenGL ES 3.0 Essentials*

▸ *Reading and writing buffer objects with mapping*

Managing VBO with Vertex Array Objects

In *Chapter 2*, *OpenGL ES 3.0 Essentials*, we introduced two features to load the vertex attributes using vertex arrays and **Vertex Buffer Object** (**VBO**). Both these features allow us to load the vertex attribute in the OpenGL ES rendering pipeline. The VBO are considered efficient compared to vertex arrays because they store the vertex data in the GPU memory. This reduces the cost of data copy between CPU and GPU. In this recipe, we will understand a new feature: **Vertex Array Objects** (**VAO**) of OpenGL ES 3.0. This feature is more efficient compared to VBO.

When a vertex attribute is loaded, it requires some additional calls to set the attribute states in the OpenGL ES rendering pipeline. For example, prior to rendering, the buffer object is bound using the `glBindBuffer` API, the data array is assigned using the `glVertexAttributePointer` API, and the vertex attribute is enabled using the `glEnableVertexAttribArray` API. The VAO stores all such states into a single object in order to remove the overhead caused by these calls.

This allows the application to quickly switch among available vertex array buffers and set their respective states. This makes the rendering efficient and also helps keep the programming code compact and clean.

How to do it...

This recipe demonstrates a simple grid geometry rendering using VAO in conjunction with VBO. There is no change required in shaders for programming VAO. Perhaps previous recipes from this chapter can be used.

The steps to create VAO are very straightforward:

1. Create a `Grid` class and define the geometry in the `CreateGrid` function. This function takes the dimension and division of the grid. Inside this function, create a VBO, IBO, and VAO, as shown in the following code:

```
void Grid::CreateGrid(GLfloat XDim, GLfloat ZDim, int XDiv,
int ZDiv)
{
    // Define geometry using Dimension and divisions
    // Create VBO and IBO for grid geometry
    // Create Vertex Array Object
    // Enable VBO and set attribute parameters
    // Unbind VAO, VBO and IBO
}
```

2. Create a VBO, generate the buffer, and fill in the buffer object with the vertex information:

```
// Create VBO ID
glGenBuffers(1, &vIdGrid);
glBindBuffer( GL_ARRAY_BUFFER, vIdGrid);
glBufferData( GL_ARRAY_BUFFER,size,0, GL_STATIC_DRAW);
glBufferSubData( GL_ARRAY_BUFFER, 0, size,gridVertex);
```

3. Similarly, create an IBO and fill in the buffer with the element indexes:

```
// Create IBO for Grid
unsigned short indexSize=sizeof(unsigned short)*indexNum;
glGenBuffers(1, &iIdGrid);
glBindBuffer( GL_ARRAY_BUFFER, iIdGrid );
glBufferData(GL_ARRAY_BUFFER,indexSize,0,GL_STATIC_DRAW);
glBufferSubData(GL_ARRAY_BUFFER,0,indexSize,gridIndices);
```

4. Generate the VAO ID using the `glGenVertexArrays` API. Bind this generated `Vertex_VAO_Id` using `glBindVertexArray`. The code written after the creation of the VAO is recorded in the state vector of the VAO object. Therefore, use the VBO and bind the data to the required vertex attribute for rendering purposes:

```
// Create Vertex Array Object
glGenVertexArrays(1, &Vertex_VAO_Id);
glBindVertexArray(Vertex_VAO_Id);
// Create VBO and set attribute parameters
glBindBuffer( GL_ARRAY_BUFFER, vIdGrid );
glEnableVertexAttribArray(VERTEX_LOCATION);
glVertexAttribPointer(VERTEX_LOCATION,3,GL_FLOAT,
GL_FALSE,0, (void*)0);
glBindBuffer( GL_ELEMENT_ARRAY_BUFFER, iIdGrid );
```

5. Unbind the VAO, VBO, and IBO, once the vertex states and attributes are set properly:

```
glBindVertexArray(0);
glBindBuffer( GL_ARRAY_BUFFER, 0 );
glBindBuffer( GL_ELEMENT_ARRAY_BUFFER, 0 );
```

6. Render the geometry with VAO using the `Render()` function, as shown here:

```
// void Grid::Render()
// Use shader program and apply transformation
.  .  .  .  .
glBindVertexArray(Vertex_VAO_Id); // Bind VAO
glDrawElements(GL_LINES,((XDivision+1)+(ZDivision+1))*2,
GL_UNSIGNED_SHORT, (void*)0); }
```

How it works...

The VAO stores the vertex array client states and the buffer binding in a state vector. When the VAO ID is bound, the subsequent operation calls, such as calls to bind with VBO, enable client states, and attach data buffer to generic attributes, are stored in the state vector of the VAO. This way, when the VAO is bound, the state vector provides the full state of current settings, configurations, and client states of the vertex array. Instead of making several calls, this one binding call will be sufficient to enable vertex array configurations and states.

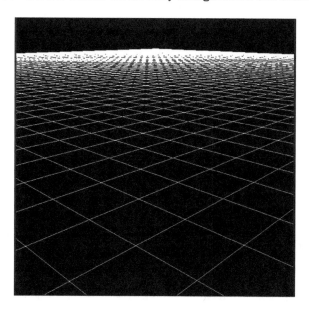

See also

▸ Refer to the _Rendering primitives with vertex arrays_ recipe in _Chapter 2, OpenGL ES 3.0 Essentials_

Reading and writing buffer objects with mapping

The previous recipe introduced a new feature to access vertex arrays using VAO. This object minimizes the overhead of switch among vertex arrays and their respective states. This recipe will go one step ahead in order to teach you how to update the data of the buffer objects using buffer mapping. The VBO can be updated using `glBufferData` and `glBufferSubData` as demonstrated in many recipes. These APIs can be used to upload or download data to the device. In contrast, the buffer mapping is an efficient way to update the buffer objects that are residing in the GPU memory.

This recipe will demonstrate buffer object range mapping. In this recipe, we will reuse the cube geometry and render each vertex of the cube as a point primitive, instead of a triangle primitive. Each vertex of the cube is programmed to change its colors randomly using the buffer object range mapping feature after a fixed interval of time.

Getting ready

Before we start with a step-by-step description, here is the overview of buffer object range mapping:

1. Bind the buffer that needs to be mapped using glBindBuffer.
2. Get the pointer to the memory location from driver memory space using the glMapBufferRange API.
3. Use this pointer to perform any read/write operations on the acquired memory.
4. Invalidate the acquire pointer using the glUnmapBuffer API. This API allows us to send updated memory contents to the GPU memory space.

How to do it...

This recipe does not require any special change in the vertex and fragment shaders. For this recipe, we used a new GL shading language API called gl_PointSize. This API is used to specify the size of the GL_POINTS primitives. Make use of the *Efficient rendering with Vertex Buffer Object* recipe in *Chapter 2, OpenGL ES 3.0 Essentials*, and proceed with the following steps to program range mapping onto a buffer object:

1. First, create the VAO of the cube geometry using the previous VAO recipe.
2. Program the map range buffer inside the Render() function as shown here. The following steps will describe this function:

```
void Cube::RenderCube(){
    if (clock() - last >= CLOCKS_PER_SEC * 0.1){
        // Bind the Buffer Object for vertex Array.
        glBindBuffer( GL_ARRAY_BUFFER, vId );
        // Get the mapped memory pointer.
        GLfloat* colorBuf = (GLfloat* )glMapBufferRange(
   GL_ARRAY_BUFFER, size, size, GL_MAP_WRITE_BIT);
        for(int i=0; i<size/sizeof(GLfloat); i++)
   {   colorBuf[i] = float(rand()%255)/255; }
        last = clock();
        // Invalidate the mapped memory.
        glUnmapBuffer ( GL_ARRAY_BUFFER );
    }
```

```
// Perform Transformation.
. . . . . . .
// Bind the VAO and Render the cube
// with Point primitive.
glBindVertexArray(Vertex_VAO_Id);
glDrawElements(GL_POINTS,36,GL_UNSIGNED_SHORT,(void*)0);
}
```

3. First, bind the VBO in order to map the color buffer data using the `glBindBuffer` API. Map the pointer to the color data memory. The color data in the VBO starts from the size index and is also size bytes long:

```
colorBuf = (GLfloat*)glMapBufferRange (GL_ARRAY_BUFFER,
  size, size, GL_MAP_WRITE_BIT);
```

On successful mapping of the buffer object, it returns a valid pointer to the memory mapped location. If an error occurs, the API would return the `NULL` pointer.

   ❑ **Syntax:**

```
void *glMapBufferRange(GLenum target, GLintptr offset,
                  GLsizeiptr length, GLbitfield access);
```

Variable	Description
target	This specifies the type of buffer, which is expected to bind for memory mapping, for example, GL_MAP_READ_BIT and GL_MAP_WRITE_BIT
offset	This specifies the starting offset within the buffer object that is the subject of interest for mapping
length	This specifies the range of the buffer that needs to be mapped
access	This is the symbol constant flag combination that indicates the desired access to the buffer range

4. Copy the new color values in this mapped memory buffer:

```
// size/sizeof(GLfloat) gives total number of elements
// that needs to be updated with new color, the formula
// is- total size of buffer / unit item size
for(int i=0; i<size/sizeof(GLfloat); i++){
    colorBuf[i] = float(rand()%255)/255;
}
```

5. Unmap the memory mapped buffer to indicate the OpenGL ES rendering pipeline to transfer this data to the GPU memory space:

```
glUnmapBuffer ( GL_ARRAY_BUFFER );
```

The `UnmapBuffer` API returns the Boolean `TRUE` if it successfully unmaps the current mapped buffer. If some error occurs, it returns `FALSE`.

   ❑ **Syntax**:

```
GLboolean glUnmapBuffer(GLenum target);
```

Variable	Description
target	This specifies the type of the buffer that needs to unbound

6. Bind the VAO and render the geometry using the `GL_POINTS` primitive. The `GL_POINTS` primitive renders small dots on the screen. In order to increase the dimension of these dots, the `gl_PointSize` API can be used in the vertex shader, as shown in the next step:

```
glBindVertexArray(Vertex_VAO_Id);
glDrawElements(GL_POINTS, 36, GL_UNSIGNED_SHORT, (void*)0);
```

7. Create `BufferMappingVertex.glsl` as follows:

```
layout(location = 0) in vec4 VertexPosition;
layout(location = 1) in vec4 VertexColor;
uniform mat4 MODELVIEWPROJECTIONMATRIX;
out vec4 Color;
void main(){
   gl_Position = MODELVIEWPROJECTIONMATRIX * VertexPosition;
   gl_PointSize= 80.0; // Size of GL_POINTS primitive
   Color       = VertexColor;
}
```

How it works...

In the VBO, `glBufferData` and `glBufferSubData` use the user data and copy it into a hooked/pinned location in the device memory location. This hooked location can be accessed by the GPU. The user data is copied to this memory location like `memcpy` internally. As the data copying process gets completed, the driver starts **direct memory allocation (DMA)** without intervening the CPU cycles.

The target destination of the DMA depends upon the usage hints from the (GL_STREAM_ DRAW, GL_STREAM_READ, GL_STREAM_COPY, GL_STATIC_DRAW, GL_STATIC_READ, GL_ STATIC_COPY, GL_DYNAMIC_DRAW, GL_DYNAMIC_READ, or GL_DYNAMIC_COPY) APIs.

In contrast, the `glMapBufferRange` method is considered much more efficient. The API first hooks a memory location directly into the driver memory space. This pinned memory location is available through a pointer to the application. This pointer can be directly used to update the location for the uploading or downloading of data for read/write purposes. Once the operation on the mapped location for read/write is completed, the pointer can be made invalid by calling `glUnMapBuffer`. This API call hints the OpenGL ES pipeline to push the updated data to the GPU memory using DMA calls.

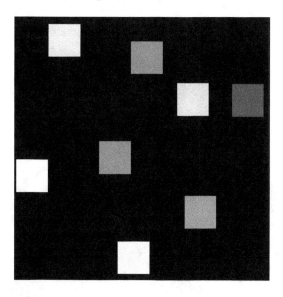

See also

▸ Refer to the *Swizzling* recipe in *Appendix, Supplementary Information on OpenGL ES 3.0*

▸ Refer to the *Transform feedback particle system with sync objects and fences* recipe in *Chapter 12, Real-time Shadows and Particle System*

Render multiple objects with geometry instancing

The geometry instancing allows us to render multiple instances of the same object in a single rendering API call. These multiple instances differ in their generic attributes, such as transformation matrices, color, scale, and so on. This feature is very useful to implement particle systems, crowd simulation, rendering of jungle trees, and so on. Compared to the traditional way of rendering multiple objects that use multiple rendering calls, this technique is very efficient as it requires a single API call. This reduces the overhead of CPU processing in sending multiple rendering calls to the OpenGL ES rendering engine.

This recipe demonstrates the rendering of 1000 cubes using geometric instancing. For this, we will use 1000 matrices in a VBO. Each matrix contains a transformation to place a cube in the 3D space. The information of the matrices are updated using the range map buffer feature as discussed in the previous recipe. This allows us to pass new transformation data on the fly at run time. The transformed data contains new rotation and translated positions.

How to do it...

So far, in our recipes, the model-view-projection matrix is always treated as uniform in the vertex shader. For this recipe, we will make use of the VAO and declare the model-view-projection matrix as a generic attribute instead of a uniform. Since the matrix is an attribute, a new VBO is required. This VBO is stored in the `matrixId` variable. `RenderCube()` uses the map buffer to update transformation matrix data.

Here are the steps to implement geometric instancing:

1. Create the vertex shader and add the following code. There is no change required for the fragment shader. It can be reused:

    ```
    #version 300 es
    layout(location = 0) in vec4 VertexPosition;
    layout(location = 1) in vec4 VertexColor;
    ```

```
layout(location = 2) in mat4 MODELVIEWPROJECTIONMATRIX;
out vec4 Color;
void main() {
  gl_Position = MODELVIEWPROJECTIONMATRIX * VertexPosition;
  Color = VertexColor;
}
```

2. In `Cube::InitModel()`, use the existing code and add a new VBO for matrix transformation. Get the ID of the generated buffer object in `matrixId`:

```
// Create VBO for transformation matrix
glGenBuffers(1, &matrixId);
glBindBuffer (GL_ARRAY_BUFFER, matrixId);
```

3. Allocate the memory to the VBO for matrix transformation. The dimension variable is initialized with 10. It gives the number of cubes along an axis. Therefore, along x, y, and z axes, *10 x 10 x1 0 = 1000 cubes*. The total size of the buffer would be size of *(GLfloat) * 16 (16 float elements in mat4) * 1000 (cubes)*:

```
glm::mat4 transformMatrix[dimension][dimension][dimension];
glBufferData(GL_ARRAY_BUFFER, sizeof(transformMatrix) , 0, GL_
DYNAMIC_DRAW);
```

   The `glBufferData` uses `GL_DYNAMIC_DRAW`. This symbolic constant specifies that the buffer is going to contain some data that is dynamic in nature. In other words, the data will require updates in the buffer. This symbolic constant helps the graphics driver to manage buffer memory in the best possible way to achieve high-performance graphics rendering.

4. In the same function, after creating the VAO (`Vertex_VAO_Id`), define the generic attribute states and configuration of the transformation matrix buffer object. This helps in saving the vertex array client states and the buffer binding in the VAO (`Vertex_VAO_Id`). The `glVertexAttribDivisor` calculates the instance ID from the total number of instances given. For more information, refer to the *There's more...* section in this recipe:

```
// Create VBO for transformation matrix and set attributes
glBindBuffer( GL_ARRAY_BUFFER, matrixId );
glEnableVertexAttribArray(MATRIX1_LOCATION);
glEnableVertexAttribArray(MATRIX2_LOCATION);
glEnableVertexAttribArray(MATRIX3_LOCATION);
glEnableVertexAttribArray(MATRIX4_LOCATION);

glVertexAttribPointer(MATRIX1_LOCATION,4,GL_FLOAT,GL_FALSE,
   sizeof(glm::mat4),(void*)(sizeof(float)*0));
glVertexAttribPointer(MATRIX2_LOCATION,4,GL_FLOAT,GL_FALSE,
   sizeof(glm::mat4),(void*)(sizeof(float)*4));
```

```
glVertexAttribPointer(MATRIX3_LOCATION,4,GL_FLOAT,GL_FALSE,
   sizeof(glm::mat4), (void*)(sizeof(float)*8));
glVertexAttribPointer(MATRIX4_LOCATION,4,GL_FLOAT,GL_FALSE,
   sizeof(glm::mat4), (void*)(sizeof(float)*12));

glVertexAttribDivisor(MATRIX1_LOCATION, 1);
glVertexAttribDivisor(MATRIX2_LOCATION, 1);
glVertexAttribDivisor(MATRIX3_LOCATION, 1);
glVertexAttribDivisor(MATRIX4_LOCATION, 1);
```

5. In `Cube::RenderCube()`, use range buffer mapping to map the transformation buffer on the client-side memory. Update the data in the memory and unmap it. Use VAO and render the cube of cubes using the geometric instance API called `glDrawElementsInstanced`. This API's last argument specifies the number of instances the given primitive will be rendered:

```
void Cube::RenderCube()
{
   glBindBuffer( GL_ARRAY_BUFFER, matrixId );
   glm::mat4* matrixBuf = (glm::mat4*)glMapBufferRange
   (GL_ARRAY_BUFFER, 0, sizeof(glm::mat4*)*(dimension
   *dimension*dimension), GL_MAP_WRITE_BIT);
   static float l = 0;
   TransformObj->TransformRotate(l++, 1, 1, 1);
   TransformObj->TransformTranslate
   (-distance*dimension/4,-distance*dimension/4, -
   distance*dimension/4);
   glm::mat4 projectionMatrix = *TransformObj->
   TransformGetProjectionMatrix();
   glm::mat4 modelMatrix = *TransformObj->
   TransformGetModelMatrix();
   glm::mat4 viewMatrix = *TransformObj->
   TransformGetViewMatrix();
   int instance= 0;
   for ( int i = 0; i < dimension; i++ ){
   for ( int j = 0; j < dimension; j++ ){
   for ( int k = 0; k < dimension; k++ ){
   matrixBuf[instance++] = projectionMatrix *
   viewMatrix * glm::translate(modelMatrix, glm::vec3(
   i*distance , j*distance, k*distance)) * glm::rotate(
   modelMatrix, l, glm::vec3(1.0, 0.0, 0.0));
                                      }
                                      }
                                      }
```

```
glUnmapBuffer ( GL_ARRAY_BUFFER );

glBindVertexArray(Vertex_VAO_Id);
glDrawElementsInstanced(GL_TRIANGLES,36,
GL_UNSIGNED_SHORT, (void*)0, dimension*dimension*dimension);
}
```

How it works...

The application first compiles the shader programs. This makes us aware of all the generic attribute locations used in the shader program. Create a VBO of 1000 matrix elements. Each element represents a transformation matrix. This matrix element is updated with new values of the transformation of every frame in the RenderCube function.

The generic attributes are first enabled using glEnableVertexAttribArray. The data array is attached to the generic location with glVertexAttribPointer. The following figure shows how the OpenGL ES program API is attached to the layout location of the vertex shader to send data:

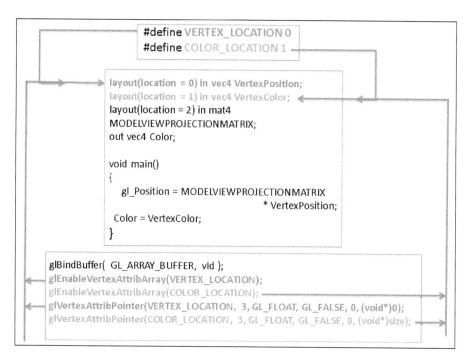

Note that the generic attributes are sent as a group of four. Therefore, for a 4 x 4 matrix, we will need four attribute locations. The start location of the attribute should be mentioned into the vertex shader using a layout qualifier:

```
layout(location = 2) in mat4 MODELVIEWPROJECTIONMATRIX;
```

The following figure shows how the attribute locations are managed by the compiler:

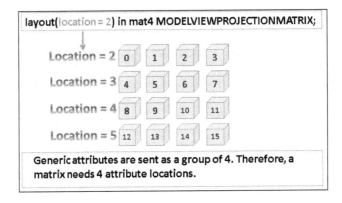

Similar to the other locations such as VERTEX_LOCATION (0) and COLOR_LOCATION (1), the transformation matrix locations (2, 3, 4, 5) also need to be enabled and attached to the array data.

The glVertexAttribDivisor API is responsible for controlling the rate at which OpenGL ES advances the data from an instanced array. The first parameter of this API specifies the generic attribute that needs to be treated as an instanced array. This tells the OpenGL ES pipeline to use this attribute per instance rendering. For example, in this example, the generic attributes, 2, 3, 4, 5, are instanced attributes. Therefore, OpenGL ES consumes the data from the transformation matrix array as an instance ID. We will see how this instance ID is calculated in a moment.

The default value of the divisor is 0 when it is not specified in the program explicitly. If the divisor is 0, the attribute index is advanced once per-vertex. If the divisor is not 0, the attribute advances once per divisor instance of the set(s) of the vertices being rendered.

Syntax:

```
void glVertexAttribDivisor(GLuint index, GLuint divisor);
```

Variable	Description
index	This specifies generic attribute layout location
divisor	This specifies the number of instances that will pass between updates of the generic attribute at the index slot

The rendering of the geometric instancing requires special instanced-based drawing APIs from OpenGL ES 3.0, as mentioned here for array- and index-based geometric data.

Syntax:

```
void glDrawElementsInstanced(GLenum mode, GLsizei count,
GLenum type, const void * indices, GLsizei primcount);
```

Variable	Description
mode	This specifies the type of the primitive that needs to be rendered
count	This specifies the number of indices considered in the drawing
type	This is used by glDrawElementsInstanced, this specifies the data type of the indices stored
indices	This specifies the arrays containing the order of the indices
primcount	This specifies the number of copies to be rendered

In the present recipe, the glDrawElementsInstanced API is used to render multiple instances of the same object. This API works in conjunction with another API called glVertexAttribDivisor. In order to update the VBO matrix elements, buffer mapping is used, which is an efficient way to update the buffer elements. If the geometric data is not index based but array based, then glDrawArraysInstanced can be used. This API accepts almost the same parameters. Refer to the online *OpenGL ES 3.0 Reference Manual* for more information.

There's more...

The second attribute of `glVertexAttribDivisor` specifies the divisor. This divisor helps in calculating the instance ID from the total number of instances. The following figure shows a simple example of the working logic of this API. In this figure, we assumed that there are total five instances to be rendered, and the figure contains five matrices. When the divisor is 5, it produces 5 instance ID of the (0, 1, 2, 3, 4). This instance ID will be used as an index to the transformation matrix array. Similarly, when the divisor is 2, it generates three instances (0, 1, 2). It generates two instances (0, 1) when the divisor is 3.

	INSTANCES	0	1	2	3	4
			instanceID = INSTANCES/Divisor			
Divisor	1	0/1 = 0	1/1=1	2/1=2	3/1=3	4/1=4
	2	0/2 = 0	1/2=0	2/2=1	3/2=1	4/2=2
	3	0/3 = 0	1/3=0	2/3=0	3/3=1	4/3=1

0 1 2 3 4

See also

▶ *Managing VBO with Vertex Array Objects*

▶ Refer to the *Efficient rendering with ETC2 compressed texture* and *Implementing Skybox with seamless cube mapping* recipes in *Chapter 7, Texture and Mapping Techniques*

Rendering multiple primitives with primitive restart

OpenGL ES 3.0 introduced a new feature called primitive restart, where multiple disconnected geometry primitives can be rendered using a single API. This feature uses a special marker in the vertex data or the index data to concatenate different geometries of the same drawing type into a single batch. The restart primitive feature executes on the GPU. Therefore, it eliminates the communication overhead per drawing call. This provides high-performance graphics by avoiding multiple drawing calls from CPU to GPU.

The recipe shows us how to use the primitive restart technique to render a cube using two sets of geometries, which are separated by a special marker.

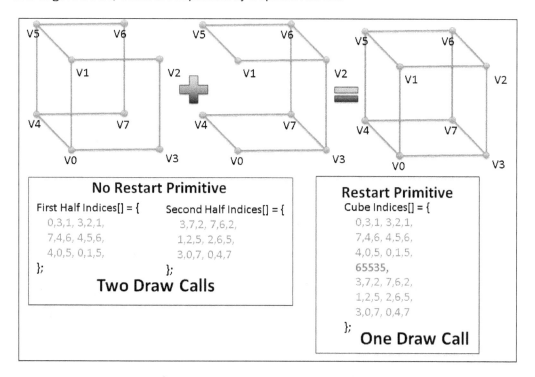

Getting ready

The marker used by the restart primitive feature to separate geometries is the highest value of the data type with which the element index or vertex data array is specified. For instance, an index value of GLushort and GLint should be _0 x FFFF_ (65535) and _0 x FFFFFFFF_ (4294967295), respectively.

How to do it...

To render multiple primitives, follow these steps:

1. Define the cube vertices and indices, as shown here:

Cube vertices	Indices

<pre>GLfloat
cubeVerts[][3] =
{
  -1, -1, 1 , // V0
  -1, 1, 1 , // V1
  1, 1, 1 ,   // V2
  1, -1, 1 , // V3
  -1, -1, -1 ,// V4
  -1, 1, -1 , // V5
  1, 1, -1 , // V6
  1, -1, -1   // V7
};</pre>
	<pre>// 36 indices
	GLushort
	cubeIndices[] =
	{
	  0,3,1, 3,2,1,
	  7,4,6, 4,5,6,
	  4,0,5, 0,1,5,
	  0xFFFF, 3,7,2,
	  7,6,2, 1,2,5,
	  2,6,5, 3,0,7,
	  0,4,7
	};</pre>

2. In order to render the cube with primitive restart, it must first of all be enabled, using glEnable(GL_PRIMITIVE_RESTART_FIXED_INDEX). Specify the total size of the indice and include the number of markers that are used in the geometry indices:

```
//Bind the VBO
glBindBuffer( GL_ARRAY_BUFFER, vId );
glVertexAttribPointer(VERTEX_LOCATION, 3, GL_FLOAT,
GL_FALSE, 0, (void*)0);
glVertexAttribPointer(COLOR_LOCATION, 3, GL_FLOAT,
GL_FALSE, 0, (void*)size);

glEnable(GL_PRIMITIVE_RESTART_FIXED_INDEX);
glBindBuffer( GL_ELEMENT_ARRAY_BUFFER, iId );
// Plus 36 + 1 because it has 1 Primitive Restart Index.
glDrawElements(GL_TRIANGLES, 36+1, GL_UNSIGNED_SHORT,
(void*)0);
glDisable(GL_PRIMITIVE_RESTART_FIXED_INDEX);
```

There's more...

The other way in which the disconnected geometry primitives can be rendered is called triangle degeneration. Triangle degeneration is the capability of the GPU to recognize disconnected primitives in the triangle strip or triangle fan index information on the basis of some special pattern.

For example, the following figure shows the special index pattern data that can be used to render degenerated triangles using the `glDrawElement` or `glDrawElementsInstanced` API.

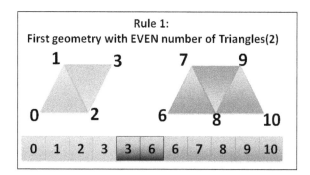

The degeneration between the two geometries is achieved by repeating the last index of the previous geometry and the first index of the next primitive. This rule of degeneration is only applicable when the previous geometry contains an odd number of triangles. Behind the curtains, the triangle would be drawn in the following order: (0, 1, 2), (2, 1, 3), (2, 3, 3), (3, 3, 6), (3, 6, 6), (6, 6, 7), (6, 7, 8), (8, 7, 10). The repeated indices form an area equivalent to zero, allowing the GPU to discard the triangles. These zero area triangles are mentioned using the bold font.

The second type of degeneration case is where the first geometry contains an odd number of triangles. For instance, the following image demonstrates the first geometry with three (odd) triangles. As per this case rule, the last index of the first geometry is repeated twice, followed by the first index of the second geometry.

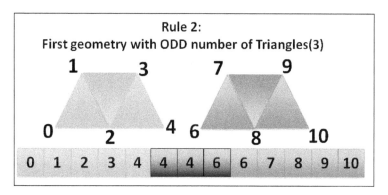

For instance, the indices specified for degenerate triangles (0, 1, 2, 3, 4, 4, 4, 8, 8, 9, 10, 11) generate the following triangles: (0, 1, 2), (2, 1, 3), (2, 3, 4), (4, 3, 4), (4, 4, 4), (4, 4, 6), (4, 6, 6), (6, 6, 9), (6, 7, 8), (8, 7, 9), (9, 8, 10).

See also

- ▶ Refer to the *Using the per-vertex attribute to send data to a shader* recipe in *Chapter 1, OpenGL ES 3.0 on Android/iOS*
- ▶ Refer to the *Efficient rendering with Vertex Buffer Object* recipe in *Chapter 2, OpenGL ES 3.0 Essentials*

4
Working with Meshes

In this chapter, we will cover the following recipes:

- ▸ Creating polygon meshes with Blender
- ▸ Rendering the wavefront OBJ mesh model
- ▸ Rendering the 3Ds mesh model

Introduction

In previous chapters, you learned the essentials of OpenGL ES to create 3D geometrical objects and place them in the 3D space and also understood and programmed new features in OpenGL ES 3.0. We also programmed a simple 3D cube model using various attributes, such as vertex positions and colors. A procedural geometry modeling (geometry built using only code without any aid of an external data-file reference or tools) in OpenGL ES is not only time consuming, but it can also be very complex to program if the geometry is very complicated. For example, rendering a 3D car model is much more difficult compared to a simple 3D cube. If the user is not careful enough, it becomes very cumbersome to program the geometry.

The best way to deal with such complicated geometry shapes is to create them using computer aided design tools; such tools not only saves time, but also the created model to visualize. The main advantage of using these tools is that you can create extremely complex geometrical shapes without having to worry about the mathematical concepts involved behind it. After the model is created, you can export them in a variety of 3D file formats in your program. These 3D geometry models are also called meshes.

In this chapter, you will learn how to create simple meshes using Blender, which is an open source 3D modeling tool. We will discuss and understand two very famous 3D mesh model types, OBJ and 3Ds, and try to understand their specifications. You will also learn how to write a parser for these models in your OpenGL ES recipes. In addition, this chapter will cover various aspects of the 3D mesh model that will be helpful to render them to 3D graphics.

Creating polygon meshes with Blender

A polygon mesh is a collection of vertices, faces, normal, colors, or textures that collectively define a 3D model. This 3D model can be directly used in various 3D applications, such as computer graphics, simulator, animation movies, and CAD/CAM. In this section, you will learn how to create mesh models in Blender, which we will use throughout the course of this book to demonstrate our recipes.

In this chapter, we will use Blender 2.68 to develop our 3D model meshes. Blender is a free and open source 3D computer graphics tool. You may use other similar software of your choice, such as 3Ds Max, Maya, Google Sketch, and so on.

Getting ready

You can download the latest version of Blender from `http://www.blender.org/download` and install it as per the instructions given on the website.

Blender is cross-platform and runs on several popular computing platforms. Blender allows a number of geometric primitives, including various polygon meshes, subdivision surface modeling, and smart geometric editing tools. It also allows various texture techniques to be implemented to geometry surfaces. When Blender is launched for the first time, you will find the tool interface, as given in the following screenshot:

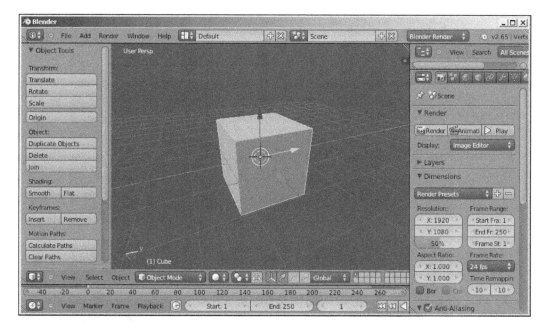

How to do it...

This section will provide a step-by-step procedure to create mesh models in Blender 2.68. We will understand the simple steps to create these meshes and export them to `wavefront.obj` and 3Ds formats so that they can be used for demonstration purposes in later recipes.

1. When Blender is launched for the first time, a cube-shaped object will be displayed in the middle of the canvas grid. If you are not interested to use this cube, you can delete this. In order to delete an object from the canvas grid, select it (by placing the cursor on it and right-clicking on it) and click on the delete key on the keyboard. Alternatively, you can select an object and click on the **X** and *Enter* key to delete the selected object.

2. By default, there are 10 basic mesh models available in Blender, which can be collectively used to create more complex shapes. Depending on the Blender version type, the UI interface may appear different. However, the basic functionality is the same. In order to add a new mesh model, navigate to menu, click on **Add | Mesh**, and select the desired model (for example, UV sphere). In the newer Blender versions (such as 2.7.0 and later versions), you may find this option on the left-hand side panel under the **Create** tab, as shown in the following screenshot:

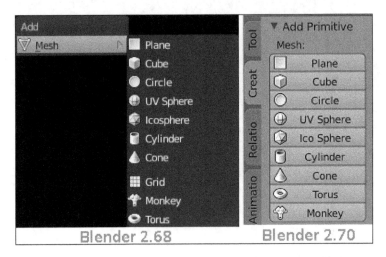

3. You can change the model properties for each model from the left-hand side pane, as shown in the following screenshot:

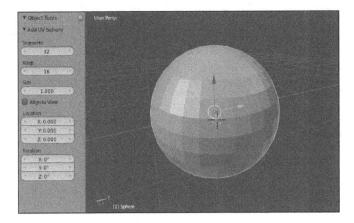

For each mesh, you can change the location and apply rotations as well. For all our recipes, we will use Location as (0.0, 0.0, and 0.0) so that the mesh always appears on the origin of the canvas grid.

4. The model can be edited in the edit mode by selecting the mesh object and clicking on the *Tab* button. In the edit model, the geometry of the mesh can be enhanced. For example, the surface of the mesh object can be subdivided into many smaller surfaces in order to enhance the smoothness of surfaces. In the edit mode, you can select the subdivide menu option to subdivide the selected objects surface. The following image shows how subdivision works:

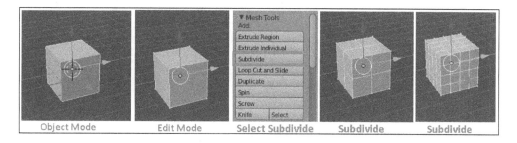

5. Export the created model using the **File | Export** menu option. We will export the created model in the wavefront and the 3Ds mesh formats. In the following sections, we will see how of these mesh formats are used in our recipes:

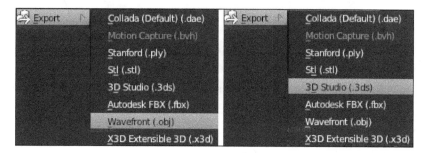

6. While exporting in the wavefront (.obj) format, you may need to select the following options, depending on your requirements:

   ❑ **Include edges**: This exports edges as two-sided faces.

   ❑ **Triangulate faces**: Instead of writing faces as a quad, each quad is represented using three triangles. We must select this option for our mesh models.

   ❑ **Include UVs (optional)**: This writes the texture coordinate information about the geometry surface

❑ **Include normals (optional)**: This writes the face and vertex normal depending on the face smooth settings:

The **Include Normals** is optional; it calculates the face normal and writes to the file-exported file format. Additionally, calculating normal at runtime will incur some extra processing cost. This feature is useful to minimize runtime calculations at the expense of a large file and the memory utilized while reading this file.

Alternatively, you can calculate the normal with the face information provided within the mesh model. Later in this recipe, you will learn how the normal is calculated using the face information.

7. To export the 3Ds format, use all the default export options.

The meshes (created in this chapter) do not contain any texture-based information. We will use texture-based models in our later chapter.

8. While using Blender, the settings can be restored to default factory settings at any time by selecting **File | Load Factory Settings**.

The exported models from Blender and other sample models in the wavefront and 3Ds format can be found in the GLPIFramework folder under Models. Feel free to explore them. *Chapter 5, Light and Materials*, makes extensive use of wavefronts models to demonstrate various types of lights.

- ▶ *Rendering the wavefront OBJ mesh model*
- ▶ *Rendering the 3Ds mesh model*

Rendering the wavefront OBJ mesh model

The wave file format is a famous 3D mesh model format developed by wavefront technologies. It contains the mesh geometry information in a readable text format.

The wavefront format mainly consists of two types of files: .obj and .mtl. The .obj file is responsible for describing the geometrical information of the 3D model, such as vertex position, normal, texture coordinates faces, and so on. The .mtl file is optional and contains material information for individual mesh parts, such as the texture and shading (diffuse, specular, and so on) information. Also, the .mtl file is exported automatically if it contains the texture information; otherwise, you must set **Write Materials**. The term material here refers to the color or texture of an object. The models that we have exported do not contain any texture information. Therefore, these models only consist of .obj files.

File format: As the wave front format is readable, you can open it in any text editor and read it. It uses special keywords to recognize specific types of information. The following table will help you to understand the keywords used for the wavefront file format:

Keyword	Meaning	Sample
#	Anything starting with # is considered as a comment.	This file is created using Blender 2.65
v	This is the vertex position that specifies x, y, and z coordinates.	▶ v 1.000000 -1.000000 -1.000000 ▶ v 1.000000 -1.000000 1.000000 ▶ v -1.000000 -1.000000 1.000000
vt	This specifies texture coordinates in the range of 0.0 to 1.0.	▶ vt 0.0 0.0 ▶ vt 1.0 0.0 ▶ vt 1.0 1.0 ▶ vt 0.0 1.0

Keyword	Meaning	Sample
vn	This represents Normals at each vertex position.	▸ vn 0.0 1.0 0.0 ▸ vn 0.0 0.0 1.0
f	This contains the face information. Each face is defined with vertex (v) followed by texture coordinates (u) and vertex normal (n). The syntax for the face information is [v]/[u]/[n].	Face information various formats: ▸ Vertex coordinates: f 1 2 3 ▸ Vertex and texture coords: f 1/1 3/2 4/3 ▸ Vertex and texture normal: f 1/1/2 3/2/1 4/3/2 ▸ Vertex and normal coords: f 1//2 3//1 4//2

The following image shows a sample wavefront (.obj) file when it's opened in a text editor. This sample only contains the vertex and face information, which is a minimal requirement of a mesh model to render to any 3D graphics visualization tool. Depending on the chosen export options, more mesh attributes can be seen with new keywords:

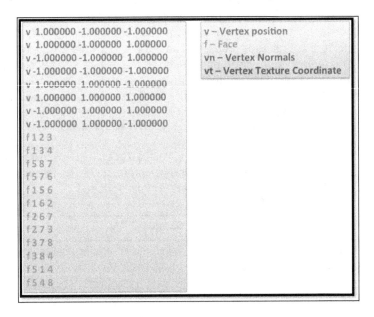

The actual capabilities of the wavefront OBJ model are way beyond what we have specified in the file format. Covering all the specifications of .obj is beyond the scope of this book. You can refer to http://paulbourke.net/dataformats/obj for the full set of specifications. This recipe essentially covers the most important and critical parts of the specification, in which you will learn how to parse the geometrical information. Our tiny parser and renderer will help you to understand the concept of meshes in-depth and allow you to program any other kind of mesh file formats.

You can explore more about wavefront OBJ file format specifications at `http://paulbourke.net/dataformats/obj/`.

Getting ready

The 3D models we created in Blender need to be imported into the project. Android and iOS have different ways to access their resources:

- **Android**: On Android, 3D mesh models need to copy from `GLPIFramework/Models` and store it in the memory card under the `sdcard/Models` folder
- **iOS**: Add the `GLPIFramework/Models` folder to the project using **File | Add Files to [Project Name]**

Class and data structure: The `OBJMesh` class is responsible for parsing wavefront OBJ mesh models; it uses necessary data structures to store the parsed wavefront OBJ information. This class is defined in `WaveFrontObj.h/.cpp` under our `GLPIframework/WaveFrontOBJ` folder. Here are the necessary data structure that are used by this class:

- **Vertex**: This structure will store the information of each vertex, which exists in the 3D geometry. It contains position coordinates of each vertex along the x, y, and z axis in the position variable. Texture coordinates are stored in the *uv* variable. Normal coordinates are stored in the normal variable. The tangential information at each vertex is stored in the tangent:

```
struct Vertex
{
public:
    glm::vec3 position;  //Store X/Y/Z coordinate.
    glm::vec2 uv;        //Store Tex coordinate.
    glm::vec3 normal;    //Store Normal information.
    glm::vec3 tangent;   //Store Tangent information.
    . . . . .
};
```

- **Face Index**: This structure is responsible for storing the face-related information. For example, it stores all indexes of the vertices, texture coordinates, and normals that are helpful in defining the face:

```
struct FaceIndex
{
    short vertexIndex; // Face's vertex Index
```

```
        short normalIndex;  // Face's normal Index
        short uvIndex;      // Face's texCoord Index
        . . . . .
};
```

▶ **Mesh**: The mesh data structure is responsible for storing the Mesh geometry information. It contains the complete path of the OBJ file in the `fileName` variable that needs to be parsed. The class contains the information on vertex, texture, and normal in the form of a vector array. This is stored in the positions, UVs, and normals vector list variables respectively. The `vecFaceIndex` stores the information of each face in the form of an index for each vertex making the face.

The indices stores the vertex index for each face and is used to calculate normals if the normal information is not available in the `.obj` mesh file:

```
struct Mesh
{
    // Obj File name
    char fileName[MAX_FILE_NAME];

    // List of Face Indices For vertex, uvs, normal
    std::vector<FaceIndex> vecFaceIndex;

    // List of vertices containing interleaved
 // information forposition, uv, and normals
    std::vector<Vertex>    vertices;

    // List of vertices containing positions
    std::vector<glm::vec3> positions;

    // List of vertices containing normal
    std::vector<glm::vec3> normals;

    // List of vertices containing uvs
    std::vector<glm::vec2> uvs;

    //! List of tangents
    std::vector<glm::vec4> tangents;

    // List of face indices
    std::vector<unsigned short> indices;
};
```

How to do it...

This section will provide a step-by-step procedure to parse and render the wavefront OBJ mesh model in OpenGL ES 3.0. Let's start the recipe using the following steps:

1. Create a `ObjLoader` class derived from the `Model` class. It will inherit all the member functions of `Model` necessary for the life cycle of `ObjLoader`.

   This class contains member variables to store the wavefront model mesh information. The mesh model is parsed using `ObjMesh` function's `waveFrontObjectModel` object. This object calls the `parseObjMesh` function, which accepts the path for the 3D wavefront OBJ model as an argument that we are interested to load on:

   ```
   OBJMesh waveFrontObjectModel;
   objMeshModel = waveFrontObjectModel.ParseObjModel(fname);
   ```

2. The `ParseObjModel` function further calls a set of helper functions to store and process the mesh information from the `.obj` file. This function returns the `Mesh` object pointer. This function accepts the path of the file to be loaded and another argument that specifies whether the normal needs to be calculated as flat or smooth:

   ```
   Mesh* OBJMesh::ParseObjModel(char* path, bool flatShading)
   {
       ParseFileInfo(path);          // Parse's the obj file
       CreateInterleavedArray();     // Interleaved data array
       CalculateNormal(flatShading);// Generate the normal
       if(objMeshModel.uvs.size())
           { CalculateTangents(); } // Generate tangents
       ClearMesh();                  // Release alloc resources
       return &objMeshModel;
   }
   ```

3. The `ParseFileInfo` reads the path of the mesh model to validate its existence. This function parses the file by reading each line in it. Each line contains a keyword at the beginning that specifies the type of information it contains. The #, u, s, or g keywords are ignored as they are not used in the parser. The # keyword is used to write comments in the wavefront file. The parsed information from this function is collected in the mesh's object pointer:

   ```
   strcpy(objMeshModel.fileName, path);
   while(!eofReached)
   {
       c = fgetc(pFile);
       switch(c)
       {
           case '#': // Ignore (This is a comment)
   ```

```
            case 'u': // Ignore
            case 's': // Ignore
            case 'g': // Grouping not supported
                    while(fgetc(pFile) != '\n');
// Skip till new next line not reached.
                    break;

#ifdef __IPHONE_4_0
        case EOF:
#else
        case (unsigned char)EOF:
#endif
                    eofReached = true;
                    break;

            case 'v': // Load the vertices.
                    c = fgetc(pFile);
// The next character will
                    // let us know what vertex attribute to load
                    ScanVertexNormalAndUV( pFile, c );
                    break;

            case 'f':
// 'f' means it is a face index information
// in the form of v/u/n
                    ScanFaceIndex( pFile, c );
                    break;
        }
}
```

4. The line starting with the `v` keyword represents vertex attributes, which could be of three types of information: vertex position (`v`), vertex texture coordinate (`vt`), and vertex normal (`vn`). This information is read using the `ScanVertexNormalAndUV` function.

   This function parses each line and stores the information of vertex position, texture coordinate, and vertex normal in `objMeshModel.positions`, `objMeshModel.uvs`, and `objMeshModel.normals` respectively:

```
        bool OBJMesh::ScanVertexNormalAndUV( FILE* pFile,
char c )
{
float  x, y, z, u, v;
switch(c)
{
```

```
   case ' ': // Load vertices
      fscanf(pFile,"%f %f %f\n",&x,&y,&z);
      objMeshModel.positions.push_back(glm::vec3(x, y, z));
   break;
   case 'n': // Loading normal coordinate comp. x,y,z
       fscanf(pFile,"%f %f %f\n",&x,&y,&z);
      objMeshModel.normals.push_back(glm::vec3(x, y, z));
      break;
   case 't': // Loading Texture coordinates (UV)
fscanf(pFile,"%f %f\n",&u,&v);
        objMeshModel.uvs.push_back(glm::vec2(u, v));
break;
   default:
       return false;
}
}
```

5. Similarly, the line starting with the f keyword and followed by a " " space represents faces. A face is made up of three vertices and each vertex may consist of three attributes: vertex position, texture coordinates, and vertex normal.

   Each face stores information in the form of an index. An index here refers to the index of an actual element in the stored arrays (calculated in step five). For example, an index of two for the vertex position in a given face means a third vertex element in the objMeshModel.positions vector array.

   Gather the face index information in the objMeshModel.vecFaceIndex vector list. This list contains all faces that have the indices of vertex attributes belonging to each vertex of the face. For more information, refer to the ObjMesh::ScanFaceIndex function.

6. Using the face index information gathered in objMeshModel.vecFace, populate the objMeshModel.vertices vector list. This list contains vertex attributes to be used to create the Vertex Buffer Object:

```
   // Allocate enough space to store vertices and indices

 objMeshModel.vertices.resize(obMeshModl.vecFacIndex.size());
      objMeshModel.indices.resize(obMeshModl.vecFacIndex.
      size());

   // Get the total number of indices.
      objMeshModel.indexCount = objMeshModel.indices.size();

   // Create the interleaved vertex information
```

```
    // containing position, uv and normal.
        for(int i = 0; i < objMeshModel.vecFaceIndex.size(); i++)
        {
//Position information must be available always
int index = objMeshModel.vecFaceIndex.at(i + 0).vertexIndex;
objMeshModel.vertices[i].position =
                    objMeshModel.positions.at(index);
objMeshModel.indices[i] =
            (GLushort)objMeshModel.vecFaceIndex.at(i).
vertexIndex;

// If UV information is available.
if(objMeshModel.uvs.size()){
index = objMeshModel.vecFaceIndex.at(i).uvIndex;
    objMeshModel.vertices[i].uv =
 objMeshModel.uvs.at(index);
}

// If Normal information is available.
if(objMeshModel.normals.size()){
index = objMeshModel.vecFaceIndex.at(i ).normalIndex;
objMeshModel.vertices[i].normal =
objMeshModel.normals.at(index);
}
}
```

7. If the normal attribute is missing in the OBJ file, it can be calculated using `OBJMesh::CalculateNormal()`. For more information, refer to the *There's more...* section in this recipe.

8. Similarly, the tangent information at each vertex is calculated using `OBJMesh::CalculateTangents()`. You can refer to bump mapping in *Chapter 5, Light and Materials*, to understand the working of this function thoroughly.

9. Once the OBJ mesh information is parsed and stored in mesh's object, clear all the temporary data structure using the `ClearMesh` function:

```
bool OBJMesh::ClearMesh()
{
  objMeshModel.positions.clear();  // Clear positions
  objMeshModel.normals.clear();    // Clear normals
  objMeshModel.uvs.clear();        // Clear tex Coords
```

```
    objMeshModel.indices.clear();      // Clear indices
    objMeshModel.vecFaceIndex.clear(); // Clear FaceIdx
    return true;
}
```

10. After parsing the OBJ file, create the VBO within the `ObjLoader` constructor:

```
// Function ObjLoader::ObjLoader( Renderer* parent )
ObjLoader::ObjLoader( Renderer* parent )
{
. . . . . . .
objMeshModel= waveFrontObjectModel.ParseObjModel(fname);
IndexCount  = waveFrontObjectModel.IndexTotal();
stride      = (2 * sizeof(glm::vec3) )+ sizeof(glm::vec2);
        offset      = (GLvoid*) (sizeof(glm::vec3) +
sizeof(glm::vec2));


        // Create the VBO for our obj model vertices.
        GLuint vertexBuffer; glGenBuffers(1, &vertexBuffer);
        glBindBuffer(GL_ARRAY_BUFFER, vertexBuffer);
    glBufferData(GL_ARRAY_BUFFER, objMeshModel->vertices.size()
            * sizeof(objMeshModel->vertices[0]),
            &objMeshModel->vertices[0], GL_STATIC_DRAW);


// Create the Vertex Array Object (VAO)
        glGenVertexArrays(1, &OBJ_VAO_Id);
        glBindVertexArray(OBJ_VAO_Id);
// Bind VBO, enable attributes and draw geometry
    glBindBuffer(GL_ARRAY_BUFFER, vertexBuffer);
    glEnableVertexAttribArray(VERTEX_POSITION);
        glEnableVertexAttribArray(NORMAL_POSITION);
        glVertexAttribPointer
    (VERTEX_POSITION, 3, GL_FLOAT, GL_FALSE, stride, 0);
        glVertexAttribPointer
    (NORMAL_POSITION, 3,GL_FLOAT,GL_FALSE,stride,offset);
        glBindVertexArray(0); //Use default VAO
```

How it works...

The `ParseObjMesh` function in the `OBJMesh` class is responsible for parsing the wavefront OBJ file and storing the information in the mesh's `objMeshModel` object variable. This function parses the file and recognizes vertex attributes, such as vertex position, texture coordinates, and vertex normals. It stores these attributes in the `objMeshModel.positions`, `objMeshModel.uvs`, and `objMeshModel.normals` respective vector arrays. These vector arrays are contiguous in nature. Therefore, these arrays can be used directly to pick elements using the index information.

The vertex texture and vertex normal are optional attributes. Without these, the geometry can still be produced. Texture coordinates only get stored if the model contains any texture. The normal can be saved in the OBJ file by selecting **Include Normals** in export options. For more information on .OBJ mesh model export options, refer to, the *How to do it...* section under the *Creating polygon meshes with Blender* recipe in this chapter for more information on OBJ mesh model export options.

After parsing the vertex attribute information, the face information needs to be parsed. Each face is made up of three vertices. These vertices can contain the position, texture, and normal information. The information for each vertex attribute in the face is stored in the form of an index. The face information in the `objMeshModel.vecFaceIndex` must be stored in the vector array list.

The `objMeshModel.vertices` is another vector-based array that is contiguous in nature and in the interleaved form. Each record in array represents a vertex element, which contains vertex positions, texture coordinates, and normal attributes. The `OBJMesh::CreateInterleavedArray` function is responsible for generating this array. The Interleaved fashion array is highly recommended as it contains different attribute data in a single array, thereby sufficient to store a single VBO. However, if the data is not stored interleaved, each attribute will be stored in a separate array. For each data array, a separate VBO is required. Use of too many VBOs is performance killing because the rendering pipeline spends more time binding and switching VBOs.

The OBJ model data are to be drawn using `GL_TRIANGLES`. The fragment shader used will provide different effects based on the information passed (for example, texture coordinates, lighting information, and so on) in the upcoming chapters. We will apply various vertex and fragment shaders to OBJ meshes in order to produce mind-blowing real-time rendering effects:

Wavefront Obj model rendered from left to right with (a) GL_TRIANGLES (b) GL_LINES and (c) GL_POINTS

There's more...

Normal's information plays an important role in the light shading of 3D objects. Our wavefront exported models do not contain any normal information. This section will help us in calculating normals using the face information.

There are two ways in which the normal can be calculated:

▸ **Face normal**: This is calculated using a single face information. This type of normal results in flat shading. It's calculated using a cross product of any two edges formed by the triangle face. In other words, it's perpendicular to the surface generated by coplanar vertices.

▸ **Vertex normal**: This is calculated by taking the average of the face normal created by faces that share common vertices:

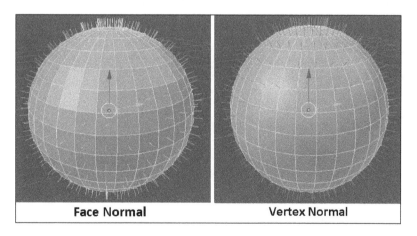

| Face Normal | Vertex Normal |

The preceding image shows the face and vertex normal. Each face normal is calculated using four vertices, which form a plane surface. Out of these four vertices, any of the three vertices can be used to form two edges. The cross product of these two edges results a perpendicular vector to plane. Normalizing this vector produces a face normal.

In contrast, each vertex shows the vertex normal in the blue colored line, which is formed by four planes or four faces surrounded around each vertex. The average of these four planes face normal results a vertex normal. Vertex normal is extremely important to generate highly detailed and smooth geometrical appearance without requiring too many vertices.

The flat shade or smooth shade normal can be calculated using `ParseObjMesh` with the second parameter as Boolean `true` for flat shading and Boolean `false` for smooth shading. Internally, this function calls `OBJMesh::CalculateNormal`, which is responsible for the mathematical calculation of normal:

```
    // Calculates the flat or smooth normal on the fly
Function OBJMesh::CalculateNormal(bool flatShading)
{
if ( objMeshModel.normals.size() == 0 ){
    // Make space to store the normal information
objMeshModel.normals.resize(objMeshModel.positions.size());
int index0, index1, index2;
glm::vec3 a, b, c;
for(int i=0; i<objMeshModel.indices.size();i += 3){
    // Use indices to retrieve the vertices
        index0 = objMeshModel.indices.at(i);
        index1 = objMeshModel.indices.at(i+1);
        index2 = objMeshModel.indices.at(i+2);
    // Retrieve each triangles vertex
        a = objMeshModel.positions.at(index0);
        b = objMeshModel.positions.at(index1);
        c = objMeshModel.positions.at(index2);
    // Calculate the normal triangle face.
        glm::vec3 faceNormal =  glm::cross((b - a), (c - a));

        if ( flatShading ){
    // Calculate normals for flat shading
            objMeshModel.vertices[i].normal += faceNormal;
            objMeshModel.vertices[i+1].normal += faceNormal;
            objMeshModel.vertices[i+2].normal += faceNormal;
        }
        else{
            objMeshModel.normals[index0] += faceNormal;
            objMeshModel.normals[index1] += faceNormal;
```

```
                objMeshModel.normals[index2] += faceNormal;
            }
    }

        // Calculate normals for smooth shading
        if ( !flatShading ){
        for(int i = 0;i<objMeshModel.vecFaceIndex.size(); i++){
        int index=objMeshModel.vecFaceIndex.at
(i +0).vertexIndex;
        objMeshModel.vertices[i].normal=
                              objMeshModel.normals.at(index);
        }
    }
        // Store the calculated normal in normalized form
    for (int j=0;j<objMeshModel.vertices.size(); j++){
    objMeshModel.vertices[j].normal =
    glm::normalize (objMeshModel.vertices[j].normal);
    }
    }
    }
```

The face normal points to the direction where polygons face. However, vertex normal changes the gradient of the polygon. If we change the direction of the vertex normal, the shading around that vertex will http://change.at/" \t "_blank, this gradient is as same as a flat polygon that's rotated in the same direction. The computer fakes a gradient over the polygon.

The following image shows how a simple sphere on the left-hand side appears without a light shading technique. In fact, it's difficult to believe that it's a sphere mesh model. The middle and rightmost mesh models are demonstrated using light shades. The prior mesh model uses the flat light shading, which is achieved using face normals, whereas the latter mesh model renders the same mesh model with vertex normals:

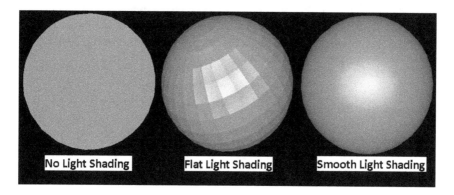

▸ Refer to the *Efficient rendering with Vertex Buffer Object* recipe *Chapter 2, OpenGL ES 3.0 Essentials*

▸ Refer to the *Phong shading – per-fragment shading technique* recipe in *Chapter 5, Light and Materials*

▸ Refer to the *Gouraud shading – the per-fragment shading technique and Phong shading – the per-fragment shading technique recipes* recipes in *Chapter 5, Light and Materials*

▸ Refer to the *Implementing bump mapping* recipe in *Chapter 7, Texture and Mapping Techniques*

▸ Refer to the *Managing VBO with Vertex Array Objects* recipe in *Chapter 3, New Features of OpenGL ES 3.0*

Rendering the 3Ds mesh model

The 3Ds mesh format is a well-known 3D mesh file format used in computer graphics. Unlike wavefront, it's not text-based and stores the mesh information in a binary form. This is used widely in Autodesk 3D Studio Max and is a professional 3D graphics program software to create 3D animation and models.

File format: This section will provide an overview of the 3Ds file format. This mesh format contains information in the form of a hierarchy of chunks. A chunk is a structured piece of information in the memory. Its unique ID recognizes each chunk, which contains the size information (in bytes) that can be used to read or skip chunks. The size information of the current chunk is always relative to its start memory position; skipping this much size will point to the next chunk.

The following table shows that each chunk is represented with the **Start** field, which contains the memory location within the 3Ds file. The **Size** field tells us how big is the chunk in bytes, whereas the **End** field specifies the memory location where the chunk finishes. The **End** field can be calculated with the help of the *Size – Start + 1* formula. The next chunk information is always relative to the current chunk position:

Start	End	Size	Name
0	1	2	Chunk ID
2	5	4	Next chunk

Each chunks ID in the 3Ds file has a predefined meaning associated with it. For example, the first chunk ID of this file format is always `0x4d4d`. This chunk is called the primary or main chunk ID. The other important chunks exist under this primary chunk as child nodes, as shown in the following screenshot:

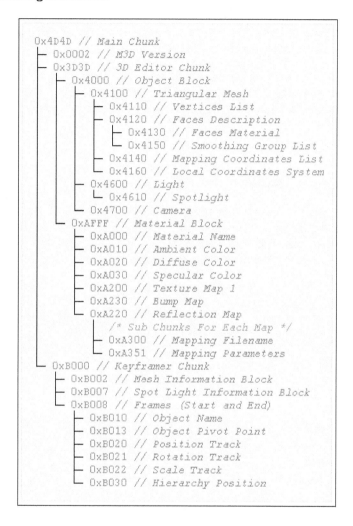

```
0x4D4D // Main Chunk
 ├─ 0x0002 // M3D Version
 ├─ 0x3D3D // 3D Editor Chunk
 │   ├─ 0x4000 // Object Block
 │   │   ├─ 0x4100 // Triangular Mesh
 │   │   │   ├─ 0x4110 // Vertices List
 │   │   │   ├─ 0x4120 // Faces Description
 │   │   │   │   ├─ 0x4130 // Faces Material
 │   │   │   │   └─ 0x4150 // Smoothing Group List
 │   │   │   ├─ 0x4140 // Mapping Coordinates List
 │   │   │   └─ 0x4160 // Local Coordinates System
 │   │   ├─ 0x4600 // Light
 │   │   │   └─ 0x4610 // Spotlight
 │   │   └─ 0x4700 // Camera
 │   └─ 0xAFFF // Material Block
 │       ├─ 0xA000 // Material Name
 │       ├─ 0xA010 // Ambient Color
 │       ├─ 0xA020 // Diffuse Color
 │       ├─ 0xA030 // Specular Color
 │       ├─ 0xA200 // Texture Map 1
 │       ├─ 0xA230 // Bump Map
 │       └─ 0xA220 // Reflection Map
 │           /* Sub Chunks For Each Map */
 │           ├─ 0xA300 // Mapping Filename
 │           └─ 0xA351 // Mapping Parameters
 └─ 0xB000 // Keyframer Chunk
     ├─ 0xB002 // Mesh Information Block
     ├─ 0xB007 // Spot Light Information Block
     └─ 0xB008 // Frames (Start and End)
         ├─ 0xB010 // Object Name
         ├─ 0xB013 // Object Pivot Point
         ├─ 0xB020 // Position Track
         ├─ 0xB021 // Rotation Track
         ├─ 0xB022 // Scale Track
         └─ 0xB030 // Hierarchy Position
```

The detailed specification of 3Ds is beyond the scope of this book. You can find more information about this specification at `http://www.martinreddy.net/gfx/3d/3DS.spec`.

Getting ready

In this recipe, we will parse the 3Ds file format using a third-party library called lib3ds. This is an open source library that helps us to parse the file and provide us the file data in the form of a data structure. This library is written in ANCI-C. Therefore, it's portable across platforms. The lib3ds is available for commercial application under GNU **Lesser General Public License (LGPL)**. The library can be download from https://code.google.com/p/lib3ds/.

In our GLPI framework, this library is present under the GLPIFramework/3DSParser/ lib3ds folder. We have used the 1.30 version for this library. Rendering 3DS mesh models to the application requires these to be stored at some appropriate location on the device or simulator.

On the Android device, you can store 3DS mesh model files under the sdcard/ GLPIFramework/Model folder. For iOS, these models can be added to the project using **File | Add Files to [Project Name]**.

Android: On the Android platform, we need the makefile to build the lib3ds library. Add the Android.mk makefile under GLPIFramework/3DSParser/lib3ds. Edit this makefile, as shown in the following code. This library will be compiled as a shared library, which is named as mylib3ds. You can also directly add the source code in the main project makefile, instead of compiling a shared library:

Android.mk:

```
LOCAL_PATH := $(call my-dir)
include $(CLEAR_VARS)
# Name of the shared library
LOCAL_MODULE    := mylib3ds
LOCAL_SRC_FILES := \
    lib3ds/viewport.c \
    lib3ds/vector.c \
    lib3ds/tracks.c \
    lib3ds/tcb.c \
    lib3ds/shadow.c \
    lib3ds/quat.c \
    lib3ds/node.c \
    lib3ds/mesh.c \
    lib3ds/matrix.c \
    lib3ds/material.c \
    lib3ds/light.c \
    lib3ds/io.c \
    lib3ds/file.c \
```

```
    lib3ds/ease.c \
    lib3ds/chunk.c \
    lib3ds/camera.c \
    lib3ds/background.c \
    lib3ds/atmosphere.c
# Included libraries and compile time flags
LOCAL_LDLIBS := -lz
LOCAL_CFLAGS := -I. -g
# Build as shared library
include $(BUILD_SHARED_LIBRARY)
```

Open the `Android.mk` makefile present in the project directory under the `JNI` folder and include the path of the `lib3ds` library `Android.mk` file that we have created in the preceding code:

```
MY_CUR_LOCAL_PATH := $(call my-dir)
FRAMEWORK_DIR    = ../../../../GLPIFramework
LIB3DS_DIR = $(FRAMEWORK_DIR)/3DSParser

include $(CLEAR_VARS)

include$(MY_CUR_LOCAL_PATH)/../GLPIFramework/zlib/Android.mk \
$(MY_CUR_LOCAL_PATH)/../GLPIFramework/3DSParser/Android.mk
# Source file for compilation
LOCAL_SRC_FILES := $(FRAMEWORK_DIR)/GLutils.cpp \
. . . . .
. . . . .
$(SCENE_DIR)/Renderer.cpp \
$(SCENE_DIR)/3DSLoader.cpp \
../../NativeTemplate.cpp
# Include the 3DS library
LOCAL_SHARED_LIBRARIES := zlib mylib3ds
```

In `GLESNativeLib.java`, edit the `GLESNativeLib` class and add the reference of our shared library, so that it will be linked at runtime:

```
public class GLESNativeLib {
static {
    System.loadLibrary("zlib");
    System.loadLibrary("mylib3ds");
    System.loadLibrary("glNative");
}
    . . . . . . Other code
}
```

iOS: On the iOS platform, you need to add `lib3ds` library source files to your project using **File | Add Files to [Project Name]**.

How to do it...

Here are the steps to create a 3Ds mesh renderer class. This class will be responsible for loading and rendering 3Ds mesh models:

1. For this recipe, we have derived a new class called `Loader3DS` from the `Scene`. This class contains a `load3dsModel` function, which will be used to load the 3Ds mesh model file.

2. Implement the `load3dsModel` function, as described in the following code snippet. This function parses the 3Ds model file using the `lib3ds` library's function called `lib3ds_file_load` and returns the `Lib3dsFile` pointer. The `Lib3dsFile` structure contains the parsed information of the 3Ds mesh file:

```
Lib3dsFile* Loader3DS::load3dsModel(const char* fileName){
    Lib3dsFile* file = lib3ds_file_load(fileName);
    if (!file) {
    LOGI("*ERROR*\nLoading file %s failed\n", fileName);
        return NULL;
    }
    .  .  .  .  .  .
    .  .  .  .  .  .
    return file;
}
```

3. When a 3Ds mesh file is parsed successfully, it loads the mesh data (geometry attributes and material information) of the mesh model in the file object type called `Lib3dsFile`. This object contains all the necessary information to read nodes. A node in the 3Ds specification is a special data structure called `Lib3dsNode` that corresponds to a subpart or submodel of the complete 3D mesh model. For example, a `car` model is made up of many different subparts, such as body frame, tires, doors, engine, and so on. Each of these individual parts correspond to a child node of the parent node that represents the 3D car model.

   Depending on the complexity of the model, there may be more than one node. These nodes are arranged in a hierarchical fashion. The nodes are created using `lib3ds_node_new_object()` and are arranged in a hierarchal order with `lib3ds_file_insert_node()`:

```
if( !file->nodes )
{
    Lib3dsMesh *mesh;
    Lib3dsNode *node;
```

```
for(mesh=file->meshes; mesh!=NULL; mesh=mesh->next){
    node = lib3ds_node_new_object();
    strcpy(node->name, mesh->name);
    node->parent_id = LIB3DS_NO_PARENT;
    lib3ds_file_insert_node(file, node);
}
}
```

4. Render the 3Ds mesh model by recursively iterating through all the nodes. Call `RenderNodes()` to render each node:

```
void Loader3DS::Render(Lib3dsFile* file)
{
    . . . . . . .
    Lib3dsNode *p;
    for (Lib3dsNode* p=file->nodes; p!=0; p=p->next ){
        RenderNodes( file, p );
    }
    . . . . . . .
}
```

5. `RenderNodes()` is a recursive function that creates VBO for each node and renders them. Each node contains a pointer to `Lib3dsMesh`; the `Lib3dsMesh` is a data structure that contains the geometrical information for each node:

```
void RenderNodes(Lib3dsFile* file,Lib3dsNode *node){
    . . . . . . .
// Use appropriate shader
glUseProgram( program->ProgramID );

Lib3dsNode *tempNode;
for(tempNode=node->child;tempNode!=0;
tempNode=tempNode->next)       {
        RenderNodes(file, tempNode);
                                }
}
```

6. The `Lib3ds` library contains a structure called `Lib3dsUserData`. It allows you to add custom variables to `lib3ds`. We will use this structure to store vertex buffer object variables like vertex:

```
// Check the user.p variable if empty is assigned
MyLib3dsUserData
if (!mesh->user.p){
  MyLib3dsUserData* myPObject = new MyLib3dsUserData;
  mesh->user.p = (void*)myPObject;
}
```

7. Build the VAO for each mesh using the `BuildMesh()` function. Cache the VAO, VBO, and IBO information in the `MyLib3dsUserData` object:

```
void Loader3DS::BuildMesh(Lib3dsMesh *mesh)
{
 MyLib3dsUserData* userObj=(MyLib3dsUsrData*)mesh->user.p;

    // Allocation memory for vertex positions
    meshVert = new float[ mesh->points * 3 ];
    . . . . .

    // Allocate memory for texture
    meshTexture = new float[ mesh->texels * 2 ];
    . . . . .

    // Allocate memory for normal
    meshNormal = new Lib3dsVector[ 3 * mesh->faces ];
    lib3ds_mesh_calculate_normals(mesh, meshNormal);

    // Allocate memory for face information
    faceIndex = new unsigned short[mesh->faces*3];
    . . . . .

    // Create the VBO and populate the VBO data
    glGenBuffers( 1, (GLuint *)&vId );
    glBindBuffer( GL_ARRAY_BUFFER, vId );
    . . . . .

    // Create and populate the IBO with index info.
    glGenBuffers( 1, (GLuint *)&iId );
    glBindBuffer( GL_ARRAY_BUFFER, iId );
    . . . . .

    // Create and Bind Vertex Array Object
    glGenVertexArrays(1, &VAOId);
    glBindVertexArray(VAOId);
    . . . . .

    // Cache the information in the User data structure
    userObj->vertexId   = vId;
    userObj->indexId    = iId;
    userObj->VAOId      = VAOId;

    . . . . .
}
```

8. In `RenderNodes()`, use the VAO information to render the 3Ds mesh model:

```
MyLib3dsUserData* userObj=(MyLib3dsUserData*)mesh->user.p;
// If VAO is not created, create using BuildMesh.
if ( !userObj->VAOId ) {
     BuildMesh( mesh );
}
else {
     // Apply Transformation & set material information
     SetMaterialInfo( mesh );
     //Bind to VAO & draw primitives
     glBindVertexArray(userObj->VAOId);
     glDrawElements(GL_TRIANGLES, userObj->indexNum,
              GL_UNSIGNED_SHORT, (void*)0);
     glBindVertexArray(0); //Bind to default VAO
}
```

How it works...

The 3Ds mesh file is parsed with lib3ds library's `lib3ds_file_load`. This function successfully populates the `Lib3dsFile` file pointer that contains all the parsed information from the 3Ds file. Using this data variable, we create nodes that are populated and assembled in a hierarchical order using `lib3ds_file_insert_node`. Each node represents a mesh, which is read from the node structure and cached in the form of a **Vertex Array Objects** (**VAO**). Each VAO stores the **Vertex Buffer Object** (**VBO**), states, and attributes.

The `RenderNodes` is a recursive function that creates the VAO and VBO for each node and renders them. Each node contains a pointer to `Lib3dsMesh`, which further contains a `Lib3dsUserData` that we will use to check whether the corresponding node contains the VAO. The VAO is recognized with a vertex array ID. These IDs are bound to runtime and used to render the geometry. Once the VAO IDs are generated, these are stored with each node in the `Lib3dsUserData` structure:

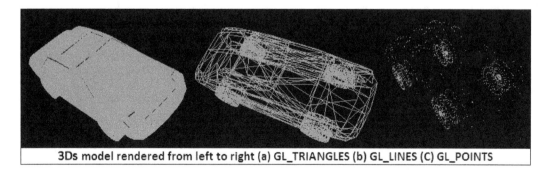

3Ds model rendered from left to right (a) GL_TRIANGLES (b) GL_LINES (C) GL_POINTS

There's more...

So far in this recipe, you learned how to render 3Ds mesh models. We rendered these using a single color. The 3Ds file format also has the provision to render faces with colors. This information is stored in `Lib3dsMaterial` of `Lib3dsMesh`. The following code shows how the material information is read from the material data structure and sends it as a uniform variable to the `3dsFragmentShader.glsl` to apply as face colors:

```
void Loader3DS::SetMaterialInfo( Lib3dsMesh *mesh )
{
    Lib3dsMaterial *material = 0;
    if ( mesh->faces ) {
        // Get associated material with the mesh
        material = lib3ds_file_material_by_name
                        (file, mesh->faceL[0].material);
    }

    if( !material ){
        return;
    }

    // Set Ambient, Diffuse and Specular light component
    glUniform4f(UniformKa, material->ambient[0],
    material->ambient[1], material->ambient[2],
    material->ambient[3]);
    glUniform4f(UniformKd, material->diffuse[0],
    material->diffuse[1], material->diffuse[2],
    material->diffuse[3]);
    glUniform4f(UniformKs,material->specular[0],
    material->specular[1], material->specular[2],
    material->specular[3]);
    glUniform1f(UniformKsh, material->shininess);
}
```

The color information is stored in the form of material colors. For more information on light and material, refer to the *Chapter 5*, *Light and Materials*. The following image illustrates a car model with colored faces, where the mesh model is rendered with triangle, line, and point primitives:

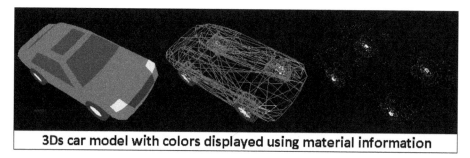

3Ds car model with colors displayed using material information

Pivot position: The pivot position renders mesh models to the translation information. This helps the mesh to render with correct positioning. Without pivot positioning, each node renders at the origin. This behavior causes all node meshes to cluster at the origin because each model does not know its position relative to other models.

See also

▶   Refer to the *Managing VBO with Vertex Array Objects* recipe in *Chapter 3, New Features of OpenGL ES 3.0*

5
Light and Materials

In this chapter, we will cover the following recipes:

- ▸ Implementing the per-vertex ambient light component
- ▸ Implementing the per-vertex diffuse light component
- ▸ Implementing the per-vertex specular light component
- ▸ Optimizing the specular light with the halfway vector
- ▸ Gouraud shading – the per-vertex shading technique
- ▸ Phong shading – the per-fragment shading technique
- ▸ Implementing directional and point light
- ▸ Implementing multiple lights in a scene
- ▸ Implementing two-side shading

Introduction

This chapter will introduce the concepts of light and material in 3D graphics. We will understand the concept of light from the aspect of physics and its dual nature. We will discuss the different types of light components, such as ambient, diffuse and specular, with their implementation techniques. Later in this chapter, we will cover some important common illumination techniques (such as Phong shading and Gouraud shading). This will help us in implementing realistic-looking lighting models in computer graphics. In addition, you will learn the difference between directional and positional light and see how optimization can be achieved in the specular lighting by using the halfway vector technique. At the end of this chapter, we will demonstrate how to set up multiple lights in a scene and render objects with two-sided shading.

Light is an electromagnetic radiation; it exists with an enormous range of frequencies or wavelengths. Human eyes can only see a portion of this wavelength of the electromagnetic spectrum and this range of portion is called visible light. Our eye receives these visible wavelengths as colors and the visible light spectrum varies from 400 nm (violet) to 700 nm (red):

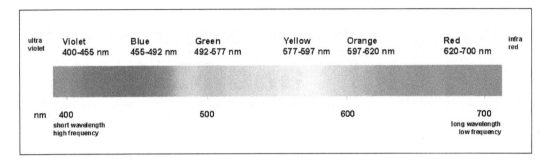

Light possesses important properties (such as intensity, direction, color, and location). In 3D graphics, we use these important properties of light to simulate various light models. In this chapter, we will use the OpenGL ES programmable pipeline to program various light models using shaders. This chapter will be helpful in providing an insight into all of the mathematics and physics required for lighting purposes.

Back in 1600s, colors were believed to be a mixture of light and darkness. In 1672, Sir Issac Newton published a series of experiments and provided us with the modern understanding of light. He successfully refracted that white light consists of a mixture of seven different colors: red, orange, yellow, green, blue, indigo, and violet. He also proposed that light is composed of particles or corpuscles.

Much later, in 1802, Thomas Young proved that light behaves as a wave through one of his experiments. He related colors to wavelength and managed to calculate the approximate wavelength of the seven colors discovered by Sir Isaac Newton.

The final proposition of light was given by Albert Einstein in March, 1905. That year, he published his quantum theory of light, where he proposed light as particles and named these particles **photons**. In June, 1905, he completed his theory of special relativity, which added a twist to his earlier proposal where light was believed to be a particle. The special theory of relativity sees light as a wave. Such contradiction gave enough proof to Einstein to propose the dual nature of light. According to him, light behaves both as a particle and a wave:

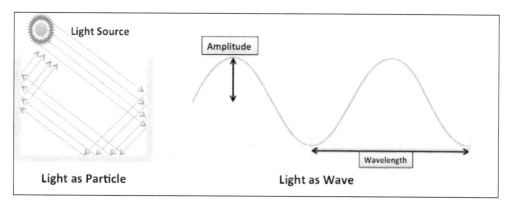

Light has a dual nature; it can behave as a particle and wave at the same time. Let's take a look in more detail:

- **Light as a particle**: Light behaves as particles. These particles are small packets of energy that are not same as the small physical particles of atoms. These packets of energy have a constant velocity and no mass, which exhibit reflection properties that are similar to the billiard balls used in a pool game. When particles hit each other, they propagate in the direction of the force and are reflected as a result of obstacles. When photon particles hit obstacles, they lose energy in the form of absorption. As a result of continuous reflection, these particles strike and diminish. As a result of collision, the obstacle from these particles gains energy and preserves the law of conservation of energy.

- **Light as waves**: Light behaves as waves. These are electromagnetic waves with electric and magnetic properties. The electromagnetic waves do not need any medium to travel through space because they are capable of traveling through vacuum. Each wave looks like a sine wave. The intensity of the wave is measured with amplitude, as shown in the preceding figure. The length of one complete sine wave is called as **wavelength**. The greater the wavelength, more visible is the color. Treating light as waves in 3D computer graphics opens up many possibilities, which one cannot achieve with the particle nature of light. For example, the particle exhibits propagation as rays; it cannot simulate diffraction and interference which is an important property of waves.

In a computer graphic simulation, the wave nature of light is represented by wave fronts stored as 2D arrays of complex numbers. The study of light in computer graphics in itself is a vast subject; covering wave-based illuminations is beyond the scope of this chapter. This chapter will help in modeling particle-based local light illumination modeling techniques.

Light is composed of three types of components: ambient (**A**), diffuse (**D**), and specular (**S**). They are explained as follows:

- ▸ **Ambient (A)**: This light component comes from all directions equally and is scattered in all the directions equally by the objects on which it falls; this makes the objects on the surface appear with constant light intensity.

- ▸ **Diffuse (D)**: This light component comes from a particular direction from the light source. It hits the surface of an object with variable intensity, which depends on the Lambert law of illumination. In other words, the intensity depends on the direction of light appearing on the face of the object and the direction of object face point to.

- ▸ **Specular (S)**: This light component also comes from a particular direction and reflects the most in the direction of the camera's view or the observer's eye. It gives an effect of shininess on the model's surface:

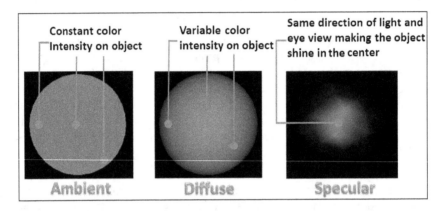

In computer graphics, light and material are both mathematically treated as colors. The color associated with an object is called material and the color associated with illumination is called light. The color intensity of light and material are specified with RGB (red, blue, green) components. Objects are visible because they reflect the light that falls up on them. For example, when sunlight falls on a green material color ball, the green material absorbs all other wavelengths and reflects the green portion of the light spectrum. As a result, it appears green to the viewer. Mathematically, the reflected or resultant color is the product of light and material color intensities:

Reflected color   =   Light intensity   *   Material color

[R1*R2, G1*G2, B1*B2]   [R1, G1, B1]   [R2, G2, B2]

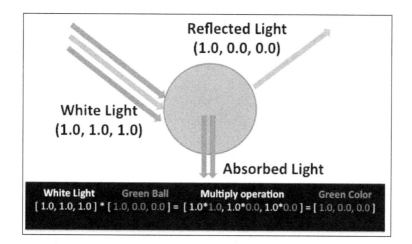

In modern computer graphics, there are two ways in which light shading equations can be calculated: per-vertex and per-fragment. They are explained as follows:

- **Per-vertex light shading**: In this type of shading, the mathematical equations to calculate light shading colors are formulated in the vertex shader. Each vertex color is calculated within the vertex shader and then passed on to the fragment shader. These vertex colors are then interpolated to the geometry faces to result each fragment or pixel color. As the colors are calculated in the vertex shader, it's called per-vertex shading.

- **Per-fragment light shading**: This calculates light colors within the fragment shader for each fragment. The quality of per-fragment shading is considerably better than the vertex shader. The performance of per-fragment shading is slower than per-vertex shading. This is because processing fewer vertices, as compared to thousands of pixels, is quicker. In today's modern graphics, processors are capable of performing several parallel operations at lightning speed; therefore, it may not be very expensive for general purpose application requirements.

One disadvantage of per-vertex light shading is that it may not be helpful for specular light to generate shading as expected because fragment colors are calculated at each vertex and shared among faces; therefore, instead of generating a smooth oval shining surface, it will generate a flat shining surface.

Implementing the per-vertex ambient light component

The ambient light illuminates the object's surface equally in all directions on which it's applied. All faces receive an equal amount of light; therefore, no change in color can be observed on the complete object. Ambient is basically a mixture of two components: the color intensity of light and material.

 Mathematically, this is the product ambient light (L_a) and ambient material (K_a).

$$I_a = L_a K_a$$

An ambient light plays a vital role in Phong and Gouraud shadings; the diffuse and specular color components of these shadings are computed by using the direction of the light that falls on the object. Therefore, an object may receive less or no light on its side or back faces depending on the direction of light on the object. In such cases, the faces may appear invisible because of the black light that is generated; choosing the correct ambient light and material color will help in making these darkened faces visible.

Getting ready

This chapter will make use of the Wavefront 3D mesh models that we implemented in *Chapter 4*, *Working with Meshes*. We will reuse the ObjLoader recipe from the same chapter to implement new recipes in this chapter.

How to do it...

The step-by-step implementation of ambient light is as follows:

1. Reuse the ObjLoader recipe from the previous chapter and create a new vertex shader file called AmbientVertex.glsl and add the following code:

```
// Geometry vertex position
layout(location=0) in vec4 VertexPosition;
uniform mat4 ModelViewProjectionMatrix;

// Ambient Light and Material information
uniform vec3 MaterialAmbient, LightAmbient;

// Shared calculated ambient from vertex shader
out vec4 FinalColor;
```

```
void main(){
   // Calculate the ambient intensity
   vec3 ambient = MaterialAmbient  * LightAmbient;
   FinalColor   = vec4(ambient, 1.0);
   gl_Position  = ModelViewProjectionMatrix*VertexPosition;
}
```

2. Similarly, create the `AmbientFragment.glsl` fragment shader file as:

```
precision mediump float;
in vec4 FinalColor;
layout(location = 0) out vec4 outColor;
void main() {
outColor = FinalColor; // Apply ambient intensity
}
```

3. In the `InitModel()` of the `ObjLoader` class, compile these shaders and set the uniform variable parameters for the ambient light and material:

```
void ObjLoader::InitModel(){
   // Compile AmbientVertex and AmbientFragment shader.
   Many line skipped here . . . . .
   // Use the shader program
   glUseProgram( program->ProgramID );

   // Query uniforms for light and material
   MaterialAmbient =
   GetUniform(program,("MaterialAmbient");
   LightAmbient    = GetUniform(program,"LightAmbient");

   // Set Red colored material
   if (MaterialAmbient >= 0)
   { Uniform3f(MaterialAmbient, 1.0f, 0.0f, 0.0f); }

   // Set white light
   if (LightAmbient >= 0)
   { glUniform3f(LightAmbient, 1.0f, 1.0f, 1.0f); }

   // Get Model-View-Projection Matrix location
   MVP = GetUniform(program, "ModelViewProjectionMatrix");
}
```

4. The `Render()` function is the same as before; it uses the VAO to render the Wavefront OBJ model.

How it works...

When the `ObjLoader` class object is created, it initializes the necessary parameters in the constructor. The `InitModel` function compiles the shader program and sets any necessary uniform variables; the vertex shader contains two uniform variables called `MaterialAmbient` and `LightAmbient`. The former is used to define the ambient color property of the material property of the object and the latter is used to specify the color of the light.

These variables are sent to the vertex shader and the ambience color shade is calculated as the product of these two variables; the result is stored in a new output variable called `FinalColor`. This variable is sent to the fragment shader and applied as a final color to each fragment. The `gl_position` is the clip coordinate value, which is a product of the vertex position and `ModelViewProjectionMatrix`. The `ModelViewProjectionMatrix` uniform variable is a product of the projection, view, and model matrix.

See also

▶ Refer to the *Rendering the wavefront OBJ mesh model* recipe in *Chapter 4, Working with Meshes*

▶ Refer to the *Managing VBO with Vertex Array Objects* recipe in *Chapter 3, New Features of OpenGL ES 3.0*

▶ Refer to the *Efficient rendering with Vertex Buffer Object* recipe in *Chapter 2, OpenGL ES 3.0 Essentials*

Implementing the per-vertex diffuse light component

Diffuse light comes from a particular direction and is reflected in various directions after collision with the surface of the object. In this section, we model this behavior by using the Phong Reflection Model, which was developed by Bui Tuong Phong in 1973. This model proposed an illumination shading technique that uses a normal surface and the direction of incident light. When light strikes on an object's surface, some of its parts are reflected and the rest is partially absorbed. Therefore, we can calculate either the intensity of light absorbed or reflected, if one of the components is given.

Total light intensity = reflection light intensity + absorption light intensity

When 100 percent light intensity falls on a plain surface and 50 percent of it is reflected, it's obvious that 50 percent of light intensity is being absorbed or lost in the surroundings. In 3D graphics, we are only concerned with the reflected light intensity because we see objects as a result of the reflection of light on them. The diffuse and specular components of light basically use the Phong reflection model as a result of light and surface interaction to model illumination techniques.

The Phong reflection model uses the Lambert cosine law to demonstrate the reflection. The Lambert cosine law uses the direction of incident light and the direction of surface geometry to calculate the intensity of light on the surface of geometry.

 The Lambert cosine law states that the intensity of illumination on a diffuse surface is directly proportional to the cosine of the angle made by the surface normal vector and the direction of light.

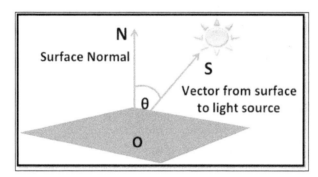

Getting ready

The general mathematical equation to calculate diffuse light is:

$$I_d = L_d K_d (N.S)$$

The L_d and K_d are the diffuse components of the light and material; the $(N.S)$ is the dot product used to calculate the cosine of the angle between the surface normal (N) and the incident light vector (S); both these vectors must be normalized first before calculating the dot product. A normalized vector is a vector whose length is unity; it's also called unit vector. For this recipe, we will reuse our first recipe, that is, ambient and make changes, as described in the next section.

How to do it...

Use the following instructions to implement the diffuse light component:

1. Reuse the last recipe for the per-vertex ambient light component (Ambient recipe) and create a new vertex shader file called `DiffuseVertex.glsl` in it, as shown in the following code:

```
layout(location = 0) in vec4  VertexPosition;
layout(location = 1) in vec3  Normal;

uniform mat4 ModelViewProjectionMatrix;
uniform mat4 ModelViewMatrix;
uniform mat3 NormalMatrix;

// Diffuse Light and Material information
uniform vec3 MaterialDiffuse, LightDiffuse;

// Position of the light source
uniform vec3 LightPosition;

out vec4 FinalColor; // Output color to frag. shader

void main(){
    // Calculate normal, eye coord and light vector
    vec3 nNormal    = normalize ( NormalMatrix * Normal );
    vec3 eyeCoord   = vec3 (ModelViewMatrix* VertexPosition);
    vec3 nLight     = normalize( LightPosition - eyeCoord );

    // Calculate cosine Normal and light vector
    float cosAngle = max( 0.0, dot( nNormal, nLight ));
    vec3 diffuse = MaterialDiffuse  * LightDiffuse;
    FinalColor   = vec4(cosAngle * diffuse, 1);
    gl_Position = ModelViewProjectionMatrix*VertexPosition;
}
```

2. There is no change in the fragment shader; we can reuse it from the last recipe, except we will rename it as `DiffuseFragment.glsl`.

3. In the `InitModel` after the shader are compiled successfully, set the configuration for diffuse light and material color and specify the position of light in world coordinates:

```
// ObjLoader::InitModel()
. . . .

glUseProgram( program->ProgramID );

// Query Light and Material uniform for ambient comp.
MaterialDiffuse  = GetUniform(program, "MaterialDiffuse");
LightDiffuse     = GetUniform(program, "LightDiffuse");
LightPosition    = GetUniform(program, "LightPosition");

// Set Red colored diffuse material uniform
glm::vec3 color = glm::vec3(1.0, 0.0, 0.0);
if (MaterialDiffuse >= 0)
    { glUniform3f(MaterialDiffuse,1.0, 0.0, 0.0); }

// Set white diffuse light
if (LightDiffuse >= 0)
    { glUniform3f(LightDiffuse, 1.0f, 1.0f, 1.0f); }

// Set light position
glm::vec3 lightPosition(0.0, 0.0, 5.0);
glUniform3fv(LightPosition,1,(float*)&lightPosition);
```

4. In the `Render()` function, specify the normal matrix, model view matrix, and model view project matrix, along with the generic vertex attributes:

```
// ObjLoader::Render()
mat3 matrix=*(TransformObj->TransformGetModelViewMatrix());
mat3 normalMat = glm::mat3( glm::vec3(matrix[0]),
            vec3(matrix[1]), glm::vec3(matrix[2]) );
glUniformMatrix3fv(NormalMatrix,1,GL_FALSE,
                (float*)&normalMat );
glUniformMatrix4fv( MV,1,GL_FALSE,(float*)TransformObj->
                    TransformGetModelViewMatrix() );
glUniformMatrix4fv( MVP,1,GL_FALSE,(float*)TransformObj->
TransformGetModelViewProjectionMatrix());

// Bind with Vertex Array Object and Render
glBindVertexArray(OBJ_VAO_Id);
glDrawArrays(GL_TRIANGLES, 0, IndexCount );
```

How it works...

The diffuse light vertex shader uses vertex position, vertex normal, and light position to calculate the light shading using the Phong reflection model; each `VertexPosition` is transformed into an eye coordinate by multiplying it with `ModelViewMatrix`. Similarly, vertex normal also needs to convert to an eye coordinate so that the transformation is also applied to normal as well. This is achieved by multiplying the `Normal` with the `NormalMatrix`.

 Unlike vertex positions, which are transformed into eye coordinates using the `ModelView` matrix, vertex normal are transformed by using the `NormalMatrix`. The normal matrix is a submatrix of the model view matrix, but its specialty is that it preserves the normal of the geometry when an affine transformation is applied. `NormalMatrix` is the inverse transpose of the upper-left 3 x 3 matrix of the model view matrix.

The `nLight` light vector is calculated by subtracting eye coordinates of the `eyeCoord` vertex position from `LightPosition`; the `nLight` direction is calculated from the surface to the light source. The `nLight` and `nNormal` must be normalized before taking the dot product in order to find the cosine angle between them.

Light intensity is stored as the cosine angle between the surface normal vector and light vector. The color information of the material and light is specified in two uniform variables, namely, `MaterialDiffuse` and `LightDiffuse`; the product of these two variables is stored in the new variable called diffuse. The cosine angle is calculated as the dot product of the `nLight` and `nNormal` and stored in the `cosAngle` variable.

 The intensity of light and material are basically used in terms of RGB components, which are always non-negative. Each component of R, G, and B is stored as a floating point number in the range between `0.0f` and `1.0f`. Light intensity is calculated as a cosine function, which can result in a range value between -1 and 1. We do not want negative light intensities because they do not make sense. Therefore, we should only consider light intensity within the range of 0.0 and 1.0; for this reason, the `max()` function is used in the resultant light intensity.

The diffuse color shade is calculated as the product of diffuse and `cosAngle` and stored in a new out variable called `FinalColor`. This variable is sent to the fragment shader and applied to each fragment. The last line of the vertex shader helps to calculate clipped coordinates by multiplying the vertex position with the model view projection matrix.

See also

▸ *Implementing the per-vertex ambient light component*

Implementing the per-vertex specular light component

Specular light is responsible for producing shininess on the surface of an object. Unlike diffuse light, which uses the incident ray and surface normal to find the intensity of light, specular light uses the reflected ray and the direction of the viewer to find the intensity of light.

Getting ready

The following figure illustrates the scenario in which the viewer's position (camera) is brought in to the picture to demonstrate the mathematical calculations for specular light. The angle made by the incident ray of light with the normal of the surface is always equal to an angle of reflection with the same normal. Therefore, both **S** and **R** vectors create a **θ** angle with **N**. The **S** vector is represented by the opposite direction (**-S**); this is because we are interested in calculating the **R** reflection vector:

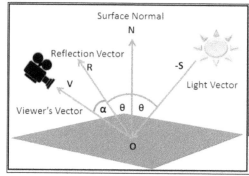

N = Normal vector of the surface.

S = Incident light vector from light to surface position, making θ angle with N.

R = Reflected light vector from surface to space, making θ angle with N.

V = View vector from surface to camera position, making α angle with R.

This shininess is dependent on the angle made between the viewer and the reflected light; if the angle between the viewer's vector and the reflected vector is small, then the surface is shinier.

Mathematically, in the Phong reflection model, the specular component's reflection vector (**R**) is calculated as:

$$R = 2N (N.S) + (-S)$$

However, in the OpenGL ES shading language, we can use the `reflect()` function to calculate vector R:

```
R = reflect( -S, N )
```

The α angle between the *R* and *V* vectors can be calculated as the dot product between these two vectors. The *V* vector is in the eye coordinates; the vertices that are closer to the *R* vector in the same direction will cause shininess on the surface. Given *R* and *V*, the specular illumination can be calculated mathematically as:

$$I_s = L_s K_s (R.V)_G$$

The G superscript in the preceding formula is used for glossy factor; its practical significance is to produce larger or smaller glossy spot on the surface of an object. Its value ranges between 1 and 200; the larger the value, smaller and brighter and vice versa.

How to do it...

Reuse the previous implemented recipe for diffuse shading and make necessary changes in the shaders and program code, as described in the following steps:

1. Create `SpecularVertex.glsl` and use the following instruction for the vertex shader; there is no change in the fragment shader. We can reuse the existing code:

```
#version 300 es
layout (location = 0) in vec4   VertexPosition;
layout (location = 1) in vec3   Normal;

uniform mat4    ModelViewProjectionMatrix, ModelViewMatrix;
uniform mat3    NormalMatrix;

// Specular Light and Material information
uniform vec3 MaterialSpecular, LightSpecular,LightPosition;
   uniform float    ShininessFactor;
out vec4         FinalColor;

void main()
```

```
{
        vec3 nNormal = normalize( NormalMatrix * Normal );
        vec3 eyeCoord= vec3( ModelViewMatrix* VertexPosition
        );
        vec3 nLight   = normalize( LightPosition - eyeCoord);
        vec3 V        = normalize( -eyeCoord);
        vec3 R        = reflect( -nLight, nNormal );

        float sIntensity=pow(max(0.0,dot(R,V)),ShininessFactor);
        vec3 specular= MaterialSpecular * LightSpecular;
        FinalColor   = vec4( sIntensity * specular, 1 );

        gl_Position   = ModelViewProjectionMatrix*VertexPosition;
}
```

2. In the `InitModel`, load and compile the specular shader and set the configuration for specular light and material color. Also, specify the position of light in world coordinates:

```
// ObjLoader::InitModel()
. . . . .

if (MaterialSpecular >= 0)
      { glUniform3f(MaterialSpecular, 1.0, 0.5, 0.5); }

if (LightSpecular >= 0)
      { glUniform3f(LightSpecular, 1.0, 1.0, 1.0); }

if (ShininessFactor >= 0)
      { glUniform1f(ShininessFactor, 40); }

if (LightPosition >= 0){
   glm::vec3 lightPosition(0.0, 0.0, 10.0);
      glUniform3fv(LightPosition,1,&lightPosition);
}
```

How it works...

The specular light vertex shader calculates the `nNormal`, `eyeCoord`, and `nLight` in the same way we computed it in the previous recipe. Calculate the direction of the viewer or the (*V*) camera by normalizing eye coordinates and the *R* reflection vector with the help of the reflect() function. The dot product of *R* and *V* is clamped by the max function within the range 0.0 and 1.0. This result is used to calculate the power function with `ShininessFactor`, which is responsible for producing a glossy spot on the surface; the calculated result is stored in sIntensity. The `FinalColor` is calculated as a product of `sIntensity`, `MaterialSpecular`, and `LightSpecular`. This color information is sent to the fragment shader as an out variable and applied to respective fragments created by primitives formed by vertices:

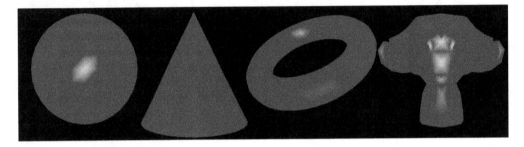

See also

▸   *Implementing the per-vertex ambient light component*

▸   *Implementing the per-vertex diffuse light component*

Optimizing the specular light with the halfway vector

The specular illumination that we have implemented in the previous recipe uses the reflection vector from the incident light ray to demonstrate the spotty illumination. This reflection vector is calculated by the `reflect()` function in the GLSL. This function is slightly expensive to calculate. Therefore, instead of calculating the dot product between the reflection and the (`R.V`) camera vector, we can also calculate (`nNormal.H`), which is the dot product between our surface normal vector and the halfway vector. The `H` halfway vector is the vector between the camera (viewer's) vector and incident light. In the following figure, you can see the resultant of the `V` and `S` vector (Note: not `-S`):

Mathematically, the halfway vector is calculated as:

Halfway vector (H) = incident light vector (S) + camera vector (V)

The equation to calculating the halfway specular light is:

$$H = S + V$$

$$I_s = L_s K_s (N.H)_G$$

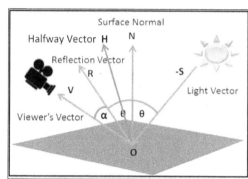

N = Normal vector of the surface.
S = Incident light vector from light to
    surface position, making θ angle with N.
R = Reflected light vector from surface to space,
    making θ angle with N.
V = View vector from surface to camera position,
    making α angle with R.
H = Halfway vector.

How to do it...

Use the previous recipe, *Implementing the per-vertex specular light component*, and make the following changes in the `SpecularVertex.glsl`. The changes in the following code are marked in bold. There is no change required in the fragment shader:

```
// No change in the global variables
. . . . . .
void main()
{
    vec3 nNormal = normalize( NormalMatrix * Normal );
    vec3 eyeCoord= vec3( ModelViewMatrix * VertexPosition );
    vec3 nLight  = normalize( LightPosition - eyeCoord);
```

```
    vec3 V        = normalize ( -eyeCoord);
    vec3 H        = normalize (nLight + V);
    float sIntensity = 0.0;
    sIntensity=pow(max(0.0,dot(H,nNormal)),ShininessFactor);

    vec3 specular   = MaterialSpecular * LightSpecular;
    FinalColor      = vec4( sIntensity * specular, 1 );
    gl_Position     = ModelViewProjectionMatrix * VertexPosition;
}
```

How it works...

In this technique, we use the `nLight` incident light vector and the (V) camera vector to find the (H) resultant vector by adding them. Both vectors must be in the eye coordinates; the resultant halfway vector must be normalized in order to generate correct results. Calculate the dot product between the (nNormal) normal surface vector and the (H) halfway vector and substitute it in the equation mentioned previously to calculate specular illumination:

```
sIntensity = pow(max(0.0, dot(H, nNormal)), ShininessFactor)
```

The current technique is considered to be more efficient as compared to the prior specular technique we implemented. The preceding image shows the difference between the two techniques. There is no doubt that using the halfway vector technique is an approximation and generates less obvious result characteristics in comparison to the original technique. This approximation is very close to reality; therefore, if you are not too bothered about precise quality, you can use the halfway vector to calculate the shininess of the surface.

 Remember to always use (-S) to calculate the reflection vector and use (S) to calculate the (H) halfway vector.

See also

▶ *Implementing the per-vertex specular light component*

Gouraud shading – the per-vertex shading technique

This recipe implements the Phong reflection model with all the three components of light, that is, ambient (A), diffuse (D), and specular (S), which we looked at in the previous recipes. This illumination technique is also known as ADS or Gouraud shading. The Gouraud shading technique is per-vertex shading because the fragment's color is calculated in the vertex shader by using each vertex's position information.

Getting ready

This recipe combines the effect of our ambient (A), diffuse (D), and specular (S) illumination, which we have implemented in our previous recipes, using the Phong reflection model technique. Mathematically, it's the summation of ambient, diffuse, and specular fragment colors:

Gouraud shading color = ambient color + diffuse color + specular color

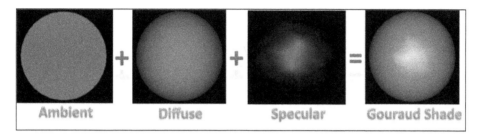

Before implementing the Gouraud shading, it's advisable to understand ambient, diffuse, and specular illumination techniques thoroughly, as mentioned in this chapter.

How to do it...

The Gouraud shading recipe implementation will make use of the existing vertex shader files from the ambient, diffuse, and specular recipes in the current vertex shader called `GouraudShadeVertex.glsl`. This recipe uses a global function called `GouraudShading()` to implement the Gouraud shading technique; the fragment shader can be completely reused as it does not require any change. The following code snippet describes the Gouraud shading vertex shader:

```
. . . . // global variables, vertex attribute and matrixes.
vec3 GouraudShading()
{
    nNormal   = normalize ( NormalMatrix * Normal );
    eyeCoord  = vec3 ( ModelViewMatrix * VertexPosition );
    nLight    = normalize( LightPosition - eyeCoord );

    // Diffuse Intensity
    cosAngle = max( 0.0, dot( nNormal, nLight ));

    // Specular Intensity
    V       = normalize( -eyeCoord );
    R       = reflect( -nLight, nNormal );
```

```
        sIntensity=pow( max(0.0, dot(R, V) ), ShininessFactor);

        // ADS color as result of Material & Light interaction
        ambient = MaterialAmbient   * LightAmbient;//Ambient light
        diffuse = MaterialDiffuse   * LightDiffuse;//Diffuse light
        specular = MaterialSpecular*LightSpecular;//Specular light

        return ambient + (cosAngle*diffuse) + (sIntensity*specular);
    }

    void main(){
        FinalColor = vec4(GouraudShading(), 1);
        gl_Position = ModelViewProjectionMatrix * VertexPosition;
    }
```

How it works...

The `GouraudShading()` function calculates the color for each vertex by adding the ambient, diffuse, and specular light colors; the resultant color information is returned to the `main()` program. The vertex shader then shares this color information to the fragment shader. The fragment shader interpolates the entire color for each fragment by using the color information received from the vertex shader.

The function definitions in OpenGL ES Shading Language is similar to the C language; it can return values and pass arguments by value. These do not support pointers or reference to send the information by address. For more information on function definition in GL Shading Language 3.0, refer to `http://www.khronos.org/files/opengles_shading_language.pdf`.

This recipe is implemented using point light; the rays from a point light form different angles with vertex when it falls on the object.

See also

▶ *Implementing directional and point light*

Phong shading – the per-fragment shading technique

This shading technique is also called as smooth shading. In this recipe, we will implement Phong shading, which is a per-fragment illumination technique. Using the per-fragment technique, light shadings add more realism to the rendering scene in comparison to the per-vertex technique. We will compare Gouraud shading with Phong shading to see the relative difference between the two techniques.

In Phong shading, color intensities are directly calculated within the fragment shader with the help of light and material properties. The vertex shader is responsible for calculating the normal and vertex position in the eye coordinates; these variables are then passed on to the fragment shader. The vertex normal and vertex positions are interpolated and normalized for every fragment to produce the resultant fragment colors.

How to do it...

Use the following steps to implement and see this technique in action:

1. Create `PhongShadeVertex.glsl` and reuse most of the variables from previous recipes. Refer to the following code. The main difference is `normalCoord` and `eyeCoord`, which are defined as the out variables. Note: we will not use the properties of light and material in vertex shader; instead, these will be used in fragment shader:

```
#version 300 es
// Vertex information
layout(location = 0) in vec4  VertexPosition;
layout(location = 1) in vec3  Normal;

// Model View Project Normal Matrix
uniform mat4 ModelViewProjectionMatrix, ModelViewMatrix;
uniform mat3 NormalMatrix;

//Out variable shared with Fragment shader
out vec3 normalCoord, eyeCoord;

void main() {
  normalCoord = NormalMatrix * Normal;
  eyeCoord    = vec3(ModelViewMatrix * VertexPosition);
  gl_Position = ModelViewProjectionMatrix * VertexPosition;
}
```

2. Create the `PhongShadeFragment.glsl` fragment shader file and add all the light and material property variables to the required precision qualifier. We will use the medium precision qualifier; this precision qualifier precedes the type in the variable declaration:

```
#version 300 es
precision mediump float;

// Material & Light property
uniform vec3 MaterialAmbient,MaterialSpecular,MaterialDiffuse;
uniform vec3 LightAmbient, LightSpecular, LightDiffuse;
uniform float   ShininessFactor;

uniform vec3 LightPosition;

in vec3     normalCoord;
in vec3     eyeCoord;

layout(location = 0) out vec4 FinalColor;

vec3 normalizeNormal, normalizeEyeCoord, normalizeLightVec, V, R,
ambient, diffuse, specular;
float sIntensity, cosAngle;

vec3 PhongShading()
{
  normalizeNormal    = normalize(normalCoord);
  normalizeEyeCoord = normalize(eyeCoord);
  normalizeLightVec = normalize(LightPosition-eyeCoord);

  // Diffuse Intensity
  cosAngle = max(0.0,
              dot(normalizeNormal,normalizeLightVec));

  // Specular Intensity
  V = -normalizeEyeCoord; // Viewer's vector
  R = reflect(-normalizeLightVec, normalizeNormal);
  sIntensity = pow(max(0.0,dot(R,V)), ShininessFactor);

  ambient     = MaterialAmbient   * LightAmbient;
  diffuse     = MaterialDiffuse   * LightDiffuse;
```

```
    specular    = MaterialSpecular * LightSpecular;

    return ambient+(cosAngle*diffuse)+(sIntensity*specular);
}

void main() {
    FinalColor = vec4(PhongShading(), 1.0);
}
```

How it works...

In Phong shading, the vertex shader calculates the vertex normal (`normalCoord`) and vertex position in the eye coordinate system (`eyeCoord`) and sends it to the fragment shader. The fragment shader uses these values and interpolates the vertex normal and vertex position for each fragment. The interpolated values must be normalized in order to produce accurate results. The remaining process to calculate ambient, diffuse, and specular light is the same as discussed in the previous recipes.

By default, the vertex shader does not require any precision in order to be defined (it's optional). If no precision is defined in the vertex shader, then it's of the highest precision. In the fragment shader, the precision qualifier needs to be defined (it's not optional).

There are three types of precision qualifier, namely, `lowp`, `medium`, and `highp`. These precision qualifiers could affect the performance of the application; it's therefore advisable to use the correct precision according to the implementation requirement. Lower precision may help to increase the FPS and power efficiency; however, it may reduce the quality of rendering. In our case, we will use the mediump precision for all the variables in the fragment shader.

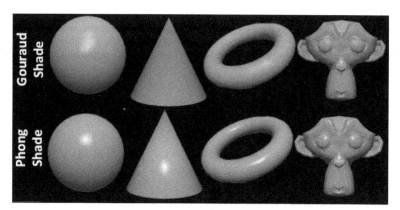

There's more...

We have used the Wavefront OBJ mesh to demonstrate the light shading effects on 3D mesh models; you can explore more on meshes in the *Chapter 4, Working with Meshes*. The same chapter describes the flat/smooth shading implementation using normal vectors.

The flat/smooth shading implementation can be enabled by using the `ObjMesh` class member function called `ParseObjModel`. This specifies the second argument as Boolean `true` (flat shading) or `false` (smooth shading). The comparative results for the two shading types are shown in the following figure:

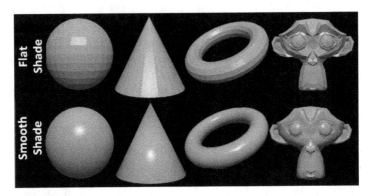

See also

▶ Refer to the *Rendering the wavefront OBJ mesh model* recipe in *Chapter 4, Working with Meshes*

Implementing directional and point light

Light can be divided into three types, namely point light, directional light, and spot light. Let's take a look in detail:

▶ **Point light or positional light**: This type of light comes from a fixed position in the 3D space. The position of light and vertices of the object on which it falls is used to calculate the direction of the light. Point light emits light in all directions. Each vertex can have different directions of light, depending on its position from the light source, as shown in the following image.

- ▸ **Directional light**: This type of light is a special case of the point light. Here, the direction of the light falling on the object is considered as nonvarying. This means that the direction of all the light rays are parallel. In directional light, the light source is considered infinitely far from the model, on which it's supposed to fall. Sometimes, it's better to assume the light direction to be parallel during the 3D scene rendering process. This is the best way to achieve nearly the same effect as point light if the distance between the source point and model is appreciably larger.

- ▸ **Spot light**: This type of light uses the direction of the light and a cutoff angle to form a cone-shaped imaginary 3D space, as shown in the following figure. The light that falls out of this shape is discarded and the light inside the cone forms the spotlight effect:

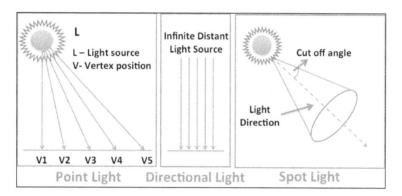

Getting ready

Sometimes, the position of the light source is considerably far from the objects. In such cases, it's advisable to implement the light-shading technique using directional lighting. The point light shading technique is a little expensive because the light direction needs to be calculated per-vertex. It's directly proportional to the number of vertices in the geometry. In contrast, directional light is treated in the constant direction where rays are assumed to be traveling in parallel directions. Unlike point light, light direction does not consider the vertex position in directional light:

Light type	Mathematical formulation	Light direction
Point	Light direction = light position - eye position	Variable
Directional	Light direction = light position	Constant

How to do it...

This recipe will demonstrate the difference between point light and directional light; all the previous recipes we have implemented so far used point light. In fact, with the previous section in this recipe, we understood which light to use when. The following instructions in bold are implemented in the fragment shader based on Phong shading; similar changes need to be performed in the vertex shader if Gouraud shading is implemented:

- **Point light or positional light**: This requires one change to implement point light:

```
vec3 PhongShading(){
    normalizeNormal    = normalize( normalCoord );
    normalizeEyeCoord = normalize( eyeCoord );
    // Calculate Point Light Direction
    normalizeLightVec = normalize( LightPosition - eyeCoord
    );
    . . . . . .
    // Calculate ADS Material & Light
    . . . . . .
    return
    ambient+(cosAngle*diffuse)+(sIntensity*specular);
}
```

- **Directional light**: Similarly, change the statement marked in bold for directional light:

```
vec3 PhongShading(){
    normalizeNormal    = normalize( normalCoord );
    normalizeEyeCoord = normalize( eyeCoord );
    // Calculate Direction Light Direction
    normalizeLightVec = normalize( LightPosition );
    . . . . . .
    // Calculate ADS Material & Light
    . . . . . .
    return ambient+(cosAngle*diffuse)+(sIntensity*specular);
}
```

How it works...

In point lighting, the light vector is used to calculate the directional vector of light, with respect to each eye coordinate of the vertex; this produces variable directional vectors, which are responsible for different amount of light intensity at each vertex.

In contrast, directional light assumes all vertexes at origin (0.0, 0.0, and 0.0). Hence, all the direction vector for each vertex are parallel. The following figure compares the point light technique and the directional light technique:

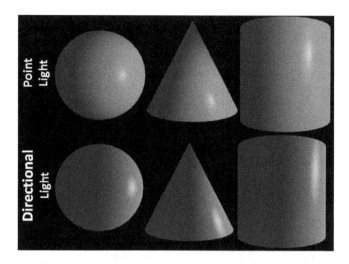

Implementing multiple lights in a scene

So far, all of our recipes are demonstrated using a single light source. This section will help us in implementing multiple lights in a scene. Unlike the fixed pipeline architecture, in which only eight lights can be added to the scene, the programmable pipeline does not impose any upper limit on the number of multiple lights. Adding multiple lights to the scene is very simple. It's similar to the way we added one light position to create one color per-fragment. Now, we add N number of light sources to generate an average of N colors per-fragment:

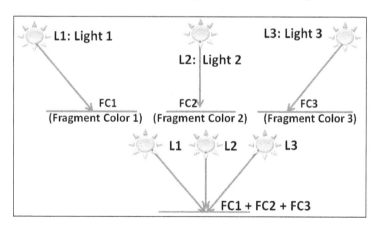

Mathematically, if light sources such as **L1**, **L2**, and **L3** create **FC1**, **FC2**, and **FC3** fragment colors individually, then the combined effect of these lights will be a single fragment color as a result of an average weight of all fragment colors.

Getting ready

The vertex shader for this recipe does not require any special changes to the source code. Therefore, we can reuse the same vertex shader (which was implemented in the Phong shading recipe). This recipe requires a few changes to the fragment shader.

How to do it...

The steps to implement multiple light recipes are as follows:

1. Create a fragment shader file called `MultiLightFragment.glsl` and highlight it, as shown in the following code:

```
// Many line skipped
. . . . .
// Light uniform array of 4 elements containing light
// position and diffuse color information.
uniform vec3    LightPositionArray[4];
uniform vec3    LightDiffuseArray[4];
uniform float   ShininessFactor;

vec3 PhongShading( int index )
{
    normalizeNormal    = normalize( normalCoord );
    normalizeEyeCoord = normalize( eyeCoord );
    normalizeLightVec = normalize
    (LightPositionArray[index] - eyeCoord );

    cosAngle = max(0.0,dot(normalizeNormal,normalizeLightVec));

    V = -normalizeEyeCoord; // Viewer's vector
    R =reflect(-normalizeLightVec,normalizeNormal);//Reflectivity
    sIntensity = pow( max( 0.0, dot( R, V ) ), ShininessFactor );

    ambient    = MaterialAmbient * LightAmbient;
    diffuse = MaterialDiffuse * LightDiffuseArray[index];
```

```
        specular  = MaterialSpecular * LightSpecular;

        return ambient+(cosAngle*diffuse)+(sIntensity*specular);
    }

void main() {
    vec4 multipleLightColor = vec4( 0.0 );
    for (int i=0; i<4; i++){
        multipleLightColor += vec4(PhongShading(i),1.0);
    }
    FinalColor = multipleLightColor;
}
```

2. There is no change required for the vertex shader; however, the main program specifies four different light positions and four different diffuse color configurations:

```
// Inside ObjLoader::InitModel()
// Compile and  use Multiple Light Shade Program
glUseProgram( program->ProgramID );
// Get Material & Light uniform variables from shaders
float lightpositions[12]={{-10.0,0.0,5.0}, {0.0,10.0,5.0},
{10.0,0.0,5.0},{0.0,-10.0,5.0}};
glUniform3fv(LightPositionArray,
sizeof(lightpositions)/sizeof(float), lightpositions);

float lightdiffusecolors[12]={{1.0,0.0,0.0}, {0.0,1.0,0.0},
{1.0,0.0,0.0}, {0.0,1.0,0.0} };
glUniform3fv(LightDiffuseArray, sizeof(lightdiffusecolors)/
sizeof(float), lightdiffusecolors);
```

How it works...

The current recipe uses four lights to demonstrate multiple-light shading in a scene. These lights are positioned around the object (left, right, top, and bottom). Lights positioned at the left-hand side and the right-hand side use red-diffused light color, whereas lights positioned at the bottom and top are set with green-diffused light color.

Programmatically, the position of lights and diffuse light colors are defined as an array in our shader program with `LightPosition` and `LightDiffuseArray` respectively.

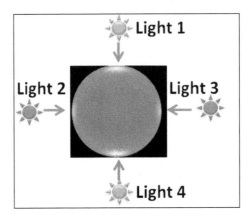

The `GouraudShading()` function is modified to accept an argument, which uses an index of the position of the light that needs to be processed. The main program loops to calculate the average fragment color intensity. This fragment color is returned to the main program.

Light positions that are closer to the surface of the sphere receive more intensity; therefore we can clearly see that the sphere is illuminated with green and red color at the top, bottom, left and right faces. The front part of the sphere is a mixture of green and red color because the intensities received by the sphere at the front face from all four light directions are equal.

Implementing two-side shading

In *Chapter 2, OpenGL ES 3.0 Essentials*, we looked at the culling technique, which is a quick way to improve performance. This technique avoids rendering polygon faces that face backwards; it's not always desirable to clip the back faces (objects that are not completely enclosed are generally rendered with back faces). Sometimes, it makes sense to view these back faces with different colors. This will help the geometry shape to define characteristics that may not be visible with the same color on both sides of the faces (back and front).

In this recipe, we will render a semi-hollow cylinder with different face colors (inside and outside). The first thing we need to do is to turn off the back culling. We can turn off the back culling with (`glDisable (GL_CULL_FACE)`).

In order to apply different colors on the front and back faces, we need to recognize them first. The OpenGL ES shading language provides a simple global-level variable called `gl_FrontFacing` in the fragment shader, which helps us to recognize the fragments belonging to front facings. This API returns Boolean as `true` if the face is front facing and vice versa.

The normal position of the face helps in defining the direction in which it's pointing. The normal position of the front face is always in the opposite direction of the back face; we will use this clue to shade the front face and the back face with different colors.

Getting ready

The multiple lights shading recipe can be reused to implement two-side shading.

 Make sure that culling is disabled in the program code; otherwise, two-side shading will not work.

How to do it...

There is no change required in the vertex shader. Create a fragment shader file called `TwoSideShadingFragment.glsl` and make the following changes mentioned in bold:

```
vec3 GouraudShading( bool frontSide ){
   normalizeNormal   = normalize ( normalCoord );
   normalizeLightVec = normalize ( LightPosition - eyeCoord );
   if ( frontSide ) // Diffuse Intensity
     { cosAngle=max(0.0, dot(normalizeNormal,normalizeLightVec)); }
   else
     { cosAngle=max(0.0, dot(-normalizeNormal,normalizeLightVec));}

   V = normalize( -eyeCoord );
   R = reflect(-normalizeLightVec, normalizeNormal);
   sIntensity = pow(max(0.0,dot(R,V)), ShininessFactor);
   ambient   = MaterialAmbient  * LightAmbient; // Net Ambient
   specular  = MaterialSpecular * LightSpecular;// Net Specular
   if ( frontSide ) // Front and back face net Diffuse color
   { diffuse=MaterialDiffuse*LightDiffuse; }
   else
   { diffuse=MaterialDiffuseBackFace*LightDiffuse; }

   return ambient + (cosAngle*diffuse) + (sIntensity*specular);
}

void main() {
    if (gl_FrontFacing)
       { FinalColor = vec4(GouraudShading(true), 1.0); }
    else
       { FinalColor = vec4(GouraudShading(false), 1.0); }
}
```

How it works...

The working principle for this recipe is very simple; the ideology behind is to check whether the primitive fragment belongs to the front face or the back face. If it belongs to the front face, assign it with one type of color coding; otherwise, chose another type of color. Within the fragment shader, check the front facing with `gl_FrontFacing`. Pass the fragment facing type in the `GouraudShading` function as an argument. Depending on the front and back facing Boolean value, this function will generate the color. We will use `MaterialDiffuseBackFace` and `LightDiffuse` for back facing and front facing diffuse light colors respectively. In order to calculate the Gouraud shading for back surfaces, we must use negative direction normal:

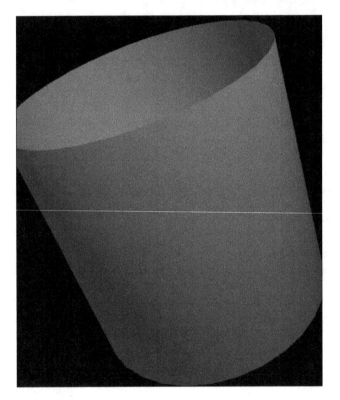

See also

▸   Refer to the *Culling in OpenGL ES 3.0* recipe in *Chapter 2, OpenGL ES 3.0 Essentials*

6

Working with Shaders

In this chapter, we will cover the following recipes:

- ▸ Implementing the wobble and ripple effect
- ▸ Procedural texture shading with object coordinates
- ▸ Creating the circular pattern and making them revolve
- ▸ Generating the brick pattern
- ▸ Generating the polka dot pattern
- ▸ Discarding fragments
- ▸ Procedural texture shading with texture coordinates

Introduction

This chapter will give you an in-depth understanding of the shaders programming technique. It discusses various techniques that can be implemented by using the vertex and fragment shaders, revealing their capabilities. We will begin this chapter by understanding the role of shaders in the OpenGL ES 3.0 programmable pipeline. You will also learn how the vertex shader and fragment shaders process information on GPU Multicores.

You will learn how to deform the geometry shape by using the vertex shader; this will produce a wobble effect on 3D mesh models. With a little modification, we will use the same deforming concept to implement the pond water ripple effect. Further, we will understand the difference between the procedural and image texturing. With the help of model coordinates, we will implement our first simple procedural texturing recipe.

Drawing a circle-shaped geometry by using vertices may be too expensive to render because it requires too many vertices to form smoother edges; the circle shader recipe demonstrates an efficient way of rendering a circle that uses procedural texturing. The brick shader recipe demonstrates how to render a pattern of bricks on the surface of an object. Using the knowledge from the circle pattern, we will program how to render polka dots on 3D mesh objects. We will extend the same recipe to show an interesting feature of the GL shading language that allows us to produce holes in the 3D geometries by using discarded fragments. Finally, you will learn how to use texture coordinates to program procedural textures. With this knowledge, we will create a grid or cage like geometry on a 3D cube mesh object.

Shader role and responsibilities: The following figure illustrates the role of vertex and fragment shaders on two overlapped models to produce the final image on the screen; the expected output is marked as label 1. The graphics engine is provided with a rectangle-shaped model (four vertices) and a triangle-shaped model (three vertices). These models are first sent to the vertex shader. The vertex and fragment shader program has syntax, such as C programming language; the program's entry point always starts from the `main()` function.

The vertex shader is compiled and executed at runtime; it's invoked once for every vertex in the geometry, as shown in the following figure with labels **2** and **3**. Shader programs are executed on the multiprocessors GPUs, which allows manipulation of several vertices at the same time. The vertex shader is always executed first before the fragment shader.

There are mainly two goals of a vertex shader:

  ▶ Calculating the transformation of the vertex coordinates
  ▶ Calculating any per-vertex calculations required by the fragment shader

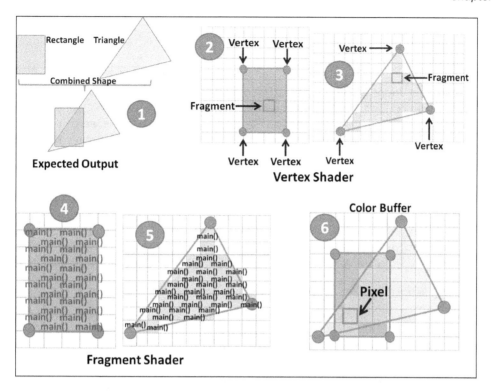

A fragment shader is always executed after the vertex shader. Unlike vertex shaders, the fragment shader also contains a `main()` function as its entry point. The fragment shader is also compiled and executed at runtime for every single fragment; label **4** and label **5** shows the execution of the fragment shader on each fragment.

The image with label **6** shows the generated fragments after the rasterization process; the pixel is shown in the red box. Each fragment may or may not correspond to a single pixel in the primitive. A pixel in the framebuffer can be composed of one or more than one fragment, as shown in the following figure; using the fragment shader, these generated fragments can be controlled programmatically to assign color, texture, and other attribute information; each fragment has position, depth, and color associated with it.

The main goal of the fragment shader is to compute the color information for each fragment or discard the fragment according to the programing decision.

A fragment has the ability to perform the following tasks:

▶ Color interpolation or computation of every fragment
▶ Texture coordinates computation
▶ Texture assignment to every pixel

- ▸ Normal interpolation for each pixel
- ▸ Calculation of light information for every pixel
- ▸ Animation effects computation

The shaders concurrent execution model: The modern graphics engine architecture is capable of rendering high performance state-of-the-art graphics. Thanks to modern graphic processors that allow fast and parallel processing of large datasets at an incredible speed, this capability requires computation of a large dataset in a fraction of micro seconds. **Graphics Processor Units (GPUs)** are special dedicated processors made to fulfill these requirements; these processors are multicore where parallel processing can be achieved.

One of the major requirements of modern graphics is that it needs efficient floating-point calculations and fast polygon transformation operations. The GPU is optimized exclusively for these types of requirements; they provide a bunch of capabilities. Among these, it includes the fast trigonometric function, which is considered to be expensive on the CPU architecture. The number of processor cores in GPU can go from a few hundreds to thousands in number.

The following figure shows the concurrent execution on the GPUs for the vertex and fragment shader:

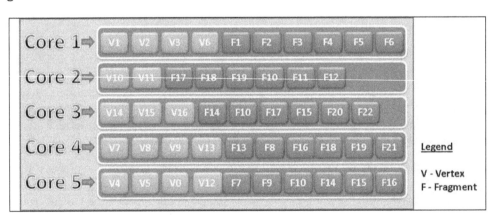

Each core of the GPU is capable of running an instance of the vertex or fragment shader; each core processes the vertices first and then the fragments, as shown in the preceding figure.

Implementing the wobble and ripple effect

This is a first simple yet effective vertex shader technique that produces a wobbling effect on the object's geometry. This shader produces animation effects on the geometric shape like a sine wave; this effect is implemented within the vertex shader. This recipe also demonstrates another animation technique that produces a water pond ripple effect.

Getting ready

For this recipe, we will reuse the existing Phong shading recipe from the previous chapter. Rename the shader files with a name of your choice; for this recipe, we will rename these to `WobbleVertex.glsl` and `WobbleFragment.glsl`. The wobble and ripple shader are both vertex shader-based recipes.

How to do it...

This section will provide the changes required to implement the vertex shader in order to produce the wobble effect. Modify the `WobbleVertex.glsl` as per the following code; there is no change required for the fragment shader:

```
#version 300 es

// Define amplitude for Wobble Shader
#define AMPLITUDE            1.2

// Geometries vertex and normal information
layout(location = 0) in vec4  VertexPosition;
layout(location = 1) in vec3  Normal;

// Model View Project and Normal matrix
uniform mat4 ModelViewProjectionMatrix, ModelViewMatrix;
uniform mat3 NormalMatrix;

uniform float Time; // Timer

// Output variable for fragment shader
out vec3     nNormal, eyeCoord;

void main(){
    nNormal    = normalize ( NormalMatrix * Normal );
    eyeCoord   = vec3 ( ModelViewMatrix * VertexPosition );
    vec4 VertexCoord = VertexPosition;
    VertexCoord.y += sin(VertexCoord.x+Time)*AMPLITUDE;
    gl_Position = ModelViewProjectionMatrix * VertexCoord;
}
```

How it works...

A sine wave has a mathematical property of producing a smooth repetitive oscillation. The following figure shows the sine wave; the amplitude of sine wave defines the height or depth of the wave trough or crest, respectively. The wobble vertex shader displaces the Y component of each object vertex V (V_x, V_y, and V_z) to produce the wobbling effect; the displacement is done using the sine function whose value always range between -1.0 and 1.0.

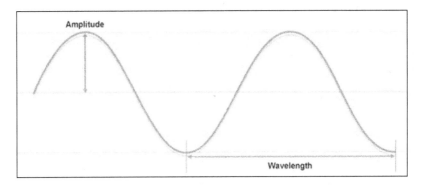

The uniform `Time` attribute variable is used for clock ticks. When these clock ticks are fed to the GLSL `sin()` function, it generates values ranging from -1.0 to 1.0. Each vertex's Y component (V_y) is added to this sine value (*VertexCoord.y += sin(Time)*) to produce a hopping effect animation. Try this equation, it will make the object hop:

$$V_y = V_y + Sin(\varphi)$$

Further, in order to produce the wobble animation, take the X (V_x) or Z (V_z) component of each vertex into consideration to produce a wave like oscillation animation using (*VertexCoord.y += sin(VertexCoord.x + Time)*). Multiplying the Y (V_y) component of the resultant with `AMPLITUDE` will affect the height of the wobbling wave animation:

$$V_y = V_y + Sin(V_x + \varphi)$$

With the new Y (V_y) component of each vertex, the clip coordinates of the vertex are calculated by multiplying it with the `ModelViewProjection` matrix.

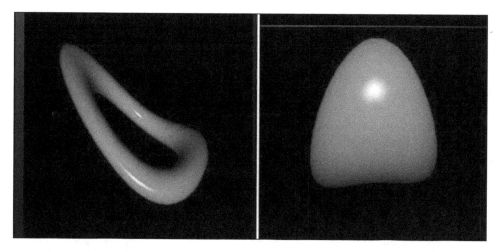

There's more...

The wobble shader recipe also exhibits a pond water ripple animation, as shown in the preceding image in this section. Mathematically, the sine wave as a function of time is defined as follows:

$$y(t) = A\sin(2\pi ft + \varphi)$$

Where *t* is the time, *A* is the amplitude of the wave, and *f* is the frequency. Using this formula, the ripple effect can be programmed as follows. The change in phase (φ) is assumed to be *t* here:

$$V_y = Sin(2 * PI * distance * FREQUENCY + \varphi) * Amplitude$$

Modify the existing vertex shader according to the instructions given in the following code snippet, highlighted in bold:

```
#define RIPPLE_AMPLITUDE 0.05
#define FREQUENCY 5.0
#define PI 3.14285714286
void main(){
    nNormal    = normalize ( NormalMatrix * Normal );
    eyeCoord   = vec3 ( ModelViewMatrix * VertexPosition );
    vec4    VertexCoord = VertexPosition;
    float distance = length(VertexCoord);
```

```
VertexCoord.y = sin( 2.0 * PI * distance * FREQUENCY + Time)
* RIPPLE_AMPLITUDE;
gl_Position = ModelViewProjectionMatrix * VertexCoord;
}
```

The distance variable is used to calculate distances of each variable from its origin; this distance is calculated using the OpenGL ES shading language `length()` API. Finally, the clipped coordinates are calculated by taking product between the `VertexCoord` and `ModelViewProjection` matrix.

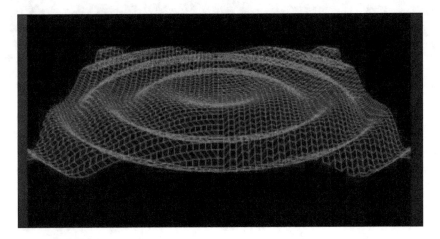

See also

▶ Refer to the *Phong shading – the per-fragment shading technique* recipe in *Chapter 5, Light and Materials*

Procedural texture shading with object coordinates

In this recipe, you will learn how to produce a texture pattern on the surface of the 3D geometry with the help of procedural textures. Basically, texturing on a 2D/3D mesh object can be divided into two categories:

▶ **Procedural texturing**: A procedure texture is an image or a texture produced mathematically using an algorithm; such algorithms use various attributes of a 2D/3D object to create an image; this type of texturing is highly controllable. Procedural texturing is used to create patterns, such as clouds, marble, wood, blending, noise, musgrave, voronoi, and so on.

▶ **Image texturing**: In this type of texture, a static image is wrapped on the object; this image could be distorted on affine scaling transformation because this is a raster type of image. You will learn more about image texturing in the next chapter called textures.

In this chapter, we will produce a number of procedural textures, with the help of object and texture coordinates. The current recipe makes use of object coordinates to demonstrate how it can be used to control fragment colors on a 3D model.

An object coordinate is a coordinate system in which the original shape of the object is defined. For example, the square in the following image is a 2 x 2 unit along the x-z plane; the origin is located in the middle of the square. The x axis and z axis divides the square into four quadrants around the origin. This recipe uses this logic to logically divide the mesh's 3D space into four quadrants, with each quadrant colored with a different color:

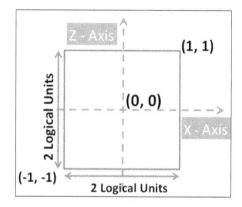

How to do it...

Perform the following steps to implement this simple recipe:

1. Create the `SimpleVertexShader.glsl` and add it to the following code snippet:

```
#version 300 es
// Vertex information
layout(location = 0) in vec4  VertexPosition;
layout(location = 1) in vec3  Normal;

// Model View Project and Normal matrix
```

```
uniform mat4 ModelViewProjectionMatrix, ModelViewMatrix;
uniform mat3    NormalMatrix;

// output variable to fragment shader
out vec3 nNormal, eyeCoord, ObjectCoord;

void main() {
    nNormal     = normalize ( NormalMatrix * Normal );
    eyeCoord    = vec3 (ModelViewMatrix * VertexPosition);
    ObjectCoord = VertexPosition.xyz;
    gl_Position = ModelViewProjectionMatrix * VertexPosition;
}
```

2. Modify the `SimpleFragmentShader.glsl` as follows:

```
// Reuse the Light and Material properties. .
in vec3 eyeCoord;       // Vertex eye coordinate
in vec3 ObjectCoord; // Vertex object coordinate
layout(location = 0) out vec4 outColor;

vec3 PhongShading(){
    . . . . . .    // Reuse Phong shading code.
}

void main() {
    if (objectCoord.x  > 0.0 && objectCoord.z  > 0.0)
        FinalColor = vec4(1.0, 0.0, 0.0, 1.0);
    else if (objectCoord.x  > 0.0 && objectCoord.z  < 0.0)
        FinalColor = vec4(0.0, 01.0, 0.0, 1.0);
    else if (objectCoord.x  < 0.0 && objectCoord.z  > 0.0)
        FinalColor = vec4(0.0, 01.0, 1.0, 1.0);
    else if (objectCoord.x  < 0.0 && objectCoord.z  < 0.0)
        FinalColor = vec4(1.0, 0.0, 1.0, 1.0);

    FinalColor = FinalColor  * vec4(PhongShading(), 1.0);
}
```

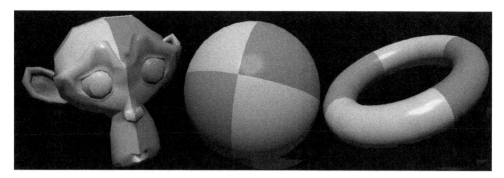

The preceding figure shows the result of our simple procedural shader The models are divided into four quadrants along the *x-z* plane , with each quadrant shown in a different color. Use the single tap on the screen in order to switch between these models.

How it works...

The shader job starts from the vertex shader where object coordinates are received by the vertex program as a vertex attribute in the VertexPosition variable; this variable contains the vertex position in the local 3D space in which the object was defined. This value is stored in the ObjectCoord and passed on to the fragment shader. In the fragment shader, the object coordinate value is checked with the origin in order to test the quadrant to which it belongs to in the *x-z* plane. Depending on the quadrant outcome, a color is assigned to the fragment. The following image shows the division of 3D space into four quadrants using object coordinates:

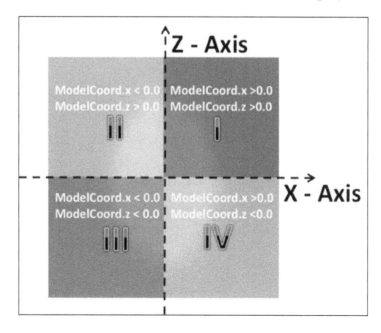

There's more...

The shader program does not provide any print statements that can be used for debugging purposes; one of the easiest solutions to debug coordinate values in the shader is to assign colors to fragments. If you are interested to deal with a coordinate range of a model in the 3D space, you can assign various colors using conditional statements. For example, if the previous fragment shader is replaced with the following code, it will render strips with various colors depending on the coordinate range:

```
// Reuse the Light and Material properties. .
in vec3 eyeCoord;    // Vertex eye coordinate
in vec3 ObjectCoord; // Vertex object coordinate
layout(location = 0) out vec4 outColor;

vec3 PhongShading(){
    . . . . . .// Reuse Phong shading code.
}

void main() {
    //Debuging Shader with Model coordinates
    if (objectCoord.x  > 0.9 )
        FinalColor = vec4(1.0, 0.0, 0.0, 1.0);
    else if (objectCoord.x  > 0.8 )
        FinalColor = vec4(1.0, 1.0, 0.0, 1.0);
    else if (objectCoord.x  > 0.7 )
        FinalColor = vec4(1.0, 0.0, 1.0, 1.0);
    else if (objectCoord.x  > 0.6 )
        FinalColor = vec4(0.60, 0.50, 0.40, 1.0);
    else if (objectCoord.x  > 0.5 )
        FinalColor = vec4(0.30, 0.80, 0.90, 1.0);
    else
        FinalColor = vec4(1.0, 1.0, 1.0, 1.0);

    if (objectCoord.z  > 0.9 )
        FinalColor = vec4(1.0, 0.0, 0.0, 1.0);
    else if (objectCoord.z  > 0.8 )
        FinalColor = vec4(1.0, 1.0, 0.0, 1.0);
    else if (objectCoord.z  > 0.7 )
        FinalColor = vec4(1.0, 0.0, 1.0, 1.0);
    else if (objectCoord.z  > 0.6 )
        FinalColor = vec4(0.60, 0.50, 0.40, 1.0);
```

```
    else if (objectCoord.z  > 0.5 )
        FinalColor = vec4(0.30, 0.80, 0.90, 1.0);

    FinalColor = FinalColor  * vec4(PhongShading(), 1.0);
}
```

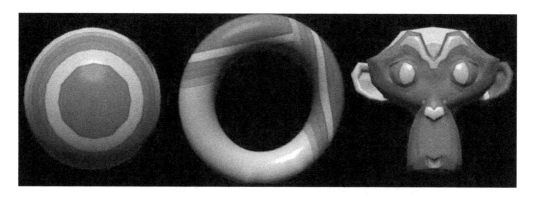

Each unique color specifies a range of object coordinates along *x* or *z* axes. The following image shows that each color represents a band of 0.1 logical units from 0.5 to 1.0 units along the *x-z* plane:

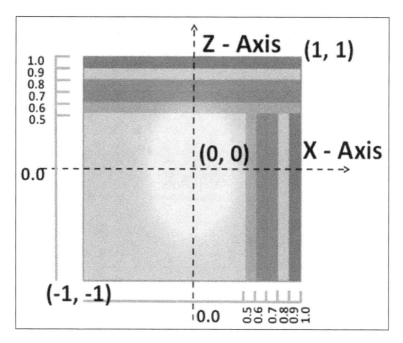

► Refer to the *Applying texture with UV mapping* recipe in *Chapter 7, Textures and Mapping Techniques*

Creating the circular pattern and making them revolve

This procedural texture recipe will make use of fragment coordinates to demonstrate a circular pattern using gl_FragCoord. The gl_FragCoord is a keyword available in the fragment shader that is responsible to store the window position of the current fragment in x and y coordinates; the z coordinate stores the depth of the fragment in the range [0, 1].

These coordinates are always relative to the OpenGL ES surface window; the gl_ FragCoords is a result of a fixed functionality in which primitive are interpolated after the vertex processing stage to generate fragments. By default, the gl_FragCoord assumes the lower-left corner of the OpenGL ES rendering surface window as the origin. The following image shows the origin in the OpenGL ES surface window with different dimensions:

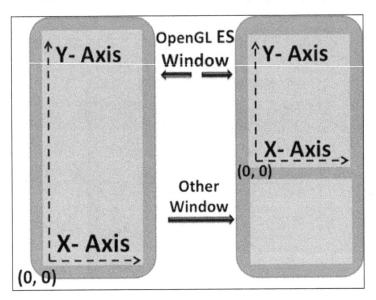

How to do it...

The light shading technique for this recipe will remain similar to the previous recipe; for more information, refer to the *Phong shading – the per-fragment shading technique* recipe in *Chapter 5, Light and Materials*. Create the `CircleVertexShader.glsl` vertex shader and reuse the code from previous recipe; for the `CircleFragmentShader.glsl` fragment shader, make the following changes:

```glsl
#version 300 es
// Reuse the variables . . . no change
vec3 PhongShading(){
    // Reuse Phong shading code.
    . . . . . .
    return ambient + diffuse + sIntensity * specular;
}

// Model and Dot color
uniform vec3 ModelColor, DotColor;

// Output color for fragment
layout(location = 0) out vec4 FinalColor;

// Size of the logical square
uniform float Side;

// Dot size 25% of Square size
float DotSize    = Side * 0.25;
vec2 Square      = vec2(Side, Side);

void main() {
    vec2 position = mod(gl_FragCoord.xy, Square) - Square*0.5;
    float length = length(position);
    float inside = step(length,DotSize);

    FinalColor = vec4(mix(ModelColor, DotColor, inside), 1.0);
    FinalColor = FinalColor * vec4(GouraudShading(), 1.0);
}
```

The following image shows the output of this recipe:

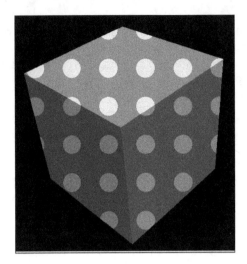

How it works...

For each fragment's window position received from `gl_Fragcoord`, it's manipulated by shifting the bottom-left coordinate to the center of the imaginary square region; this square region is used to inscribe a circle in it. The following code is responsible for displacing each coordinate relative to the center of the logical square, as shown in the following image:

```
vec2 position = mod(gl_FragCoord.xy, Square) - Square*0.5;
```

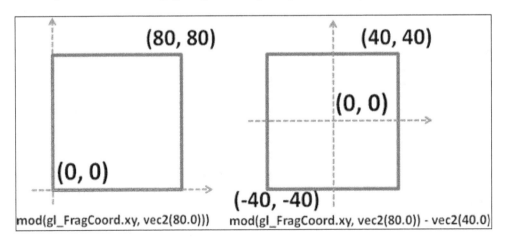

As the `position` is relative to the center of the imaginary square, we can calculate the distance of each coordinate from the center using the standard length formula in vector graphics. This length is used to render the fragment with the color of the circle, which is specified using the `DotColor`; if the length is smaller than the `DotSize`, then the body color is rendered using the `ModelColor`.

Mathematically, a circle is the locus of a point, which is always equidistant from a given point; as the origin is moved to the center, we can inscribe a circle within the square, as shown in the following figure. The coordinates falling under the circle can be rendered with `DotColor` to produce a circle pattern on the model. In order to check whether the length is greater or lesser than `DotSize`, we have used the `step()` GLSL API:

```
inside  = step(length,DotSize);
```

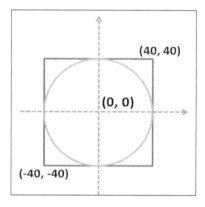

Syntax:

```
float step(float edge,  float x);
```

Variable	Description
edge	This specifies the location of the edge of the step function
x	This specifies the value to be used to generate the step function
Return value	This step function returns 0.0 if x is smaller than edge; otherwise, it returns 1.0

There's more...

The current implementation of the circle pattern is very static; it does not show any movement on the patterns of the circle. In this section, we will apply a general form of the 2D rotation matrix to perform a single rotation in the Euclidean space; the general form of the rotation matrix is:

$$R = \begin{bmatrix} \cos\theta & -\sin\theta \\ \sin\theta & \cos\theta \end{bmatrix}$$

Modify the existing fragment shader recipe to see the circular patterns rotation in action; the highlighted code is responsible for calculating the rotation matrix according to the 2D equation:

```
uniform float   RadianAngle;
void main() {
    float cos  = cos(RadianAngle); // Calculate Cos of Theta
    float sin  = sin(RadianAngle); // Calculate Sin of Theta

    mat2 rotation  = mat2(cos, sin, -sin, cos);
    vec2 position  = mod( rotation * gl_FragCoord.xy, Square)
    - Square*0.5;
    float length  = length(position);
    float inside  = step(length,DotSize);

    FinalColor = vec4(mix(ModelColor, DotColor, inside), 1.0);
    FinalColor = FinalColor * vec4(PhongShading(), 1.0);
}
```

See also

  ▸   *Generating the polka dot pattern*

Generating the brick pattern

The brick shader generates a pattern the bricks on the given surface of the 3D mesh object; this is another very good example of procedural texturing. The brick pattern is made up of two components (a brick and the mortar); these are represented using two different colors, as shown in the following figure. These colors are defined using BrickColor and MortarColor as the global variables in the vertex shader.

The rectangular size of the brick consists of brick and mortal materials; the total dimension of the rectangular region is 0.40 x 0.10 square units, out of which 90 percent of the horizontal dimension (0.40) is reserved for the dimension of the bricks along the *x* axis; the remaining 10 percent is used for the mortar along the same axis. Similarly, the brick vertical dimension is 85 percent along the *y* axis and the remaining 15 percent is used by the mortar's vertical dimension:

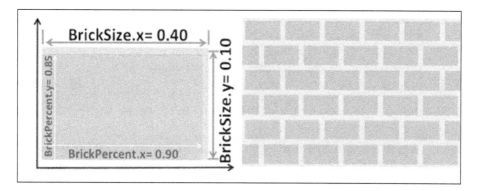

How to do it...

Perform the following steps to implement the brick shader:

1. Create `BrickVertex.glsl` and reuse the code of the vertex shader from the previous recipe.

2. Create `BrickFragment.glsl` and modify the following code:

```
// Brick uniform parameters
uniform vec3  BrickColor, MortarColor;
uniform vec2  RectangularSize, BrickPercent;

// Object coordinates of the mesh
in vec3    ObjectCoord;

vec3 PhongShading(){ //Reuse code for Phong shading
    . . . . . .
    return ambient + diffuse + specular;
}

vec3   color;
vec2   position, useBrick;

void main() {
    position = ObjectCoord.xy / RectangularSize;
```

```
// Displace rows alternately after 0.5 decimals
if (fract(position.y * 0.5) > 0.5){
    position.x += 0.5;
}

position = fract(position);
useBrick = step(position, BrickPercent);
color    = mix(MortarColor, BrickColor,
                    useBrick.x * useBrick.y);
FinalColor  = vec4(color * PhongShading(), 1.0);
}
```

3. Use the main program and specify the color for `BrickColor` and `MortarColor` uniform variables:

```
BrickColor = ProgramGetUniformLocation(program, "BrickColor");
MortarColor= ProgramGetUniformLocation(program,
"MortarColor");

if (BrickColor >= 0)
    {glUniform3f(BrickColor, 1.0, 0.3, 0.2 );}
if (MortarColor >= 0)
    {glUniform3f(MortarColor, 0.85, 0.86, 0.84);}
```

4. Similarly, specify the total rectangular size and brick percentage:

```
RectangularSize= ProgramGetUniformLocation(program,
"RectangularSize");
BrickPercent = ProgramGetUniformLocation(program,
"BrickPercent");
if (RectangularSize >= 0)
    {glUniform2f(RectangularSize, 0.40, 0.10 );}
if (BrickPercent >= 0)
    {glUniform2f(BrickPercent, 0.90, 0.85 );}
```

How it works...

Each incoming object coordinate `ObjectCoord` in the fragment shader is divided by the `BrickSize`; the outcome position contains rows and columns of the brick to which `ObjectCoord` belongs. For each alternative row, the position of the brick is advanced by 0.5 units in the horizontal direction using the following code snippet in the program:

```
if (fract(position.y * 0.5) > 0.5)
{
    position.x += 0.5;
}
```

The `fract` GLSL API calculates the fractional part of the position and stores it in the `position` variable; as it's a fractional value, it must be in a range between 0.0 and 1.0; we must use this new value to compare it with `BrickPercent` using the GLSL step function. The step function takes two arguments, a threshold and a parameter against which the threshold needs to be compared; if the parameter value is less than the threshold value, the function return `0`; otherwise, it will return `1`:

```
position = fract(position);
useBrick = step(position, BrickPercent);
color    = mix(MortarColor,BrickColor,useBrick.x * useBrick.y);
```

The mix function mixes two colors using a weight parameter; this weight parameter in the current recipe is provided as a product between `useBrick.x` and `useBrick.y`. The resultant color is multiplied with `PhongShading()`, which produces the final light shading on the brick shader.

There's more...

The mix function that is used in the brick shader is responsible for performing linear interpolation between two given values based on the weight value.

Syntax:

```
genType mix(genType x, genType y, genType a);
```

Variable	Description
x	This specifies the start of the range in which to interpolate
y	This specifies the end of the range in which to interpolate
a	This specifies the value to use to interpolate between x and y

Mathematically, the *mix(x, y, and a)* function calculates the linear interpolation between x and y, using a as weight. The resultant value is computed as $x * (1 - a) + y * a$.

See also

▸ Refer to the *Gouraud shading – the per-fragment shading technique* recipe in Chapter 5, *Light and Materials*

Generating the polka dot pattern

This recipe is another procedural texture, which is an extension of our circle pattern shader. In that recipe, we looked at the logic behind producing a 2D circle pattern on a planar surface; this planar surface was created using fragment coordinates. In this recipe, we will create a polka dot pattern on the surface of the 3D mesh object; the main difference here is that instead of producing a logical circle in the square, we will use an inscribed logical sphere within the logical cube of dimensions **Side** x **Side** x **Side** units:

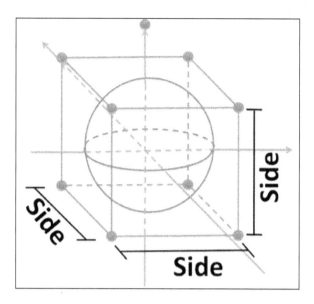

Getting ready

In this recipe, we have reused the lighting technique using the *Implementing two-side shading* recipe in *Chapter 5, Light and Materials*. The generic vertex attributes for vertex positions, normals, and texture coordinates are laid out with 0, 1, and 2 indexes, respectively.

How to do it...

Perform the following steps to implement the polka dot recipe:

1. Create `PolkaDotsVertex.glsl` and reuse the code of the vertex shader from the previous recipe.

2. Create `PolkaDotsFragment.glsl`; edit the following fragment shader file:

```
#version 300 es
precision mediump float;
layout (location = 0) out vec4 outColor;

in vec3  ObjectCoord;

// Size of the logical cube
uniform float Side;
uniform float DotSize;
vec3 Cube        = vec3(Side, Side, Side);
```

```
vec3 RenderColor= vec3(0.0, 0.0, 0.0);

// Front and Back face Model(mesh)/polka dot color
uniform vec3 ModelColor, DotColor, BackSideModelColor,
BackSideDotColor;

void main() {

    float insideSphere, length;
    vec3 position = mod(ObjectCoord, Cube) - Cube*0.5;
    // Note: length() can also be used here
    length = sqrt( (position.x*position.x) +
    (position.y*position.y) + (position.z*position.z) );
    insideSphere = step(length,DotSize);

    // Determine color based on front/back shading
  if (gl_FrontFacing){
    RenderColor=vec3(mix(ModelColor,DotColor,insideSphere));
        outColor = vec4(RenderColor , 1.0);
    }
    else{
        RenderColor==vec3(mix(BackSideModelColor,
        BackSideDotColor, insideSphere));
         outColor = vec4(RenderColor, 1.0);
    }
}
```

The following image shows the output of the polka shader on various 3D mesh models; among these, the hollow cylinder shows the two-sided shading technique, where the inside and outside faces are rendered with different color polka dots from inside and outside:

How it works...

The polka dot shader uses object coordinates to produce polka dot on the surface of the mesh model; these object coordinates are shared by the vertex shader in the form of the `ObjectCoord` input vertex attribute variable. A modulus operation is performed on `ObjectCoord` using the `Cube` variable, which is a `vec3` of `Side`. This results in a logical cube, which is further subtracted by the half cube dimension in order to bring the origin at the center of the logical cube:

```
vec3 position = mod(ObjectCoord, Cube) - Cube/0.5;
```

Calculating the distance of the translated `ObjectCoord` with respect to this center will provide the length of the position vector from the translated origin:

```
length = sqrt( (position.x*position.x) +
  (position.y*position.y)+(position.z*position.z));
```

Finally, the length is compared with the `DotSize` using the GLSL step function in order to check whether it's inside the imaginary sphere of the `DotSize` radius or not:

```
insideSphere = step(length,DotSize);
```

Depending on the outcome of the `insideSphere`, the color value is assigned to the body and polka dots; the colors used for the front face are different from the color used for back faces in order to exhibit the two-side shading.

▶ Refer to the *Implementing two-side shading* recipe in *Chapter 5, Light and Materials*

▶ *Procedural texture shading with object coordinates*

▶ *Creating the circular pattern and making them revolve*

Discarding fragments

The OpenGL ES shading language provides an important feature of discarding fragments using the `discard` keyword; this keyword is used only in the fragment shader to prevent updating the framebuffer. In other words, using this keyword throws away the current fragment and stops execution of the fragment shader. This feature of the OpenGL ES shading language is a simple yet effective feature, which opens up possibilities of producing cross-sectional views of 3D geometries, holes, or perforated surfaces.

Getting ready

This recipe reuses the last recipe; this requires a few changes in the fragment shader to demonstrate discarded fragment capabilities.

How to do it...

Rename the polka shader vertex and the fragment shader file as `DiscardFragVertex.glsl` and `DiscardFragFragment.glsl`. Open the fragment shader file and add the highlighted code:

```
#version 300 es
// Many lines skipped . . .
layout(location = 0) out vec4 FinalColor;
vec3 GouraudShading( bool frontSide )
{
    // Reuse two sides shade recipe PhongShading code here
    return ambient + diffuse + specular;
}

in vec3  ObjectCoord;
```

```
uniform float Side, DotSize;
vec3 Square       = vec3(Side, Side, Side);
vec3 RenderColor;

// Front and Back face polka dot color
uniform vec3 ModelColor, DotColor, BackSideModelColor,
BackSideDotColor;

// Variable for toggling the use of discard keyword
uniform int toggleDiscardBehaviour;

void main() {

    float insideCircle, length;
    vec3 position = mod(ObjectCoord, Square) - Square/2.0;

   length = sqrt( (position.x*position.x) +
          (position.y*position.y)+(position.z*position.z));
    insideCircle       = step(length,DotSize);

    // The toggleDiscardBehaviour change the behavior
    // automatically after fixed interval time.
    // The timer is controlled from the OpenGL ES program.
    if(toggleDiscardBehaviour == 0){
          if (insideCircle != 0.0)
             discard;
    }
    else{
          if (insideCircle == 0.0)
             discard;
    }

    // Determine final color based on front and back shading
    if (gl_FrontFacing){
     RenderColor = vec3(mix( ModelColor, DotColor, insideCircle));
     FinalColor = vec4(RenderColor * PhongShading(true), 1.0);
    }
    else{
     RenderColor=vec3(mix(BackSideModelColor,
```

```
        BackSideDotColor, insideCircle));
        FinalColor=vec4(RenderColor * PhongShading(false), 1.0);
    }
}
```

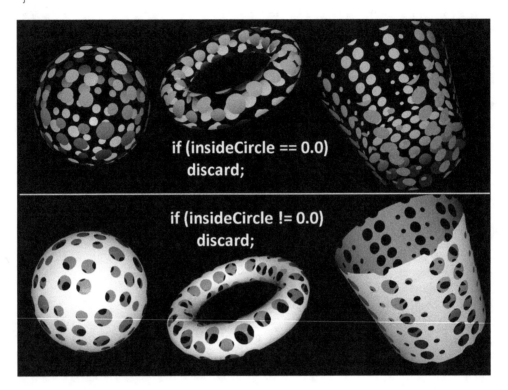

How it works...

The preceding output shows the application of the discard keyword in the polka fragment shader program. In this recipe, fragments are judged on the basis of the `insideCircle` variable. This variable checks whether the fragment is falling inside the circle or outside the circle. If it's falling inside the circle, then the fragment is thrown away; this results in a perforated look, as shown in the previous image.

In the vice versa condition, fragments residing outside of the circle are discarded, as shown in previous images. In general, it's not advisable to use the `discard` keyword extensively because it increases the overhead on the graphics pipeline to perform additional operations. According to Imagination Technologies, for PowerVR architecture, it advises limited use of the `discard` keyword in programming practices. Although this is very much dependent on the application itself, it's advisable to profile your application to see whether the `discard` produces a significant loss in its performance.

See also

- *Generating the polka dot pattern*
- *Procedural texture shading with texture coordinates*

Procedural texture shading with texture coordinates

Texture coordinates control the wrapping of texture on the surface of a model; these are 2D coordinates used to map texture on the 3D surface of the geometry. Texture coordinates are mapped to a different coordinate system called **UV** Mapping. Letters **U** and **V** denote the axis of the texture along the *x* and *y* axis, respectively:

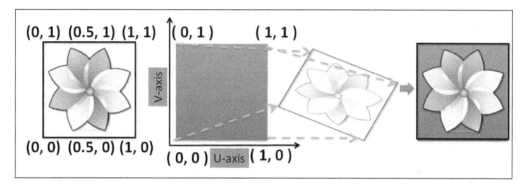

The preceding extreme left image shows an icon that needs to be mapped to a blue-colored square of some arbitrary dimension. An image (irrespective of its dimensions) is always treated in the UV mapping between a range of 0 to 1 along the U and V axis, respectively. Therefore, the bottom-left image is always **(0, 0)** and the top-left image is **(1, 1)**; there is no need to assign these values in the OpenGL ES program. By default, it's understood by the graphics pipeline.

What needs to be mentioned is the texture coordinates of the 2D/3D model; for example; in the previous image, the blue color square is assigned with four UV coordinates, which shows how the image is going to be completely mapped to the surface of the square:

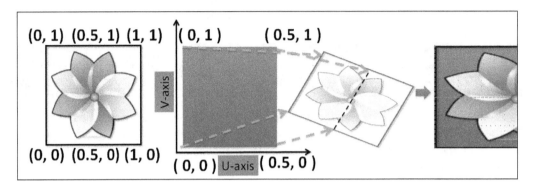

In the preceding image, the blue-colored square is assigned with new texture coordinates with bottom-left and top-right at (0, 0) and (0.5, 1), respectively; the resultant mapped image is shown in the right-hand side corner, where we can clearly see that new texture coordinates are pasted on half of the image along the *U* axis.

Texture coordinates are compulsory for image-based texturing; however, they are not must for procedural texturing. Texture coordinates in procedural texturing have their own importance and their applications are endless. This recipe will demonstrate one of the applications of texture coordinates, where a grid like procedural texture is produced on the surface of a 3D cube mesh model. For more information on UV Mapping and its related application, refer to the next chapter.

Getting ready

For this recipe, the mesh model must contain texture coordinates information. For more information on how to create Wavefront object models with texture coordinates, refer to *Chapter 8, Working with Meshes*.

How to do it...

In order to implement this recipe, perform the following steps:

1. Create the `GridVertex.glsl` vertex shader program and add the following code:

```
#version 300 es
// Vertex layout information
layout(location = 0) in vec4  VertexPosition;
layout(location = 1) in vec3  Normal;
```

```
layout(location = 2) in vec2  TexCoords;


// Model View Projection Normal matrix
uniform mat4    ModelViewProjectionMatrix, ModelViewMatrix;
uniform mat3    NormalMatrix;

out vec3    nNormal, eyeCoord;
out vec2    TextureCoord;

void main()
{
    nNormal      = normalize ( NormalMatrix * Normal );
    eyeCoord     = vec3 ( ModelViewMatrix * VertexPosition
);
    TextureCoord = TexCoords;

    gl_Position = ModelViewProjectionMatrix *
VertexPosition;
}
```

2. For the programming grid shader, we need to make changes in the fragment shader. Create a new fragment shader file called `GridFragment.glsl` and use the following code:

```
vec3 PhongShading( bool frontSide ){
    // Reuse the Phong shading code.
    return ambient + diffuse + specular;
}


in vec2    TextureCoord;
layout(location = 0) out vec4 FinalColor;

    // Scale factor of the texture coord & Grid strip width
    uniform float texCoordMultiplyFactor, stripWidth;

void main() {
    // multiplicationFactor scales number of stripes
    vec2 t = TextureCoord * texCoordMultiplyFactor;

    // The stripWidth is used to define the line width
    if (fract(t.s) < stripWidth  || fract(t.t) < stripWidth
){
    // Front Face coloring
```

```
        if (gl_FrontFacing){
            FinalColor = vec4(PhongShading(true), 1.0);
        }
        // Back Face coloring
        else{
            FinalColor = vec4(GouraudShading(false), 1.0);
        }
    }
        // Throw the fragment
        else{
        discard;
    }
}
```

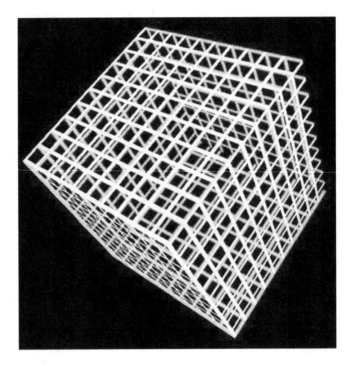

How it works...

The vertex shader receives texture coordinates from the OpenGL ES program in the `TexCoord` vertex attribute; this attribute is defined with index **2** as the layout location. Texture coordinates are passed on to the fragment shader as an out variable using `TextureCoord`. In this recipe, we have used a cube made of six square faces; each of these faces has texture coordinates defined in the UV mapping. Each of these UV mapping coordinates is multiplied by a multiplier factor variable called `texCoordMultiplyFactor`, which produces surface mapping coordinates called **ST** coordinates. Note that ST coordinates are logical coordinates, which are used to create surface mapping calculations; in many places, both are used interchangeably:

```
vec2 t = TextureCoord * texCoordMultiplyFactor;
```

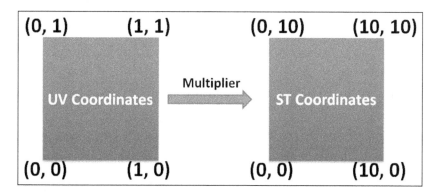

The practical significance of `texCoordMultiplyFactor` is to define the number of strips along horizontal and vertical dimensions. The width of the strip is controlled by the `stripWidth` variable. As coordinates are converted to ST mapping, we can now assume that there are 10 strips along the horizontal and vertical axis and each strip is **1** unit wide. The stripWidth is compared against ST coordinate fractional values using the GLSL `frac()` API; this API returns the fractional value of the decimal number. If the fractional values are greater than the `stripWidth`, then they are discarded; otherwise, depending on the front and back facing of the fragment, they are assigned with colors:

```
if (fract(t.s) < stripWidth  || fract(t.t) < stripWidth ){
//Front Face coloring
if (gl_FrontFacing)
{ outColor = vec4( GouraudShadingGouraud(true), 1.0); }
//Back Face coloring
else{
{ outColor = vec4( GouraudShadingGouraud(false), 1.0); }
}
// Throw the fragment
```

```
else{
discard;
}
```

See also

▶ Refer to the *Implementing two-side shading* recipe in *Chapter 5, Light and Materials*

▶ *Discarding fragments*

▶ Refer to the *Applying texture with UV mapping* recipe in *Chapter 7, Textures and Mapping Techniques*

7
Textures and Mapping Techniques

In this chapter, we will cover the following recipes:

- Applying texture with UV mapping
- Efficient rendering with ETC2 compressed texture format
- Applying multiple textures
- Implementing Skybox with seamless cube mapping
- Implementing reflection and refraction with environment mapping
- Implementing render to texture with Frame Buffer Objects
- Implementing terrain with displacement mapping
- Implementing bump mapping

Introduction

This chapter will shed some light on textures, which is a very interesting part of the 3D computer graphics study. Texturing is a technique by which the surface of a 3D mesh model is painted with static images. In our previous chapter, we described the procedural and image texturing technique. The former uses a special algorithm to calculate the colors of the fragments in order to generate specific patterns. On the other hand, the latter one uses static images, which are wrapped onto the 3D mesh or geometry.

This chapter is all about image texturing that explains its various applications in the field of 3D computer graphics. We will begin this chapter with a simple recipe that demonstrates the UV mapping to render a texture on the 2D planar surface; moving ahead from single texture, you will learn how to apply multiple textures on 3D objects. OpenGL ES 3.0 has introduced many new features. Among these, nonpower of two (NPOT) texture support, ETC2/EAC texture compression support, and seamless cube mapping are explained in detail in this chapter, with the help of a few practical recipes. In the later sections of this chapter, we will implement the environment mapping recipes to simulate the reflection and refraction behavior on the surface of objects. The chapter will continue to explain an effective technique called render to texture; this allows you to render scenes to user-defined texture buffers. Further, we will discuss the displacement mapping technique, which can be used to render a geographical terrain; the last recipe in this chapter will discuss the bump mapping technique, which is used to produce a high quality, detailed surface using a low polygon mesh.

Applying texture with UV mapping

A texture is basically an image represented by a chunk of memory in the computer; this memory contains color information in the form of red (R), green (G), blue (B), and alpha (A) component; each component is represented as a series of bits/bytes, depending on the format of the type of texture.

In this recipe, we will create a simple square and apply texture to it; three things are required for texture mapping:

1. An image first needs to be loaded into the OpenGL ES texture memory with the help of texture objects.

2. A texture is mapped to the geometry using texture coordinates.

3. Use texture coordinates to get the corresponding color from texture in order to apply it on the surface of the geometry.

Getting ready

The GLPI framework allows to load **Portable Network Graphics** (**PNG**) image files using a high-level abstracted class called .png image, which is derived from image; this class loads the .png image and stores image metrics in the class, such as name, dimensions, raw bits, and OpenGL ES texture name (ID). Internally, this class uses libpng, which is a platform-independent library that allows you to parse .png images.

How to do it...

The following procedure describes the steps to render geometry with the `.png` image texture:

1. The `libpng` library is available under the `GLPLFramework` folder; this book will use version 1.5.13 of `libpng`.

   ❑ **iOS**: On iOS, this library needs to be added to the project. In Xcode, under your project, you can include this library using **File | Add to <Project Name>**.

   ❑ **Android**: For Android, `libpng` can be compiled as a shared library called `GLPipng`; for this, create `Android.mk` in the `libpng` folder and add the following code:

```
LOCAL_PATH := $(call my-dir)
include $(CLEAR_VARS)

LOCAL_MODULE     := GLPipng
LOCAL_SRC_FILES := png.c pngerror.c pngget.c \
pngmem.c pngpread.c pngread.c pngrio.c \
pngrtran.c pngrutil.c pngset.c pngtrans.c \
pngwio.c pngwrite.c pngwtran.c pngwutil.c

LOCAL_LDLIBS := -lz
LOCAL_CFLAGS := -I. -g
include $(BUILD_SHARED_LIBRARY)
```

This makefile (`<GLPIFramework>/libpng/Android.mk`) needs to be included in the makefile main project (`SimpleTexture/Android/JNI/ Android.mk`) and the following line must be included in order to compile it in the makefile of your main project:

```
include $(MY_CUR_LOCAL_PATH)/../
../../../GLPIFramework/libpng/Android.mk
```

The generated shared library called `GLPipng` must be added to the project, as given in the following code:

```
LOCAL_SHARED_LIBRARIES := GLPipng
```

2. In order to read or write files on the external storage, your app must acquire the system permissions:

 Beginning with Android 4.4, these permissions are not required if you're reading or writing only files that are private to your app.

```
<manifest ...>
    <uses-permission
android:name="android.permission.WRITE_EXTERNAL_STORAGE" />
    ...
</manifest>
```

3. Create a `SimpleTexture` class derived from `Model`; inside the constructor of this class, use the `PngImage` class member variable image to load an image:

```
SimpleText::SimpleText( Renderer* parent ){
    . . . .
    modelType           = ImageDemoType;
    char fname[MAX_PATH] = {""};

    #ifdef __APPLE__
       GLUtils::extractPath( getenv( "FILESYSTEM" ), fname );
    #else
        strcpy( fname, "/sdcard/Images/" );
    #endif

    strcat( fname, "cartoon.png" );
    image = new PngImage();
    image->loadImage(fname);
}
```

4. The `PngImage::loadImage()` is responsible for loading an image and assigning a unique name to the loaded texture, which is provided by OpenGL ES to recognize a texture uniquely in the system.

   ❏ **Syntax:**

   ```
   void PngImage::loadImage(char* fileName, bool generateTexID
   = true, GLenum target = GL_TEXTURE_2D );
   ```

Variable	Description
`fileName`	This is the name of the image file that needs to be loaded.
`generateTexID`	This is the Boolean value that decides whether the image needs a unique name ID or not. If the Boolean value is `true`, then the loaded image is assigned with a unique ID and if the Boolean value is `false`, no ID is assigned to the image. The default value of this parameter is Boolean `true`.
`target`	This specifies the target to which the texture needs to be bound. The possible targets are GL_TEXTURE_2D, GL_TEXTURE_3D, GL_TEXTURE_2D_ARRAY, or GL_TEXTURE_CUBE_MAP. The default value of this parameter is GL_TEXTURE_2D.

❑ **Code**: The working code for the `loadImage` function of the `PngImage` class is as follows:

```
bool PngImage::loadImage(char* fileName,
              bool generateTexID, GLenum target ){

// Get the image bits from the png file.
memData.bitsraw = read_png_file( fileName);

    // Generate the texture ID if it is not produced before
    if ( generateTexID ){
        GLuint texID;
        glGenTextures ( 1,&texID );
        memData.texID = texID;

        // Depending upon the target type bind the
        // texture using generated texture ID handler

        if (target == GL_TEXTURE_2D){
            glBindTexture(GL_TEXTURE_2D,texID );
        }
    // Similarly, handle cases like GL_TEXTURE_2D,
        // GL_TEXTURE_3D, and GL_TEXTURE_2D_ARRAY etc.
    }

    // Get the colorType from ligpng for current
    // image and prepare the texture accordingly
    switch (colorType) {
        case PNG_COLOR_TYPE_RGB_ALPHA: {
            glTexImage2D ( target,  0, GL_RGBA,
```

```
                memData.width, memData.height, 0, GL_RGBA,
                GL_UNSIGNED_BYTE,memData.bitsraw);
        break;
        }
    // Similarly, handle other cases: -
    // PNG_COLOR_TYPE_GRAY,PNG_COLOR_TYPE_RGBetc.


    }

                // Release the allocate memory for image bits.
        free(memData.bitsraw);
        memData.bitsraw=NULL;return true;
    }
```

5. The `loadImage` function parses the specified image filename and stores the read image buffer in the `bitraw` class member of `PngImage`.

   The unique texture name is generated using the `glGenTexture` OpenGL ES API. This API generates a number of unused names in textures as specified by `n`. This name exists in the form of an unsigned integer ID; the generated ID is stored in the `texID` PngImage's member variable.

   ❑ **Syntax**:

   ```
   void glGenTextures(GLsizei n, GLuint * textures);
   ```

Variable	Description
n	This specifies the number of texture names to be generated
textures	This specifies an array of unused generated texture names

   ❑ Consider the following code:

   ```
   GLuint texID;
   glGenTextures    ( 1,&texID );
   memData.texID = texID;
   ```

   Bind the generated `texID` into a specified target using `glBindTexture`; this API of OpenGL ES 3.0 specifies the pipeline and what kind of texture it needs to manage. For example, the following code mentions that the current state of OpenGL ES contains a 2D type texture:

   ```
   if (target == GL_TEXTURE_2D){
       glBindTexture ( GL_TEXTURE_2D,texID );
   }
   ```

This API is very important to be called to perform any operation on a texture; it binds the correct texture name to OpenGL ES, which allows you to perform any texture operation on it.

❑ **Syntax**:

```
void glBindTexture(GLenum target, GLuint texture);
```

Variable	Description
target	This specifies the target to which the texture is bound. This must be either GL_TEXTURE_2D, GL_TEXTURE_3D, GL_TEXTURE_2D_ARRAY, or GL_TEXTURE_CUBE_MAP.
texture	This specifies an array of unused generated texture names.

6. Load the image in the OpenGL ES texture memory using the glTexImage2D OpenGL ES 3.0 API:

```
glTexImage2D ( target, 0, GL_RGBA,  memData.width,
memData.height,0,GL_RGBA,GL_UNSIGNED_BYTE,memData.bitsraw);
```

The syntax of the glTexImage2D API describing each parameter is as follows:

❑ **Syntax**:

```
void glTexImage2D(GLenum target, GLint level, GLint
internalFormat, GLsizei width, GLsizei height, GLint
border, GLenum format, GLenum type, const GLvoid * data);
```

Variable	Description
target	This specifies the target to which the texture is bound.
level	This is the level of detail number for mipmapping.
internalFormat	This specifies the number of components in the texture. For example, this recipe uses an image with four components (red, green, blue, and alpha). Therefore, the format will be GL_RGBA.
width	This specifies the width of the texture; the new version of OpenGL ES 3.0 supports 2048 texels for all implementations.
height	This specifies the height of the texture; the new version of OpenGL ES 3.0 supports 2048 texels for all implementations.
border	This value must be 0.
format	This specifies the pixel data format; for this recipe, it's GL_RGBA.
type	This specifies the data type of the pixel data; in this recipe, all components used 8 bits unsigned integer. Therefore, the type must be GL_UNSIGNED_BYTE.
data	This is a pointer to the image parsed data.

7. Create a vertex shader file called `SimpleTexutreVertex.glsl` and add the following code; this shader file receives the vertex and texture coordinate information from the OpenGL ES program; the received texture coordinates are further sent to the fragment shader for texture sampling purposes:

```
#version 300 es
layout (location = 0) in vec3  VertexPosition;
layout (location = 1) in vec2  VertexTexCoord;
out vec2 TexCoord;
uniform mat4 ModelViewProjectMatrix;

void main ( void ) {
   TexCoord = VertexTexCoord;
   gl_Position=ModelViewProjectMatrix*vec4
(VertexPosition,1.0);
}
```

Similarly, create a shader file called `SimpleTexureFragment.glsl`; this is responsible for receiving the texture coordinate from the vertex shader and the texture image. The texture is received in sampler2D, which is a built-in data type in GLSL to access texture in the shader. Another GLSL API texture is used to retrieve the fragment color; this API accepts the texture and texture coordinate as an argument:

```
#version 300 es
precision mediump float;
in vec2 TexCoord;
uniform sampler2D Tex1;
layout (location = 0) out vec4 outColor;

void main() {
    outColor = texture (Tex1, TexCoord);
}
```

8. Define the geometry vertices of the square and texture coordinates to map the texture on the geometry:

```
float quad[12] = { -1.0, -1.0,  0.0, 1.0, -1.0,  0.0,
                   -1.0, 1.0, -0.0, 1.0, 1.0, -0.0 };
float texCoords[8] = { 0.0, 1.0, 1.0, 1.0, 0.0, 0.0, 1.0, 0.0 };
```

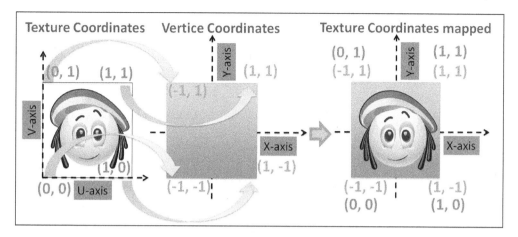

A single texture is always represented in the UV coordinate system from (0.0, 0.0) bottom-left to (1.0, 1.0) top-right. If the texture coordinates goes beyond these dimensional ranges, then the special wrapping rule can be applied to control texture wrapping. For more information, refer to the *There's more...* section in this recipe.

9. The OpenGL ES shader accesses loaded images using texture units; texture units are pieces of hardware that have access to images. Each texture unit has an ID that ranges from 0 to GL_MAX_COMBINED_TEXTURE_IMAGE_UNITS -1. In order to make a texture unit active, use glActiveTexture. In the current recipe, the loaded texture is made accessible to the shader through texture unit 0 (GL_TEXTURE0). Bind the texture to this texture unit:

```
glActiveTexture(GL_TEXTURE0); //Make texture unit 0 active.
glBindTexture(GL_TEXTURE_2D, image->getTextureID());
```

Send the texture unit ID to the fragment shader using a glUniform1i. In the fragment shader, the Tex1 uniform variable receives this information; query the location of this uniform variable in order to provide the texture unit information. Note that 0 here is the texture unit number, not the handle of the texture:

```
TEX = ProgramManagerObj->ProgramGetUniformLocation
                         ( program, (char *) "Tex1" );
    glUniform1i(TEX, 0);
```

10. Set the minification, magnification, and wrapping behavior on the texture using `glTexParameterf`:

```
    glTexParameterf(GL_TEXTURE_2D,GL_TEXTURE_MAG_FILTER,
GL_LINEAR);
    glTexParameterf(GL_TEXTURE_2D,GL_TEXTURE_MIN_FILTER,
GL_LINEAR);
    glTexParameteri(GL_TEXTURE_2D,GL_TEXTURE_WRAP_S,
GL_CLAMP_TO_EDGE);
    glTexParameteri(GL_TEXTURE_2D,GL_TEXTURE_WRAP_T,
GL_CLAMP_TO_EDGE);
```

11. Use the current shader program and send the vertex and texture coordinate information to the shader to render geometry:

```
glUseProgram(program->ProgramID);
glDisable(GL_CULL_FACE); // Disable culling
glEnable(GL_BLEND);      // Enable blending
glBlendFunc(GL_SRC_ALPHA,GL_ONE_MINUS_SRC_ALPHA);
                         //Send Vertices
glEnableVertexAttribArray(VERTEX_POSITION);
glEnableVertexAttribArray(TEX_COORD); //Send Tex
Coordinate
glVertexAttribPointer
TEX_COORD, 2, GL_FLOAT, GL_FALSE, 0, texCoords);
glVertexAttribPointer
(VERTEX_POSITION, 3, GL_FLOAT, GL_FALSE, 0, quad);
glUniformMatrix4fv
( MVP, 1, GL_FALSE,( float * )TransformObj->
TransformGetModelViewProjectionMatrix() );
```

How it works...

The GLPI framework provides a high-level PNG image parsing class called `PNGImage`; it internally uses the `libpng` library to parse PNG files and stores vital information in a local data structure. This class generates texture objects, binds them with an OpenGL state machine, and loads the image buffer data in it.

OpenGL ES supports texture through texture objects; these texture objects are prepared using the `glGenTextures` API within the `loadImage` function. This API generates a texture object behind the curtains and returns the (`texID`) unique name ID. OpenGL ES is a state machine; therefore, before applying any operation on a texture, it needs to set it as a current texture; this can be achieved using `glBindTexture`. This API will bind the `texID` to the current OpenGL ES state as current texture, which allows the OpenGL ES state machine to apply all texture-related operations to the current texture object.

The OpenGL ES loads the texture in the form of an image buffer in its texture memory; this information is provided through `glTexImage2D`, which specifies the format of the image to the underlying programmable pipeline. The `glActiveTexture` API is used to bind the texture with a texture unit; the texture units in OpenGL ES are meant to access textures in the fragment shader. In our recipe, the loaded texture is attached to texture unit 0 (GL_TEXTURE0). The fragment uses a uniform `Sampler2D` data type that contains the handle of texture unit through which the texture is attached. The `glUniform1i` is used to send information to the sampler `Tex1` variable in the fragment shader:

```
TEX = ProgramManagerObj->ProgramGetUniformLocation
( program, (char *) "Tex1" );
glUniform1i(TEX, 0);
```

The vertex shader has two generic attributes, namely, `VertexPosition` and `VertexTexCoord`, which receive the vertex coordinates and the texture coordinates. Per-vertex texture coordinates (received in the vertex shader) are sent to the fragment shader using `TexCoord`.

The fragment shader is responsible for sampling the texture; sampling is a process of selecting a desire `texel` using texture coordinates; this `texel` provides the color information that needs to be applied to the corresponding pixel in the primitive. It uses the incoming per-vertex generic attribute called `TexCoord` to retrieve texture coordinates and a texture handle in the sampler2D. Texture handles allow you to access the texture from the OpenGL ES texture memory to be used in shaders to perform the sampling operation. The shading language provides a texture for sampling purposes; it uses the texture handle, which is 0 for this recipe, and the `TexCoord` texture coordinate.

There's more...

In this section, we will discuss the various built-in filtering and wrapping techniques available in the OpenGL ES 3.0 pipeline. These techniques are applied through `glTexParamterf`, `glTexParameteri`, `glTexParameterf`, `glTexParameteriv`, or `glTexParameterfv` by specifying various symbolic constants.

 Unlike texture, coordinates have the UV coordinate system; the sampling texels have a convention of the ST coordinate system, where S corresponds to the horizontal axis and T corresponds to the vertical axis. This can be used to define the filtering and wrapping behavior along S and T in the sampling process.

Filtering

The texture filtering technique allows you to control the appearance of the texture quality; sometimes, at correct depth, one texel corresponds to exactly one pixel on screen. However, in other cases, mapping a smaller texture on to a bigger geometry may cause the texture to appear stretched (magnification). Similarly, in the vice versa case, many texels are shader by a few pixels (minification).

This type of situation is called minification and magnification. Let's look at them in detail:

- **Minification**: This occurs when many texels exist for a few screen pixels.
- **Magnification**: This occurs when many screen pixels exist for a few texels.

In order to deal with minification and magnification, OpenGL ES 3.0 provides the following two types of filtering techniques:

- `GL_NEAREST`: This uses the pixel color closest to texture coordinates
- `GL_LINEAR`: This uses the weighted average of four surrounding pixels closest to texture coordinates

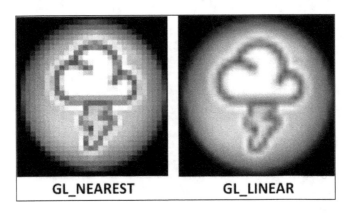

GL_NEAREST   GL_LINEAR

OpenGL ES 3.0 provides GL_TEXTURE_MAG_FILTER and GL_TEXTURE_MIN_FILTER as symbolic constants, which can be used in glTexParamterf as a parameter to specify the filtering technique on magnification and minification respectively.

Wrapping

One obvious question that comes to mind is what happens when the range of texture mapping is greater than 1.0; the OpenGL ES 3.0 sampling allows three types of wrapping mode:

- ▸ GL_REPEAT: This produces repeating patterns
- ▸ GL_MIRRORED_REPEAT: This produces a repeating pattern where adjacent texture is mirrored
- ▸ GL_CLAMP_TO_EDGE: This produces border edges pixels that are repeated

The following image uses 2 x 2 texture coordinates and demonstrates the use of wrapping modes:

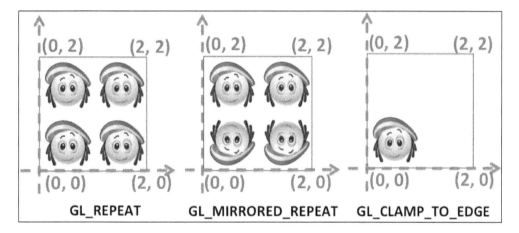

MIP mapping

This is a texture mapping technique that improves the visual output by reducing the aliasing effect and increases the performance of the system by reducing the texture bandwidth. MIP mapping uses precalculated versions as a texture (where each texture is half of the resolution of the previous one). An appropriate texture is selected at runtime according to how far away the viewer is.

Textures can be viewed from a far or near viewer's distance; this changes the shape and size of the texture that causes the texture to undergo the minification and magnification artefacts. These artefacts can be minimized using the previously mentioned filters, but the effective result can only be produced if the texture size scales in a factor of half or double; beyond these scales, the filter may not produce pleasing results. The MIP mapping improves the quality by picking the correct resolution based on the viewer's distance from the given texture. Not only does it improve the quality of the image by minimizing the minification/magnification artefacts, but it also increases the performance of the system by picking a correct resolution texture instead of using the full resolution image:

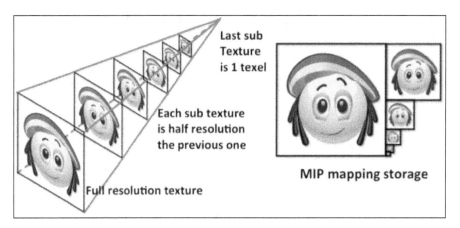

The `glGenerateMipmap` API can be used to generate mipmaps.

Syntax:

```
void glGenerateMipmap(GLenum target);
```

Variable	Description
`target`	This specifies the target type to which the texture mipmaps are going to generate and bound. The target must be either of GL_ TEXTURE_2D, GL_TEXTURE_3D, GL_TEXTURE_2D_ARRAY, or GL_TEXTURE_CUBE_MAP.

The generated mipmaps can be bound to a particular level of depth using the `glTexImage2D` API; the second parameter of this API can be used to specify the level of detail. Refer to step 2 under *How to do it...* section of current recipe to see the full description of the `glTexImage2D` API.

See also

- ▸ Refer to the *Procedural texture shading with texture coordinates* recipe in *Chapter 6, Working with Shaders*
- ▸ *Applying multiple textures*
- ▸ *Efficient rendering with the ETC2 compressed texture*

Efficient rendering with the ETC2 compressed texture

For many reasons, compressed texture is desirable over uncompressed textures; the major benefit is reduced memory footprint on the device, smaller size of the downloadable application, and an increase in performance. The OpenGL ES 3.0 specifications made it compulsory for all vendors to support ETC2 and EAC texture compression formats. Prior to this, in OpenGL ES 2.0, texture compression was not standard, as a result of which various hardware specific extensions were evolved. Developers have to support programs of various extensions in order to achieve texture compression on different types of devices.

In this recipe, we will demonstrate ETC2, which is very famous among different texture compression schemes. ETC stands for **Ericson Texture Compression**, which is a lossy texture compression technique; this scheme supports both RGB and RGBA formats. Additionally, this recipe also demonstrates the new feature of OpenGL ES 3.0, which is capable of loading the **nonpower of two** (**NPOT**) texture.

Getting ready

The ETC2 compressed texture can be stored in two types of file formats, that is, KTX and PKM. The KTX file format is a standard Khronos Group compression format, which stores multiple textures under a single file; for example, mipmaps in KTX require only one file to contain all mipmapped textures. On the other hand, PKM is a very simple file format that stores each compressed texture as a separate file. Therefore, in case of mipmaps, it will generate multiple files. For this recipe, we will use the PKM file format. It consists of a header and is followed by the payload; the following c structure declaration describes the header:

```
struct ETC2Header {
  char name[4];              // "PKM "
  char version[2];           // "20" for ETC2
  unsigned short format;     // Format
  unsigned short paddedWidth;   // Texture width,(big-endian)
  unsigned short paddedHeight;  // Texture height,(big-endian)
```

```
    unsigned short origWidth;     // Original width(big-endian)
    unsigned short origHeight;    // Original height(big-endian)
};
```

OpenGL ES 3.0 supports compressed textures using the `glCompressedTexImage2D` API.

Syntax:

```
void glCompressedTexImage2D(GLenum target, GLint level, GLint
internalFormat, GLsizei width, GLsizei height, GLint border,
GLenum imageSize, const GLvoid * data);
```

Except the `internalFormat` and `imageSize`, most of the parameters are similar to glTexImage2D, which was described in the first recipe. The former is a format of the compressed texture and the latter specifies the image size, which is specifically calculated using formula. For example, in this recipe, the `internalFormat` is a GL_COMPRESSED_RGB8_PUNCHTHROUGH_ALPHA1_ETC2 format, which is an RGBA. The `imageSize` is calculated using the *ceil(width/4) * ceil(height/4) * 8* formula, where width and height are the image dimensions.

 For more information on the internal formation and image size calculations, refer to OpenGL ES 3.0 reference pages at `https://www.khronos.org/opengles/sdk/docs/man3/html/glCompressedTexImage2D.xhtml`.

How to do it...

Perform the following steps to program compressed textures; you can refer to the `CompressedTexture` sample recipe of this chapter. In this recipe, we will render a compressed image on to a square plane:

1. This recipe reuses our first `SimpleTexture`; there is no change in the vertex or fragment shader; the code to render the square geometry has also been reused. For more information, refer to *Applying texture with UV mapping*.

2. In order to process the compressed PKM format image, the GLPI framework provides a high-level helper class called `CompressImage`. This class is responsible for loading the compressed PKM image using the `loadImage` function. The compressed image can be loaded using the following code:

```
char fname[MAX_PATH] = {""};
#ifdef __APPLE__
GLUtils::extractPath( getenv( "FILESYSTEM" ), fname );
#else
strcpy( fname, "/sdcard/Images/" );
#endif
strcat( fname, "SmallEarth.pkm" );
```

```
compressImage = new CompressedImage();
compressImage->loadImage(fname);
```

3. In `CompressedImage::loadImage`, open the compressed image and read the header bytes specified by the ETC2 header specification mentioned previously:

```
FILE *fp = fopen(fileName, "rb");
if (!fp){ return false; }
ETC2Header pkmfile;
fread(&pkmfile, sizeof(ETC2Header), 1, fp);
```

4. Convert read bytes to the Big Endian format:

```
pkmfile.format       = swap_uint16(pkmfile.format);
pkmfile.paddedWidth  = swap_uint16(pkmfile.paddedWidth);
pkmfile.paddedHeight = swap_uint16(pkmfile.paddedHeight);
pkmfile.origWidth    = swap_uint16(pkmfile.origWidth);
pkmfile.origHeight   = swap_uint16(pkmfile.origHeight);
```

5. Calculate the size of the compressed image as per the specified formula mentioned in the *Getting ready* section of this recipe; use it to read the payload image buffer:

```
memData.width  = pkmfile.paddedWidth;  // Texture Width
memData.height = pkmfile.paddedHeight; // Texture Height

// This only handles the pkmfile format
unsigned int imageSize =
ceil(memData.width/4)*ceil(memData.height/4)*8;
memData.bitsraw = (unsigned char*) malloc(imageSize);

fread(memData.bitsraw, imageSize, 1, fp); //Load Payload
if (!memData.bitsraw){ return false; }
```

6. Generate and bind the `texID` named texture and use `glCompressedTexImage2D` to load the compressed texture image buffer:

```
GLuint texID;
glGenTextures( 1,&texID );
glBindTexture( GL_TEXTURE_2D,texID );
glCompressedTexImage2D(GL_TEXTURE_2D, 0,
GL_COMPRESSED_RGB8
_PUNCHTHROUGH_ALPHA1_ETC2, memData.width,memData.height,
0,imageSize, memData.bitsraw);
```

How it works...

The `CompressedTexture` class helps in loading the PKM format ETC2 compressed texture images. The PKM file format is simple; the header `ETC2Header` size is 16 bytes long and the payload is variable. The first four bytes of the header must be PKM and the next two bytes must be 20 to ensure the ETC2 scheme. The format provides the internal format of the compressed image, the next two bytes provide the padded dimension of the image, and the last two each byte represents the original dimension of the image in pixels. The internal format helps to identify the correct formula to calculate the size of the image:

```
imageSize = ceil(memData.width/4) * ceil(memData.height/4) * 8;
```

Finally, the compressed texture is loaded using the `glCompressedTexImage2D` OpenGL ES 3.0 API; this API will also provide a table reference for all compressed internal formats, which is very helpful to know the image size calculation formula, as mentioned in the preceding code. Refer to the previous recipe for more information on texture rendering using UV texture coordinates.

There's more...

There are a variety of texture compression tools available that can be used for texture compression; among them, the famous tools are PVRtexTool, Mali GPU Texture Compression Tool, and so on. You can use them to compress a desired image into the PKM format.

See also

> ▸ *Applying texture with UV mapping*

Applying multiple textures

The multitexturing allows you to apply more than one texture on a given geometry to produce many interesting results; modern graphics allow you to apply multiple textures on to geometry by means of texture units. In this recipe, you will learn how to make use of multiple texture units in order to implement multitexturing.

Getting ready

This recipe is similar to our first recipe, that is, `SimpleTexture`. The only difference is that we will use more than one texture. Instead of using the 2D plane geometry, we will use a 3D cube. Additionally, there are some changes required in the fragment shader. We will discuss this in the next section.

How to do it...

This section will discuss all the important changes made to support multiple textures:

1. Modify the fragment shader to support two given textures simultaneously; these two textures are referenced using the `TexFragile` and `Texwood` handles:

```
#version 300 es
precision mediump float;

in vec2 TexCoord;
uniform sampler2D TexFragile; // First Texture
uniform sampler2D TexWood;    // Second Texture

layout(location = 0) out vec4 Color;

void main() {
   vec4 TextureFragile = texture(TexFragile, TexCoord);
   vec4 TextureWood    = texture(TexWood, TexCoord);
   Color=mix(TextureWood,TextureFragile,TextureFragile.a);
}
```

2. Create a function called `loadMultiTexture`, which will be responsible for loading multiple textures in the `MultipleTexture` class; it must be called after the loading and compilation of the shader programs. In this function, query the location of `TexFragile` and `Texwood` uniform sampler variables:

```
void MultipleTexture::loadMultiTexture(){
    glUseProgram( program->ProgramID );
    // Query uniform samplers location
    TEX  = ProgramManagerObj->ProgramGetUniformLocation
                    ( program, (char *) "TexFragile" );
    TEX2 = ProgramManagerObj->ProgramGetUniformLocation
                    ( program, (char *) "TexWood" );
}
```

3. Activate the texture unit `1` and load the `fragile.png` image using the PngImage's class and the `loadImage` function. This takes care of creating the named texture ID and binds it to the current OpenGL ES state. Internally, this API uses `glGenTextures`, `glBindTexture`, and `glTexImage2D` to load the image; this wrapper API makes the job of loading images easy:

```
    glActiveTexture(GL_TEXTURE1);
     image = new PngImage();
     image->loadImage(creatPath(fname,
(char*)"fragile.png"));
```

4. Set the texture filtering and wrapping properties:

```
glTexParameterf
(GL_TEXTURE_2D, GL_TEXTURE_MAG_FILTER, GL_LINEAR);
glTexParameterf
(GL_TEXTURE_2D, GL_TEXTURE_MIN_FILTER, GL_LINEAR);
glUniform1i(TEX, 1);
```

5. Using the `TEX` location of `TexFragile`, send the texture unit information to the shader using the `glUniform1i` API. The Fragile.png texture can be accessed using texture unit 1; therefore, send 1 as parameter in the `glUniform1i` API:

```
glUniform1i(TEX, 1); // Attached to texture unit 1
```

6. Similarly, for the second texture, that is, wooden.png, follow the same procedure mentioned from the third to the fifth steps:

```
glActiveTexture(GL_TEXTURE2);
image->loadImage(creatPath(fname, (char*)"woodenBox.png"));
image2 = new PngImage();
image2->loadImage(fname);
glTexParameterf
(GL_TEXTURE_2D, GL_TEXTURE_MAG_FILTER, GL_LINEAR);
glTexParameterf
(GL_TEXTURE_2D, GL_TEXTURE_MIN_FILTER, GL_LINEAR);
glUniform1i(TEX2, 2); // Attached to texture unit 2
```

How it works...

The fragment shader uses two samplers, namely `TexFragile` and `TexWood`; these are used to access texture images in the shader. It stores the handle of texture units; therefore, it's very important to query their locations from the fragment shader and is stored in the `TEX` and `TEX1`. Texture images are loaded in the OpenGL texture memory using the `PngImage::loadImage` function. For single or multiple textures, it's compulsory to activate texture units so that they become available in the shader program; the texture unit is made active using the `glActiveTexture` API. It accepts the handle of the texture unit as an argument. Refer to the next section for more information on texture units.

The texture unit 1 is activated for the first texture object (`fragile.png`) and a corresponding uniform variable is set with `1` using `glUniform1i(TEX1, 1)`. Similarly, the second texture unit (`woodenBox.png`) is activated and its corresponding uniform variable `TEX1` is set to value `2`. There is no special change required for the vertex shader because it sets clip coordinates for the incoming position and shares texture coordinates with the fragment shader. The fragment shader utilizes these texture coordinates for texture sampling from the available two textures; the sampling provides two color values stored in the `TextureFragile` and `TextureWood`; these colors are mixed together with the help of the mix GLSL API to produce mixed color effect; this API takes three parameters as an input. The first two parameters specifies the colors that need to be mixed together, whereas the third parameter specifies the proportion of the colors in which these need to be mixed.

There's more...

Texture units can be thought of as buffers that contain texture information and the number of texture units fixed; the number is very specific to the hardware implementation of the OpenGL ES 3.0. This number can be checked by using the `GL_MAX_COMBINED_TEXTURE_IMAGE_UNITS` macro. The texture object is not directly bound with the shader program. Instead, they are bound to the index of the texture unit.

In the following figure, the texture memory shows 16 texture units. Out of these, only three seem unoccupied (blue in color) and the rest of them are utilized by various texture images. Texture units are uniquely recognized by their index; these can be accessed in the shader program directly, thereby giving a unique capability of multitexturing. Texture units 1 and 2 are accessed in the fragment shader to produce the desired output, as shown in the following figure:

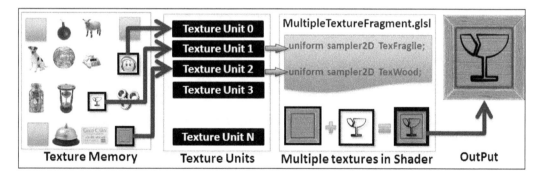

Implementing Skybox with seamless cube mapping

Cube mapping is a texturing technique used in 3D graphics to fill the background of a scene with a given set of images. This technique reduces the number of objects required to draw a scene in order to make the scene look populated (the scene looks bigger). It is commonly used in gaming to render sky horizons, rooms, mountains, day/night effect, reflection, and refraction.

A cube map is achieved by wrapping six sets of images on six faces of the cube; these images perfectly stitch with each other on the edges. In the cube mapping technique, the viewer or camera is always in the center of the cube. When camera displaces in the 3D space, the cubes are also displaced with respect to it. This way, the camera never reaches close to any face of the cube and creates an illusion of a horizon that always remains at the same distance from the viewer.

Getting ready

This recipe uses six images named bottom, top, left, right, front, and back for each face of the cube to be mapped on, as shown in the following image. When these images are wrapped around the cube and viewed from inside, it produces an illusion of the sky environment. So far, we have already learned the mapping of texture on to a given geometry in our previous recipes using the UV texture coordinate mapping. However, OpenGL ES provides a special mapping called cube mapping; this mapping makes the job easier to wrap images to a cube-shaped geometry.

Creating the cube map in OpenGL ES 3.0 is simple:

1. Create a texture object using `glGenTexture`.

2. Bind the texture using the `glBindTexture` API with the `GL_TEXTURE_CUBE_MAP` argument. This will help the OpenGL ES to understand the type of texture it needs to store.

3. Load six images in the OpenGL ES texture memory, using `glTexImage2D` with `GL_CUBE_MAP_{POSITIVE, NEGATIVE}_{X, Y, Z}` as the target parameter:

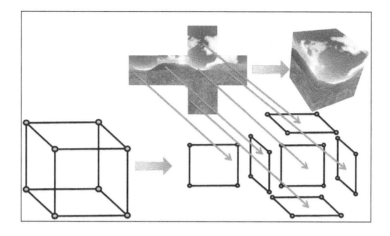

How to do it...

This section will describe the practical steps required to implement this recipe:

1. Create a class called Skybox to render cube geometry; you can reuse the *Efficient rendering with Vertex Buffer Object* recipe from *Chapter 2, OpenGL ES 3.0 Essentials.*

2. Implement the vertex and fragment shader, as given in the following code. For cube mapping, we require the vertex information in the fragment shader. Therefore, each incoming per-vertex needs to be shared with the fragment shader:

Vertex shader	Fragment shader
| ```
//CubeMappingVertex.g
lsl
#version 300 es

layout(location = 0)
in vec4
VertexPosition;
uniform mat4 MVP;
out vec4 Vertex;

void main( void ) {
   Vertex = VertexPosition;
   gl_Position

=MVP*VertexPosition;
}
``` | ```
//CubeMappingFragment.
glsl
#version 300 es
precision mediump
float;
uniform samplerCube
CubeMapTexture;
in vec4 Vertex;
layout(location = 0) out vec4
outColor;

void main() {
  outColor = texture(
    CubeMapTexture,
Vertex.xyz);
}
``` |

3. Create a function called `createCubeMap` in the `Skybox` class and call the following function after the shaders are loaded and compiled:

```
void Cube::InitModel(){
   //Load and compile shaders . . . .
   . . . .
   createCubeMap(); // Create the Cube Map
}

void Skybox::createCubeMap(){
   glActiveTexture(GL_TEXTURE1);
   char fname[MAX_PATH]= {""};
   image = new PngImage();

   image->loadImage(creatPath(fname, (char*)"Right.png"),
               true,  GL_TEXTURE_CUBE_MAP_POSITIVE_X);
   image->loadImage(creatPath(fname, (char*)"Left.png"),
               false, GL_TEXTURE_CUBE_MAP_NEGATIVE_X);
   image->loadImage(creatPath(fname, (char*)"Top.png"),
               false, GL_TEXTURE_CUBE_MAP_POSITIVE_Y);
   image->loadImage(creatPath(fname, (char*)"Bottom.png"),
               false, GL_TEXTURE_CUBE_MAP_NEGATIVE_Y);
   image->loadImage(creatPath(fname, (char*)"Front.png"),
               false, GL_TEXTURE_CUBE_MAP_POSITIVE_Z);
   image->loadImage(creatPath(fname, (char*)"Back.png"),
               false, GL_TEXTURE_CUBE_MAP_NEGATIVE_Z);

   glTexParameterf(GL_TEXTURE_CUBE_MAP,
               GL_TEXTURE_MAG_FILTER, GL_LINEAR);
   glTexParameterf(GL_TEXTURE_CUBE_MAP,
               GL_TEXTURE_MIN_FILTER, GL_LINEAR);

   // The clamping is important for Skyboxes
   // due to texel filtering
   glTexParameterf(GL_TEXTURE_CUBE_MAP,
               GL_TEXTURE_WRAP_R, GL_CLAMP_TO_EDGE);
   glTexParameterf(GL_TEXTURE_CUBE_MAP,
               GL_TEXTURE_WRAP_S, GL_CLAMP_TO_EDGE);
   glTexParameterf(GL_TEXTURE_CUBE_MAP,
               GL_TEXTURE_WRAP_T, GL_CLAMP_TO_EDGE);

   uniformTex=ProgramManagerObj->ProgramGetUniformLocation
```

```
                    (program, (char*) "CubeMapTexture" );

        if (uniformTex >= 0)
            { glUniform1i(uniformTex, 1); }
    }
```

4. In the `createCubeMap` function, make the texture unit 1 active; this allows you to access the cube map texture from the fragment shader:

   ```
   glActiveTexture(GL_TEXTURE1);
   ```

5. The `createCubeMap` function first loads six images using `PngImage::loadImage`. This function creates the texture objects into the OpenGL ES texture memory. Only the first image needs to send with the `true` value in the second argument; this parameter will tell the function to generate the named texture (an ID is given to the texture object). The rest of the images will use the same texture name (ID); therefore, the rest must be sent with a `false` argument. If the image appears at the right-hand side corner of the cube box and (`Right.png`) is located at the positive *x* axis, then use `GL_TEXTURE_CUBE_MAP_POSITIVE_X` as the fourth argument. Similarly, for other images, use the appropriate argument, as shown in the preceding code.

6. Set linear filtering for the minification/magnification and wrapping scheme.

7. Query the location of the `CubeMapTexture` uniform sampler from the fragment shader and set the handle of texture unit as 1.

8. Render the scene using the `Skybox::Render` function:

   ```
   void Skybox::Render(){
   glDisable(GL_CULL_FACE); glDisable(GL_DEPTH_TEST);
   glUseProgram( program->ProgramID );
   // Transform as per your scene requirement. . .
   glBindBuffer( GL_ARRAY_BUFFER, vId );
   glBindBuffer( GL_ELEMENT_ARRAY_BUFFER, iId );
   glDrawElements(GL_TRIANGLES,36,GL_UNSIGNED_SHORT,(void*)0);
       }
   ```

How it works...

The cubemap texturing requires six sets of 2D images; these images are mapped to the six faces of the cube geometry. Select a texture unit and make it active. In the present case, its texture unit is 1 (GL_TEXTURE1). Load the image using PngImage::loadImage; this function is called in the Skybox::InitModel. After the shaders are loaded, it accepts three arguments. The first argument specifies the image file to be loaded and the second argument decides whether to create a texture object or not. For example, in the case of cubemap, only the first image is required to create a texture object; the remaining images will share the same texture object. The final argument specifies the face to which the image belongs to in the cubemap. In this function, it creates a texture object using glGenTexture and bounds it using glBindTexture with the GL_TEXTURE_CUBE_MAP parameter. The glTexImage2D API will allocate the necessary storage space for all textures; this API accepts important parameters, such as GL_TEXTURE_CUBE_MAP_POSITIVE_X, GL_TEXTURE_CUBE_MAP_NEGATIVE_X, and so on and helps OpenGL ES to know what texture to apply on which surface. Share the cubemap texture stored in the texture unit 1 to the fragment shader.

In order to render the cubes, we have reused the *Efficient rendering with Vertex Buffer Object* recipe, *Chapter 2, OpenGL ES 3.0 Essentials*. The rendering process takes place in the Render() function, the cube is scaled in order to fill up the screen and the culling and depth testing should be disabled.

From the shader's perspective, cube vertices are received in the vertex shader; these are shared to the fragment shader in the form of the position vector as the origin is at (0.0, 0.0, 0.0). The position vector turns out to be the same as vertex positions. This vertex position in the fragment shader is used for sampling purposes where the texture API is provided with the sampler and vertex position; it returns the corresponding color of the fragment.

See also

- ▶ *Implementing reflection and refraction with environment mapping*
- ▶ Refer to the *Efficient rendering with Vertex Buffer Object* recipe in *Chapter 2, OpenGL ES 3.0 Essentials*

Implementing reflection and refraction with environment mapping

Environment mapping is a simple yet effective and efficient technique that allows you to map the surrounding environment effect to render 3D objects. There are two ways in which environment mapping can be used: reflection and refraction. In the former technique, rendered objects are mapped with the reflection of the surroundings, which shows the reflection of the surrounding view of objects. However, in the latter case, objects mapped with the refraction allow you to see through objects. These environment mapping techniques require cube mapping that we programmed in the previous recipe Skybox with seamless cube mapping. In this recipe, we will implement the reflection and refraction environment mapping.

Getting ready

For this recipe, we can reuse the *Implementing Skybox with seamless cube mapping* recipe and *Rendering the wavefront OBJ mesh model* recipes in *Chapter 5, Working with Meshes*. The former recipe does not require any special changes. However, we will program a new shader for the latter case.

Reflection is a phenomenon in which light/wave changes its direction when it interacts with other mediums. As a result, it bounces back to the same medium from which it was coming from. The angle of incidence of the light is always equal to the angle of reflection after bouncing, as shown in the following figure:

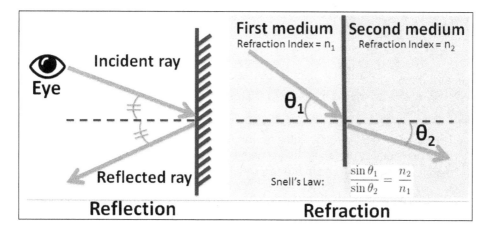

Refraction is a phenomenon that bends the direction of the wave/light through the transmission medium in which it is traveling. The reason for this bending is the difference between the optical densities of these two mediums. For example, a straw in a glass of water appears bent because light travels at different speeds in the given medium/material, such as air and water. This characteristic of the medium or material that affects the speed of light is called the refractive index. The refractive index of a medium tells us how fast the light travels in a given medium; it's the ratio of the speed of light in vacuum (c) to the speed of light in that medium (v), $n=c/v$, therefore, the bending of the light is determined by its refractive index.

Snell's law gives the relation between the refractive index and the direction of propagation. Mathematically, $n1.sin\theta1 = n2.sin\theta2$. As per this law, the ratio of the sine angle of incidence and refraction ($sin\theta1/sin\theta2$) is equivalent to the opposite ratio of refractive index of the mediums ($n2/n1$).

How to do it...

In this section, you will learn the step-by-step procedure to program environment mapping for reflection and refraction:

1. The surrounded environment required in environment mapping is created using the cube mapped Skybox from the previous recipe in this chapter. Inside the Skybox simple 3D waveform, objects are rendered (refer to the *Rendering the wavefront OBJ mesh model* recipe *Chapter 5, Working with Meshes*). Add the Skybox and the ObjLoader model in the createModels function and include the required headers:

   ```
   #include "ObjLoader.h"
   #include "Skybox.h"

   void Renderer::createModels(){
       clearModels();
       addModel( new Skybox ( this ) );
       addModel( new ObjLoader ( this ) );
   }
   ```

   The Skybox model is responsible for rendering the Skybox environment using the cube mapped texture; there is no change required for shader programs. The cube mapped texture is stored in the texture unit 1.

2. The ObjLoader model renders mesh objects and uses the texture unit 1 (containing the cube mapped texture) to apply the reflection and refraction mapping.

3. Define new shader programs (ReflectionVertex.glsl) for the vertex shader:

   ```
   #version 300 es

   // Vertex information
   layout(location = 0) in vec4  VertexPosition;
   ```

```
layout(location = 1) in vec3   Normal;
uniform vec3    CameraPosition;

// Model View Project matrix
uniform mat4    MODELVIEWPROJECTIONMATRIX, MODELMATRIX;
uniform mat3    NormalMatrix;

vec3 worldCoordPosition, worldCoordNormal;
out vec3 reflectedDirection;

void main( void ) {
    worldCoordPosition = vec3(MODELMATRIX * VertexPosition);
    worldCoordNormal   = normalize(vec3( MODELMATRIX *
    vec4(Normal, 0.0)));

    // Make negative normals positive so that the face
    // of back side will still remain illuminated,
    // otherwise these will appear complete black
    // when object is rotated and back side faces
     // the camera.
    if(worldCoordNormal.z < 0.0){
      worldCoordNormal.z = -worldCoordNormal.z;
     }
    worldView = normalize(CameraPosition -
    worldCoordPosition);
    reflectedDirection = reflect(worldView,
    worldCoordNormal );
    gl_Position = MODELVIEWPROJECTIONMATRIX *
    VertexPosition;
}
```

4. Use the following code reflection mapping fragment shader in
   ReflectionFragment.glsl:

```
#version 300 es
precision mediump float;
uniform samplerCube CubeMap;
in vec3    reflectedDirection;

layout(location = 0) out vec4 outColor;
void main() {
    outColor = texture(CubeMap, reflectedDirection); }
```

Similarly, for refraction, reuse the preceding reflection shader and define a uniform float variable for the refraction index called `RefractIndex`. Additionally, replace the GLSL `reflect` API with the refract API and rename the `reflectedDirection` with `refractedDirection`:

```
uniform float    RefractIndex;
out vec3 refractedDirection;
void main() {
    . . . . . .
  refractedDirection =
      -refract(worldView, worldCoordNormal, RefractIndex);
  gl_Position = MODELVIEWPROJECTIONMATRIX * VertexPosition;
}
```

5. Create `RefractionFragment.glsl` and reuse the code from `ReflectionFragment.glsl`; the only change required is renaming the incoming shared attribute called `reflectedDirection` with `refractedDirection`.

6. Load and compile the shader in the `ObjLoader::InitModel` function and initialize all uniform variables required by the reflection and refraction shaders. Set the current texture in `CubeMap` from the texture unit `1` as it contains the cube mapped texture. Note that this texture unit was loaded from the Skybox model class:

```
void ObjLoader::InitModel()
{
    glUseProgram( program->ProgramID );
    char uniformTex = ProgramManagerObj>
    ProgramGetUniformLocation(program, (char*)"CubeMap");
    if (uniformTex >= 0) {
    glUniform1i(uniformTex, 1);
    }
    char Camera = ProgramManagerObj->
    ProgramGetUniformLocation(program, "CameraPosition");
    if (Camera >= 0){
    glm::vec3 cp = RendererHandler->getCameraPosition();
    glUniform3fv(Camera, 1, (float*)&cp);
    }

    MVP = ProgramManagerObj->ProgramGetUniformLocation
    ( program, ( char* )"MODELVIEWPROJECTIONMATRIX" );
    M   = ProgramManagerObj->ProgramGetUniformLocation
    ( program, ( char* )"MODELMATRIX" );
    NormalMatrix  = ProgramManagerObj->
    ProgramGetUniformLocation(program, (char*)"NormalMatrix");
    return;
}
```

How it works...

The working model of the reflection and refraction environment mapping is very similar; both use the cube map texturing to produce the reflection and refraction effect. The following image shows the logic behind this working model. Here, the top view of the cube map is represented with a green rectangle and all the labeled edges are faces of the cube. The camera position is depicted by an eye, which looks toward the sphere direction that are placed inside the cube map Skybox. Each vertex position produces an incident ray from the camera position, which is used with the normal vector at the vertex position to calculate the reflected vector. This reflected vector is used with the cube-mapped texture to look up the corresponding texel. For example, in the following image, the vertex v1, v2, and v3 after reflection corresponds to the right, back and left face of the cube map. Similarly, refracted rays correspond to the front face of the cube map:

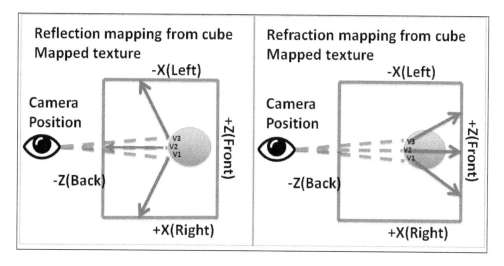

The reflected and refracted positional vector is calculated in the vertex shader; these vectors are shared with the fragment shader, where the cubemap texture is used to look up the texel for the corresponding texture.

Now, we know that the working of the environment mapping is at a higher level; let's understand the code for reflection environment mapping. The vertex shader calculates the world position of each vertex position (VertexPosition) and normal vector (Normal) in the world coordinate using the model matrix (MODELMATRIX) and stores it in worldCoordPosition and worldCoordNormal respectively. The incident ray for each vector with respect to camera position is calculated and stored in the incidenceRay. The OpenGL ES shading language provides a high level reflect() API to calculate the reflected vector. This API takes an incident ray, normal vector, and returns the reflected vector.

Syntax:

```
genType reflect(genType I, genType N);
```

Variable	Description
I	This is the incidence ray from coming from source to destination
N	This is the normal of the surface
Return	This is the reflected vector given by *I - 2.0 * dot(N, I) *N*

The reflected vector is shared with the fragment shader using an out variable called reflected direction. The fragment shader uses this vector to find the corresponding texel in the cube map using the `texture()` API.

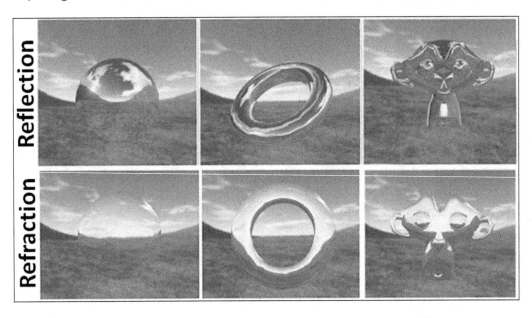

Similarly, the refraction is calculated using the `refract()` GLSL API; unlike the reflect API, this accepts an additional parameter called refract index of the material and returns the refracted vector.

Syntax:

```
genType refract(genType I, genType N, float RI);
```

Variable	Description
I	This is the incidence ray from coming from source to destination
N	This is the normal of the surface
RI	This is the refractive index of the medium
Return	This is the refracted vector

The refracted vector is shared with the fragment shader using `refractedDirection`. The texel color is calculated for the corresponding fragment.

See also

- *Implementing Skybox with seamless cube mapping*
- Refer to the *Rendering the wavefront OBJ mesh model* recipe in *Chapter 4, Working with Meshes*

Implementing render to texture with Frame Buffer Objects

OpenGL ES renders a scene on framebuffer; this framebuffer is called the default framebuffer. A framebuffer consist of various buffers, such as color, depth, and the stencil buffer. **Frame Buffer Objects** (**FBO**) allows you to create user-defined framebuffers, which can be used to render scenes on non-default framebuffers. The rendered scene on the nondefault framebuffer can be used as a texture to map objects. In this recipe, we will demonstrate render to texture in which a scene is rendered to a texture and this texture is mapped to a 2D plane surface; the 2D plane can be rotated in a 3D space using touch gesture events.

How to do it...

The detailed procedure to implement the render to texture recipe using FBO is as follows. We will reuse the *Generating the polka dot pattern* recipe from *Chapter 6, Working with Shaders*:

1. Create a `DemoFBO` class derived from the `Model` base class and add `SimpleTexture` and `ObjLoader` pointer objects; initialize these objects in the constructor of `DemoFBO`. For more information on dependent recipes, refer to the *See also* subsection in this recipe:

   ```
   #include "ObjLoader.h"
   #include "SimpleTexture.h"
   ```

```
class DemoFBO : public Model
{
 private:
    void InitModel();
    ObjLoader* objModel;
    SimpleText* textureQuad;
    GLuint fboId, rboId, textureId, depthTextureId;
 public:
    DemoFBO( Renderer* parent = 0);
    ~DemoFBO();
    unsigned int generateTexture
(int width,int height,bool isDepth=false);
    void GenerateFBO(); . . . .
};
```

2. Define the `generateTexture` function; this function is responsible for generating the color or depth texture depending on the (`isDepth`) Boolean argument passed to it:

```
unsigned int DemoFBO::generateTexture
(int width, int height, bool isDepth) {
unsigned int texId;
glGenTextures(1, &texId);
    glBindTexture(GL_TEXTURE_2D, texId);
    . . . . Set Minification and Maxification filters
    if (isDepth){
      glTexImage2D( GL_TEXTURE_2D, 0, GL_DEPTH_COMPONENT32F,
          width, height, 0,GL_DEPTH_COMPONENT, GL_FLOAT, 0);
    }
    else{
      glTexImage2D(GL_TEXTURE_2D, 0, GL_RGBA, width, height,
          0, GL_RGBA, GL_UNSIGNED_BYTE, 0);
    }

    int error;
    error = glGetError();
    if(error != 0){
        std::cout<<"Error: Fail to generate texture."<<error;
    }
    glBindTexture(GL_TEXTURE_2D,0);
    return texId;
}
```

3. Define the `GenerateFBO` and use the following code. This function is responsible for generating the FBO; it uses the color buffer and the depth buffer from the framebuffer. This recipe also contains the `GenerateFBOWithRenderBuffer` alternate function, which uses Render buffer's depth buffer to create FBO. For more information, refer to *There's more...* subsection in this recipe:

```
void DemoFBO::GenerateFBO(){
    // create a frame buffer object
    glGenFramebuffers(1, &fboId);
    glBindFramebuffer(GL_FRAMEBUFFER, fboId);

    textureId = createTexture(TEXTURE_WIDTH,TEXTURE_HEIGHT);
    depthTextureId = createTexture(
    TEXTURE_WIDTH,TEXTURE_HEIGHT, true);
    // attach texture to FBO color attachment point
    glFramebufferTexture2D(
    GL_FRAMEBUFFER,          //1.fbo target: GL_FRAMEBUFFER
    GL_COLOR_ATTACHMENT0,    //2.Color attachment point
    GL_TEXTURE_2D,           //3.tex target: GL_TEXTURE_2D
    textureId,               //4.Color texture ID
    0);                      //5.mipmap level: 0(base)

    // Attach texture to FBO depth attachment point
    glFramebufferTexture2D(
    GL_FRAMEBUFFER,          //1.fbo target: GL_FRAMEBUFFER
    GL_DEPTH_ATTACHMENT,     //2.Depth attachment point
    GL_TEXTURE_2D,           //3.tex target: GL_TEXTURE_2D
    depthTextureId,          //4.depth texture ID
    0);                      //5.mipmap level: 0(base)

    // check FBO status
    GLenum status = glCheckFramebufferStatus(GL_FRAMEBUFFER);
    if(status != GL_FRAMEBUFFER_COMPLETE){
    printf("Framebuffer creation fails");
    }
}
```

4. Define the `InitModel` function and initialize the Polka dots and simple texture classes. Also, generate the FBO using the following code:

```
void DemoFBO::InitModel(){
    objModel->InitModel();
    textureQuad->InitModel();
    GenerateFBO();
}
```

5. In the `Render()` function, render the polka dots in the FBO texture and map this texture to the 2D plane:

```
void DemoFBO::Render(){// Render to Texture
    int CurrentFbo;
    glGetIntegerv(GL_FRAMEBUFFER_BINDING, &CurrentFbo);
    glBindFramebuffer(GL_FRAMEBUFFER,fboId);
    glViewport(0, 0, TEXTURE_WIDTH, TEXTURE_HEIGHT);
    glClear(GL_COLOR_BUFFER_BIT|GL_DEPTH_BUFFER_BIT);
    objModel->Render();
    glBindFramebuffer(GL_FRAMEBUFFER, CurrentFbo);
    TransformObj->TransformError();

    // Render Quad with render buffer mapped.
    glViewport(0, 0, RendererHandler->screenWidthPixel()*2,
                RendererHandler->screenHeightPixel()*2);
    glClearColor(0.710,0.610,0.30,1.0);
    glClear(GL_COLOR_BUFFER_BIT|GL_DEPTH_BUFFER_BIT);
    glActiveTexture (GL_TEXTURE0);
    glBindTexture(GL_TEXTURE_2D, textureId);
    textureQuad->Render();
    TransformObj->TransformError();

}
```

Shader programs can be reused completely without any changes. The only exception being that we rename shader from `SimpleTexture` to FBO.

How it works...

The final destination of all the rendering commands in the rendering pipeline is the default framebuffer; OpenGL ES 3.0 provides means to create additional framebuffers using FBO. FBO allows you to render a scene directly to a texture, which can be used like any other texture for mapping purposes. It can also be used for post processing of a scene. Similar to the default framebuffer, FBO also contains color, depth, and stencil buffers; these buffers are accessed through the (`GL_COLOR_ATTACHMENT0..N`, `GL_DEPTH_ATTACHMENT`, `GL_STENCIL_ATTACHMENT`) attachment points, as shown in the following image given in the *There's more...* section..

First, like any other buffer object in OpenGL ES, create an FBO and bind it using `glGenFramebuffer` and `glBindFrameBuffer`. Use the `generateTexture` function and create an empty 256 x 256 color and depth buffer texture object and store the handles in `textureId` and `depthTextureId` respectively. The FBO implementation of OpenGL ES 3.0 allows one color buffer and one depth buffer, which can be attached to the FBO, using the `glFramebufferTexture2D` API; more color buffers may be defined depending on the OpenGL ES Driver implementation. This is defined via the macro `MAX_COLOR_ATTACHMENTS`.

The `glFramebufferTexture2D` API attaches the handle of the created color and depth buffer:

```
glFramebufferTexture2D(GL_FRAMEBUFFER,GL_COLOR_ATTACHMENT0,
    GL_TEXTURE_2D,textureId,0);
glFramebufferTexture2D(GL_FRAMEBUFFER,GL_DEPTH_ATTACHMENT,
    GL_TEXTURE_2D,depthTextureId,0);
```

Syntax:

```
void glFramebufferTexture2D(GLenum target, GLenum attachment,
GLenum textarget, GLuint texture, GLint level);
```

Variables	Description
`target`	This specifies the framebuffer target and should be `GL_FRAMEBUFFER`, `GL_DRAW_FRAMEBUFFER`, or `GL_READ_FRAMEBUFFER`.
`attachment`	This specifies the framebuffer target. For this recipe, it should be `GL_COLOR_ATTACHMENT0` for the color buffer and `GL_DEPTH_ATTACHMENT` for the depth buffer.
`textarget`	This specifies the 2D texture target, which in the present case is `GL_TEXTURE_2D`.
`texture`	This specifies the handle of the texture buffer. In the current recipe, it should be `textureID` for the color buffer and `depthTextureId` for the depth buffer.
`level`	This specified the Mipmap level.

Check the status of the created framebuffer using the `glCheckFramebufferStatus` API; this API must return `GL_FRAMEBUFFER_COMPLETE` if the framebuffer is created successfully.

Now, we have an FBO with the color and depth buffer attached; the second thing we need to do is to render the scene to this texture. For this, we need to redirect the rendering command to our FBO instead of a default framebuffer. We need to query the handle of the default framework using `glGetIntergerv` with the `GL_FRAMEBUFFER_BINDING` parameter and store it in `currentFbo`; we will use this handle to restore the default framebuffer once the render to texture operation is accomplished. Bind the rendering pipeline with the `fboID` frame buffer object handle using `glBindFramebuffer`. Prepare the viewport and clear the color and depth buffer of the FBO using `glViewPort` and `glClearColor` APIs respectively. Finally, rendering the Polka dots will redirect all the procedural texture-patterned meshes to our `textureId` FBO color texture object. After the rendering is completed, restore the default framebuffer by binding its handle to the rendering pipeline using `glBindFramebuffer` with `CurrentFbo`.

The third important thing is to use the (textureId) FBO texture and apply it to this 2D square; this process of applying texture is similar to our first recipe, that is, simple texture; the only difference here is that instead of a static texture, we will use the FBO texture. As we have switched to the default buffer, we need to set the viewport and clear the color and depth buffer. Set the active texture unit ID to 0 using glActiveTexture with the GL_TEXTURE0 parameter or make sure that this texture unit is the same as what is sent to the fragment shader. Finally, render the square geometry and see the render to texture in action:

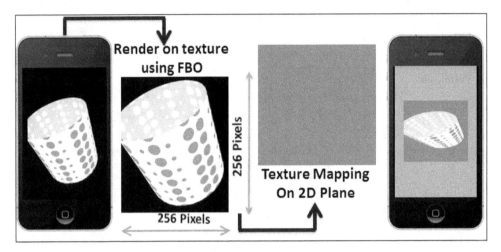

Make sure that the FBO is deleted using the glDeleteFramebuffers API when it's not required by any application.

There's more...

The current FBO recipe uses the depth buffer from the Texture object. Alternatively, we can also use the depth buffer of the render buffer for this purpose. The render buffer is a special OpenGL ES object used with the FBO that allows you to render off screen; it renders the scene directly to the render buffer object instead of a texture object. The render buffer can only store a single image in its internal format.

In the following code, we will see how we can use the render buffer's depth buffer instead of using the depth buffer from the texture object; the process of creating an FBO object and attaching with the color buffer of texture images is the same as described in the previous section:

```
void DemoFBO::GenerateFBOWithRenderBuffer()
{
    // create a frame buffer object
    glGenFramebuffers(1, &fboId);
    glBindFramebuffer(GL_FRAMEBUFFER, fboId);
    // attach the texture to FBO color attachment point
```

```
    textureId = generateTexture(TEXTURE_WIDTH,TEXTURE_HEIGHT);
    glFramebufferTexture2D(GL_FRAMEBUFFER,GL_COLOR_ATTACHMENT0,
                        GL_TEXTURE_2D,textureId,0);

    // create a renderbuffer object to store depth info
    glGenRenderbuffers(1, &rboId);
    glBindRenderbuffer(GL_RENDERBUFFER, rboId);
    glRenderbufferStorage(GL_RENDERBUFFER, GL_DEPTH_COMPONENT16,
                        TEXTURE_WIDTH,TEXTURE_HEIGHT);

    // attach the renderbuffer to depth attachment point
    glFramebufferRenderbuffer(GL_FRAMEBUFFER, GL_DEPTH_ATTACHMENT,
                        GL_RENDERBUFFER, rboId);

    // check FBO status
    GLenum status = glCheckFramebufferStatus(GL_FRAMEBUFFER);
    if(status != GL_FRAMEBUFFER_COMPLETE)
        {printf("Framebuffer creation fails"); }
}
```

The render buffer is created using `glGenRenderBuffers`, this API returns a non-zero value when a **Render Buffer Objects** (**RBO**) is created successfully. Unlike the other OpenGL ES objects also need to be bound first before using it with the help of the `glBindRenderBuffer` API. The created object is empty. Therefore, it's allocated to the memory space using the `glRenderbufferStorage` API; this API takes four arguments. The first argument specifies the target of the allocation (which is `GL_RENDERBUFFER`), the second argument is the internal format render buffer image (which may be a color-renderable, depth-renderable, or stencil-renderable format). For this recipe, we will use the depth renderable format. The last two parameters are used to specify the dimensions of the render buffer.

Syntax:

```
void glRenderbufferStorage(GLenum target, GLenum internalformat,
GLsizei width, GLsizei height);
```

Finally, the `glFramebufferRenderbuffer` API helps the RBO depth buffer to attach to the FBO depth attachment point. The first parameter of this API specifies the framebuffer target, which should be `GL_FRAMEBUFFER` in this case. The second argument is the attachment point of the FBO; as we want to attach to the depth attachment point, it should be `GL_DEPTH_ATTACHMENT`. The third argument specifies the render buffer target and must be `GL_RENDERBUFFER`. The last argument specifies the handle of the `rboId` render buffer object. When RBO is no longer in need, it can be deleted using `glDeleteRenderbuffers`.

Syntax:

```
GLsync glFramebufferRenderbuffer(GLenum target, GLenum
    attachment, GLenum renderbuffertarget, GLuint renderbuffer);
```

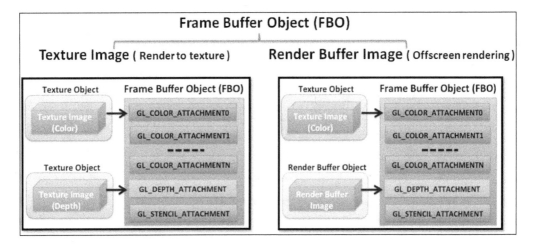

See also

▸ *Applying texture with UV mapping*

▸ Refer to the *Generating the polka dot pattern* recipe in *Chapter 6, Working with Shaders*

Implementing terrain with displacement mapping

The displacement map technique modifies the surface of a geometric shape using procedural texture or texture image. This recipe uses the texture image called height maps to implement a geographical terrain surface on a 2D plane. A height map is a grayscale image where each texel stores the elevation information in the range of 0.0 to 1.0 (white is mapped to 1.0 and black is mapped to 0.0). The 2D plane is represented by a set of vertices arranged in a grid fashion; the elevation information for each vertex in this 3D grid space is read from the height map. This recipe uses another texture image, which is used to map the grass texture on the generated terrain, to make it more realistic.

How to do it...

Perform the following steps to implement the displacement mapping height field recipe:

1. Create a `HeightField` class and declare the following member variables in it:

```
class HeightField: public Model
{

public:
    HeightField(Renderer* parent, float rDimension, float
                cDimension, int Rows = 10, int Columns =
10);
    ~HeightField();

    void InitModel();              // Initialize Model class
    void Render();                 // Render the Model class

private:
    Image* image;                  // Image object
    int imageHeight, imageWidth;   // Image texture dimension
    char MVP, TEX;                 // uniform attrib locations
    float rot;

    GLint NormalMatrix;
    GLuint HeightFieldVAO_Id;       // VAO of Height Field
    GLuint vId, iId;                // VBO and IBO
    int faces;                      // Number of faces

    // Size of vertices, texture, faces indexes, color
    int sizeofVertex, sizeofTex, sizeofFace, sizeofColor;
    float *v, *n, *tex;             // temporary buffers
    unsigned short *faceIdx;
};
```

Define the parameterize constructor; the first argument specifies the parent of the `HeightField` class, the next two parameters define the dimensions of the terrain, and the final two parameters specify the row and column used to create the vertex grid for the terrain plane.

In this function, load the `HeightMap.png` and `grass.png` textures for the displacement mapping and texture mapping respectively; this will generate two texture objects. We are interested only in the front face of the terrain; the total number of faces will be the product of the rows and columns. Allocate the memory space for the total number of vertices (`v`), normals (`n`), texture coordinates (`tex`), and populate them with their respective information. Calculate vertex coordinates using the dimension argument; the normal information is assumed to be a positive unit vector along the *y* axis for each vertex. Assign texture coordinates for each vertex in the grid plane. Finally, use this populated buffer information to generate the VBO and IBO:

```
        HeightField::HeightField(Renderer*parent, float
rDimension,
                        float cDimension, int Rows,
int Columns)
{
    . . . .
    // Load height map image & grass texture file.
    . . . . . .

    // Load HeightMap.png
    imageHeightMap->loadImage(fname);

    // Load grass.png
        imageGrass->loadImage(fname);

        faces = Rows * Columns; // Front side faces
        v     = new float[3 * (Rows + 1) * (Columns + 1)];
        n     = new float[3 * (Rows + 1) * (Columns + 1)];
    tex   = new float[2 * (Rows + 1) * (Columns + 1)];

        faceIdx= new  unsigned short [6 * Rows * Columns];
        sizeofVertex = sizeof(float)*3*(Rows+1)*(Columns+1);
        sizeofTex    = sizeof(float)*2*(Rows+1)*(Columns+1);
    sizeofFace  = sizeof(unsigned short) * 6 * Rows *
Columns;

    float x2, z2;
    x2      = rDimension/2.0f;
    z2      = cDimension/2.0f;

    float zFactor, xFactor;
    zFactor    = cDimension/Columns;
```

```
xFactor    = rDimension/Rows;

float texi, texj;
texi       = 1.0f/Columns;
texj       = 1.0f/ Rows;

float x, z; int vidx = 0, tidx = 0;

// Calculate the Vertices,Normals and TexCoords
   for( int i = 0; i <= Columns; i++ ) {
      z = zFactor * i - z2; // Column

      for( int j = 0; j <= Rows; j++ ) {
         x = xFactor * j - x2; // Row

         // Vertex position
         v[vidx]    =x;
         v[vidx+1]  =0.0f;
         v[vidx+2]  =z;

         // Normals along +Y direction
         n[vidx]    =0.0f;
         n[vidx+1]  =1.0f;
         n[vidx+2]  =0.0f;

         // Jump to the next vertex index
          vidx += 3;

         // Texture coordinates
         tex[tidx]   =j*texj;
         tex[tidx+1] =i*texi;

         // Jump to the next vertex index
         tidx += 2;
      }
   }

// Calculate the face indices
 unsigned int rowStart, nextRowStart, idx = 0;
 for( int i = 0; i < Columns; i++ ) {
     rowStart = i * (Rows+1);
     nextRowStart = (i+1) * (Rows+1);
     for( int j = 0; j < Rows; j++ ) {
```

```
            faceIdx[idx]      = rowStart + j;
            faceIdx[idx+1]    = nextRowStart + j;
            faceIdx[idx+2]    = nextRowStart + j + 1;
            faceIdx[idx+3]    = rowStart + j;
            faceIdx[idx+4]    = nextRowStart + j + 1;
            faceIdx[idx+5]    = rowStart + j + 1;
            idx += 6;
        }
    }


    // Generate and bind the VBO and IBO
    // Create the Vertex Array object for height field
    . . . . . . .

    // Refer to:- Managing VBO's with vertex array
    // objects (VAO), OpenGL ES 3.0 New Features

    // Bind the VBO and IBO for VAO and
    // Delete temporary buffer
    . . . . . . .
}
```

2. In the `initModel` function, link and compile the vertex and fragment shader. Activate texture units and bind it with the height map and grass texture objects. The height map texture is used by the vertex shader to read the elevation information for each vertex. However, the grass texture is used in the fragment shader to paint the geometric surface. The vertex shader uses a `heightFactor` uniform variable to control the elevation value for each vertex:

```
    void HeightField::InitModel(){
. .Compile and Link shaders

    glUseProgram( program->ProgramID );
    TEX_HEIGHT = ProgramManagerObj->
    ProgramGetUniformLocation(program, "ImageTexture");
    glActiveTexture (GL_TEXTURE0);
    if (imageHeightMap) {
    glBindTexture(GL_TEXTURE_2D, imageHeightMap->getTextureID());
    glTexParameterf(GL_TEXTURE_2D,GL_TEXTURE_MAG_FILTER,
GL_LINEAR);
```

```
glTexParameterf(GL_TEXTURE_2D,GL_TEXTURE_MIN_FILTER,GL_LINE
AR);
glTexParameteri(GL_TEXTURE_2D,GL_TEXTURE_WRAP_S,GL_REPEAT);
glTexParameteri(GL_TEXTURE_2D,GL_TEXTURE_WRAP_T,GL_REPEAT);

TEX_GRASS = ProgramManagerObj->
ProgramGetUniformLocation(program,"ImageGrassTexture");
glActiveTexture (GL_TEXTURE1);
if (imageGrass) {
   glBindTexture(GL_TEXTURE_2D, imageGrass->getTextureID());

   glTexParameterf(GL_TEXTURE_2D,GL_TEXTURE_MAG_FILTER,GL_LINEAR);
   glTexParameterf(GL_TEXTURE_2D,GL_TEXTURE_MIN_FILTER,GL_LINEAR);
   glTexParameteri(GL_TEXTURE_2D,GL_TEXTURE_WRAP_S,GL_REPEAT);
   glTexParameteri(GL_TEXTURE_2D,GL_TEXTURE_WRAP_T,GL_REPEAT);
}

   MVP = ProgramManagerObj->ProgramGetUniformLocation
   ( program, (char*)"ModelViewProjectionMatrix" );
   FACTOR = ProgramManagerObj->ProgramGetUniformLocation
   ( program, (char*)"heightFactor" );
   if ( FACTOR >= 0 ){
   glUniform1f(FACTOR, 3);
   }
}
```

3. Create the `HeightFldVertex.glsl` vertex shader and add the following code. In this shader, use texture coordinates and read the elevation information for each vertex from the height map texture stored in the `HeightMapTexture`:

```
#version 300 es
layout(location = 0) in vec4  VertexPosition;
layout(location = 2) in vec2  TexCoords;
uniform mat4     ModelViewProjectionMatrix;

out vec2     TextureCoord;
out vec3     vertexColor;
uniform sampler2D HeightMapTexture;
uniform float heightFactor;
void main()
{
    TextureCoord     = TexCoords;
```

```
    vec4 height     = texture(HeightMapTexture, TexCoords);
    if(heightFactor>0){
        height /= heightFactor;
    }else{
        height = 0.333; // Assumption, some arbitrary value
    }

    gl_Position = ModelViewProjectionMatrix * vec4(
            VertexPosition.x, height.r, VertexPosition.z,
1.0);
}
```

4. Similarly, for the `HeightFldFragment.glsl` fragment shader, add the following code. Make use of texture coordinates and map the grass texture from the `ImageGrassTexture` texture unit to the surface of the terrain:

```
#version 300 es
precision mediump float;

layout(location = 0) out vec4 FinalColor;
uniform sampler2D ImageGrassTexture;
in vec2    TextureCoord;

void main() {
    FinalColor = texture(ImageGrassTexture, TextureCoord);
}
```

5. In the `Renderer.cpp`, add the `HeightField` model, as shown in the following code; the model is 5 units in horizontal and vertical dimensions and contains 50 rows and columns:

```
void Renderer::createModels(){
    clearModels();
    addModel( new HeightField( this, 5, 5, 50, 50 ));
}
```

How it works...

The following image shows the working of displacement mapping that renders the dummy geographical terrain. In this simple example, we assumed the terrain plane with dimension as 1 x 1 units with three rows and columns, resulting in a 3 x 3 vertex grid. Vertex positions are calculated in such a way that the origin always resides in the center; all vertex elevations by default are at 0.0. The vertex shader is responsible for calculating the elevation for each given vertex using the gray scale height map texture. This texture is loaded and accessed using the HeightMapTexture texture unit (image part **A**), the height information is read using the TexCoords texture coordinate (image part **D**) from the height map and is assigned to elevation coordinates (image part **B: H0, H1. . . H8**). Finally, the output of the displacement mapping looks like part **C**, as shown in the following image. This is the screenshot of the practical recipe, in which the terrain is 5 x 5 wide and contains 50 x 50 rows and columns.

In the fragment shader, the grass image texture is applied to the surface of the terrain geometry with the help of a simple texture mapping technique; this makes the geometry more realistic. The image parts **D**, **E**, and **F** show the output of the fragment shader:

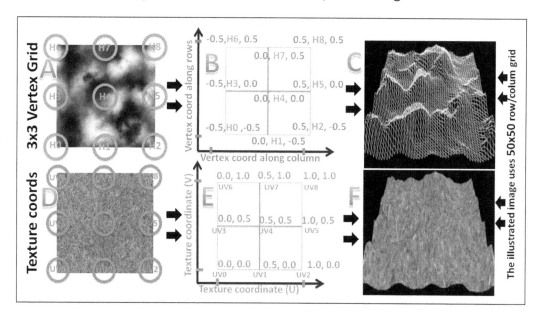

See also

▶ Refer to the *Efficient rendering with Vertex Buffer Object* recipe in *Chapter 2, OpenGL ES 3.0 Essentials*

▶ Refer to the *Managing VBO with Vertex Array Objects* recipe in *Chapter 3, New Features of OpenGL ES 3.0*

Implementing bump mapping

The bump mapping technique is a very efficient technique as compared to displacement mapping. This technique is also used to add depth details or elevations to the surface of the geometry. However, this depth or elevation is fake. The geometry vertices do not undergo any change in the elevation. Instead, it uses the light illumination to simulate the depth appearance on a smooth surface. Light illumination uses the vertex normal information stored in normal maps to add depth. Like height maps, which store the height or elevation information, the normal map stores normal information. The idea in normal maps is to avoid calculation of normal maps for each triangular face; these can be sampled from the texture.

The designer responsible for designing mesh models first create a very high polygon (100,000+) mesh model, then they create a normal map out of it in an image file. Finally, they reduced the high-resolution model to a low polygon mesh (between 3000 and 5000 depends). Depth details are applied at runtime to the low poly mesh using a normal map, which results in a similar appearance like the high poly mesh. Therefore, bump mapping is used to add high details in a low poly mesh model.

In this recipe, we will implement an earth globe, which makes use of the normal map to produce the bump mapping effect; this makes the 3D depth information more obvious on the globe surface.

Getting ready

In order to implement this recipe, we need two textures. The first texture contains the color information to apply texture on the geometric surface. The second texture is the normal map of the first texture. There are many tools available to generate normal maps, such as CrazyBump, GIMP, PixPlant, Photoshop plugins, XNormals, and so on.

How to do it...

The step-by-step instructions to implement bump mapping are as follows:

1. Load the `sphere.obj` with `ObjLoader::LoadMesh()`; this function uses the `OBJMesh` class to load the mesh data. This recipe requires the tangent information from the loaded mesh in order to implement the bump mapping; this is automatically calculated by the `OBJMesh` class with the help of the `CalculateTangents` function. For more information on this function and mathematics calculations, refer to the *There's more...* section of this recipe.

2. Load the `earthcolor.png` earth texture and its normal (`earthnormal.png`) to create texture objects in the `ObjLoader::initModel`, as shown in previous recipes. Attach and bind these two texture objects to the texture unit 0 and 1 respectively so that they become available to the shader programs.

3. Create the `BumpVertex.glsl` and add the following code snippet; this code is responsible for calculating the bi-normal tangent (B) with the help of the cross product of normal (N) and tangent (T). All these vertex parameters are in the tangent space; these must be normalized and stored as a 3x3 tangent space matrix represented by (`[Tx, Bx, Nx]`, `[Ty, By, Ny]`, and `[Tz, Bz, Nz]`). This is used to convert the eye space to a tangent space. The eyecoord in the present case is converted to the tangent space and shared with the fragment shader:

```
#version 300 es
// Vertex information
layout(location = 0) in vec4  VertexPosition;
layout(location = 1) in vec3  Normal;
layout(location = 2) in vec2  TexCoords;
layout (location = 3) in vec4 VertexTangent;

// Model View Project matrix
uniform mat4    ModelViewProjectionMatrix, ModelViewMatrix;
uniform mat3    NormalMatrix;
uniform mediump vec3 LightPosition;
out vec2    textureCoord;
out vec3    eyeCoord;
out mat3    tangentSpace;

void main(){
    // Transform normal and tangent to eye space
    vec3 norm = normalize(NormalMatrix * Normal);
    vec3 tang = normalize(NormalMatrix * vec3(VertexTangent));

    // Compute the binormal
```

```
    vec3 binormal = cross( norm, tang );

    // Matrix for transformation to tangent space
    tangentSpace = mat3(tang.x, binormal.x, norm.x, tang.y,
           binormal.y, norm.y, tang.z, binormal.z, norm.z );

    // Transform view direction to tangent space
    eyeCoord=vec3(ModelViewMatrix*VertexPosition)*tangentSpace;
    textureCoord = TexCoords;
    gl_Position  = ModelViewProjectionMatrix * VertexPosition;
}
```

4. Create the `BumpFragment.glsl` and use the following code; the fragment shader coverts the light direction from eye coordinates to the tangent space; this is helpful in calculating the diffuse and specular intensity:

```
#version 300 es
precision mediump float;

// Light information
uniform vec3 LightAmbient,LightSpecular,LightDiffuse,
                                    LightPosition;

// Material information
uniform vec3 MaterialAmbient,MaterialSpecular,
                                    MaterialDiffuse,;
uniform float ShininessFactor;

in vec2 textureCoord;
in vec3 eyeCoord;
in mat3 tangentSpace;
layout(location = 0) out vec4 FinalColor;

vec3 normalizeNormal, normalizeEyeCoord, normalizeLightVec;

vec3 V, R, ambient, diffuse, specular;

float sIntensity, cosAngle;

vec3 PhongShading( vec3 norm, vec3 MaterialDiffuse ) {
    normalizeNormal   = normalize( norm ) ;
    normalizeEyeCoord = normalize( eyeCoord);
```

```
normalizeLightVec = normalize( (LightPosition-eyeCoord)
                        *tangentSpace);

    // Diffuse Intensity
    cosAngle = max( 0.0, dot(normalizeNormal,
                        normalizeLightVec ));

    // Viewer's vector
    V = -normalizeEyeCoord;
    R = reflect( -normalizeLightVec, normalizeNormal);
    sIntensity = pow(max(0.0,dot(R,V)),ShininessFactor);

    // ADS as result of Material & Light interaction
    ambient = MaterialAmbient * LightAmbient;
    diffuse = MaterialDiffuse * LightDiffuse * cosAngle;
    specular= MaterialSpecular*LightSpecular*sIntensity;

    return  ambient + diffuse + specular;
}

uniform sampler2D ImageTexture, ImageTextureNormal;

void main() {
  //Lookup normal map
    vec4 normalMap = texture(ImageTextureNormal, vec2(1.0-
                    textureCoord.x, textureCoord.y));

  //Convert [0,1] -> [-1,1]
    normalMap     =  (2.0*normalMap-1.0);
    vec4 texColor = texture(ImageTexture, vec2(1.0 -
                    textureCoord.x, textureCoord.y));
    FinalColor    = vec4( PhongShading(normalMap.xyz,
                    texColor.rgb), 1.0 );
}
```

How it works...

The bump map requires two texture files. The first texture file contains color information and is used in the diffuse shading. The second texture is called the normal map, which contains the normal information for the geometry; this information is helpful for specular shading. Both these textures are loaded and stored in texture units in order to make it accessible to the shader.

Bump mapping heavily relies on the tangent information calculated in the `ObjMesh` class when the mesh is loaded. For more information on the tangent calculation, refer to the next section in this recipe. The tangents that are calculated are stored within the mesh VBO and are available to the vertex shader unlike other vertex attributes. In the vertex shader, this information in conjunction with the normal information helps to calculate per-vertex bi-tangent vectors. Once the normal (N), tangent (T), and bi-tangent (B) vectors are available, they are normalized and used to create a tangent space matrix, as shown in the following figure:

$$\text{Tangent Space Matrix} \begin{bmatrix} T_x & B_x & N_x \\ T_y & B_y & N_y \\ T_z & B_z & N_z \end{bmatrix}$$

The obtained tangent space matrix (`tangentSpace`) is multiplied with the eye coordinates of the `VertexPosition` to yield tangent space eye coordinates (`eyeCoord`). These are then shared with the fragment shader, along with the tangent space matrix and the `TexCoords` texture coordinates.

In the fragment shader, the image texture and normal texture are sampled using texture coordinates and are stored in the `texColor` and `normalMap`. It's necessary to change the normal map values from the range `[0, 1]` to `[-1, 1]`. Once changed, these two texture values are then sent to the `GouraudShading`. In this function, the light direction for each vertex is calculated and multiplied with the `tangentSpace` in order to transform into the tangent space. This modified `normalizeLightVec` and `eyeCoord` are then used to calculate diffuse and specular illumination components in the same way we calculated in the Gouraud shading technique. For more information on this technique, refer to *Chapter 5, Light and Materials*.

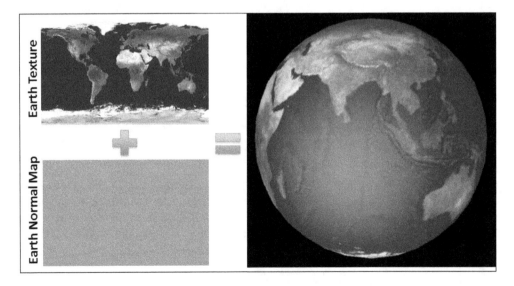

There's more...

The normal map used in the bump mapping technique stores normal information of the geometry with respect to some default direction when normal map was generated. When this texture is mapped on the geometry and used for rendering purposes, it may generate incorrect results because not all faces of the geometry have the same direction as the mapped normal map. Therefore, the normal map needs to be manipulated on the fly at runtime, depending on the direction of the face, which is done using tangent planes. In the ObjMesh class, this tangent plane is calculated using OBJMesh::CalculateTangents; the tangent plane consists of Tangent (T) and BiTangent (B) vectors.

A tangent is a vector that touches a curved surface at a given point; there could be too many tangents at a given point. Hence, it's very important to choose the correct tangent. Therefore, we want our tangent space to be aligned in such a way that **X** direction corresponds to the **U** direction of texture coordinates and **Y** direction corresponds to the **V** direction of texture coordinates.

Consider a scenario where there is a triangle with vertices P_0, P_1, and P_2 and corresponding texture coordinates as (U_0, V_0), (U_1, V_1), and (U_2, V_2), the following image explains the calculation of the tangent space (see the equations). This gives the un-normalized Tangent (T) and BiTangent (B) for the triangle face created using P_0, P_1, and P_2. In order to calculate the tangent for a given vertex, take the average tangents of all triangle faces that share this vertex:

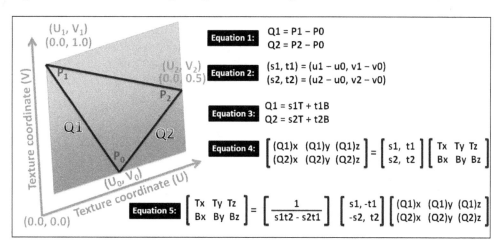

The preceding pictorial illustration and given equations in it, the tangent information is calculated in the OBJMesh class, as shown in the following code:

```
bool OBJMesh::CalculateTangents(){
    vector<vec3> tan1Accum, tan2Accum; // Accumulated tangents
```

```
        objMeshModel.tangents.resize(objMeshModel.positions.size());

        for( uint i = 0; i < objMeshModel.positions.size(); i++ ) {
         tan1Accum.push_back(vec3(0.0f));tan2Accum.push_back(vec3(0.0f));
         objMeshModel.tangents.push_back(vec4(0.0f));
        }

        int index0, index1, index2, index0uv, index1uv, index2uv;

        // Compute the tangent vector
        for( uint i = 0; i < objMeshModel.vecFaceIndex.size(); i += 3
    ){
            index0 = objMeshModel.vecFaceIndex.at(i).vertexIndex;
            index1 = objMeshModel.vecFaceIndex.at(i+1).vertexIndex;
            index2 = objMeshModel.vecFaceIndex.at(i+2).vertexIndex;

           const vec3 &p0 = objMeshModel.positions.at(index0);
           const vec3 &p1 = objMeshModel.positions.at(index1);
           const vec3 &p2 = objMeshModel.positions.at(index2);

           index0uv = objMeshModel.vecFaceIndex.at(i).uvIndex;
           index1uv = objMeshModel.vecFaceIndex.at(i+1).uvIndex;
           index2uv = objMeshModel.vecFaceIndex.at(i+2).uvIndex;

           const vec2 &tc1 = objMeshModel.uvs.at(index0uv);
           const vec2 &tc2 = objMeshModel.uvs.at(index1uv);
           const vec2 &tc3 = objMeshModel.uvs.at(index2uv);

           // Using Equation 1
           vec3 q1 = p1 - p0;
            vec3 q2 = p2 - p0;

           // Using Equation 2
           float s1 = tc2.x-tc1.x, s2 = tc3.x-tc1.x;
           float t1 = tc2.y-tc1.y, t2 = tc3.y-tc1.y;

       // From Equation 5
           float r = 1.0f / (s1 * t2 - s2 * t1);

           // Using Equation 5
           vec3 tan( (t2*q1.x - t1*q2.x) * r,
                     (t2*q1.y - t1*q2.y) * r,
                     (t2*q1.z - t1*q2.z) * r);
```

```
    vec3 bTan( (s1*q2.x - s2*q1.x) * r,
               (s1*q2.y - s2*q1.y) * r,
               (s1*q2.z - s2*q1.z) * r);


      tan1Accum[index0] += tan1; tan1Accum[index1] += tan1;
      tan1Accum[index2] += tan1; tan2Accum[index0] += bTan;
      tan2Accum[index1] += bTan; tan2Accum[index2] += bTan;
    }

    for( uint i = 0; i < objMeshModel.positions.size(); ++i ){
      objMeshModel.tangents[i] = vec4(
                    glm::normalize(tan1Accum[i] ),1.0);
    }

    for(int i = 0; i < objMeshModel.vecFaceIndex.size(); i++){
      int index = objMeshModel.vecFaceIndex.at(i + 0).vertexIndex;
    objMeshModel.vertices[i].tangent=objMeshModel.tangents.at(index);
    }

  // Clear & Return
   tan1Accum.clear();tan2Accum.clear();
  return true;
}
```

See also

▸ Refer to the *Gouraud shading – the per-vertex shading technique* recipe in *Chapter 5, Light and Materials*

▸ Refer to the *Rendering the wavefront OBJ mesh model* recipe in *Chapter 4, Working with Meshes*

8

Font Rendering

In this chapter, we will cover the following recipes:

- ▶ Font rendering with the FreeType project
- ▶ Rendering different languages with Harfbuzz
- ▶ Rendering text on Head Up Display

Introduction

Font rendering is an essential part of computer application programs; it helps users to interact with the system and understand information in a readable form. OpenGL ES does not provide a built-in support for font rendering; instead, the font engine needs to be programed by a developer. There are many font-rendering techniques; this chapter will cover the most popular technique for font rendering, which is rendered using the **FreeType** project in conjunction with the **Harfbuzz** library. The former is used to rasterize symbolic characters or glyphs using font files; this library supports different types of font file formats, such as TTF, BDF, OTF, Windows FNT, and so on. The latter library is used for multilingual support. Using this library, almost all world-famous language scripts can be rendered.

This chapter will provide you with a detailed description on how to build the font engine; we will implement simple text rendering with the help of FreeType. We will use the capabilities of the Harfbuzz library to print multilingual text rendering, such as Arabic, Thai, Tamil, Punjabi, and so on. Last but not least, you will learn the technique to render text in the screen coordinate system on the **Head Up Display** (**HUD**) or overlays.

Font rendering with the FreeType project

In this recipe, we will render a simple Latin text in the 3D space. For this, we can create a texture bitmap for each character and render it in a quad geometry (rectangle) shape. However, creating each character bitmap could be expensive in terms of memory management and performance because it is required to load several bitmaps in the texture memory. Instead, the better solution is to create a big texture embedded with all characters in it and use their texture coordinates to map them on the geometry quad.

An overview of the process to render fonts using the FreeType library is as follows:

1. Initialize the FreeType library. This initializes the necessary FreeType data structure.

2. Load the font face. This loads the font file and generates the font style (font face) information.

3. Specify the font size. With the specified size of the font, create an empty texture big enough to contain all glyphs. In order to make the texture backward compatible with OpenGL ES 2.0, choose its texture size to be a power of two.

4. Access the font face data contents. This uses the font face and metric information to create glyph images on an empty texture, which is called texture atlas. Glyphs will be drawn in the form of row and columns, as shown in the next image.

5. Map the glyph. This stores the texture coordinates of each glyph image from the texture atlas in a data structure and maps it to its respective charcode.

6. Render the text. The glyph map contains all character codes, picks the desired character, and maps the respective texture coordinate from the texture atlas to the quad geometry of each character. For example, the following image shows the printing of the Hello World from the texture atlas:

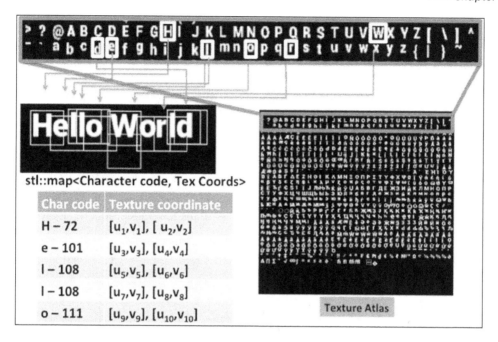

stl::map<Character code, Tex Coords>

Char code	Texture coordinate
H – 72	$[u_1,v_1], [u_2,v_2]$
e – 101	$[u_3,v_3], [u_4,v_4]$
l – 108	$[u_5,v_5], [u_6,v_6]$
l – 108	$[u_7,v_7], [u_8,v_8]$
o – 111	$[u_9,v_9], [u_{10},v_{10}]$

Texture Atlas

Classes and data structure:

The following is a brief description of all the classes and related data structures used in font rendering:

- FontGenerator: This class loads the font file with the help of the FreeType library. It stores important information from the font file in the related data structure. It uses the FreeType library data structure to build the bitmap texture; the bitmap information for each character/glyph is stored locally in a quick accessible map:
  - library: This is the handle of the FreeType library instance.
  - fontface: Each font may contain one or more font faces or typeface; it has a specific weight, style, condensation, width, slant, italicization, ornamentation, and designer or foundry.
  - glyphs: This is the STL map of glyph and character code.
  - atlasTex: This contains the handle of the atlas texture object.

- ▶ `Glyph`: This data structure stores information related to a glyph present in the font file:

  - ❑ `Metric`: Glyph metric is used to position the glyph when rendered in the 2D/3D space.

  - ❑ `texCoordX`, `texCoordY`, `atlasX`, and `atlasY`: These store texture coordinates of glyphs present in the texture atlas.

  - ❑ `advanceHorizontal` and `advanceVertical`: The advance information is helpful in placing next adjacent character with respect to current glyph.

- ▶ `Font`: This class is derived from `FontGenerator` and provides an interface to load the font file and a helper function to render text.

- ▶ `FontSample`: This class acts as a consumer of the font renderer; it renders sample text for demonstration purposes.

The following diagram shows the class diagram of the design; the `Font` class is derived from `FontGenerator` and `Model`:

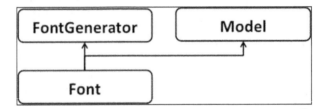

Getting ready

The FreeType project is an open source library used for font rasterization; it reads font files and is able to generate bitmaps from the vector/curve information stored in such files. This library is written in ANSI-C, which makes it portable across platforms.

 The library is freely available under the download section at `http://www.freetype.org`.

The **FreeType License** (**FTL**) is the most commonly used one. This is a BSD-style license with a credit clause and is compatible with the GNU Public License (GPL) version 3 and not with the GPL version 2. In our GLPI framework, we will use the 2.5.4 version, which is placed under the `GLPIFramework/Font/FreeType` folder.

Build process: The following points provide a detailed description of the build process for the FreeType library and other source files required to implement this recipe:

- ▶ **Android platform**: We need the makefile to build the FreeType project library. Add the `Android.mk` makefile under `GLPIFramework/Font/FreeType`; edit this makefile, as shown in the following code. This will be compiled as a shared library, which is named as GLPift2. Optionally, you can also add the source code directly in the main project makefile instead of compiling a shared library:

```
ifndef USE_FREETYPE
USE_FREETYPE := 2.4.2
endif
ifeq ($(USE_FREETYPE),2.4.2)

LOCAL_PATH:= $(call my-dir)
include $(CLEAR_VARS)

LOCAL_SRC_FILES:= \
src/base/ftbbox.c src/base/ftbitmap.c \
src/base/ftfstype.c src/base/ftglyph.c \
src/base/ftlcdfil.c src/base/ftstroke.c\
src/base/fttype1.c src/base/ftxf86.c \
src/base/ftbase.c src/base/ftsystem.c \
src/base/ftinit.c src/base/ftgasp.c \
src/raster/raster.c src/sfnt/sfnt.c \
src/smooth/smooth.c src/autofit/autofit.c \ src/truetype/
truetype.c src/cff/cff.c \ src/psnames/psnames.c src/pshinter/
pshinter.c

LOCAL_C_INCLUDES += $(LOCAL_PATH)/builds $(LOCAL_PATH)/include

LOCAL_CFLAGS+=-W -Wall -fPIC -DPIC -O2
LOCAL_CFLAGS+="-DDARWIN_NO_CARBON" "-DFT2_BUILD_LIBRARY"

LOCAL_MODULE:= libGLPift2
include $(BUILD_SHARED_LIBRARY)
```

Open the `Android.mk` makefile present in the project directory under the `JNI` folder (`<Source code path>/SimpleFont/Android/JNI`) and include the path of the FreeType library `Android.mk` file that we have created in the preceding code:

```
FONT_PATH= $(FRAMEWORK_DIR)/Font
$(MY_CUR_LOCAL_PATH)/../../../../GLPIFramework/Font/FreeType/
Android.mk
LOCAL_C_INCLUDES += $(FONT_PATH)/FreeType/include
```

```
LOCAL_SRC_FILES += $(SCENE_DIR)/FontGenerator.cpp \
                   $(SCENE_DIR)/Font.cpp \
                   $(SCENE_DIR)/FontSample.cpp \
                   $(SCENE_DIR)/SimpleTexture.cpp
LOCAL_SHARED_LIBRARIES += GLPift2
```

In `GLESNativeLib.java`, edit the `GLESNativeLib` class and add the reference of our `GLPift2.so` shared library in order to link at runtime:

```
public class GLESNativeLib {
static {
System.loadLibrary("GLPift2");
    . . . . . . Other code
}
```

▶ **iOS platform**: On the iOS platform, we need to add the same FreeType project source files (mentioned under the `LOCAL_SRC_FILES` makefile variable) to your project using the **Build Phase | Compile Sources** project properties; click on add to select source files.

Provide a path to include header files for the free type project using **Build Settings | Search Paths | Header Search Paths**. For the present case, it should be:

```
../../../../GLPIFramework/Font/FreeType/Include
```

Add the following preprocessor macro under **Apple LLVM <compiler version> | Preprocessing | Preprocessor Macros**:

```
FT2_BUILD_LIBRARY=1 DARWIN_NO_CARBON
```

Add the `FontGenerator.h/cpp`, `Font.h/cpp` project source files and `FontSample.h/cpp` using **File | Add Files to <Project Name>**.

How to do it...

Perform the following steps to understand the procedure of implementing this recipe:

1. Create the `FontGenerator` class and add the following code body to it; the important data structure is already covered in the previous section under classes and data structures:

```
struct Glyph {
FT_Glyph_Metrics metric; // Glyph metric
    float advanceHorizontal; // Horizontal advance
    float advanceVertical;   // Horizontal advance
    float texCoordX, texCoordY; // Atlas Texture Coords
    float atlasX, atlasY;    // Position in texture Altas
```

```
};

class FontGenerator {
  public:
    FontGenerator ();       // Constructor
    ~FontGenerator ();      // Destructor
    bool errorState ();     // Error check flag
    bool loadFont(const char* filename, int resolution);

    GLuint          atlasTex;       // Texture atlas handle
    std::map<unsigned long, Glyph>  glyphs; // Glyph map
    float           texDimension;
    float           squareSize;     // Glyph square size
    LanguageType    languageType;   // Current language
    FT_Face         fontFace;       // typeface information

  private:
    bool readFont (const FT_Face& fontFace,
    int resolution, int glyphMargin);

    bool getCorrectResolution(const FT_Face& fontFace,
    int resolution, int& newResolution, int& newMargin);

    void generateTexFromGlyph (FT_GlyphSlot glyph, GLubyte*
    texture, int atlasX, int atlasY, int texSize,
    int resolution, int marginSize, bool drawBorder);

    void setPixel (GLubyte* texture, int offset,
    int size, int x, int y, GLubyte val);

    bool                    errorStatus;
    FT_Library              library;  // FreeType lib handle
};
```

2. Make sure that the `<ft2build.h>` header file is included in the source.

3. Initialize the FreeType library in the constructor with the `FT_Init_FreeType` function; this constructor will be called from the Font class when its object is created from the `Renderer::createModels` function. This function creates a new instance of the FreeType library and sets the handle to the library:

```
FontGenerator::FontGenerator () : errorStatus(false),
 atlasTex(0), texDimension(0), squareSize(0)  {
    if (FT_Init_FreeType(&library)){
```

```
    errorStatus = true;return;
    }
  }
```

4. The `loadFont` function is responsible for loading the font file using FreeType's `FT_New_Face` function. This function creates a new face with the available typeface and style information in the font file. For example, Arial Bold and Arial Italic correspond to two different faces. This function calls the `getCorrectResolution` function, which is described in the next step:

```
bool FontGenerator::loadFont(char* file,int resolution){
    // Generate the face object, return on error
     if(FT_New_Face(library,filename,0 &fontFace))
    {
    return false;
    }

    // Check if current resolution is supported?
    int calculatedResoution; int calculatedMargin;
    if( getCorrectResolution(fontFace, resolution,
    calculatedResoution, calculatedMargin)){
    return readFont(fontFace, calculatedResoution,
    calculatedMargin);
    }
    return true;
}
```

Before creating the texture atlas, it's important to check whether the texture size is supported by a device using the `getCorrectResolution` function. The maximum texture size can be queried using the `GL_MAX_TEXTURE_SIZE` symbolic flag. If the texture exceeds the maximum supported limit, this function falls back to the next immediate smaller available power of two sizes:

 The texture altas we generated for this recipe is made of power 2.0 in order to make it compatible with OpenGL ES 2.0 version.

```
bool FontGenerator::getCorrectResolution(const FT_Face&
fontFace, int resolution, int&
newResolution, int& newGlyphMargin){

    int glyphMargin = 0;
    GLint MaxTextureSize;
    glGetIntegerv(GL_MAX_TEXTURE_SIZE, &MaxTextureSize);

    while(resolution>0){
    glyphMargin = (int)ceil(resolution*0.1f);
```

```
      const long numGlyphs = fontFace->num_glyphs;
      const int squareSize = resolution + glyphMargin;

      const int numGlyphsPerRow = (int)ceilf(sqrt((double)numGlyphs));
      const int texSize         = (numGlyphsPerRow)*squareSize;
      int realTexSize           = GLUtils::nextPowerOf2(texSize);

      if(realTexSize<=MaxTextureSize )
      {     break; }

      resolution  = resolution - 5; // Decrease 5 units.
      }

      if(resolution > 0){
      newResolution    = resolution;
      newGlyphMargin   = glyphMargin;
      return true;
      }
      else{
      return false;
      }
    }
```

Read the font information from the FreeType library in the `readFont` function. This function sets the font size using `FT_Set_Pixel_Sizes` in pixels:

```
bool FontGenerator::readFont (const FT_Face& fontFace,
int resolution, int glyphMargin) {
  FT_Set_Pixel_Sizes(fontFace, resolution, resolution);
  const int numGlyphs = fontFace->num_glyphs;
  . . . .
}
```

5. The `fontFace` contains information about the total number of characters in the font file. Using this information and the provided font size, the total size of the texture atlas is calculated in the power of two dimensions. A two channel texture memory is allocated and stored in the `textureData` variable for luminance and alpha:

```
// Inside FontGenerator::readFont() function
squareSize = resolution + glyphMargin;

// Texture size for all glyphs in power of 2
const int numGlyphsPerRow = ceilf(sqrt(numGlyphs));
```

```
const int texSize = numGlyphsPerRow*squareSize;
int realTexSize  = GLUtils::nextPowerOf2(texSize);

// Two channel texture (luminance and alpha)
GLubyte* textureData = NULL;
textureData = new GLubyte[realTexSize*realTexSize*2];

// if there exist an old atlas delete it.
if (atlasTex){
glDeleteTextures(1,&atlasTex);
atlasTex=0;
}

glGenTextures(1, &atlasTex);
glBindTexture(GL_TEXTURE_2D, atlasTex);
glTexParameteri
(GL_TEXTURE_2D,GL_TEXTURE_MAG_FILTER, GL_LINEAR);
glTexParameteri
(GL_TEXTURE_2D, GL_TEXTURE_MIN_FILTER, GL_LINEAR);
GLUtils::checkForOpenGLError(__FILE__, __LINE__);
```

6. Each glyph in the font face is recognized with a unique index; the face object contains one or more tables called character maps (charmaps), which are used to map glyph indices to character codes. For example, A has a character code of 65 in ASCII encoding.

    Loop through all the available glyph in the font and load the information for a current glyph image using FT_Load_Glyph. This function stores the glyph image in a special object called glyph slot. The FT_Load_Glyph accepts three parameters, handles the font face object, glyphs indexes, and loads flags:

```
// Inside FontGenerator::readFont() function
int texAtlasX  = 0;       int texAtlasY  = 0;
FT_UInt gindex = 0;    FT_ULong charcode = 0;

for (FT_ULong charcode=FT_Get_First_Char(fontFace,
&gindex); gindex != 0;charcode=FT_Get_Next_Char
(fontFace, charcode, &gindex)) {

if(FT_Load_Glyph(fontFace,gindex,FT_LOAD_DEFAULT)){
LOGE("Error loading glyph with index %i and charcode %i.
Skipping.", gindex, charcode);
continue;
}
// Many lines skipped.
}
```

7. A glyph slot is a container that stores only one type of image at a time. This can be bitmap, outline, and so on. The glyph slot object can be accessed using **fontFace | glyph**. The bitmap information is generated out of the glyph slot using the `FT_Render_Glyph` API; it accepts two arguments, the first argument is the glyph slot and the second argument is the render mode flag, which specifies how to render the glyph image.

    The glyph information is loaded into the glyph data structure and stored as a value in the STL map glyphs with the character code as a key:

    ```
    // Inside FontGenerator::readFont() function
    // This is part of the glyph loading loop.
    FT_GlyphSlot glyph = fontFace->glyph;
    FT_Render_Glyph(glyph, FT_RENDER_MODE_NORMAL);

    // Calculate glyph information
    Glyph glyphInfo;
    glyphInfo.metric       = glyph->metrics;

    // Get texture offset in the image
    glyphInfo.atlasX=texAtlasX*squareSize/realTexSize;
    glyphInfo.atlasY=texAtlasY*squareSize/realTexSize;

    // Advance stored as fractional pixel format
    // (=1/64 pixel), as per FreeType specs
    glyphInfo.advanceHorizontal=glyph->advance.x/64.0f;
    glyphInfo.advanceVertical=glyph->advance.y/64.0f;
    glyphs[charcode] = glyphInfo;
    ```

8. Load the glyph bitmap in the texture atlas using the `generateTexFromGlyph` function. This function writes the raster information from the glyph slot to the texture data. After all the characters are rastered, load the texture atlas in the OpenGL ES texture object with the help of `glTexImage2D` and delete the local texture atlas:

    ```
    // Inside FontGenerator::readFont()
    {
    . . . . .
    // Copy the bits to the texture atlas
    generateTexFromGlyph(glyph, textureData, texAtlasX,
    texAtlasY, realTexSize, resolution, glyphMargin, false);

    texAtlasX++;
    if (texAtlasX >= numGlyphsPerRow){
    texAtlasX=0;
    texAtlasY++;
    ```

```
}

        // set texture atlas to OpenGL ES tex object
        glTexImage2D (GL_TEXTURE_2D, 0, GL_LUMINANCE_ALPHA,
        realTexSize, realTexSize, 0, GL_LUMINANCE_ALPHA,
        GL_UNSIGNED_BYTE, textureData);

        // Delete local texture atlas
        delete[] textureData;
        GLUtils::checkForOpenGLError(`_FILE__, __LINE__);
        texDimension = (squareSize)/(float)realTexSize;
        return true;
}
```

9. The `generateTexFromGlyph` function is responsible for loading the current specified glyph in to the glyph slot to load it into a particular position in the texture atlas specified by `atlasX`, `atlasY`, and `texSize`. The last parameter for this function is used to draw a border around the character, which can be very helpful in debugging the positioning of a character in texture rendering. For example, see the preceding **Hello World** sample text image; it contains a border around each character:

```
        void FontGenerator::generateTexFromGlyph (FT_GlyphSlot
        glyph, GLubyte* texture, int atlasX, int atlasY, int
        texSize,int resolution,int marginSize,bool drawBorder){

        int squareSize = resolution + marginSize;
        baseOff
        set=atlasX*squareSize+atlasY*squareSize*texSize;

        if (drawBorder) {
        for (int w=0; w<squareSize; w++)
        { setPixel(texture,baseOffset,texSize, w, 0, 255); }

         for (int h=1; h<squareSize; h++){
         for (int w=0; w<squareSize; w++){
         setPixel(texture,baseOffset,texSize,w,h,
         (w==0||w==squareSize-1)?255:
         (h==squareSize-1)?255:0);
                                          }
                                          }
        }

        const int gr = glyph->bitmap.rows;
        const int gw = glyph->bitmap.width;
```

```
        for (int h=0; h<gr; h++) {
        for (int w=0; w<gw; w++) {
        setPixel(texture, baseOffset+marginSize, texSize,
        w, marginSize+h, glyph->bitmap.buffer[w+h*gw]);
        }
        }
    }
```

10. Create the `Font` class derived from `Model` and `FontGenerator`:

```
    class Font : public Model, public FontGenerator {
    public:
    Font(const char* ttfFile, int Size, Renderer* parent,
    LanguageType Language= English);
    ~Font();
    void Render();
    void InitModel();
    void printText (const char* str, GLfloat Red = 1.0f,
    GLfloat Green = 1.0f, GLfloat Blue = 1.0f,
    GLfloat Alpha = 1.0f);
    private:
    void drawGlyph (const Glyph& gi);
    char MVP, TEX, FRAG_COLOR;
    };
```

Create a vertex shader file called `fontVertex.glsl` and add the following code; this shader file receives the vertex and texture coordinate information from the OpenGL ES program. The received texture coordinates are further sent to the fragment shader for the purpose of texture sampling purpose:

```
#version 300 es
layout(location = 0) in vec3  VertexPosition;
layout(location = 1) in vec2  VertexTexCoord;
out vec2 TexCoord;
uniform mat4 ModelViewProjectMatrix;

void main( void ) {
  TexCoord       = VertexTexCoord;
  gl_Position    =ModelViewProjectMatrix  *
                  vec4(VertexPosition,1.0);
}
```

11. Create the `fontfrag.glsl` fragment shader; it contains a sampler2D variable for the texture input and a uniform `TexColor` for the text color:

```
#version 300 es
precision mediump float;

in vec2 TexCoord;
uniform sampler2D FontTexture;
uniform vec4 TextColor;
layout(location = 0) out vec4 outColor;

void main() {
    vec4 texcol = texture(FontTexture, TexCoord);
    outColor    = vec4(vec3(TextColor.rgb), texcol.a);
}
```

12. Load and compile the shader in the `initModel` function and query the vertex shader attributes:

```
void Font::InitModel() {
    . . . . . // Other code . . . .
    program->VertexShader  = ShaderManager::ShaderInit
            (VERTEX_SHADER_PRG, GL_VERTEX_SHADER);
    program->FragmentShader  = ShaderManager::ShaderInit
            (FRAGMENT_SHADER_PRG, GL_FRAGMENT_SHADER);
    . . . . . // Other code . . . .

    MVP = ProgramManagerObj->ProgramGetUniformLocation
            (program,"ModelViewProjectMatrix");
    TEX = ProgramManagerObj->ProgramGetUniformLocation
            (program, (char*) "Tex1");
    FRAG_COLOR = ProgramManagerObj->ProgramGetUniformLocation
            (program, (char*)"TextColor");
}
```

13. The `drawGlyph` function is responsible for rendering the glyph. The glyph is rendered on a logical square by mapping texture coordinates stored in the glyph data structure. Initialize the texture sample with texture unit 0:

```
void Font::drawGlyph(const Glyph& gi) {
    glUseProgram(program->ProgramID);

    // Using the glyph metrics to get the glyph info.
    float xmargin = flot(gi.metric.width)/(2.0*64.0);
    float ymargin =float(gi.metric.horiBearingY)/(2.0*64.0);

    // Calculate texture coord for glyph rendering
```

```
    float texCoords[8] = {
        gi.atlasX, gi.atlasY,
        gi.atlasX + texDimension, gi.atlasY,
        gi.atlasX, gi.atlasY + texDimension,
        gi.atlasX + texDimension, gi.atlasY + texDimension
    };

    // 1x1 glyph Quad.
    float quad[12]    = {
        {-0.5f, 0.5f,  0.0f},{ 0.5f, 0.5f,  0.0f},
        {-0.5f, -0.5f, 0.0f},{0.5f, -0.5f, 0.0f }};

for (int i = 0; i<12;){
    quad[i] *= squareSize/2.0;
    quad[i+1] *= squareSize/2.0;
    quad[i+2] *= 0.0;
    i += 3;
}

    // Initialize the texture with texture unit 0
    glUniform1i(TEX, 0);
    TransformObj->TransformPushMatrix();
    TransformObj->TransformTranslate(-xmargin, ymargin,
                                          0.0f );
    glUniformMatrix4fv(MVP, 1, GL_FALSE, (float*)
    TransformObj->TransformGetModelViewProjectionMatrix());
    TransformObj->TransformPopMatrix();

    // Send the vertex and texture info to shader
    glEnableVertexAttribArray(VERTEX_POSITION);
    glEnableVertexAttribArray(TEX_COORD);
    glVertexAttribPointer(VERTEX_POSITION, 3, GL_FLOAT,
        GL_FALSE, 0, quad);
    glVertexAttribPointer(TEX_COORD, 2, GL_FLOAT,
        GL_FALSE, 0, texCoords);
    glDrawArrays(GL_TRIANGLE_STRIP, 0, 4);
}
```

14. The message string is printed with the help of the `printText` function. This function loops through the message string and calls the `drawGlyph` function to render each character in it. After rendering each character, the next glyph is advanced by the horizontal offset `advanceHorizontal` information stored in the glyph data structure for the corresponding character code:

```
void Font::printText(char* str, GLfloat Red,
     GLfloat Green, GLfloat Blue, GLfloat Alpha) {
    // Initialize OpenGL ES States
    glDisable(GL_CULL_FACE);
    glDisable(GL_DEPTH_TEST);
    glEnable(GL_BLEND);
    glBlendFunc(GL_SRC_ALPHA, GL_ONE_MINUS_SRC_ALPHA);

    // Use font program
    glUseProgram(program->ProgramID);

    // Activate Texture unit 0 and assign the altas
    glActiveTexture (GL_TEXTURE0);
    glBindTexture(GL_TEXTURE_2D, atlasTex);

    TransformObj->TransformPushMatrix();
    GLfloat color[4] = {Red, Green, Blue, Alpha};
    glUniform4fv(FRAG_COLOR, 1, color);

    for (const char* c = str; *c != '\0'; c++) {
        const Glyph& gi = glyphs[((unsigned long) *c)];
        TransformObj->TransformTranslate
          (gi.advanceHorizontal/ 2.0, 0.0, 0.0);
        drawGlyph(gi);
    }
    TransformObj->TransformPopMatrix();
    return;
}
```

The present case of `drawGlyph()` can be optimized by bunching multiple draw calls into a single one. Multiple glyphs can be defined and drawn in one go if all glyph quads are computed and specified along with their texture coordinates in vertex attribute buffers. We will leave this optimization as an exercise to our readers.

15. Create a `FontSample` class derived from `Model` and override the `Render()` method in order to render the sample text, as shown in the following code:

```
void FontSample::Render(){
    Font* English = dynamic_cast<Font*>
                    (RendererHandler->getModel(FontEnglish));
    static float angle = 0.0;
    TransformObj->TransformPushMatrix();
    TransformObj->TransformTranslate(-0.50, 0.0, 0.0);
    TransformObj->TransformRotate(angle++, 1.0, 0.0, 0.0);
    English->printText((char*)"Hello World !!!",1,1,0,1);
    TransformObj->TransformPopMatrix();
}
```

16. In the `Renderer::createModel` function, load the font file with the desired font size and add the `FontSample` model. Make sure that the font file is added to the project:

```
void Renderer::createModels(){
    clearModels();
    char fname[500]= {""};
#ifdef __APPLE__
    GLUtils::extractPath( getenv("FILESYSTEM"), fname);
#else
    strcpy( fname, "/sdcard/GLPIFramework/Font/");
#endif
    addModel(new Font(strcat(fname,"ACUTATR.TTF"),
        50, this, English) );
    addModel( new FontSample(this) );
}
```

How it works...

The initialization of FreeType is necessary in order to use it properly and without any unexpected surprises during use; this initialization is done in the constructor of the `Font` class using the `FT_Init_FreeType` API. This ensures that all the modules in the library are ready for use. On successful initialization, this API returns `0`; otherwise, it returns an error and sets the handle with a `NULL` value.

The constructor also calls the loadFont function; this function loads the font file using the FT_New_Face API and creates the face object. One font file may contain one or more than one font faces; the face contains the font style information. It describes a given typeface and style. For example, *Times New Roman Regular* and *Times New Roman Italic* correspond to two different faces. The loadFont function calls getCorrectResolution to make sure that the hardware device supports the requested texture size of the texture atlas allocation. The maximum texture size limit can be queried using GL_MAX_TEXTURE_SIZE; if the texture size is bigger than the supported limit, it falls back to the next smallest available size and returns the new updated resolution and margin size in the calculatedResolution and calculatedSize.

The readFont function sets the font size information using the FT_Set_Pixel_Size API. This function takes three arguments, namely, font face, pixel width, and pixel height. The total number of glyphs in the font file, pixel resolution, and the margin size are used to calculate the size of texture atlas, which is allocated in the power of two and stored in the textureData. The allocated texture is stored as two channel information: one for the color information and another for the alpha component.

Each glyph present in the library is traversed and loaded using the FT_Load_Glyph API. This loads the current glyph in the glyph slot that can be retrieved with fontFace | glyph and passed to FT_Render_Glyph and rasters the bitmap bits. These bits are written in the textureData using the generateTexFromGlyph function. The glyph writing in the texture is done from the left to right direction. When the number of the glyph reaches the maximum number of glyphs per row, the write pointer is set to the next row. After all the glyphs are written in the textureData texture atlas, create an OpenGL ES texture object and set it with this information:

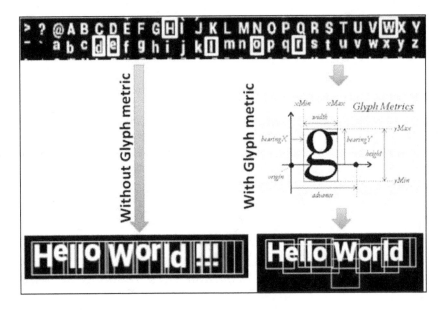

The `Font` class provides the interface to the external world for texture rendering purposes. This class first initializes the shaders in the `initModel` function, similar to other GLPI framework models. The `printText` function can be used to render the text information; this function accepts a text message string as the first argument and colors information in the RGBA format as next four parameters. The printing function should disable the culling and depth testing. The former testing is disabled because we want to view the font on the back faces as well; otherwise, it will surprise the user when texture goes suddenly missing. The latter case is helpful to keep the text rendered at the top always; we don't want this if it gets occluded by some other objects. The alpha blending must be turned on with the `glBlendFunc (GL_SRC_ALPHA, GL_ONE_MINUS_SRC_ALPHA)` blending function. Traversing through each character prints the string; the corresponding glyph is obtained from the glyphs map for the current character code and passed on to the `drawGlyph` function. The `drawGlyph` function makes use of the glyph structure and generates the necessary information to draw the bitmap image in the 2D or 3D space. Each glyph is rendered to a square and mapped with texture coordinates from the texture atlas; glyphs need to be placed according to font metrics or the glyph metric in the 2D/3D space.

The glyph metric contains the distance information associated with a particular glyph to help it in positioning while creating a text layout.

There's more...

The `printText` function renders a simple text where the transformation can be applied to the string to achieve various effects. We have seen that each string is rendered as a single glyph at a time. Therefore, it's possible to perform transforming animations on a single glyph. The following image is an example of the glyph animation, where glyphs are arranged in a circular fashion and rotates along the *y* axis:

In the current recipe, the `animateText` function can be used to render glyphs in an animated fashion. The function definition is explained later on; it accepts two more parameters: radius and rotation in addition to the `printText` parameter. This function renders glyphs that are arranged in a circular fashion and rotate along the *y* axis.

Based on the number of characters in the string and the given radius, a locus is calculated, and each character is placed in such a way that it always faces the camera. This way, the letter always faces the camera, irrespective of its position and angle along the *y* axis:

```
void Font::animateText(const char* str, GLfloat Red, GLfloat Green,
    GLfloat Blue, GLfloat Alpha,float radius,float rotation){
      // Same code as printText, reuse it
      int num_segments = strlen(str); int index = 0;
      float theta = 0;
      for (const char* c = str; *c != '\0'; c++) {
          TransformObj->TransformPushMatrix();
          TransformObj->TransformRotate(rot , 0.0, 1.0, 0.0);

           // position of character on the locus
           theta = 2.0f * PI_VAL * (index++)/num_segments;
           TransformObj->TransformPushMatrix();
           TransformObj->TransformTranslate
                 (radius*cosf(theta), 0.0, radius * sinf(theta));
           const Glyph& gi = glyphs[((unsigned long) *c)];
           TransformObj->TransformRotate(-rot , 0.0, 1.0, 0.0);

        // Draw Glyph
        drawGlyph(gi);
         TransformObj->TransformPopMatrix();
         TransformObj->TransformPopMatrix();
      }
      TransformObj->TransformPopMatrix();
}
```

See also

▶ *Rendering different languages with Harfbuzz*
▶ Refer to the *Applying texture with UV mapping* recipe in *Chapter 7, Textures and Mapping Techniques*

Rendering different languages with Harfbuzz

The FreeType library performs the rasterization operation in which each character is associated with a glyph index; this glyph index maps to the bitmap image. This information is more or less sufficient for simple scripts like English, which does not change its shape with the context. For example, based on the context, Arabic language has four different types of shape forms, where a character may change its shape depending on the own location or surrounding characters. With Unicode, there was a need for different languages to allow them to create complex transformations of glyphs, such as substitution, positioning, bi-directional text, context-sensitive shaping, and ligatures. Therefore, we need some special library that understands the context of the language and does the job of shaping for us; this is where Harfbuzz comes into the picture.

Harfbuzz is a text shaping engine that manages complex text; it performs the shaping job on the given Unicode text using the language script and layout direction specified by the user. This library does not provide text layout or rendering.

Here are some of the characteristics of complex text:

- **Bi-directionality**: Text written/displayed from left to right and vice versa direction. Arabic and Hebrew scripts use the right to left direction. However, most other languages, including Latin, are written from left to right. The following image shows the mix of English numerals and Arabic text in the bidirectional order.

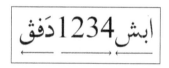

- **Shaping**: The character shape depends on the context. For example, the shape of the Arabic character changes when it connects to the adjacent characters. The following example shows contextual shaping in Arabic.

- **Ligatures**: A ligature is a special character that combines two or more characters into a single character. Here is an example of the Arabic ligature.

- ▶ **Positioning**: Glyphs are adjusted with respect to a given character vertically or horizontally; the following image demonstrates the concept of positioning in Thai.

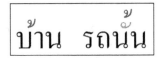

- ▶ **Reordering**: The position of a character depends on the context. In the following example, the last character of the Hindi text (Devanagri script) is placed in front of the second last character in the final output.

- ▶ **Split characters**: In this case, the same character appears in more than one position.

 Image courtesy: `http://scripts.sil.org`

This recipe will demonstrate text rendering in different types of languages, such as Arabic, Thai, Punjabi, Tamil, and English altogether.

Classes and data structure:

This recipe will introduce a new class, which is responsible for shaping the text as per the specified language.

FontShaping: This class is derived from `FontGenerator`. It inherits all the vital information from the FreeType library that is necessary for rasterization. This class uses the `Harfbuzz-ng` library for text shaping:

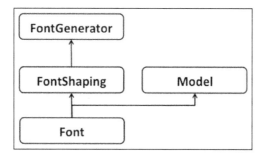

Getting ready

The `Harfbuzz-ng` library is an open source library written in ANSI-C. This library is freely available under the MIT license.

 The library can be downloaded at `http://freedesktop.org/wiki/Software/HarfBuzz/`.

Build process: The following steps provide a detailed description of the installation process for the `Harfbuzz-ng` library and other source files required to implement this recipe:

- ▸ **Android**: On the Android platform, we need the makefile to build the `Harfbuzz-ng` library. Add the `Android.mk` makefile under `GLPIFramework/Font/harfbuzz-ng`. Edit this makefile, as given in the following code. This will be compiled as a shared library and named as `GLPiharfbuzz`:

```
LOCAL_SRC_FILES:= \
    src/hb-blob.cc src/hb-buffer-serialize.cc \
src/hb-buffer.cc src/hb-common.cc \
src/hb-fallback-shape.cc src/hb-font.cc \
    src/hb-ft.cc src/hb-ot-tag.cc src/hb-set.cc \
src/hb-shape.cc src/hb-shape-plan.cc \
src/hb-shaper.cc src/hb-tt-font.cc \
    src/hb-unicode.cc src/hb-warning.cc \
src/hb-ot-layout.cc src/hb-ot-map.cc \
src/hb-ot-shape.cc src/hb-ot-shape-complex-arabic.cc\
    src/hb-ot-shape-complex-default.cc \
    src/hb-ot-shape-complex-indic.cc \
    src/hb-ot-shape-complex-indic-table.cc \
    src/hb-ot-shape-complex-myanmar.cc \
    src/hb-ot-shape-complex-sea.cc \
    src/hb-ot-shape-complex-thai.cc \
```

```
        src/hb-ot-shape-normalize.cc \
        src/hb-ot-shape-fallback.cc \

LOCAL_CPP_EXTENSION := .cc

LOCAL_C_INCLUDES += $(LOCAL_PATH)/src external/icu4c/common \
            $(LOCAL_PATH)/src
$(LOCAL_PATH)/../freetype/include

LOCAL_CFLAGS := -DHAVE_OT
LOCAL_MODULE:= GLPiharfbuzz
LOCAL_STATIC_LIBRARIES := GLPift2
include $(BUILD_SHARED_LIBRARY)
```

In `GLESNativeLib.java`, edit the `GLESNativeLib` class and add the reference of our `GLPiharfbuzz.so` shared library in order to link at runtime:

```
public class GLESNativeLib {
static {
 System.loadLibrary("GLPiharfbuzz");
       . . . . . . Other code
}
```

Open the `Android.mk` makefile in the present project directory under the (`<Source code path>/Localization/Android/JNI`) JNI folder and include the path of the `Android.mk` makefile that we have created in the `harfbuzz` library. Additionally, add the following source files in order to build this recipe:

```
FONT_PATH= $(FRAMEWORK_DIR)/Font
include $(MY_CUR_LOCAL_PATH)/..//..//../GLPIFramework/Font/
harfbuzz-ng/Android.mk

LOCAL_C_INCLUDES += $(FONT_PATH)/FreeType/include
LOCAL_C_INCLUDES += $(FONT_PATH)/harfbuzz-ng/src

LOCAL_SRC_FILES += $(SCENE_DIR)/FontGenerator.cpp \
                   $(SCENE_DIR)/FontShaping.cpp \
                   $(SCENE_DIR)/Font.cpp \
                   $(SCENE_DIR)/FontSample.cpp \
                   $(SCENE_DIR)/SimpleTexture.cpp
LOCAL_SHARED_LIBRARIES += GLPiharfbuzz
```

▸ **iOS**: On the iOS platform, we need to add the same FreeType project source files (mentioned under the `LOCAL_SRC_FILES` makefile variable) to your projects using the **Build Phase | Compile Sources** project properties. Click on add to select source files.

Provide a path to include the header files for the Harfbuzz project using **Build Settings | Search Paths | Header Search Paths**. For the present case, it should be:

```
../../../../GLPIFramework/Font/harfbuzz-ng/src/
```

In addition, add `FontGenerator.h/cpp`, `FontShaping.h/cpp`, `Font.h/cpp`, and `FontSample.h/cpp` using **File | Add Files to <Project Name>**.

How to do it...

Reuse the first implemented recipe, *Font rendering with FreeType project*, and proceed to the following procedure to program this recipe:

1. Create the `FontShaping` class derived from `FontGenerator` and add the following code. This class contains two major functions: `setDirectionAndScript` and `produceShape`:

```
class FontShaping : public FontGenerator{
 public:
     FontShaping(){ font = NULL; buffer = NULL; }
     ~FontShaping(){}
     void setDirectionAndScript
           (hb_buffer_t *&buffer, LanguageType languageType);
     bool produceShape(const char* string, vector<FT_UInt >&);

  private:
     hb_font_t   *font;
     hb_buffer_t  *buffer;
};
```

2. The `produceShape` function is responsible for text shaping using the `Harfbuzz-ng` library. It accepts a string that needs to be shaped as an input parameter and returns the code points after processing the shape. These code points are nothing but glyph indexes:

```
bool FontShaping::produceShape(const char* str,
std::vector< FT_UInt >& codePoints){
    FT_UInt glyph_index = 0;
    hb_glyph_info_t *glyph_info;
    FT_Face     ft_face = fontFace; //handle to face object
    if (!ft_face)
```

```
            { return false; }

    int num_chars = (int)strlen(str);
    if (!font) { font=hb_ft_font_create(ft_face, NULL); }

    /* Create a buffer for harfbuzz to use */
    if (buffer){ hb_buffer_destroy(buffer); buffer=NULL; }

    buffer = hb_buffer_create();

    // The languageType is an enum containing enum of
    // different supported languages
    setDirectionAndScript(buffer, languageType);

    /* Layout the text */
    hb_buffer_add_utf8(buffer, str, num_chars, 0, num_chars);
    hb_shape(font, buffer, NULL, 0);

    glyph_count = hb_buffer_get_length(buffer);
    glyph_info  = hb_buffer_get_glyph_infos(buffer, 0);
    for (int i = 0; i < glyph_count; i++) {
        glyph_index = glyph_info[i].codepoint;
        codePoints.push_back(glyph_index);
    }

    if (buffer) {hb_buffer_destroy(buffer); buffer=NULL;}
    if (codePoints.size() <=0 ) { return false; }
    return true;
}
```

3. The Harfbuzz requires scripting and layout direction hints in order to perform the text shaping. Therefore, the end user must provide the script type and the direction of the text layout:

```
void FontShaping::setDirectionAndScript
(hb_buffer_t *&buffer, LanguageType languageType){
    switch( languageType ){
        case Thai:{
            hb_buffer_set_direction(buffer, HB_DIRECTION_LTR);
            hb_buffer_set_script(buffer, HB_SCRIPT_THAI);
        }break;

        case Punjabi:{
```

```
            hb_buffer_set_direction(buffer,
                                    HB_DIRECTION_LTR);
            hb_buffer_set_script(buffer,
                                 HB_SCRIPT_GURMUKHI);
        }break;

        case Arabic:{
            hb_buffer_set_direction(buffer,
                                    HB_DIRECTION_RTL);
            hb_buffer_set_script(buffer, HB_SCRIPT_ARABIC);
        }break;

        case Tamil:{
            hb_buffer_set_direction(buffer,
                                    HB_DIRECTION_LTR);
            hb_buffer_set_script(buffer, HB_SCRIPT_TAMIL);
        }break;

        default:{
            hb_buffer_set_direction(buffer,
                                    HB_DIRECTION_LTR);
            hb_buffer_set_script(buffer, HB_SCRIPT_COMMON);
        }break;
    }
}
```

4. In the `FontGenerator::readFont` function, replace the following code. This will be useful to map the Harfbuzz-generated code points after text shaping:

```
for (FT_ULong charcode=FT_Get_First_Char(fontFace, &gindex);
        gindex != 0; charcode=FT_Get_Next_Char
        (fontFace, charcode, &gindex)) { . . }
```

Replace the preceding code with this code:

```
for(int myc = 0; myc < numGlyphs; myc++) {  . . . }
```

5. With respect to the preceding code changes done in the `FontGenerator::readFont` function, replace the following code in the `Font::printText` function:

```
    for (const char* c = str; *c != '\0'; c++) {
        const Glyph& gi = glyphs[((unsigned long) *c)];
        TransformObj->TransformTranslate
            (gi.advanceHorizontal / 2.0, 0.0, 0.0);
```

```
            drawGlyph(gi);
        }
```

Replace the preceding code with this code:

```
    std::vector< FT_UInt > codePointsPtr;
int glyph_count = 0;
if ( !produceShape(str, codePointsPtr, glyph_count) ){
    LOGI("Error in producing font shape");return;}

glyph_count = (int) codePointsPtr.size();
FT_UInt glyph_index = 0;
for (int i = 0; i < glyph_count; i++) {
    glyph_index = codePointsPtr.at(i);
    const Glyph& gi = glyphs[glyph_index];
    TransformObj->TransformTranslate
        (gi.advanceHorizontal / 2.0, 0.0, 0.0);
    drawGlyph(gi);
}
```

6. In the `Renderer::createModels` function, add the necessary font files as per the supported languages:

```
void Renderer::createModels(){
    clearModels();
    . . . . // Other code . . .
    addModel( new Font(strcat(fname,"ae_Nagham.ttf"),
        50, this, Arabic) );
    addModel( new Font(strcat(fname,"Roboto-Black.ttf"),
        50, this, English) );
    addModel( new Font(strcat(fname,"DroidSansThai.ttf"),
        50, this, Thai) );
    addModel( new Font(strcat(fname,"Uni Ila.Sundaram-
        03.ttf"),
        50, this, Tamil) );
    addModel(new Font(strcat(fname,"AnmolUni.ttf"),
        50, this, Punjabi) );
    addModel( new FontSample(this) );
}
```

How it works...

The working logic to render fonts in the current recipe is the same as the previous recipe. Therefore, it's strongly advisable to understand the first recipe before reading this section, which will only cover the text shaping working concept.

This recipe has introduced a new class called FontShaping, which is derived from FontGenerator. From now on, the Font class will be inheriting from FontShaping, instead of FontGenerator. The FontShaping class is the core engine for text shaping. Internally, this class makes use of the Harfbuzz-ng library.

We send UTF-8 encoding as an input parameter for multilingual text rendering in the Font::printText function. This function calls the FontShaping::produceShaping, which accepts one more argument in addition to the UTF-8 text, which is a vector list of code points that are returned from this function to the caller function. Code points are basically indexes of glyphs in the font file. In the multilingual text rendering, we have used the index of glyphs instead of character code in the glyphs map.

The Harfbuzz-ng library uses its own temporary buffer (of the hb_buffer_t type) to calculate the shaping information; this temporary buffer is allocated using the hb_buffer_create API. The created buffer is used to set the text layout direction (hb_buffer_set_direction) and language script (hb_buffer_set_script) in the setDirectionAndScript function.

Use the hb_buffer_add_utf8 API and provide the UTF8 encoded text to the Harfbuzz library. In addition, the font face information is required from FreeType in order to create its own font (hb_font_t). This font is created using the hb_ft_font_create API. The hb_shape API does the shaping job for the input string. It accepts the hb_font_t and hb_buffer_t object as an argument.

After the shaping process is completed in the library, the number of glyphs may change. The `hb_buffer_get_length` API provides the new glyph count. The shaping information can be retrieved with the `hb_buffer_get_glyph_infos` API, which returns the `hb_glyph_info_t` object that contains all the glyph code points. These code points are collected in a vector list and sent back to the `printText` function. Make sure that the temporary buffer must be released from the memory at the end of the process.

In the `Font::printText`, the `codePoint` or glyph indexes are retrieved from the vector list and render the same way (we have described in the first recipe).

See also

▸ *Font rendering with the FreeType project*

Rendering text on Head Up Display

Text rendering on the screen coordinate system is a very common use case of printing text. The HUD, also known as overlays, allows you to render the text on top of a normal scene. The depth of the scene object does not change the size of the text. Examples of HUD are menu items, status bar, game scoreboards, and so on.

Technically, HUD is an orthographic view where the dimensions of left, right, top, and bottom are set equal to the viewport of the scene. In this recipe, we will print the vertex position of a rotating 3D cube in the screen coordinates. All vertices in the cube (near or far) have text in equal size. It is not affected by the distance of vertices from the camera position:

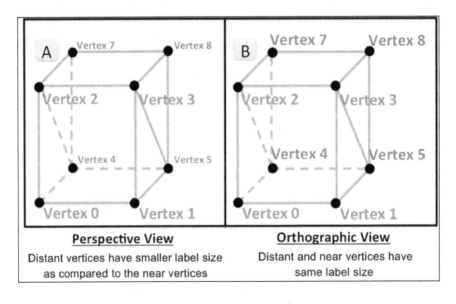

Perspective View

Distant vertices have smaller label size as compared to the near vertices

Orthographic View

Distant and near vertices have same label size

In the current recipe, we will reuse the *Drawing APIs in OpenGL ES 3.0* recipe from *Chapter 2, OpenGL ES 3.0 Essentials*. This will render a rotating cube in the 3D space. We will use the HUD mechanism to display the positions of each vertex in the screen coordinates.

Getting ready

Reuse the last recipe, *Rendering different languages with Harfbuzz*, and add the following files from another recipe *Drawing APIs in OpenGL ES 3.0* in *Chapter 2, OpenGL ES 3.0 Essentials*:

1. Open the `Cube.h` and `Cube.cpp` GL ES program files
2. Open the `CubeVertex.glsl` and `CubeFragment.glsl` GLSL shader files

How to do it...

The following instructions will provide a step-by-step procedure to implement HUD:

1. Edit the `Cube.h/cpp` and define a new method called `GetScreenCoordinates`. This will produce the screen coordinates from the logical coordinates of the cube vertices and collect them in a `screenCoordinateVector` vector list. There is no change required for imported shaders:

```
void Cube::GetScreenCoordinates(){
    // Get Screen Coordinates for cube vertices
    int    viewport_matrix[4];
    float screenCoord[3];
    glGetIntegerv( GL_VIEWPORT, viewport_matrix );
    screenCoordinateVector.clear(); // Clear vector

    for(int i=0; i<sizeof(cubeVerts)/(sizeof(GLfloat)*3);i++){
        GLfloat x = cubeVerts[i][0]; // Vertex X coordinate
        GLfloat y = cubeVerts[i][1]; // Vertex Y coordinate
        GLfloat z = cubeVerts[i][2]; // Vertex Z coordinate

        int success = TransformObj->TransformProject
                (x, y, z,
                TransformObj->TransformGetModelViewMatrix(),
                TransformObj->TransformGetProjectionMatrix(),
                viewport_matrix, &screenCoord[0],
```

```
                              &screenCoord[1], &screenCoord[2]);

            if (!success)
                {memset(screenCoord,0,sizeof(float)*3);continue;}
            int screenX  = screenCoord[0];
            int screenY  = viewport_matrix[3] - screenCoord[1];
            screenCoordinateVector.push_back
                        (glm::vec2(screenX,screenY));

        }
    }
```

2. Call the `GetScreenCoordinates` in the `Cube::Render` function after rendering the primitives. For this recipe, we change the rendering primitive from `GL_TRIANGLES` to `GL_LINE_LOOP`:

```
void Cube::Render(){

    . . . . Other Rendering Code . . . .
    glVertexAttribPointer(attribVertex, 3, GL_FLOAT,
            GL_FALSE, 0, vertexBuffer);
    glDrawArrays(GL_LINE_LOOP, 0, 36);
    GetScreenCoordinates();
}
```

3. In `FontSample.h/cpp`, create a function called `HeadUpDisplay`; this function will be responsible for setting the correct projection system and its dimensions for the head up display. The projection system for HUD must be orthographic and the dimension must be set to the viewport dimension:

```
void FontSample::HeadUpDisplay(int width, int height){
    TransformObj->TransformSetMatrixMode( PROJECTION_MATRIX );

    TransformObj->TransformLoadIdentity();
    // Left ,Right ,Bottom , Top, Near, Far
    TransformObj->TransformOrtho(0, width, 0, height,-1,1);

    TransformObj->TransformSetMatrixMode( VIEW_MATRIX );
    TransformObj->TransformLoadIdentity();

    TransformObj->TransformSetMatrixMode( MODEL_MATRIX );
    TransformObj->TransformLoadIdentity();
}
```

4. In `FontSample::Render()`, call the `HeadUpDisplay` function before rendering any drawing primitive. This will enable the HUD viewing. Get the vector list from the `Cube` class and render the vertex position with the `Font::printText` function:

```
void FontSample::Render(){
    int viewport_matrix[4];
    glGetIntegerv( GL_VIEWPORT, viewport_matrix );
    HeadUpDisplay(viewport_matrix[2], viewport_matrix[3]);

    Font* English = dynamic_cast<Font*>
                    (RendererHandler->getModel(FontEnglish));
    Cube* cubeObject = dynamic_cast<Cube*>
                    (RendererHandler->getModel(CubeType));
    std::vector<glm::vec2>* vertexVector =
                    cubeObject->getScreenCoordinateVertices();

    char buffer[500];
    for(int i = 0; i<vertexVector->size(); i++) {
        TransformObj->TransformPushMatrix();
        TransformObj->TransformTranslate
        (vertexVector->at(i).x, vertexVector->at(i).y, 0.0);
        TransformObj->TransformScale(2.0, 2.0, 2.0);
        memset(buffer, 0, 500);
        sprintf(buffer, "Vertex pos: %d,%d", (int)
        vertexVector->at(i).x, (int)vertexVector->at(i).y);
        English->printText(buffer, 1.0, 1.0, 1.0, 1.0f );
        TransformObj->TransformPopMatrix();
    }
}
```

How it works...

The projection system for head up display must always be in the orthographic view. The `FontSample::HeadUpDisplay` function sets the projection matrix to an orthographic view with the help of the `Transform::TransformOrtho` API. It accepts eight parameters, in which the left-right and top-bottom must be specified with the correct dimension matched to the viewport size. Set the `Model` and `View` as the identity matrix:

```
TransformObj->TransformSetMatrixMode( PROJECTION_MATRIX );
TransformObj->TransformLoadIdentity();
```

```
// Left, Right, Bottom, Top, Near, Far
TransformObj->TransformOrtho(0, width, 0, height,-1,1);
```

The `HeadUpDisplay` function must be called before rendering primitives. For this recipe, we have collected screen coordinates of each vertex from the Cube class and displayed them using the `Font::printText` function with their respective screen coordinates position. The screen space coordinates of a vertex can be calculated in the logical coordinate system using the `Transform::TransformProject` function:

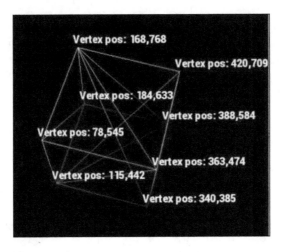

See also

 ▸ *Rendering different languages with Harfbuzz*

 ▸ Refer to the *Understanding projection system in GLPI* recipe in *Chapter 2, OpenGL ES 3.0 Essentials*

 ▸ Refer to the *Drawing APIs in OpenGL ES 3.0* recipe in *Chapter 2, OpenGL ES 3.0 Essentials*

9
Postscreen Processing and Image Effects

In this chapter, we will cover the following recipes:

- ▸ Detecting scene edges with the Sobel operator
- ▸ Making the scene blur with the Gaussian blur equation
- ▸ Making a scene glow real time with the bloom effect
- ▸ Painting the scene like a cartoon shading
- ▸ Generating an embossed scene
- ▸ Implementing grayscale and CMYK conversions
- ▸ Implementing fisheye with barrel distortion
- ▸ Implementing the binocular view with procedural texturing
- ▸ Twirling the image
- ▸ Sphere illusion with textured quadrilateral

Introduction

This chapter will unfold the endless possibilities of a scene and its image-based effects, which are widely used in the field of data visualization and after effects. Practically, objects are represented as a set of vertices in the 3D space. As the number of vertices go higher, the time complexity of the scene increases. Moreover, representing the object in terms of an image has a time complexity proportional to the number of fragments in the scene. Additionally, many effects can only be efficiently possible in the image space rather than implementing in the vertex space, such as blurring, blooming, cloud rendering, and so on.

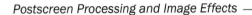

The term post screen processing is a texel manipulation technique applied on an OpenGL ES scene once it's rendered. To be more specific, the scene is first rendered to an offscreen surface where effects are applied. Then, this manipulated offscreen texture is rendered back to the screen surface.

In post processing, the outcome of a given texel is affected by its surrounding texels. Such techniques cannot be applied on live scenes because the vertex and fragment shader works locally. This means a vertex shader is only aware of the current vertex and the fragment shader about the current fragment; they cannot use elements information of their neighbors. This limitation can be fixed easily by rendering the scene into a texture, which allows the fragment shader to read any texel information present in the texture. After the scene is rendered to a texture, the image/texture-based techniques are applied to the texture.

The image-based effects are applied to an image texture using the fragment shader. During the post-processing implementation, the rendered scene goes through a number of passes, depending on the complexity of the effect. At each pass, it saves the processed output in a texture and then passes it on to next pass as an input.

The post screen processing execution model for post processing can be majorly divided into four sections:

- ▶ **Creation of the framebuffer**: The first stage requires creation of an offline texture to render the scene into it. This is achieved by creating the **Frame Buffer Objects** (FBO). Depending on the requirements of the scene, various textures or buffers, such as color, stencil, and depth are attached to the FBO.

- ▶ **Render the scene to texture**: By default, the OpenGL ES scene renders to a default framebuffer. As a prerequisite of post processing, this rendering must be diverted to an offline texture (the FBO texture) by binding the FBO handle to the current rendering pipeline. This ensures that rendering must happen on the FBO texture rather than the default framebuffer.

- ▶ **Apply texture effects**: After the scene is rendered into the texture, it's like an image in the memory where various image effects can be applied. Depending on the post processing complexities, you may require multiple passes to process the desired effect. In the multipass post processing, we may require two or more FBO's in order to hold the intermediate processed result of the current pass in it and to be used in the next or later passes.

- ▶ **Render to the default framebuffer**: Finally, the post processed textured scene is rendered back to the default framebuffer, which becomes visible on the scene. The following figure shows an edge detection example, in which various stages of the post screen processing are illustrated:

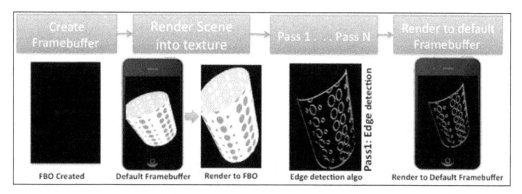

| FBO Created | Default Framebuffer | Render to FBO | Edge detection algo | Render to Default Framebuffer |

Detecting scene edges with the Sobel operator

Edge detection is an image-processing technique used to detect boundaries in an image. It is widely used in the field of computer vision, data visualization, and surface topology. For example, the pencil sketch effect of an image is nothing, but an application of edge detection algorithm. This recipe will demonstrate the edge detection technique using the Sobel operator or filter.

A Sobel filter measures the change in the gradient of an image in which it recognizes the regions of an image where the frequency of the color transition is higher. These higher transition regions shows sharp changes in the gradient that eventually correspond to the edges. The Sobel operator uses convolution kernels to detect the edge portions in the image. A convolution kernel is a matrix that contains predefined weights that formulate the calculation of the current pixel based on the neighboring pixels intensity and weights contained in the convolution matrix itself.

A Sobel filter uses two 3 x 3 convolution kernels for edge detection processing; one operates on the neighboring pixels in the horizontal direction to the current pixel. Similarly, the other operates on the vertical neighboring pixels. The following image shows two convolution kernels:

$$Px = \begin{bmatrix} 1 & 0 & -1 \\ 2 & 0 & -2 \\ 1 & 0 & -1 \end{bmatrix} \quad Py = \begin{bmatrix} 1 & 2 & 1 \\ 0 & 0 & 0 \\ -1 & -2 & -1 \end{bmatrix}$$

Now, we know very well that the Sobel filter approximates the gradient of an image. Therefore, the RGB information of the image must be brought to some gradient form and the best way is to calculate the brightness or luminance of the image. An RGB color represents a 3D space of color in the R, G, and B direction. These colors must bring in 1D gradient space using the brightness information of the image. The brightness of an image is represented by gradient colors between white and black:

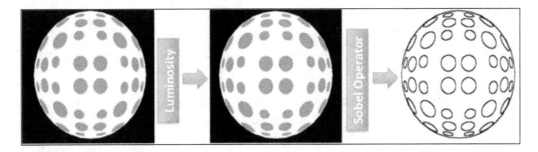

Getting ready

Post-processing techniques heavily rely on texturing basics and FBO. Therefore, as a prerequisite for this chapter, you must understand these concepts. We have covered these concepts very well in *Chapter 7, Textures and Mapping Techniques*. For more information, refer to the *See also* subsection in this recipe.

> The texture filtering technique must be GL_NEAREST to detect more edges and darker appearances. Unlike the GL_LINEAR filtering, which uses the weighted average of the four surrounding pixels closest to texture coordinates, the GL_NEAREST filtering uses the pixel color that is closest to texture coordinates, therefore resulting gradients with higher chances of sharp changes in frequency.

How to do it...

Perform the following step-by-step guidelines to understand the programming procedure. Make sure that you refer to the *See also* section for dependencies before you read this section. This recipe reuses the FBO recipe from textures and renames the class from DemoFBO to EdgeDetection:

1. In the constructor, load the SimpleTexture and ObjLoader class. The former class renders the polka dot pattern mesh and the latter class is used to render the FBO texture.

2. In this class, create two variables called `DefaultFBO` and `FboId` to hold the handles of the default framebuffer and FBO respectively. Create two more variables: `textureId` and `depthTextureId` to hold the handles of the color texture and the depth texture in the FBO.

3. Create the FBO in the `initModel()` with user-defined dimensions (width and height) as per the application requirement. This recipe uses the same dimension as the render buffer dimension. The framebuffer is created in the `GenerateFBO()` function, which creates a color buffer and a depth buffer to store the scene color and depth information:

```
void EdgeDetection::GenerateFBO(){
glGetRenderbufferParameteriv(GL_RENDERBUFFER,
GL_RENDERBUFFER_WIDTH, &TEXTURE_WIDTH);

glGetRenderbufferParameteriv(GL_RENDERBUFFER,
GL_RENDERBUFFER_HEIGHT, &TEXTURE_HEIGHT);


glGenFramebuffers(1, &FboId); // Create FBO
glBindFramebuffer(GL_FRAMEBUFFER, FboId);

// Create color and depth buffer textureobject
 textureId = generateTexture(
 TEXTURE_WIDTH,TEXTURE_HEIGHT);
 depthTextureId = generateTexture(TEXTURE_WIDTH,
 TEXTURE_HEIGHT,true);

// attach the texture to FBO color
// attachment point
glFramebufferTexture2D(GL_FRAMEBUFFER,
GL_COLOR_ATTACHMENT0, GL_TEXTURE_2D, textureId, 0);

// attach the texture to FBO color
// attachment point
glFramebufferTexture2D(GL_FRAMEBUFFER,
GL_DEPTH_ATTACHMENT, GL_TEXTURE_2D,depthTextureId, 0);

// check FBO status
GLenum status = glCheckFramebufferStatus(
GL_FRAMEBUFFER);
if(status != GL_FRAMEBUFFER_COMPLETE){
printf("Framebuffer creation fails: %d", status);
          }
glBindFramebuffer(GL_FRAMEBUFFER, 0);
      }
```

4. Render the scene using the `RenderObj()` function. The scene is rendered to the perspective projection system using `SetUpPerspectiveProjection()`, which is called before `RenderObj()`. FBO must be bound before drawing a scene. This will render the color information of scenes to FBO's color texture and depth information to FBO's depth texture.

5. Set the model-view matrix and draw a scene. Make sure to restore the default framebuffer at last after the scene is rendered to the FBO:

```
void EdgeDetection::RenderObj(){
    // Get the default Framebuffer
    glGetIntegerv(GL_FRAMEBUFFER_BINDING, &DefaultFBO);

    // Bind Framebuffer object
    glBindFramebuffer(GL_FRAMEBUFFER,FboId);
    glViewport(0, 0, TEXTURE_WIDTH, TEXTURE_HEIGHT);
    glFramebufferTexture2D(GL_FRAMEBUFFER,GL_COLOR_ATTACHMENT0,
    GL_TEXTURE_2D, textureId,0);
    glFramebufferTexture2D(GL_FRAMEBUFFER, GL_DEPTH_ATTACHMENT,
    GL_TEXTURE_2D, depthTextureId, 0);

    glClear(GL_COLOR_BUFFER_BIT|GL_DEPTH_BUFFER_BIT);
    objModel->Render();

    glBindFramebuffer(GL_FRAMEBUFFER, DefaultFBO);
}
```

6. Now, we are good to go with edge detection with the help of the `SimpleTexture` class. This class will take the saved texture from the FBO and apply the edge detection shader to it. For more information on how the `SimpleTexture` class works, refer to the *Applying texture with the UV mapping* recipe in *Chapter 7, Textures and Mapping Techniques*.

7. The FBO texture is rendered to a quad of size two. This quad fits to the complete viewport. This is why the orthographic projection system must also be defined with the same dimensions:

```
TransformObj->TransformSetMatrixMode( PROJECTION_MATRIX );
TransformObj->TransformLoadIdentity();
float span = 1.0;
TransformObj->TransformOrtho(-span,span,-span,span,-span,span);
```

8. The `EdgeDetect()` function applies the Sobel filter using the `SimpleTexture` class. This sets the required `pixelSize` uniform in the edge detection shader:

```
void EdgeDetection::EdgeDetect(){
    glDisable(GL_DEPTH_TEST);
    glBindFramebuffer(GL_FRAMEBUFFER, DefaultFBO);
    glViewport(0, 0, TEXTURE_WIDTH, TEXTURE_HEIGHT);
    glActiveTexture (GL_TEXTURE0);
    glBindTexture(GL_TEXTURE_2D,textureId);

    program = ProgramManagerObj->Program
((char*)"EdgeDetection" );
    glUseProgram( program->ProgramID );
    GLint PIXELSIZE = ProgramManagerObj-
>ProgramGetUniformLocation
(program, (char*) "pixelSize");
    glUniform2f(PIXELSIZE, 1.0/TEXTURE_HEIGHT,
1.0/TEXTURE_WIDTH);
    textureQuad->Render();
}
```

9. Implement the following `EdgeDetectionFragment.glsl` fragment shader for edge detection. There is no change required in the vertex shader. Use `SimpleTexture::InitModel()` to load this shader:

```
#version 300 es
precision mediump float;
in vec2 TexCoord;
uniform vec2 pixelSize;
uniform sampler2D Tex1;
layout(location = 0) out vec4 outColor;
uniform float GradientThreshold;
float p00,p10,p20,p01,p21,p02,p12,p22,x,y,px,py,distance;
vec3 lum = vec3(0.2126, 0.7152, 0.0722);
void main(){
    x = pixelSize.x; y = pixelSize.y;
    p00 = dot(texture(Tex1, TexCoord+vec2(-x, y)).rgb, lum);
    p10 = dot(texture(Tex1, TexCoord+vec2(-x,0.)).rgb, lum);
```

```
p20 = dot(texture(Tex1, TexCoord+vec2(-x,-y)).rgb, lum);
p01 = dot(texture(Tex1, TexCoord+vec2(0., y)).rgb, lum);
p21 = dot(texture(Tex1, TexCoord+vec2(0.,-y)).rgb, lum);
p02 = dot(texture(Tex1, TexCoord+vec2( x, y)).rgb, lum);
p12 = dot(texture(Tex1, TexCoord+vec2( x,0.)).rgb, lum);
p22 = dot(texture(Tex1, TexCoord+vec2( x,-y)).rgb, lum);

// Apply Sobel Operator

px = p00 + 1.0*p10 + p20 - (p02 + 1.0*p12 + p22);
py = p00 + 1.0*p01 + p02 - (p20 + 1.0*p21 + p22);
// Check frequency change with given threshold
if ((distance = px*px+py*py) > GradientThreshold ){
    outColor = vec4(0.0, 0.0, 0.0, 1.0);
}else{ outColor = vec4(1.0); }
}
```

How it works...

Edge detection is implemented in the EdgeDetection class. This class contains two objects of the ObjLoader and SimpleTexture class. The former class renders the 3D mesh and the latter renders the texture on the HUD. First, the scene is rendered to a frame buffer object. This allows you to capture the current scene in the texture form in the color buffer of the frame buffer object. This texture is then applied to the Sobel operator convolution filter, which detects edges. Finally, the process texture is rendered back to the HUD using the object of the SimpleTexture class.

Let's understand its functioning in detail. The EdgeDetection class first initializes the ObjLoader and SimpleTexture class objects in the constructor. In the initModel() function, it calls GenerateFBO to create an offline rendering buffer (FBO) with the same dimensions as the render buffer. In the render function, this FBO is attached to the drawing pipeline so that all drawing commands are diverted to our FBO, rather than going to the default buffer. The ObjLoader class renders the scene to this FBO's texture (with textureId). The graphics pipeline again binds back to the default framebuffer so that the output is visible on the screen. Now, the SimpleTexture class handles the remaining job of finding the scene edges through the EdgeDetectionFragment.glsl shader. This shader implements the Sobel operator and accepts a texture as an input. This texture must be the FBO's color texture (textureId). In the fragment shader program, each time a current fragment is processed, it retrieves a 3 x 3 fragment matrix around it. This matrix is then multiplied by the convolution kernel along the horizontal and vertical direction to result px and py. This result is used in calculating the intensity (distance) and compared with the given threshold (GradientThreshold). If the comparison is greater, then the fragment is colored black; otherwise, it's colored with white color:

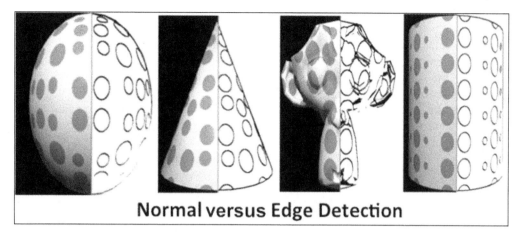

Normal versus Edge Detection

See also

▸ Refer to the *Implementing render to texture with Frame Buffer Objects* recipe in *Chapter 7, Textures and Mapping Techniques*

▸ *Implementing grayscale and CMYK conversions*

▸ Refer to the *Generating the polka dot pattern* recipe in *Chapter 6, Working with Shaders*

Making the scene blur with the Gaussian blur equation

The blur effect is an image processing technique that softens an image or makes it hazy. As a result, the image appears smoother like viewing it through a translucent mirror. It reduces the overall sharpness of the image by decreasing the image noise. It's used in many applications, such as blooming effect, depth-of-field, fuzzy glass, and heat haze effect.

The blurring effect in this recipe is implemented using the Gaussian blur equation. Like other image processing techniques, the Gaussian blur equation also makes use of the convolution filter to process image pixels. Bigger the size of the convolution filter, better and dense is the blur effect. The working principle of the Gaussian blur algorithm is very simple. Basically, each pixel's color is mixed with the neighboring pixel's color. This mixing is performed on the basis of a weight system. Closer pixels are given more weight as compared to farther ones.

The math behind the Gaussian blur equation:

The Gaussian blur equation makes use of the Gaussion function. The mathematical form of the equation and graphical representation of this function in one and two-dimensional space, as shown in the left-hand side of the following figure. This recipe uses the 2D form of this function, where σ is the standard deviation of the distribution, x and y are the texel distance in the horizontal and vertical axis from the current texel on which the convolution filter works. The Gaussian function is very useful in making high frequency values smoother:

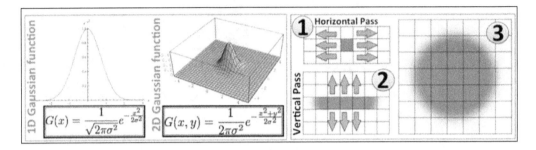

Working principle:

The Gaussian filter is applied on each and every texel. As a result, the change in its original value is based on the neighboring pixels. The number of the neighboring pixels depends on the size of the convolution kernel. For a 9 x 9 kernel, the number of computations required are 9 * 9 = 81. These can be reduced by performing the Gaussian blur in two passes, wherein the first pass is applied on each texel in the horizontal direction (s axis), as shown in the upper-right corner image by label (1), and the second pass is applied in the vertical direction (t axis) represented by label (2). This requires 18 computations and the result is the same as 81 calculations. The final output of the Gaussian blur is represented by label 3.

There are five steps required to implement the Gaussian blur:

- **Filter size**: This depends on many things, such as the processing time, image size, output quality, and so on. Bigger the filter size, more the processing time, and better the results. For this recipe, we will use the 9 x 9 convolution filter.

- **FBO**: This creates two FBO's, the first one with the color and depth information and the second one only with the color information.

- **Render to texture**: This renders the scene to the first FBO's color texture.

- **Horizontal pass**: This uses the color buffer of the first FBO and applies the horizontal Gaussian blur pass.

- **Vertical pass**: This reuses the first FBO's color buffer and applies the vertical pass.

How to do it...

This recipe makes use of the first recipe on edge detection. We renamed the class from `EdgeDetection` to `GaussianBlur`. The steps to understand the required changes are as follows:

1. Create a new vertex shader called `Vertex.glsl`, as shown in the following code. This vertex shader will be shared by horizontal and vertical Gaussian blur passes:

```
#version 300 es
// Vertex information
layout(location = 0) in vec3  VertexPosition;
layout(location = 1) in vec2  VertexTexCoord;

out vec2 TexCoord;
uniform mat4 ModelViewProjectionMatrix;
void main( void ) {
    TexCoord = VertexTexCoord;
    vec4 glPos = ModelViewProjectionMatrix *
    vec4(VertexPosition,1.0);
    vec2 Pos = sign(glPos.xy);
    gl_Position = ModelViewProjectionMatrix *
    vec4(VertexPosition,1.0);
}
```

2. Create a new fragment shader called `BlurHorizontal.glsl` and add the following code:

```
#version 300 es
precision mediump float;
in vec2 TexCoord;
uniform vec2 pixelSize;
uniform sampler2D Tex1;

layout(location = 0) out vec4 outColor;

uniform float PixOffset[5];    // Texel distance
uniform float Weight[5];       // Gaussian weights

void main(){
    vec4 sum = texture(Tex1, TexCoord) * Weight[0];
    for( int i = 1; i < 5; i++ ){ // Loop 4 times
        sum+=texture( Tex1, TexCoord + vec2(PixOffset[i],0.0)
```

```
        * pixelSize.x) * Weight[i];
        sum += texture( Tex1, TexCoord - vec2(PixOffset[i],0.0)
        * pixelSize.x) * Weight[i];
    }
    outColor = sum;
}
```

3. Similarly, create another new fragment shader called `BlurVertical.glsl`:

```
// Use same code from BlurHorizontal.glsl
void main(){
    vec4 sum = texture(Tex1, TexCoord) * Weight[0];
    for( int i = 1; i < 5; i++ ){ // Loop 4 times
        sum+=texture( Tex1, TexCoord + vec2(0.0, PixOffset[i])
        * pixelSize.y) * Weight[i];
        sum += texture( Tex1, TexCoord - vec2(0.0, PixOffset[i])
        * pixelSize.y) * Weight[i];}
    outColor = sum;
}
```

4. Compile and link these shaders in the `SimpleTexture::InitModel()`.

5. Calculate the Gaussian weight using `GaussianEquation()`. We assumed sigma (σ) as 10.0. The parameter value contains the texel distance along the horizontal or vertical direction, and the σ is the variance or standard deviation of the Gaussian distribution:

```
float GaussianBlur::GaussianEquation(float value, float sigma){
return 1./(2.*PI*sigma)*exp(-(value*value)/(2*sigma));
}
```

6. Calculate the weights for the horizontal and vertical Gaussian fragment shader, as given in the following code using the `GaussianEquation` function:

```
    gWeight[0]   = GaussianBlur::GaussianEquation(0, sigma);
    sum          = gWeight[0]; // Weight for centered texel

    for(int i = 1; i<FILTER_SIZE; i++){
        gWeight[i] = GaussianBlur::GaussianEquation(i, sigma);

        // Why multiplied by 2.0? because each weight
        // is applied in +ve and -ve direction from the
        // centered texel in the fragment shader.
```

```
        sum += 2.0 * gWeight[i];
    }

    for(int i = 0; i<FILTER_SIZE; i++){
        gWeight[i] = gWeight[i] / sum;
    }

    if (GAUSSIAN_WEIGHT_HOR >= 0){
        glUniform1fv(GAUSSIAN_WEIGHT_HOR,
        sizeof(gWeight)/sizeof(float), gWeight);
    }

    // Similarly, pass the weight to vertical Gaussian
    // blur fragment shader corresponding weight
    // variable GAUSSIAN_WEIGHT_VERT

    float pixOffset[FILTER_SIZE];
    // Calculate pixel offset
    for(int i=0; i<FILTER_SIZE; i++){ pixOffset[i] = float(i);
}
    if (PIXEL_OFFSET_HOR >= 0){
        glUniform1fv(PIXEL_OFFSET_HOR, sizeof(pixOffset)/
        sizeof(float), pixOffset);
    }
```

7. Create two FBO's within the `Gaussian::InitModel` with `GenerateBlurFBO1` (with the color and depth texture) and `GenerateBlurFBO2` (only the color buffer). These create two FBO's with the `blurFboId1` and `blurFboId2` handles respectively. The first FBO uses an additional buffer for depth because we want depth testing to be performed so that the correct image will be rendered to the color texture of this FBO.

8. Render the scene with the perspective projection system to the first FBO (`blurFboId1` color texture). This will render the scene image to the color texture of this FBO:

```
void GaussianBlur::Render(){
    // Set up perspective projection
    SetUpPerspectiveProjection();

    RenderObj();
    // Set up orthographic project for HUD display
    SetUpOrthoProjection();
    RenderHorizontalBlur();
```

```
            RenderVerticalBlur();
    }

    void GaussianBlur::RenderObj(){
            // Get the current framebuffer handle
            glGetIntegerv(GL_FRAMEBUFFER_BINDING, &CurrentFbo);

            // Bind Framebuffer 1
            glBindFramebuffer(GL_FRAMEBUFFER,blurFboId1);
            glViewport(0, 0, TEXTURE_WIDTH, TEXTURE_HEIGHT);
            glFramebufferTexture2D(GL_FRAMEBUFFER, GL_COLOR_-
            ATTACHMENT0, GL_TEXTURE_2D, textureId,0);
            glFramebufferTexture2D(GL_FRAMEBUFFER, GL_DEPTH_-
            ATTACHMENT, GL_TEXTURE_2D, depthTextureId, 0);

            glClear(GL_COLOR_BUFFER_BIT|GL_DEPTH_BUFFER_BIT);
            objModel->Render();

            glBindFramebuffer(GL_FRAMEBUFFER, CurrentFbo);
    }
```

9. Now, set the second FBO (with the `blurFboId2` handle) as a render destination, reuse the color texture from the first FBO (which contains the scene image), and pass it on to the horizontal blur pass (pass 1) with the `RenderHorizontalBlur()` function. This will produce the horizontal blur scene image on the (`textureId2`) color buffer of the second FBO. Note that the project system should be orthographic before the second FBO is set:

```
    void GaussianBlur::RenderHorizontalBlur(){
            glDisable(GL_DEPTH_TEST);

            // Bind Framebuffer 2
            glBindFramebuffer(GL_FRAMEBUFFER,blurFboId2);
            glViewport(0, 0, TEXTURE_WIDTH, TEXTURE_HEIGHT);
            glFramebufferTexture2D(GL_FRAMEBUFFER,
              GL_COLOR_ATTACHMENT0, GL_TEXTURE_2D, textureId2, 0);
            glActiveTexture (GL_TEXTURE0);
            glBindTexture(GL_TEXTURE_2D, textureId);

            // Apply the shader for horizontal blur pass
            program = textureQuad->ApplyShader(HorizontalBlurShader);
            textureQuad->Render();
            TransformObj->TransformError();
    }
```

10. Finally, use the default framebuffer and apply the pass 2 (vertical blur) using the
`RenderVerticalBlur` function in the second FBO's texture (`textureId2`):

```
void GaussianBlur::RenderVerticalBlur() {
    glDisable(GL_DEPTH_TEST);

// Restore to old framebuffer
    glBindFramebuffer(GL_FRAMEBUFFER, CurrentFbo);
    glViewport(0, 0, TEXTURE_WIDTH, TEXTURE_HEIGHT);
    glActiveTexture (GL_TEXTURE1);
    glBindTexture(GL_TEXTURE_2D,textureId2);

// Apply the shader for horizontal blur pass
    program = textureQuad->ApplyShader(VerticalBlurShader);
    GLint PIXELSIZE = ProgramManagerObj->ProgramGetUniform-
    Location( program, (char *) "pixelSize" );
    glUniform2f(PIXELSIZE, 1.0/TEXTURE_HEIGHT,
    1.0/TEXTURE_WIDTH);

    textureQuad->Render();
}
```

How it works...

The basic idea behind the Gaussian blur is to create a new texel of an image by taking a weighted average of the texels around it. Weights are applied using the Gaussian distribution function. For each texel, we need to create a square around the centered pixel. For instance, for a given texel, a square kernel of five texel contributes 25 texels weighted average to get the middle texel. Now, as the diameter of the kernel grows, the operation becomes expensive because it needs to read more texels to contribute. This expense is not linear fashioned because a 9 x 9 kernel requires 81 texels to read, which is almost four times the previous kernel.

Now, the Gaussian blur can be optimized to read less texels and yet achieve the same results. This can be done by dividing the kernel operation into two passes as the horizontal and vertical pass. In the former, only row-wise elements of the kernel are used for weighted average to calculate the middle texel of the row. Similarly, for the latter case, columnwise elements are considered. This way, it requires 18 (9 + 9) pixels to read instead of 81.

Now, let's understand the working of this recipe. The Gaussian blur is applied in two phases. Each phase works on one-dimensional row and column. The first phase is a horizontal pass, where texels in the horizontal direction are considered by the Gaussian kernel. This phase is called pass 1, which is performed using `BlurHorizontal.glsl`. Similarly, the second phase for pass 2 is carried within the `BlurVertical.glsl` fragment shader. Both these fragment shaders share a common vertex shader called `Vertex.glsl` and these shaders are managed by the `SimpleTexture` class.

When the `GaussianBlur` class is initialized, it creates two FBO's. The first FBO requires the color and depth information to render the scene. However, the second FBO does not require any depth texture information because it works on the first FBO's color texture, which is already taken the depth of the scene into consideration.

The scene is rendered to the color texture of the first FBO. This color texture is shared with the `SimpleTexture` class where the first pass (horizontal blur) is applied to it. During the second pass, the second FBO is used and provided with the horizontal, blurred color texture (from the first FBO) as an input. This texture (horizontal blurred) processes the vertical blur shader and stores the processed texture in the color buffer of the second FBO. Finally, the scene is attached to the default framebuffer, and the color buffer from the second FBO is rendered on the screen:

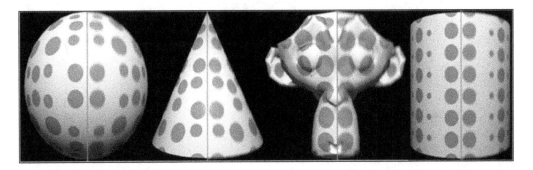

See also

▸   *Detecting the scene edges with the Sobel operator*

Making a scene glow real time with the bloom effect

Blooming is a very useful post screen processing technique that makes a real-time scene glow. With this effect, certain parts of the scene appear highly brighter and give an illusion of emitting scattered light in the atmosphere. This technique is widely used in gaming and cinematic effects.

The working principle of the bloom effect is very simple. The following image shows a pictorial representation of the working model, which is used in the current recipe. First, the scene is rendered to an offline framebuffer or texture (label **1**), where its texture is used as an input in the next stage that detects the bright portions in the scene and writes in a new texture (label **2**). This texture is then passed on to the horizontal (label **3**) and vertical blur (label **4**), which applies the Gaussian blurring effect to make it blurred and scattered a bit. This output (label **4**) is then finally combined on top of the original rendered scene (label **1**), which produces a glow-like effect:

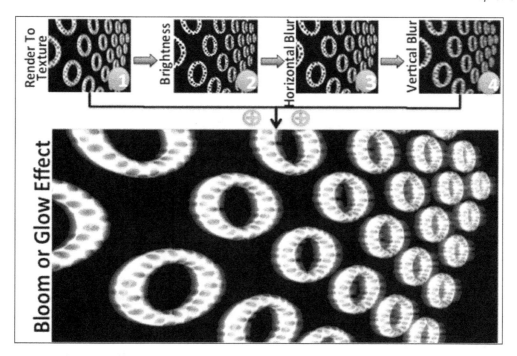

How to do it...

This recipe reuses our previous recipe on Gaussian blur. We rename the class from
`GaussianBlur` to `Bloom`. Here are the steps to implement this recipe:

1. Create a new fragment shader called `Bloom.glsl`. This fragment shader need to be
   compiled and linked within the `SimpleTexture` class. This shader is responsible for
   locating the bright portions of the scene:

   ```
   in vec2 TexCoord;
   uniform sampler2D Tex1;
   layout(location = 0) out vec4 outColor;
   void main() {
   vec4 val = texture(Tex1, TexCoord);
   float brightness = 0.212*val.r + 0.715*val.g + 0.072*val.b;
   brightness>0.6 ? outColor=vec4(1.) : outColor=vec4(0.);
   }
   ```

2. There is no change required in the `BlurHorizontal.glsl`. However, in the `BlurVertical.glsl`, add the following code. This code is responsible for mixing the blurred bright portions of the scene with the original scene (unchanged) preserved in the `RenderTex` texture:

```
void main(){
        vec4 scene = texture(RenderTex, TexCoord);
        vec4 sum = texture(Tex1, TexCoord) * Weight[0];
        for( int i = 1; i < 5; i++ ){
        sum+=texture(Tex1,TexCoord+vec2(0.0,PixOffset[i])
        *pixelSize.y)*Weight[i];
        sum+=texture(Tex1,TexCoord-vec2(0.0,PixOffset[i])
        *pixelSize.y)*Weight[i];
    }
        outColor = sum + scene;
}
```

3. Create three FBO's in `Bloom::InitModel` with `GenerateSceneFBO()` (using the color and depth texture), `GenerateBloomFBO()` (using only the color buffer), and `GenerateBlurFBO2()` (using only the color buffer). These functions will create three FBO's with the `SceneFbo`, `BloomFbo`, and `BlurFbo` handles respectively.

4. Render the bloom recipe under `Bloom::Render()`. In this function, render the scene with the perspective projection system, process the textures under the orthographic projection system, and store the handle of the default framebuffer.

5. Render different phases for the bloom effect using `RenderObj()`, `RenderBloom()`, `RenderHorizontalBlur()`, and `RenderVerticalBlur()`. All of these functions accept four arguments. The first argument (`BindTexture`) specifies the input color texture/buffer, the second argument (`Framebuffer`) specifies the handle of the framebuffer to which the scene should be attached, the third argument (`ColorBuf`), and the fourth argument (`DepthBuf`) specifies the color and depth buffer to which the scene writes. If any of the argument is not required, send `NULL` as an argument:

```
void Bloom::Render(){
    // Perspective projection
    SetUpPerspectiveProjection();
    glGetIntegerv(GL_FRAMEBUFFER_BINDING, &DefaultFrameBuffer);

    // Render scene in first FBO called SceneFBO
    RenderObj(NULL, SceneFbo, SceneTexture, DepthTexture);

    // Orthographic projection
    SetUpOrthoProjection();

    // Render Bloom pass
```

```
RenderBloom(SceneTexture, BloomFbo, BloomTexture, NULL);

    // Render Horizontal pass
    RenderHorizontalBlur(BloomTexture,
    BlurFbo, BlurTexture, NULL);
    // Render Vertical pass
    RenderVerticalBlur(BlurTexture,
    DefaultFrameBuffer,NULL,NULL);
}
```

6. The `RenderObj()` will render the scene to the `SceneFbo` framebuffer in the `SceneTexture` and `DepthTexture`.

7. Similarly, the `RenderBloom()` uses `SceneTexture`. Now, apply the `BlurHorizontal.glsl` shader to it, which will render the scene to `BlurTexture`.

8. Finally, `RenderVerticalBlur()` uses `BlurTexture` and `SceneTexture` as an input and applies the `BlurVertical.glsl` shader on it, which will apply the vertical blur pass and mix it in the scene texture.

9. Now, use the `blurFboId2` FBO and reuse the first FBO's texture and pass it on to pass 1 (the horizontal blur) using the `RenderHorizontaBlur()` function. This will store the processing result of pass 2 in `textureId2`.

10. Now, use the default framebuffer and apply the pass 2 (the vertical blur) to the second FBO's texture (`textureId2`).

How it works...

The working principle of the bloom effect is very similar to the previous recipe. Instead, a new stage for blooming is added. First, the scene is rendered to a nondefault framebuffer called `SceneFBO`, where it's written in the `SceneTexture`. The next stage called blooming is also performed on an offline framebuffer (`BloomFBO`). In this, the texture from the previous stage is used as an input and applied to the bloom fragment shader. The bloom shader converts a color image to luminance, which stores the image information in the linear gradient form. This provides the brightness information of the image, where the bright portions are detected by comparing the gradient value to the required threshold. The brightest portions are then written in the `BloomTexture` and provided to the Gaussian blur stage.

In this stage, the input stored in the `BloomTexture` from the previous stage is processed using the horizontal Gaussian blur pass where it's stored in `BlurTexture` and applied to the vertical pass. During the vertical blur pass, the blurred bright portion is mixed with the original scene using `SceneTexture`. This way, the image is mixed with the bright scattered glowing light on the scene:

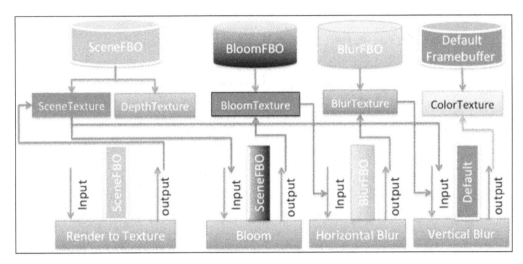

See also

▸ *Detecting the scene edges with the Sobel operator*

▸ *Making the scene blur with the Gaussian blur equation*

Painting the scene like a cartoon shading

Among various different kinds of shaders, the toon shader is well known for producing cartoon-shaded scenes. The cartoon shading technique is implemented in the fragment shader. The fundamental basis of this shader is the quantization of colors. In this, a range of colors are represented by a single type of color. Mathematically, color values are constrained from a continuous set of values (in floating numbers) to a relatively small discrete color set (represented by integer values). In addition to the quantization of color, the edges of the geometry are also highlighted using the Sobel operator.

The following image shows a screenshot from the current recipe, where quantization can be easily seen in various shades of green color. In conjunction, the Sobel operator renders thick black edges:

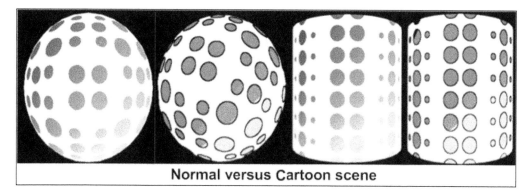

Normal versus Cartoon scene

This recipe is an extension of our edge detection recipe. With very little changes in the fragment shader, we can create a scene that looks like a painted cartoon. For this recipe, you are advised to thoroughly understand our first recipe in this chapter. This recipe will cover the changes we added to the existing edge detection's fragment shader for implementing the cartoon shader.

How to do it...

We reused the EdgeDetectionFragment.glsl and renamed it to ToonShader.glsl:

```glsl
uniform float quantizationFactor;
void main(){
    // Reuse Edge detection recipe fragment shader and
    // Calculate p00, p10, p20,p01, p21, p02, p12, p22
    px = p00 + 2.0*p10 + p20 - (p02 + 2.0*p12 + p22);
    py = p00 + 2.0*p01 + p02 - (p20 + 2.0*p21 + p22);
    // Check frequency change with given threshold
    if ((distance = px*px+py*py) > GradientThreshold ){
        outColor = vec4(0.0, 0.0, 0.0, 1.0);
    }else{ // Apply the Cartoon shading
    rgb = texture(Tex1,TexCoord).rgb*quantizationFactor;
    rgb += vec3(0.5, 0.5, 0.5);
    ivec3 intrgb = ivec3(rgb);
    rgb = vec3(intrgb)/ quantizationFactor;
    outColor = vec4(rgb,1.0);
    }
}
```

How it works...

In the cartoon shading, each incoming fragment is first passed through the Sobel operation to check whether it belongs to an edge or not. If it does, the current fragment is rendered with a black edge color; otherwise, it's shaded with the cartoon shading effect.

In the cartoon shading effect, each fragment color is multiplied by a `quantizationFactor` (which is 2.0 in the present case). This is used in the process of the image quantization. In computer graphics, image quantization is a process of limiting a large set of colors to fewer ones. In other words, it groups similar colors as one.

The obtained color components are added with 0.5 to enhance the chances of producing values greater than 1.0. This is helpful for the next step, where the floating point color space is converted to the integer type. During this process, the decimal part of the color component is chopped off.

Finally, the effect of the `quantizationFactor` multiplication is nullified (we applied this at the beginning), by dividing the integer space color components by `quantizationFactor`. The resultant value is applied on the fragment.

See also

▶   *Detecting the scene edges with the Sobel operator*

Generating an embossed scene

Embossing is a technique in which the scene appears raised or highlighted with some 3D depth. The working logic of the emboss shader is similar to the edge detection technique. Here, the detected edges are used to highlight the image based on edge angles.

Getting ready

For this recipe, we will reuse any of the previous post screen processing recipe implemented in this chapter. This recipe will directly jump to the shader part with an assumption that the reader has understood the fundamental logics of the post processing.

How to do it...

Create a new fragment shader called `EmbossFrag.glsl`, as shown in the following code. There are no changes required for the vertex shader:

```
in vec2 TexCoord;
uniform vec2 pixelSize;
```

```
uniform sampler2D Tex1;
layout(location = 0) out vec4 outColor;
uniform float EmbossBrightness, ScreenCoordX;

void main(){
   // Apply Emboss shading
   vec3 p00 = texture(Tex1, TexCoord).rgb;
   vec3 p01 = texture(Tex1, TexCoord + vec2(0.0,
 pixelSize.y)).rgb;

// Consecutive texel difference
   vec3 diff = p00 - p01;

// Find the max value among RGB
   float maximum = diff.r;
   if( abs(diff.g) > abs(maximum) ){
   maximum = diff.g;
}

if( abs(diff.b) > abs(maximum) ){
    maximum = diff.b;
}

// Choose White, Black, or Emboss color
   float gray = clamp(maximum+EmbossBrightness, 0.0, 1.0);
   outColor = vec4(gray,gray,gray, 1.0);

}
```

How it works...

In this recipe, edges are detected by taking the difference between two consecutive texels in any arbitrary direction. The difference of these two results in a new color intensity, where each component (RGB) are compared among themselves to find the greater magnitude component (max). This component is then used to clamp between low (0.0) and high (1.0). This operation results in three color intensities: white (derived from low), black (derived from high) 1.0, and emboss (derived from the max component). The result of the emboss shader is shown in the following image.

First, the scene is rendered to a FBO where it's stored in the color buffer. This color buffer is then sent to the emboss shader in the Tex1 variable. The p00 and p01 are represented as two consecutive texels, which are sampled from Tex1 for the current fragment position. The difference is stored in the diff variable. The diff variable is checked to find the maximum magnitude among RGB components, which is stored in the max variable. The max value is clamped using the clamp () function. The result is finally used as an RGB component of the current fragment:

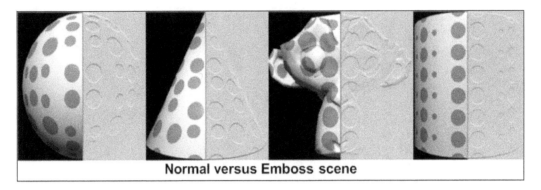

Normal versus Emboss scene

There's more...

The clamping operation we used in this recipe is performed using the clamp () GLSL function. This function takes three values: original, lower, and higher range value. If the original value lies between the minimum and maximum range, it returns the original value; otherwise, it returns the minimum range value if the value is smaller than the minimum one and vice versa.

Syntax:

```
void clamp(genType x, genType minVal, genType maxVal);
```

Variable	Description
x	This specifies the value to constrain
minVal	This specifies the lower end of the range to constrain x
maxVal	This specifies the upper end of the range to constrain x

See also

▶ *Implementing grayscale and CMYK conversions*

Implementing grayscale and CMYK conversions

The grayscale or luminance is an important topic that digital image processing is incomplete without discussing its practical implementation. Luminance is widely used in various applications of image processing. Edge detection, cartoon shading, and emboss effect are examples that we implemented in this chapter, which make use of luminance. In this recipe, you will learn how to covert an RGB color space to luminance and CMYK.

Numerically, a grayscale is a linear interpolation between black and white, depending on the color depth. A depth of 8 bits represent 256 varying shades from white to black. However, with four, only 16 shades can be represented. The black color is the darkest possible shade, which is the total absence of transmitted or reflected light. The lightest possible shade is white, which is the total transmission or reflection of light at all visible. Intermediate shades of gray are represented by equal levels of three primary colors (red, green, and blue) to transmit light or equal amounts of three primary pigments (cyan, magenta, and yellow) for reflected light.

The ITU-R BT.709 standard provides the weight of these components as follows:

RGB luminance value = 0.2125*(Red) + 0.7154*(Green) + 0.0721*(Blue)

Getting ready

This recipe onwards, we will discuss various image processing techniques that was implemented in this chapter. For these recipes, we have reused the *Applying texture with UV mapping* recipe from *Chapter 7, Textures and Mapping Techniques*. For the current image processing recipe, we only need to make changes in the fragment shader. Proceed to the next section to understand the changes that need to be made to implement grayscale and CMYK conversions.

How to do it...

Reuse the simple texture recipe, as mentioned previously, and make the following changes in the fragment shader to implement the grayscale and CMYK recipe:

Grayscale recipe:

```
in vec2 TexCoord;
uniform sampler2D Tex1;
```

```
layout (location = 0) out vec4 outColor;
// Luminance weight as per ITU-R BT.709 standard
const vec3 luminanceWeight = vec3(0.2125, 0.7154, 0.0721);
void main() {
vec4 rgb = texture(Tex1, TexCoord); // Take the color sample
// Multiply RGB with luminance weight
float luminace = dot(rgb.rgb, luminanceWeight);
outColor = vec4(luminace, luminace, luminace, rgb.a);
}
```

How it works...

Declare a `luminanceWeight` variable that contains the weight of RGB components as per the ITU-R BT.709 standard. Use the incoming texture coordinate and sample the corresponding texel from the texture in the `rgb` variable. Take the dot product between the luminanceWeight and rgb variable to produce the grayscale image (stored in the luminance variable). The grayscale image output of the current recipe is shown in the following right hand-side image:

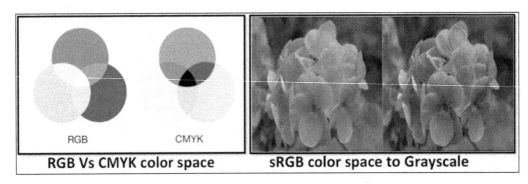

RGB Vs CMYK color space   **sRGB color space to Grayscale**

There's more...

Images are represented in the RGB color space on color computer monitors. However, when these images are published using the standard printing process, these need to be converted to the CMYK color space. The RGB model is created by adding color components to the black color. This is based on emissive colors. In contrast, the CMYK color is transmissive. Here, the colors are created by subtracting color components from white. In an RGB to CMYK conversion, the red component changes to cyan, green to magenta, blue to yellow, and black. The publishing print press uses the CMYK color format, where the RGB space image is converted to four separate single color images, which are used to create four separate printing plates to the printing process.

The CMYK color space can be calculated from RGB using the following formula:

$$\begin{bmatrix} K \\ C \\ M \\ Y \end{bmatrix} = \begin{bmatrix} \text{minimum}(1\text{-}R, 1\text{-}G, 1\text{-}B) \\ (1\text{-}R\text{-}B)/(1\text{-}B) \\ (1\text{-}G\text{-}B)/(1\text{-}B) \\ (1\text{-}B\text{-}B)/(1\text{-}B) \end{bmatrix}$$

However, this simple conversion does not truly match the desired results one would expect after conversion. The following approximation from Adobe Photoshop produces very satisfactory results. The under color removal (**ucr**) and black generation (**bg**) function is given as follows, where *Sk=0.1*, *KO = 0.3*, and *Kmax = 0.9*. These are the constant values used in the formula:

$$\begin{bmatrix} C' \\ M' \\ Y' \\ K' \end{bmatrix} = \begin{bmatrix} C \text{ - } f_{ucr}(K) \\ M \text{ - } f_{ucr}(K) \\ Y \text{ - } f_{ucr}(K) \\ f_{bg}(K) \end{bmatrix}$$

$$f_{ucr}(K) = S_K * K$$

$$f_{bg}(K) = \begin{cases} 0 & K < K_0 \\ K_{max} * \dfrac{K - K_0}{1 - K_0} & K >= K_0 \end{cases}$$

Under color removal (ucr) is the process of eliminating the overlapped yellow, magenta, and cyan color components that would be added to produce a dark neutral black color, replacing them with black ink called full black. This results in less ink and greater depth in shadows.

Black generation (bg) is the process of producing a black channel or color. This affects color channels, when color conversation is performed from the RGB to CMYK color space.

The following image shows the color version and four separated versions of CMYK in grayscale. The grayscale representation of each component shows the amount of ink required for each darker values, indicating high consumption of ink:

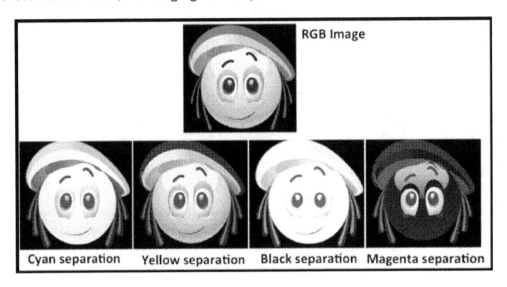

Here is the fragment shader code for the CMYK separation from an RGB color space:

```
in vec2 TexCoord;
uniform sampler2D Tex1;
uniform float ScreenCoordX;
uniform int caseCYMK;
layout(location = 0) out vec4 outColor;
void main() { // Main Entrance
vec4 rgb  = texture(Tex1, TexCoord);
vec3 cmy  = vec3(1.0)-rgb.rbg;
float k   = min(cmy.r, min(cmy.g, cmy.b));

// fucr (K)= SK*K, SK = 0.1
vec3 target  = cmy - 0.1 * k;

// fbg (K) = 0, when K<K0, K0 =0.3, Kmax =0.9
// fbg (K) = Kmax*(K-K0)/(1-K0), when K>=K0
k<0.3 ? k=0.0 : k=0.9*(k-0.3)/0.7;
vec4 cmyk = vec4(target, k);
// Since we are interested in the separation of each component
// we subtracted gray scale of each color component from white
if(caseCYMK == 0){               // CYAN conversion
   outColor = vec4(vec3(1.0 - cmyk.x),rgb.a);
```

```
    }else if(caseCYMK == 1){      // MAGENTA conversion
        outColor = vec4(vec3(1.0 - cmyk.y),rgb.a);}
    else if(caseCYMK == 2){      // YELLOW conversion
        outColor = vec4(vec3(1.0 - cmyk.z),rgb.a);}
    else if(caseCYMK == 3){      // BLACK conversion
        outColor = vec4(vec3(1.0 - cmyk.w),rgb.a);}
    else{ outColor = rgb;}       // RGB
}
```

See also

▶ Refer to the *Applying texture with UV mapping* recipe in *Chapter 7, Textures and Mapping Techniques*

Implementing fisheye with barrel distortion

Fisheye is an effect in which a scene looks sphered. As a result, edges in the scene look curved and bowed around the center of this virtual sphere. This effect makes the scene look like wrapped around a curved surface.

The barrel distortion technique is used to achieve the present effect, which can be applied to fragments or vertices. This recipe will implement the barrel distortion on the fragment shader first and then apply it to the vertex shader. The difference between the two is this; in the former shader, the geometry does not distort. However, texture coordinates are distorted, resulting in a magnifying lens effect or a fisheye lens effect. In the latter technique, the geometry is displaced and creates different amusing distorted shapes. Note that this is not a post processing technique.

Getting ready

For this recipe, we can reuse our first recipe and replace the edge detection logic with the current barrel distortion fragment shader: `BarrelDistFishEyeFragment.glsl`.

How to do it...

Modify the `BarrelDistFishEyeFragment.glsl`, as shown in the following code:

```
precision mediump float;
in vec2 TexCoord;
uniform sampler2D Tex1;
layout(location = 0) out vec4 outColor;

uniform float BarrelPower;
```

```glsl
uniform float ScreenCoordX;

vec2 BarrelDistortion(vec2 p){
    float theta  = atan(p.y, p.x);
    float radius = sqrt(p.x*p.x + p.y*p.y);
    radius = pow(radius, BarrelPower);
    p.x = radius * cos(theta);
    p.y = radius * sin(theta);
    return (p + 0.5);
}

vec2 xy, uv;
float distance;
void main(){
    if(gl_FragCoord.x > ScreenCoordX){
        // The range of text coordinate is from (0,0)
        // to (1,1). Assuming center of the Texture
        // coordinate system middle of the screen.
        // Shift all coordinate wrt to the new
        // center. This will be the new position
        // vector of the displaced coordinate.
        xy = TexCoord - vec2(0.5);

        // Calculate the distance from the center point.
        distance = sqrt(xy.x*xy.x+xy.y*xy.y);

        float radius = 0.35;
        // Apply the Barrel Distortion if the distance
        // is within the radius. Our radius is half of
        // the ST dimension.
        uv = (distance < radius?BarrelDistortion(xy):TexCoord);

        if( distance > radius-0.01 && distance < radius+0.01 ){
            outColor = vec4(1.0, 0.0, 0.0,1.0);
        }
        else{
            // Fetch the UV from Texture Sample
            outColor = texture(Tex1, uv);
        }
    }
    else{
        outColor = texture(Tex1, TexCoord);
    }
}
```

How it works...

This recipe first renders the scene to a FBO's color texture, which is then shared with the `SimpleTexture` class and applied to the quad geometry with texture coordinates ranging from (0.0, 0.0) to (1.0, 1.0). The quad vertex and texture information are provided to the vertex and fragment shader to process the geometry and fragment information. The barrel distortion technique is implemented in the fragment shader, where each incoming texture coordinate is temporarily converted to the polar coordinate to produce the fisheye effect.

Texture coordinates are first translated in the center (0.5, 0.5) and the distance of these translated texture coordinates is computed from the center. If the translated texture coordinates (xy) falls outside the given threshold of 0.35 radius, then unaltered texture coordinates (`TexCoord`) are used to fetch the sample from `Tex1`; otherwise, this coordinate (xy) is applied to the barrel distortion with the `BarrelDistortion` function. The following image shows the radius of the red circle. The `BarrelDistortion` function first calculates the length of the texture coordinate with respect to the center of the logical circle. This obtained length is altered using the barrel power, which shrinks or expands the length. The following image shows different results obtained from various barrel powers (1.0, 0.5, 0.3, and 2.0).

This altered length is then multiplied by the slope of texture coordinates along the S (horizontal) and T (vertical) components, which will result in a new set of translated texture coordinates. These texture coordinates are retranslated into their old origin (bottom, left). Finally, this retranslated texture coordinate is used to calculate the sampled texture from the input texture coordinate:

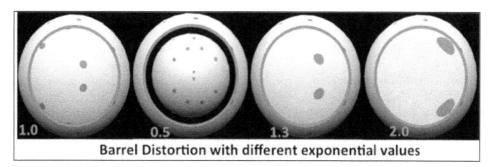

Barrel Distortion with different exponential values

There's more...

When the barrel distortion is applied to the geometry, it distorts the physical shape of the geometry. The following images show the application of the barrel distortion on different meshes. You can explore this recipe using the `BarrelDistortion_Vtx_Shdr` source code provided in this chapter:

The working logic of this recipe is similar to the previous one except the fact that it's now implemented in the vertex shader. Here, we do not need to translate the texture coordinate from the center because, by default, the origin always is the center of the Cartesian coordinate system.

Use the following code in the vertex shader to apply barrel distortion on the vertex shader:

```
layout(location = 0) in vec4  VertexPosition;
layout(location = 1) in vec3  Normal;
uniform mat4   ModelViewProjectionMatrix, ModelViewMatrix;
uniform mat3   NormalMatrix;
out vec3        normalCoord, eyeCoord, ObjectCoord;
uniform float  BarrelPower;

vec4 BarrelDistortion(vec4 p){
    vec2 v = p.xy / p.w;
    float radius = length(v);
   // Convert to polar coords
    if (radius > 0.0){
        float theta = atan(v.y,v.x);
        radius = pow(radius, BarrelPower);
   // Apply distortion
        // Convert back to Cartesian
        v.x = radius * cos(theta);
        v.y = radius * sin(theta);
        p.xy = v.xy * p.w;
    }
```

```
    return p;
}

void main(){
    normalCoord = NormalMatrix * Normal;
    eyeCoord    = vec3 ( ModelViewMatrix * VertexPosition );
    ObjectCoord = VertexPosition.xyz;
    gl_Position = BarrelDistortion(ModelViewProjectionMatrix*
    VertexPosition);
}
```

See also

> ▸ Refer to the *Generating the polka dot pattern* recipe in *Chapter 6, Working with Shaders*

Implementing the binocular view with procedural texturing

This recipe implements a binocular view effect, where a scene is rendered as if it's visualized from the binocular itself. We will implement this effect by programing a procedural shader. Alternatively, in another technique, the alpha-mapped texture is used instead. In this approach, an alpha-masked texture containing a binocular view image is superimposed on top of the scene. This way, only those parts of the scene are visible that belong to the nonmasked texture region.

The procedural textured approach is also relatively simpler. Here, the scene is programmed in the fragment shader where the binocular view effect is created using texture coordinates of the vertices. Texture coordinates are used to create a logical circular region on the rendered image. The fragment that belongs outside the circumference of this circular region are rendered with an opaque color (say black). This opacity reduces as the distance shrinks toward the center point of this circular region. The tapped point (the single tap gesture) on the device screen is used as a center point of the circular region; this way, the lens can be moved around the screen using touch gestures.

How to do it...

Use any of the existing image processing recipes and replace the following code in the fragment shader. This fragment shader accepts a few inputs from the OpenGL ES program. The image texture is stored in the `Tex1`; the tapped point must be provided in the center variable, which will be treated as the center of the circle. We also require the `horizontalAspectRatio` and `verticalAspectRatio` aspect ratios so that with different screen resolutions, a circle remains as a circle and not turned to any elliptical shape. Finally, we need the inner and outer radius (`LensInnerRadius, LensOuterRadius`) to define the width of the circular region. The color (`BorderColor`) will be used for the mask painting:

```
#version 300 es
precision mediump float;
in vec2 TexCoord;
uniform sampler2D Tex1;
uniform vec2 center;
uniform float horizontalAspectRatio, verticalAspectRatio;
uniform float LensInnerRadius,LensOuterRadius;
uniform vec4 BorderColor;

layout(location = 0) out vec4 outColor;
void main() {
outColor = texture(Tex1, TexCoord);
    float dx = TexCoord.x-center.x;
float dy = TexCoord.y-center.y;

dx *= horizontalAspectRatio;
dy *= verticalAspectRatio;
    float distance = sqrt(dx * dx + dy * dy);
    outColor = mix( outColor, BorderColor,
        smoothstep(LensInnerRadius, LensOuterRadius, distance));
    return;
}
```

How it works...

The incoming texture coordinates is subtracted by the center position and are translated into new logical coordinates, where transformed texture coordinates or positional vectors (dx, dy) are stored with reference to the center point (`center`). This coordinate must be multiplied by the `aspectRatio` in the horizontal and vertical directions to eliminate any shape distortion due to the difference in the horizontal and vertical device screen resolution.

The distance of each positional vector is calculated with the vector length formula $P(x, y) = \sqrt{(x2 + y2)}$ and fed into the smoothstep GLSL API. The smooth step API accepts three arguments (**edge1**, **edge2**, and **x**). The first two arguments are two outbound values and the third is the weight. Refer to the following left-hand side image to understand its functioning. This API returns an interpolated value between two edges, based on the weight provided. The output of the smoothstep is used as a weight to feed into another GLSL API called mix. The mix API mixes the border color with the current texture using a weighted value provided by the smoothstep function:

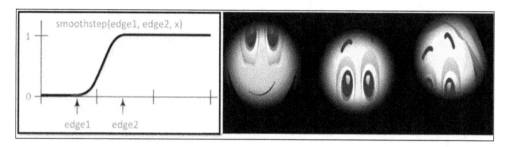

See also

> ▸ Refer to the *Applying texture with UV mapping* recipe in *Chapter 7, Textures and Mapping Techniques*

Twirling the image

Twirling is a very common effect used in animations. When applied to a rendered scene or image, it distorts the appearance within the circular region and produces a radial circular motion of the texels where these are moved around the center of the circular region, producing a whirlpool-like effect.

Programmatically, for a given image, an arbitrary texel is chosen as a center. A fixed distance from the center of the circle defines a locus of the circumference. All the texels falling under this circumference are being applied to the rotation. The rotation of the texels within the circle decreases with the distance from the center and diminishes at the circumference edge. The following image shows how the twirl effect looks:

How to do it...

Use the following code in the fragment shader to implement the twirl effect:

```
in vec2 TexCoord;
uniform sampler2D Tex1;
uniform float ScreenCoordX,twirlRadius,angle,imageHeight,
imageWidth;
uniform vec2 center;
float radiusFactor = 3.0;
layout(location = 0) out vec4 outColor;
// Note: the angle is assumed to be in radians to
// work with trigonometric functions.
vec4 Twirl(sampler2D tex, vec2 uv, float angle){
    // Get the current texture size of the image
    vec2 texSize = vec2(imageWidth, imageHeight);

    // Change the texCoordinate w.r.t. to the image dimensions
    vec2 tc = (uv * texSize) - center;

    // Calculate the distance of the current transformed
```

```
    // texture coordinate from the center.
    float distance = sqrt(tc.x*tc.x + tc.y*tc.y);
    if (distance < twirlRadius+angle*radiusFactor){
        float percent    = (twirlRadius - distance)/twirlRadius;
        float theta       = percent * percent * angle;
        float sinus       = sin(theta);
        float cosine      = cos(theta);
        tc = vec2(dot(tc, vec2(cosine, -sinus)), dot(tc,
 vec2(sinus, cosine)));
    }
 return texture(tex, (tc+center) / texSize);
 }

 void main() {
 if(gl_FragCoord.x > ScreenCoordX)
 outColor = Twirl(Tex1, TexCoord, angle);
 else
 outColor = texture(Tex1, TexCoord);
 }
```

How it works...

The twirling effect requires a center point around which the whirlpool effect is produced, this center point is provided by the OpenGL ES program in the center variable. Additionally, we need the size of the image (imageHeight and imageWidth), which is used to control the region of animation within the image boundaries.

Each incoming texture coordinate is converted to its corresponding texel position by multiplying it with the image size and is then translated with respect to the center. The translated coordinates represent the position vector, which is used to calculating the distance from the center point. If the distance is within a given radius threshold, the texels are rotated around the center with an arbitrary angle specified in the degree. The angle of rotation increases as the distance between the center and the translated coordinate decreases.

See also

▶   *Implementing the binocular view with procedural texturing*

Sphere illusion with textured quadrilateral

This recipe will demonstrate a performance efficient technique, which makes use of the procedural texture to produce the illusion of a real 3D object. In the Gouraud shading, fragments are painted with light shadings based on the direction of the light source and the geometry shape. For instance, in *Chapter 5, Light and Materials*, we implemented the diffuse light on a spherical model, which contains a very high number of vertices. This recipe technique renders the same diffused sphere, but using only four vertices. It fakes the light shading in such a way that the difference between the two becomes indistinguishable.

The performance is directly proportional to the number of fragments it renders to the screen. For example, the surface area covered by a single fullscreen rendering sphere is equivalent to several tiny spheres covering up the same surface area on the screen.

How to do it...

Use the following steps to implement sphere with textured quadrilateral:

1. Create a new class called `TextureQuadSphere` derived from the `Model` class.

2. Declare the necessary vertex information for the quad, which will have the sphere rendered in:

   ```
   float vertexColors[12] = { 0, 0, 0, 1, 0, 0, 1, 1, 0, 0, 1, 0 };
   float texCoords[8]     = { 0.f, 0.f, 1.f, 0.f, 0.f, 1.f, 1.f, 1.f };
   float quad[8]          = { -1.f,-1.f,1.f,-1.f,-1.f, 1.f, 1.f,1.f};
   ```

3. Add the following `TexQuadSphereVertex.glsl` vertex shader:

   ```
   #version 300 es
   uniform mat4 ModelViewProjectMatrix;
   layout(location = 0) in vec3  VertexPosition;
   layout(location = 1) in vec2  VertexTexCoord;
   layout(location = 2) in vec4  VertexColor;
   out vec4 TriangleColor; out vec2 TexCoord;

   void main() {
     gl_Position = ModelViewProjectMatrix*vec4(VertexPosition,1.0);
     TriangleColor = VertexColor;
     TexCoord = VertexTexCoord;
   }
   ```

4. There is no change required in the `TexQuadSphereFragment.glsl`:

```
#version 300 es
precision mediump float;
in vec4 TriangleColor;
in vec2 TexCoord;
uniform float ScreenWidth;
uniform float ScreenHeight;
uniform float ScreenCoordX;
uniform float ScreenCoordY;
out vec4 FragColor;
vec3 lightDir = normalize(vec3(0.5, 0.5, 1.0));

void main() {
vec2 resolution = vec2(ScreenWidth, ScreenHeight);
   vec2 center     = vec2(resolution.x/2.0,
resolution.y/2.0);
    lightDir = normalize(vec3((ScreenCoordX - center.x)
/(ScreenWidth*0.5), (ScreenCoordY - center.y)
/(ScreenHeight*0.5), 1.0));

    float radius   = 0.5; // Calculate the sphere radius
  vec2 position  = TexCoord.xy - vec2(0.5, 0.5);
    float z        = sqrt(radius*radius -
position.x*position.x - position.y*position.y);
     vec3 normal=normalize(vec3(position.x,position.y,abs(z)));
    if (length(position) > radius) { // Outside
        FragColor = vec4(vec3(0.0,0.0,0.0), 0.0);
    } else { // Inside
        float diffuse = max(0.0, dot(normal, lightDir));
        FragColor = vec4(vec3(diffuse), 1.0);
    }
}
```

How it works...

This technique uses a square geometry with four texture coordinates for each vertex. Texture coordinates are shared by the vertex shader in the `TexCoord` variable with the fragment shader. Texture coordinates are in the range from 0.0 to 1.0. These are subtracted by half dimensions to calculate the positional vector (`position`) with respect to the center of the circle. The radius of the circle and the arbitrary position vector from the center of the circle is used to calculate the elevation at each given position.

This elevation is used with the positional coordinate to produce a normal vector; this normal vector provides the angle it made with incidence light rays. The cosine of this angle is used on the color intensity to produce the diffuse shading effect of light on the logical hemisphere. The incident light ray is calculated with the tap coordinates on the fly using the screen resolution and tapped coordinates x and y positions.

The following figure shows the pictorial representation of the previous described working logic. P (x, y, 0.0) represents the position vector (`position`), C is the center, and Q is the point on the hemisphere which will be calculated using *CQ = CP + PQ*, as shown in the following figure:

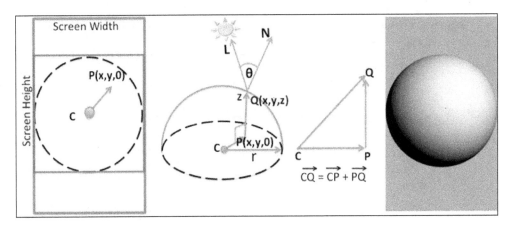

See also

  ▸   Refer to the *Implementing the per-vertex diffuse light component* recipe in *Chapter 5, Light and Materials*

10

Scene Management with Scene Graphs

In this chapter, we will cover the following recipes:

- ▶ Implementing the first scene using a scene graph
- ▶ Adding local and relative transformations
- ▶ Adding parent-child support in the scene graph
- ▶ Creating complex models with a transformation graph
- ▶ Implementing picking with the ray trace technique
- ▶ Implementing 2D textured button widgets
- ▶ Navigating the scene with a camera system
- ▶ Implementing the scene with multiple views

Introduction

In all our previous chapters, we programed various recipes in a modeled centric way where we have an engine manager (renderer) that does all the required rendering activities for models. This approach is great for learning purposes, but in a real use case, we need scalability and manageability where multiple complex scenes can be handled easily. This chapter will introduce the scene-graph paradigm that allows you to program and manage complex scenes efficiently.

Scene graph-based architecture: The present design we used in existing recipes contains a renderer engine, which works in conjunction with other helper classes to render programed models. This simple architecture is wonderful for quick prototyping purposes. This has already been demonstrated in all the recipes in previous chapters.

The modern 3D graphics use cases are not only limited to render a few chunks of objects in the 3D space, but the real-time challenge is to produce a state-of-the-art graphics engine that meets all modern graphical requirements. These include optimized rendering of complex scenes that involve a hierarchy of nodes, particles, mesmerizing shading effects, states, semantic logics, level of details, event handling, geospatial services, and so on. To meet these requirements, a modern 3D graphics application uses a scene graph-based architecture. The scene graph architecture encapsulates the hierarchical structure of a complete 3D scene, which has mainly two aspects: semantics and rendering. The semantic aspect works like a database, which manages the visual representation and state management. Think of it like a visual database that tells the graphical system the scene that's going to come and the scene that's not in use so that it can be released along with its resources for better optimization and memory management. On the other hand, the rendering aspect deals with the life cycle management of drawable entities or a model, which includes initialization, deinitialization, processing, control management and displaying them on screen.

The scene graph is a big and evolving topic. Covering all its (requirement) aspects is out of the scope of this title. In this chapter, we will create a small architecture that allows you to manage multiple scenes; each scene can consist of multiple lights, cameras, and models. Complex models can be created using the parent-child relationships, with the help of local and relative transformations. Models can be applied to predefined materials dynamically and all this will be done outside the graphics engine in a separate C++ file. This will keep the scene-graph hierarchy logic preserved at a single place so that it can be managed easily.

Difference with the existing design: This chapter uses the knowledge of our existing rendering engine to produce the scene graph-based architecture. The existing design mainly consists of a renderer and model classes. The former is responsible for managing models, creating a single view, and processing events. On the other hand, the latter contains lights, material, performs the event handling process, and renders 3D objects.

For real-time 3D applications, we need to extend our design to meet the requirements of the scene graph architecture:

- **Hierarchical relationship**: Various modules of the system can be arranged in a hierarchical fashion. For example, the `Application` module contains the `Renderer` module inside and the application works in a singleton fashion. However, it can produce many threads to run one renderer instance in each. Each `Renderer` instance contains a `Scene` module, which contains the `Model` and `Camera`. The scene module can create different views from various cameras to visualize the rendering of models on screen.

- **Objects with parent-child relationship**: The objects of the similar type must support a parent-child relationship. In the parent-child relationship, a parent manages all its children automatically. This way, semantics and rendering can be managed in an optimized way.

- **Transforming graphs**: Each renderable object in a system stores the transformation with respect to its parent. In order to understand this, let's take an example of a simple 3D model car that comprises of four tires, four doors, and a car body. If we want to translate this car by 2 units in the *x* axis direction, then using the existing design, we need to move all the nine parts of the car by 2 units. However, if we make the doors and tires as the children of the body of the car, then we do not need to worry about moving all nine parts; only the parent part (car body) will be enough to move all the related parts.

- **Multiple scene management**: In the existing design, creating multiple scenes is not possible; in fact, everything is drawn as a single scene.

- **Separating semantic and rendering**: The rendering of objects must be loosely coupled with semantics. The rendering output can be affected by a number of factors, such as change in state, user input, or both. The design should be flexible enough to manage states and events.

- **Level of Detail** (**LOD**): LOD uses the computed information of an object and reveals how far it is from the camera view or an observer. If the object is outside the viewing frustum, then it can be ignored before it consumes vital resources of the system. The object in the frustum view, which are far away from the camera, can be rendered at a lower fidelity in which a fewer polygons and small textures can be used.

- **State encapsulation**: It's important that each node or object in the system contains a state that is able to reveal the nature of the object. This way several similar types of objects can be clubbed together by traversing the parent-child hierarchy; this will be highly efficient in avoiding random state switches, for example, texture loading and binding.

This chapter will take us through a systematic approach to develop scene graphs:

- **Implementing the first scene in the scene graph** (**recipe 1**): This recipe will build the foundation of scene graph, in which it will support scene, model, light and the material module. The modeling will be done outside the rendering engine in the `NativeTemplate.cpp`.

- **Adding local and relative transformation** (**recipe 2**): This recipe will introduce the local and the relative transformation concept to the existing scene graph. Local transformation is only applicable within the renderable object, whereas relative transformation is received from a parent and propagated to its children.

- **Adding parent-child support in the scene graph** (**recipe 3**): This recipe builds the parent-child relationship between similar types of objects.

- **Creating complex models using a transformation graph** (**recipe 4**): This recipe will make use of previous recipe concepts and demonstrate how to build complex animated models, such as a revolving windmill.

▸ **Implementing picking using the ray trace technique** (**recipe 5**): This recipe will add the support of events to the scene graph and help in implementing the ray trace-based picking technique that allows you to select 3D objects in a scene.

▸ **Implementing 2D textured button widgets** (**recipe 6**): Implementing 2D widgets uses the screen coordinate system. This recipe contains another subrecipe, which implements clicking on the button widget.

▸ **Navigating a scene with the camera system** (**recipe 7**): This recipe will implement the camera support to the scene.

▸ **Implementing a scene using multiple views** (**recipe 8**): This recipe enables scene graphics to render multiple views to a single scene.

Implementing the first scene using a scene graph

Let's start by looking at the block diagram of the existing engine (left) with the new expected scene graph (right) design. This design is segregated into many simpler reusable modules, where each module is self-explanatory in the image itself. The Object module is a base class for most of the other modules. These modules exhibit the parent-child relationship. Similarly, modules that support the event handling process must be inherited from the Event.

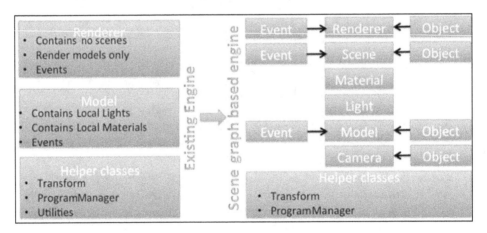

In the following image, you can see the hierarchical relationship among different modules in the scene graph. The Renderer is a graphics engine that contains various scenes. These scenes can be added to and removed from the rendering engine dynamically. A scene contains one or more cameras as per its requirements; it also contains models that the scene needs to render.

Transformation is managed in the model-view-projection analogy, where the modeling transformation is carried out in the `Model` module and the projection and viewing transformation is calculated in the `Camera` module. As we are aware, any renderable object must be derived from the `Model` class, which exhibits a parent-child relationship, where the parent is fully responsible for managing the life cycle of their children. The events in the system flow in the top-down direction and the native application receives the events and passes them on to the `Renderer`, which further propagates the event to the scene. The scene detects the view to which the event belongs to and the events are sent to all corresponding Model's derived classes in the view where it's finally handled:

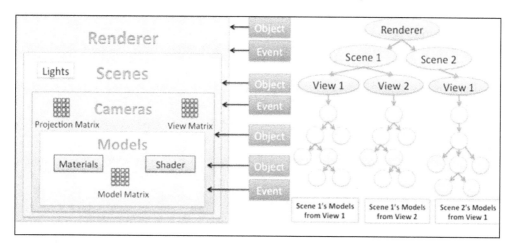

Getting ready

This first recipe will implement the basic structure of the scene graph architecture described previously in the introduction section. For this recipe, we will implement the `Renderer`, `Scene`, `Light`, and `Material` modules. For the `Model` class, the changes are very minor. In the scene graph approach, the `Renderer` has simplified with the addition of other modules. As we move on to subsequent recipes, we will break down the complexity further into simpler modules:

In the next section, we will understand the step-by-step procedure to implement our first scene. This recipe builds the foundation class of the scene graph, where we will describe the class structure and the definition of important member functions.

Coding the definition of all functions may not be possible in this recipe. We will suggest our readers to follow the `SG1_withSceneLightMaterial` recipe provided with the sample code of this chapter to view the full source.

How to do it...

Here are the steps to implement the scene graph architecture:

1. The new `Renderer` class is created in `RendererEx.h`; this new version has very less code compared to the older version. It manages all the scenes contained in it and takes care of the life cycle, such as initialization and rendering:

```
class Renderer{
std::vector <Scene*> scenes; // Scene List

public:
void initializeScenes();     // Initialize Engine
void resize( int w, int h );// resize screen
void render();               // Render the Scenes
void addScene(Scene* scene);// Add new scene
    bool removeScene( Scene* scene); // Remove the scene
};
```

2. Define the member functions of `RendererEx.cpp`, as shown in the following code:

```
// When renderer initializes it initiates each Scene
void Renderer::initializeScenes(){
    for( int i=0; i<scenes.size();  i++ )
            scenes.at(i)->initializeScene();
}

// Resize all the scenes to adapt new window size
void Renderer::resize( int w, int h ){
  for( int i=0; i<scenes.size();  i++ )
    scenes.at(i)->resize(w, h);
}

// Add a new Scene into the rendering engine
void Renderer::addScene( Scene* scene){
  if(!scene) return;

  for( int i=0; i<scenes.size();  i++ ){
```

```
        if(scenes.at(i) == scene ){
            return; // If already added return;
        }
    }

    scenes.push_back( scene );
    scene->setRenderer(this);
}

// No longer need a scene, then remove it
bool Renderer::removeScene(Scene* scene){
    for( int i=0; i<scenes.size();  i++ ){
if(scenes.at(i) == scene){
scenes.erase(scenes.begin()+i);
return true;
}
    }
    return false;
}

// Render Each Scene
void Renderer::render(){
    glClearColor(0.0f, 0.0f, 0.0f, 1.0f);
    glClear(GL_COLOR_BUFFER_BIT|GL_DEPTH_BUFFER_BIT);

    for( int i=0; i<scenes.size();  i++ )
        scenes.at(i)->render();
}
```

3. Create the `Light` class in `Light.h/.cpp` and implement it, as shown in the following code:

```
class Light {
  private:
    int lightID;
  public:
    Material material;
    glm::vec4 position;
    GLfloat constantAttenuation, linearAttenuation,
            quadraticAttenuation;
    Light() {}
    Light(Material mt, glm::vec4 p, GLfloat ca = 1.0,
              GLfloat la = 0.2, GLfloat qa = 0.05) {
```

```
        material                = mt;
        position                = p;
        constantAttenuation     = ca;
        linearAttenuation       = la;
        quadraticAttenuation    = qa;
        enabled                 = false;
    }
};
```

4. Similarly, create `Material.h`/`.cpp` and implement the `Material` class as follows:

```
class Material{
public:
    glm::vec4 ambient, diffuse, specular;
    GLfloat shines;
    std::string name;
MaterialType typeOfMaterial;
    Material(glm::vec4  ambient, glm::vec4 diffuse,
  glm::vec4 specular, GLfloat shiness);
    Material(const Material & p);
Material & operator = (const Material & p);
Material(MaterialType type = MaterialNone);
};
```

5. Define some common material types. For more information, refer to the sample code of this recipe:

```
typedef enum {
    MaterialNone,
    MaterialGold,
    MaterialCopper,
} MaterialType;

// Copper Material
const vec4 CopperAmbient(0.19f, 0.07f, 0.022f, 1.0f);
const vec4 CopperDiffuse(0.70f, 0.27f, 0.082f, 1.0f);
const vec4 CopperSpecular(0.2f, 0.13f, 0.086f, 1.0f);
const GLfloat   CopperShiness = 2.8f;

// Gold Material
const vec4 GoldAmbient(0.24f, 0.19f, 0.07f, 1.0f);
const vec4 GoldDiffuse(0.75f, 0.60f, 0.22f, 1.0f);
const vec4 GoldSpecular(0.62f,0.55f, 0.36f, 1.0f);
const GLfloat   GoldShiness=51.2f;
```

All float data type (GLfloat or float) variables should be declared explicitly with the additional f sign in the end. Otherwise, during assignment, the variables will be treated as double and casted to the floating type, which will drastically decrease the performance.

6. Create a scene class in Scene.h. This manages the models it contains inside. Currently, it does not contain any camera in it. We will add the camera later in this chapter. The scene provides many services to models, such as managing shader programs, transformation services, rendering of models, and so on. Each scene can be recognized with a unique name. While rendering each model, the scene maintains the reference of the current rendering model in the currentModel:

```
class Scene{
public:
Scene(string name="",Renderer* parentObj = NULL);
  virtual ~Scene(void);        // Destructor
   void initializeScene();        // Initialize Scene
   inline ProgramManager* SceneProgramManager(){
 return &ProgramManagerObj; }
    inline Transform*  SceneTransform() {
 return &TransformObj;   }
    void render();               // Render the Models
    void initializeModels();     // Initialize Models
    void clearModels();          // Remove models
    void addModel( Model* );     // Add into model list
    void addLight( Light* );     // Add lights
    Renderer* getRenderer();      // Get scene's renderer
    void setUpProjection();       // Set projection
    std::vector<Light*>& getLights(){ return lights; }

private:
    ProgramManager    ProgramManagerObj;
    Transform         TransformObj;
    vector<Model*> models; // Model's List
    vector<Light*> lights; // Light's List
    Renderer* renderManager;   // Scene's Renderer
    Model* currentModel;     // Current Model in use
};
```

7. A scene contains multiple lights and models; these models and lights are added to the scene using the `addModel` and `addLight` function defined in the `Scene.cpp`:

```
void Scene::addModel(Model* model){
    if(!model) { return; }
    models.push_back( model );
    model->setSceneHandler(this);
}

void Scene::addLight( Light* lightObj){
    for(int i =0; i<lights.size(); i++){
        if(lights.at(i) == lightObj) return;
    }
    lights.push_back(lightObj);
}
```

8. Create the `Model` class in `ModelEx.h`. This new version of the `Model` class contains the material and parent scene object:

```
class Model {
public:
    Model(Scene* SceneHandler, Model* model,
        ModelType type, string objectName="");

    // Define setter and getter function for Scene
    // and material class.

    // Reuse the older Model class existing methods

protected:
    Scene*  SceneHandler;
    Material materialObj;
};
```

9. As the `ObjLoader` class is also a derivative of the `Model` class, it must also contain the reference of the scene under which it will execute. Modify the `ObjLoader` constructor to hold the scene reference and create two new functions (`ApplyLight`, `ApplyMaterial`) to apply the light and material information:

```
class ObjLoader : public Model{
public:
    // Constructor for ObjLoader
    ObjLoader( Scene* parent, Model* model, MeshType
  mesh, ModelType type);
    void ApplyLight();    // Apply scenes light
```

```
    void ApplyMaterial();// Object's material

    // Rest of the function are same, for more info please
    // refer to SG1_withSceneLightMaterial recipe.
};
```

10. The new method to apply light and materials must be applied before rendering the mesh object to the `ObjLoader::render` method, as given in the following code:

```
void ObjLoader::Render(){
    glUseProgram(program->ProgramID);
    ApplyMaterial();
    ApplyLight();

    // Apply Transformation.
  // Bind with Vertex Array Object for OBJ

    // Draw Geometry
    glDrawArrays(GL_TRIANGLES, 0, IndexCount );
    glBindVertexArray(0);
}
```

11. In `NativeTemplate.cpp`, create a scene in the `GraphicsInit` function and add a light and mesh object to it. Execute the scene by adding these objects to the engine:

```
Renderer* engine   = NULL;
ObjLoader* Suzzane = NULL;
Scene* scene1      = NULL;

bool GraphicsInit(){
  // Create a new Renderer instance
   engine = new Renderer();

// Add a new scene named "Mesh Scene" to engine
   scene1 = new Scene("MeshScene", engine);

   // Create a new light and set into the scene
   scene1->addLight(new Light(Material(MaterialWhite)
 ,glm::vec4(0.0, 0.0, 10.0, 1.0)));

   // Create Suzzane,added into the scene1.
   Suzzane = new ObjLoader(scene1,NULL,SUZZANE,None);
Suzzane->SetMaterial(Material(MaterialCopper));

   // Add Suzzane into Scene
```

```
scene1->addModel( Suzzane);

// Initialize engine
engine->initializeScenes();
}
```

12. Similarly, the `GraphicsRender` function renders the mesh model and updates the scene and related modules. In this recipe, it applies various predefined material types on the mesh model for every one second:

```
bool GraphicsRender(){
    static int i=0;    static clock_t start = clock();
 // Switch material each second
    if(clock()-start > CLOCKS_PER_SEC){
        start = clock();
        (i %=6)++; //Plus one to avoid None type

        // Assign a new material
        Suzzane->SetMaterial(Material(MaterialType(i)));
    }
    engine->render();
}
```

How it works...

The `Renderer` class in the scene graph model is highly simplified compared to the earlier overloaded version; `Scenes` are a containment of the `Renderer` class. A scene must be created dynamically and added to the rendering engine. Similarly, it can be removed from the engine, which allows you to save vital memory resources and CPU cycles. Every scene has a unique name that can be used to retrieve the scene from the engine; the scene has a containment relationship with lights and models. Each scene can have multiple lights. However, the present implementation only supports a single light; the models retrieve the light information from their respective scenes. The implementation of a Model class has not changed much except for the fact that from now onwards the materials can be applied at runtime using the light information from the scene. The scene graph allows sharing the models from one scene to another without any overhead, thus making it highly flexible.

 In order to differentiate the `Renderer` and `Model` classes of the older graphics engine with the scene graph architecture, the filenames of the newer class are suffixed with Ex (`RendererEx.h/.cpp`, `ModelEx.h/.cpp`).

The scene graph architecture allows you to create modeling of the scenes and the control logic outside the engine; this is a more generic and expected way of programming. This recipe uses NativeTemplate.cpp as an external file for modeling and rendering purposes. In this file, the initialization scene is done in the GraphicsInit(). First, the graphicsEngine rendering engine object is created. This engine is set to the Scene's object called scene1 and the parameterized constructor of the Scene contains its name and the parent object of the rendering engine in which it resides. The scene contains a white light source, which is situated 10 units away in the z direction.

The Model object, namely, Suzzane, is created using the parameterized constructor of ObjLoader and is applied to the predefined copper colored material type.

The scene is controlled in GraphicsRender(). In this function, various types of materials are applied at runtime after a regular interval of one second, as shown in the following image:

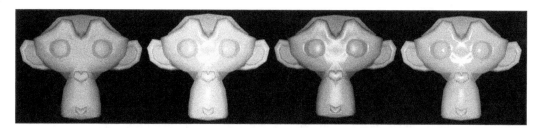

See also

▶ Refer to the *Building prototypes using the GLPI framework* recipe in *Chapter 2, OpenGL ES 3.0 Essentials*

Adding local and relative transformations

Transformation can be divided into two types:

▶ **Local transformation**: This type of transformation is only applicable to an object; it does not affect its child objects. For example, if two objects are in a parent-child relationship, then applying the local scale transformation will not scale the child object.

▶ **Relative transformation**: This type of transformation is applied with respect to the parent of the object. Here, the transformation of the parent is propagated to the children, thereby affecting the geometrical vertex positions in the 3D space. For example, in this case, the scaling transformation to the parent object will scale all its children and their children.

If an object does not have a parent (called the `root` object), then the OpenGL ES coordinate system will be considered its parent. The next recipe will discuss more about the parent-child relationship.

This recipe will create two mesh objects (`Torus`, `Suzzane`) and produce an effect similar to the moon's (`Suzzane`) revolution around the Earth (`Torus`). The moon not only revolves around Earth, but also revolves around its own axis at the same time.

For more information on the internals of the 3D transformation, you can refer to *Implementing scene with the model, view, and projection analogies* recipe in *Chapter 2, OpenGL ES 3.0 Essentials*. This topic covers various types of transformation, transformation matrix conventions, homogenous coordinates, and transformation operations, such as translation, scaling, and rotation.

Getting ready

This recipe requires the first recipe as a prerequisite; you are advised to understand the implementation of the first recipe. You can locate the source of the current recipe (`SG2_withSG1+Transformation`) that is provided with the sample code in this chapter.

How to do it...

Here are the steps to implement local- and relative-transformation in the existing scene graph architecture:

1. In `ModelEx.h`, add the following member variables in `Model` class. These variables are responsible for storing the local and relative transformation matrix. It also has a center of the origin around which the transformation will be applied:

   ```
   mat4 transformation; mat4 transformationLocal; vec3 center;
   ```

2. Go to `ModelEx.cpp` and implement the local transformation function and the relative transformation function:

   ```
   // Many line skipped, refer to source for CTOR/DTOR
   void Model::Rotate(float angle,float x,float y,float z){
   transformation = translate( transformation, center);
   transformation=rotate(transformation,angle,vec3(x,y,z));
   transformation = translate( transformation, -center);
   ```

```
}

void Model::Translate(float x, float y, float z ){
 transformation = translate(transformation,vec3(x,y,z));
}

void Model::Scale(float x, float y, float z ){
 transformation = scale(transformation,vec3(x,y,z)); }

void Model::RotateLocal(float ang,float x,float y,float z){
transformationLocal = rotate(transformationLocal, ang,
                        vec3( x, y, z ) ); }

void Model::TranslateLocal(float x, float y, float z ){
    transformationLocal = translate
(transformationLocal, vec3( x, y, z ));
}
void Model::ScaleLocal(float x, float y, float z ){
        transformationLocal=scale(transformationLocal,vec3(x,y
,z));
}
void Model::SetCenter(vec3 cntrPoint){center=cntrPoint;}
vec3 Model::GetCenter(){ return center; }
```

3. This step is extremely important; it provides the thumb rule to apply local and relative transformation in the `Model` functions derivative classes. For more information, see the implementation of the `Render()` function in the `ObjLoader.cpp` and add the following member functions to the respective variables:

```
ObjLoader::Render(){
  // USE PROGRAM, APPLY MATERIAL AND LIGHT
    // APPLY RELATIVE TRANSFORMATION
      TransformObj->TransformPushMatrix();
      *TransformObj->TransformGetModelMatrix() =
*TransformObj->TransformGetModelMatrix()
*transformation;

      // APPLY LOCAL TRANSFORMATION
      TransformObj->TransformPushMatrix();
      *TransformObj->TransformGetModelMatrix() =
*TransformObj->TransformGetModelMatrix()
*transformationLocal;
              // RENDER GEOMETRY, REUSE CODE
              // POP LOCAL TRANSFORMATION
```

```
        TransformObj->TransformPopMatrix(); // Local Level

        Model::Render();
    // POP RELATIVE TRANSFORMATION
        TransformObj->TransformPopMatrix();
    }
```

4. In `NativeTemplate.cpp`, edit the `GraphicsInit()` function, as shown in the following code:

```
// GLOBAL VARIABLES
//   Renderer* graphicsEngine;  ObjLoader* Suzzane;
//   ObjLoader* Torus; Scene* scene1;

   graphicsEngine = new Renderer();
   scene1         = new Scene("MeshScene", graphicsEngine);
   Suzzane        = new ObjLoader(scene1, NULL, SUZZANE, None);
   Torus          = new ObjLoader(scene1, NULL, TORUS, None);

// Set Light and Material
   scene1->addLight(new Light(Material(MaterialWhite),
   glm::vec4(0.0, 0.0, 10.0, 1.0)));
   Suzzane->SetMaterial(Material(MaterialCopper));
   Torus->SetMaterial(Material(MaterialGold));
   Torus->Scale(0.40, 0.40, 0.4);

   scene1->addModel( Suzzane ); //Add Suzzane to scene
   scene1->addModel( Torus );   //Add Torus to scene

// Set position in the 3D space.
   Suzzane->SetCenter(glm::vec3 (-3.0, 0.0, 0.0));
   Suzzane->Translate(3.0, 0.0, 0.0);

   graphicsEngine->initializeScenes(); //Init Scene
```

5. Use the same file and edit the `GraphicsRender()` function to apply the relative and local transformation on `Suzzane`, as shown in the following code:

```
bool GraphicsRender() {
    Suzzane->Rotate(1.0, 0.0, 1.0, 0.0);      // Relative
    Suzzane->RotateLocal(6.0, 0.0, 1.0, 0.0);// Local
    graphicsEngine->render();    return true;
```

How it works...

The transformation of each `Model` object is stored locally in the transformation and transformationLocal variable. These variables store the translate, rotate, and scaling information. The former variable accumulates all the transformation applied to the parent and its ancestors; each parent object propagates its transformation information to its children. The latter variable only stores the transformation information that is applied to the current object locally; it never passes this transformation to its children. The mechanism that differentiates between relative and local transformation needs to be implemented by a developer in the `Model` derived class in the `Render` function (see step three in the previous section):

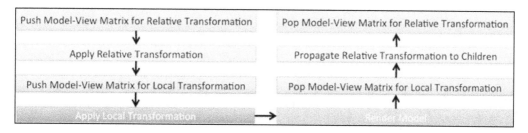

In the current recipe, Torus will act as a reference to the center point of the parent OpenGL ES coordinate system. More specifically, the Torus will render to the OpenGL ES origin, which is (0.0, 0.0, and 0.0). The model is also scaled down and it appears like a center point. The `Suzzane` performs two types of rotations in order to demonstrate the relative and local transformation. In the former transformation, the `Suzzane` will be placed 3 units away from the origin and also set with a center (0.0, 0.0, and -3.0) so that it can revolve around the new origin (center). However, in the latter transformation, `Suzzane` rotates around its own axis. In the `GraphicsRender` function, `Suzzane` is rotated by one degree on each frame locally and relatively, as shown in the following image:

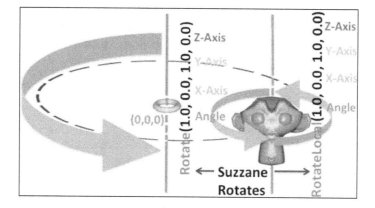

See also

▸ *Adding parent-child support in the scene graph*

Adding parent-child support in the scene graph

This recipe is a very important milestone in the architecture of scene graphs; needless to say, a scene graph is all about the hierarchical connectivity. In the current concept, we maintain the parent-child relationship among similar types of objects. This recipe contains two subrecipes:

1. Building a simple parent-child relationship among renderable objects

2. Understanding the concept of a dummy parent

 The parent-child relationship is applicable to all renderable objects (derived from the `Model` class) and logical engine entities, such as scenes, renderer, and so on. In the present scene graph architecture, this relationship is achieved through the `Object` class. This class allows you to add/remove children dynamically; each object can be recognized with a user-defined name.

How to do it...

Make use of the last recipe that we implemented in this chapter and the following steps to add the support of the parent-child relationship:

1. Create `Object.h` and edit the following code. Each object of this class has a name, a parent, and one of more children stored in the child list. The parent's information is set in the constructor. This class provides high level functions for retrieving the parent or child information, which can be added or removed at fly time. The function of each name is self-explanatory to describe the kind of job it performs:

```
class Object{
public:
    Object(string name="", Object* parentObj=NULL);
    virtual ~Object(){}
    void SetName(string mdlName){ name = mdlName;}
    string GetName() { return name; }

    void SetChild(Object* child = 0);
    void RemoveFromParentChildList();
```

```
        Object*  GetParent() { return parent; }
        vector<Object*>* GetChildren(){ return &childList; }

        void SetVisible(bool flag,bool applyToChildren=false);
        bool GetVisible(){ return isVisible; }

protected:
    string name;            // Model's name
    Object* parent;         // Model's parent
    vector<Object*> childList; // Model's child list
  bool isVisible;         // Is Model Visible
};
```

2. Create `Object.cpp` and define high level methods that cannot be defined inline in the header file. The constructor accepts the name and the parent (`parentObj`) of the object; the `RemoveParent` removes the parent of an object and ensures that none of the children exists in the parent `childList`:

```
Object::Object(std::string objectName, Object* parentObj){
    parent = NULL;            name = objectName;
    SetParent(parentObj);    return;
}

void Object::RemoveParent()
{ RemoveFromParentChildList(); parent = NULL; }

void Object::SetChild(Object* child){
    for(int i =0; i<childList.size(); i++){
if(child == childList.at(i)) { return; }
 }
    child->parent = this;
    childList.push_back(child);
}

void Object::RemoveFromParentChildList(){
   for(int i=0; parent&&i<parent->childList.size(); i++){
        if(this == parent->childList.at(i))
            { parent->childList.erase
(parent->childList.begin()+i); return; }
    }
}
```

3. Implement the `setVisible` and propagate the visibility of the children based on the last parameter: `applyToChildren`, if applicable:

```
void Model::SetVisible(bool flag, bool applyToChildren){
    isVisible = flag;
    if(applyToChildren){
      for(int i =0; i<childList.size(); i++)
        dynamic_cast<Model*>(childList.at(i))->
SetVisible( flag, applyToChildren );}
    }
```

4. Derive the `Renderer`, `Scene`, and `Model` class from the `Object` class.

5. In the derived version for `Model` classes, handle the object visibility, as given in the following code. For more information, refer to `ObjLoader::Render`:

```
ObjLoader::Render(){
   // REUSE CODE, APPLY RELATIVE TRANSFORMATION
   if(isVisible){
        // APPLY LOCAL TRANSFORMATION
   // RENDER GEOMETRY, REUSE CODE
      // POP LOCAL TRANSFORMATION
   }
      // POP RELATIVE TRANSFORMATION
      }
```

6. Implement the rendering of child models:

```
void Model::Render(){
    for(int i =0; i<childList.size(); i++)
        dynamic_cast<Model*>(childList.at(i))->Render();
}
```

7. Use `NativeTemplate.cpp` and add implement the parent-child modeling:

```
Renderer* graphicsEngine; Scene* scene1;
ObjLoader *Sphere, *BaseSphere, *Cube[2];

bool GraphicsInit(){
    graphicsEngine = new Renderer();
    scene1 = new Scene("MeshScene", graphicsEngine);
    scene1->addLight(new Light(Material(MaterialWhite)
,vec4(0.0,0.0,10.0,1.0))));
    BaseSphere =  new ObjLoader   (scene1,NULL,SPHERE,None);
    BaseSphere->SetMaterial(Material(MaterialGold));
    BaseSphere->ScaleLocal(1.5,1.5,1.5);
    int j = 0;
```

```
    for(int i=-1; i<2; i+=2){
      Cube[j] = new ObjLoader(scene1,BaseSphere,CUBE,None);
      Cube[j]->SetMaterial(Material(MaterialCopper));
      Cube[j]->Translate(10.0*i, 0.0, 0.0);
      for(int i=-1; i<2; i+=2){
        Sphere=new ObjLoader(scene1,Cube[j],SPHERE,None);
        Sphere->SetMaterial(Material(MaterialSilver));
        Sphere->Translate(0.0, -5.0*i, 0.0);
      } j++;
    }
    scene1->addModel( BaseSphere);
    graphicsEngine->initializeScenes();
}

bool GraphicsRender(){
    BaseSphere->Rotate(1.0, 0.0, 1.0, 0.0);
    Cube[0]->Rotate(-1.0, 1.0, 0.0, 0.0);
    Cube[1]->Rotate( 1.0, 1.0, 0.0, 0.0);
    graphicsEngine->render();
}
```

How it works...

Any renderable (Model and derivatives) or nonrenderable entities (Renderer, Scene, and derivative) can be derived from the Object class in order to achieve the parent-child relationship. The Object class stores the parent's information in the parent variable and child information in a vector list called childList; any other class object can access the parent and child information using the GetParent() and GetChildren() function.

Each parent is responsible for taking care of its children's execution life cycle. For example, a parent scene will automatically load the children scenes one by one. Similarly, a Model loads its children and manages their initialization to load the required shaders, propagating parent's transformation to children and rendering of each child model.

This recipe contains seven models (five sphere (one big, four small), two cubes), as shown in the following left-hand side image. The parent-child relationship is shown in the following right-hand side image in which the yellow sphere is the parent of two copper colored cubes and each cube has two silver color sphere attached to it. The yellow sphere rotates around the *y* axis; this makes all children elements to rotate around the yellow sphere, while the cubes revolve around the *y* axis. At the same time, they revolve around their own *x* axis, one in a clockwise direction and another in an anticlockwise direction:

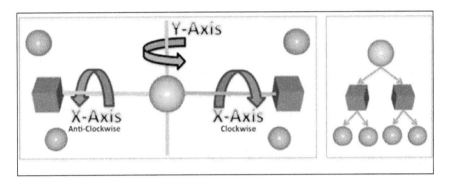

[

Refer to *Create complex models with a transformation graph* recipe. This recipe guides you to create a windmill model using the parent-child relationship and local/relative transformation.
]

There's more...

Look at the following image and try to figure out how we can solve it with the existing parent-child relationship approach.

Problem statement:

A set of semi-circumferences (created from cubes) are arranged in a concentric fashion, where each semi-circumference rotates in the opposite direction with respect to its neighboring semi-circumference:

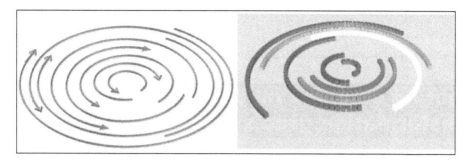

In the present situation, we have eight concentric semi-circumferences. Considering the innermost semi-circumference as the parent of others, one really has to scratch one's head to solve it (give it a try).

Sometimes, there are complex parent-child situations that can be solved easily. As a solution to this problem, we can create eight parents, apply transformations as required, create two parent objects (innermost), and add children, based on the direction of the rotation. Finally, move one parent clockwise and another anticlockwise. This recipe uses the previous solution with the dummy parent, which is described ahead.

So far, we have seen the all parent of the renderable entities, which are also renderable. This is where dummy parent concepts come into the picture. This allows you to create a parent, which does not have any geometry. Therefore, it cannot be rendered and provides a logical parent-child relationship. The `Render` method does not render anything and is only used to apply transformation. The local transformation here does not make any sense as the object's geometry does not exist:

```
class DummyModel : public Model{
public:
    DummyModel(Scene* SceneHandler, Model* model, ModelType type,
            string objectName = "");  // Constructor
    virtual ~DummyModel(){}       // Destructor
        void Render();            // Render the dummy model.
};

DummyModel::DummyModel(Scene*  parentScene, Model* model,
ModelType type,std::string objectName):Model(parentScene,
model, type, objectName){}            // DummyModel CTOR.

void DummyModel::Render(){
    SceneHandler->SceneTransform()->TransformPushMatrix();
    ApplyModelsParentsTransformation();//Parent Transformation
        Model::Render(); // Base renderer process the childs
    SceneHandler->SceneTransform()->TransformPopMatrix();
}
```

▶ *Creating complex models with transformation graph*

Creating complex models with a transformation graph

A transformation graph is a forest of semantic transformations in which each node represents a tree of models. Combining all of these tree models produces a complex 3D model structure. The following image on the left-hand side shows a semantic model of the transformation. The right-hand side image shows a tree structure represented by each of the nodes in the semantic transformation graph:

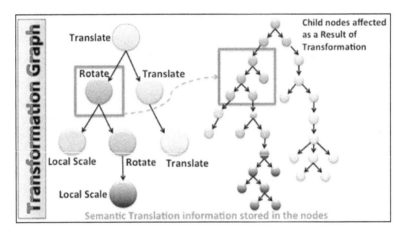

Transformation graphs use the parent-child relationship extensively. Without this, the transform graph hierarchy is very difficult to manage. A transformation graph represents node hierarchies, in which each child node contains the transformation information (translate, scale, and rotate) with respect to its parent.

This recipe is the hybrid of the previous two recipes. It will use the parent-child relationship and the local and relative transformation to produce a semantic transformation graph. In this recipe, you will learn how to create a complex windmill model with basic mesh models, such as cube, cylinder, and sphere.

How to do it...

This recipe does not require any special changes in the scene-graph engine. Use `NativeTemplate.cpp` and edit the `GraphicsInit` and `GraphicsRender`, as shown in the following code:

```
Renderer*      graphicsEngine;    Scene* scene1;
ObjLoader      *Base,    *Stand, *MotorShaft, *CubePlane;
ObjLoader      *Sphere,   *Torus, *Suzzane;

bool GraphicsInit(){
    graphicsEngine = new Renderer();
    scene1 = new Scene("MeshScene", graphicsEngine);
    scene1->addLight(new Light(
            Material(MaterialWhite),vec4(0.0, 0.0, 10.0, 1.0)));

    Base =  new ObjLoader(scene1, Sphere, CUBE);// Base
    Base->SetMaterial(Material(MaterialSilver));
    Base->SetName(std::string("Base"));
    Base->ScaleLocal(1.5, 0.25, 1.5);

    Stand = new ObjLoader(scene1,Base,SEMI_HOLLOW_CYLINDER);// Stand
    Stand->SetMaterial(Material(MaterialSilver));
    Stand->SetName(std::string("Stand"));
    Stand->Translate(0.0, 4.0, 0.0);
    Stand->ScaleLocal(0.5, 4.0, 0.5);

    MotorShaft = new ObjLoader(scene1,Stand,CUBE); // MotorShaft
    MotorShaft->SetMaterial(Material(MaterialSilver));
    MotorShaft->SetName(std::string("MotorShaft"));
    MotorShaft->Translate(0.0, 4.0, 1.0);
    MotorShaft->ScaleLocal(0.5, 0.5, 2.0);

    Sphere = new ObjLoader(scene1,MotorShaft,SPHERE);// MotorEngine
    Sphere->SetMaterial(Material(MaterialGold));
    Sphere->Translate(0.0, 0.0, 2.0);
    Sphere->SetName(std::string("Sphere"));

    for(int i=0; i<360; i+=360/18){ // 20 Fan Blades
        CubePlane =  new ObjLoader   ( scene1, Sphere, CUBE);
        CubePlane->SetMaterial(Material(MaterialCopper));
        CubePlane->SetName(std::string("FanBlade"));
```

```
            CubePlane->Translate(0.0, 2.0, 0.0);
            CubePlane->SetCenter(glm::vec3(0.0, -2.0, 0.0));
            CubePlane->ScaleLocal(0.20, 2.0, 0.20);
            CubePlane->Rotate(i, 0.0, 0.0, 1.0);
        }
        scene1->addModel( Base);
        graphicsEngine->initializeScenes(); return true;
    }
    bool GraphicsRender(){
        Sphere->Rotate(3.0, 0.0, 0.0, 1.0);
        Base->Rotate(1.0, 0.0, 1.0, 0.0);
            graphicsEngine->render(); return true;
    }
```

How it works...

The windmill model comprises of a total of 24 parts: one base, one stand, one motor shaft, one motor engine, and 20 fan blades. The base, motor shaft, and fan blades are made up of cube meshes, whereas the stand and motor engine is made up of cylinder and sphere meshes respectively. All these parts must be arranged in the correct parent-child order and at the same time applied to correct placement, using the local and relative transformation in the 3D space. A picture is worth a thousand words, by looking at the following image, you must have got the idea on how a complete model is woven part by part.

Let's understand the working of this windmill. In the `GraphicsInit()`, the first thing that we need is the base of the windmill, which is created using a perfect cube (**A**). This cube is locally scaled in order to produce a shape depicted by (**B**). Next, the stand is made from a cylinder and translated to four units (**C**) before the origin and then scaled (**D**) so that it perfectly expands in the vertical direction to fit in to the base. The base here is the parent of the stand. The motor shaft is also made up of the (**E**) cube, which translates into four units (**F**). This model is scaled locally in order to give it the (**G**) shape.

Every transformation that we apply is with respect to its parent. Therefore, in the present case, four units in the vertical direction are with respect to the stand, which is the parent of the `MotorShaft`.

Create a sphere in order to produce a `MotorEngine` (**H**) and render it to the **+Z** direction by two units (**I**). The final part is to create the fan blade. Each fan blade is made up of a cube (**J**). This cube needs to render away from the parent center by four units in the vertical direction (**K**). The translate blade is then applied to the local scaling in order to create a blade like shape (**L**). Similarly, this process of producing blades is repeated 20 times to build the complete fan (**M, N**).

Finally, once the geometry is created, the parent node (base) of the windmill is added to the scene. Why haven't the other models been added to the scene? In previous recipes, we mentioned that each parent model takes care of its children. As the base is added to the scene, it takes care of its child elements. The same rule is applicable to all child elements, which are themselves parents of other items:

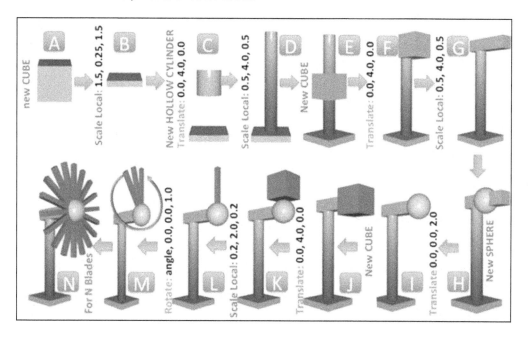

The windmill fan blades rotate by three degrees around the z axis of each frame. This transformation can be simply achieved by applying the rotation on the sphere, which is the parent of all blades. Similarly, in order to revolve the whole model around the y axis, apply a one degree rotation on the base in the GraphicsRender().

See also

▶ *Adding parent-child support in the scene graph*
▶ *Adding local and relative transformations*

Implementing picking with the ray trace technique

Picking is a process of selecting objects in the 3D space contained in a scene by user inputs. This is a very common requirement in 3D graphic applications, where you may be interested in an object tapped by an end user. The tapped point contains position in the screen coordinate system, which is a reference to the viewport. This reference point can be used in various picking techniques to detect the tapped object. In the present recipe, we will use a very versatile picking technique called "ray picking" or "ray trace pick".

In this technique, a ray is simulated using the tapped point in the scene. When the ray intersects with an object, it's assumed to be clicked on. The ray can be intersected with multiple objects in a given scene; the selected objects can be collected and sorted according to the distance from the viewpoint in order to become the closest selected object. In this recipe, we will implement the ray trace picking technique, which is highly accurate in pinpointing 3D objects.

The following steps provide an overview of implementing ray tracing picking:

1. Detect the tapped point on screen (Sx, Sy).

2. Use (Sx, Sy) and find unprojected coordinates on the near (Nx, Ny) and far plane (Fx, Fy).

3. Create a ray from (Nx, Ny) and (Fx, Fy) unprojected coordinates.

4. Consider each triangle of the mesh geometry and perform the ray triangle intersection. The test can be optimized using a low polygon mesh.

How to do it...

Here are the steps to implement ray-trace picking:

1. Create an interface class called `GestureEvent` derived from `Event` in a new file called `Event.h/.cpp`. This will provide the necessary interfaces for touch screen events. Classes that want to utilize the benefits of gesturing must be derived from the `GestureEvent` class:

```
class Event {
 public:
    Event(){          // Define CTOR };
    virtual ~Event(){ // Define DTOR };
};
class GestureEvent : public Event {
   public:
    GestureEvent():Event(){  // Define CTOR }
```

```
        virtual ~GestureEvent(){ // Define DTOR }
        virtual void TouchEventDown(float x, float y) = 0;
        virtual void TouchEventMove(float x, float y) = 0;
        virtual void TouchEventRelease(float x, float y) = 0;
};
```

2. The `Renderer`, `Scene`, and `Model` class need to be inherited with `GestureEvent` in order to support touch events. Include the `Event.h` header file in their respective classes:

```
class Renderer: public Object, public GestureEvent
class Scene    : public Object, public GestureEvent
class Model    : public Object, public GestureEvent
```

3. Propagate gesture events to all scenes in the `Renderer` class:

```
void Renderer::TouchEventDown(float x, float y){
    for( int i=0; i<scenes.size();  i++ )
        { scenes.at(i)->TouchEventDown(x, y); } }
// Similarly, implement TouchEventMove &
// TouchEventRelease like TouchEventDown.
```

4. Implement gesture interfaces in the `Scene` class and propagate the received touch events from renderer to all the models contained in the following code:

```
void Scene::TouchEventDown(float x, float y){
    for( int i=0; i<models.size(); i++ ){
      models.at(i)->TouchEventDown(x, y); }
}
//Similarly, defineTouchEventMove & TouchEventRelease
```

5. Implement gesture interfaces in the `Model` and apply them to each child:

```
void Model::TouchEventDown(float x, float y){
    for(int i =0; i<childList.size(); i++){
      dynamic_cast<Model*>
        (childList.at(i))->TouchEventDown(x, y);}
}
//Similarly, define TouchEventMove & TouchEventRelease
```

6. Create a `Ray.h/.cpp` file and define the `Ray` class, as given in the following code:

```
class Ray{
 public:
   vec3 dest, dir; // Destination and Direction
   Ray(){ dest = vec3(); dir = vec3(); }
   Ray(vec3 de, vec3 di){ dest = de; dir = di; }
   Ray(const Ray & r){ dest=r.dest; dir=r.dir; }
```

```
Ray & operator=(const Ray&r)
{dest=r.dest; dir=r.dir; return *this; }
};
```

7. Create a function called `IntersectWithRay` in the base `Model` class and implement in the `ObjLoader` derived class:

```
bool ObjLoader::IntersectWithRay(Ray ray0,vec3& intersect){
    vec4 p0, p1, p2;
    // COMPUTE EACH TRIANGLE AND CHECK INTERSECTION
    for(uint i=0; i<objMeshModel->vertices.size(); i+=3){
      p0=vec4(objMeshModel->vertices.at(i).position,1);
      p1=vec4(objMeshModel->vertices.at(i+1).position,1);
      p2=vec4(objMeshModel->vertices.at(i+2).position,1);
      mat4 mat = *TransformObj->TransformGetModelMatrix();

      p0 = mat*GetEyeCoordinatesFromRoot() * p0;
      p1 = mat*GetEyeCoordinatesFromRoot() * p1;
      p2 = mat*GetEyeCoordinatesFromRoot() * p2;

      if (intersectLineTriangle(ray0.destination,
      ray0.dir, vec3(p0.x,p0.y,p0.z),
      vec3(p1.x,p1.y,p1.z), vec3(p2.x,p2.y,p2.z),
      intersect))
      { return true; }
    }
    return false;
}
```

8. Create a function called `IntersectWithRay` in the base `Model` class and implement it in the derived version classes, such as `ObjLoader`, in the present scenario:

```
void ObjLoader::TouchEventDown( float x, float y ){
    GLint vp[4] = { 0, 0, 0, 0 }; //Store's viewport
    glGetIntegerv( GL_VIEWPORT, vp );
    vec4 viewport(vp[0], vp[1],vp[2], vp[3]);
    vec3 win(x, vp[3]-y, 0.0);
    vec3 nearPoint = glm::unProject(win, *TransformObj->
    TransformGetModelViewMatrix(), *TransformObj->
    TransformGetProjectionMatrix(), viewport);
    win.z = 1.0; // On the far plane.
    vec3 farPoint = glm::unProject(win,
```

```
*TransformObj->TransformGetModelViewMatrix(), *TransformObj-
>TransformGetProjectionMatrix(), viewport);
    Ray ray0(nearPoint, farPoint-nearPoint);
    glm::vec3 intersectionPoint;
    if(IntersectWithRay( ray0, intersectionPoint)){
      printf("Intersect with %s", GetName().c_str());
        isPicked = !isPicked;
    }


    Model::TouchEventDown(x,y); //Propagate to children
}
```

How it works...

The `GestureEvent` class receives the tap event (Sx, Sy) in the screen coordinate system from the main application in Renderer and passes it to Model classes via the respective parent scene. These coordinates are then used to calculate unprojected coordinates on the near and far plane. In the present recipe, we have used the `glm::unproject` API:

Syntax:

```
void glm::unproject(vec3 const& win, mat4 const& modelView,
mat4 const& proj, vec4 const& viewport);
```

Variable	Description
win	Components *x*, *y* specify screen coordinates. The *z* with value zero and one specify the near and far plane respectively.
modelView	This specifies the product of the view and model matrix.
proj	This specifies the project matrix of the current scene.
viewport	This specifies the current dimension of the viewport region.

The unproject inverts the operation of projection calculation in which world coordinates are used to calculate screen coordinate in the following order:

```
Screen Coordinates => Viewport => Projection => ModelView => World
coordinates
```

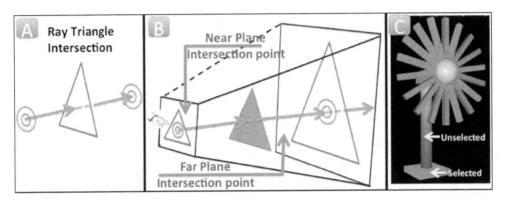

Unprojected coordinates on the near plane (Nx, Ny) and the far plane (Fx, Fy) are used to shoot a ray from the near to the far plane, as shown in the preceding image (**B**). When this ray hits a 3D object, it is considered to be picked. Mathematically, this picking is performed by taking the intersection of mesh polygons and ray produced. For the sake of simplicity, we used the line and triangle intersection in the present recipe, as shown in image (**A**). The mesh is iterated for each triangle in it and intersected by the ray using the `IntersectWithRay` function, which is inherited from `Model`. This function must be overridden in the derived version in order to perform the intersection test. The `ObjLoader` class overrides this function and calculates the ray-triangle intersection using the `glm::intersectLineTriangle` API. This recipe paints all the selected 3D mesh objects with ambient red, which are intersected by the ray. In order to find the closest selected object, sort the entire selected item and choose the closest one from the camera view.

See also

▶ *Implementing 2D textured button widgets*

Implementing 2D textured button widgets

OpenGL ES does not provide built-in UI components, such as buttons, radio box, checkbox, and so on. In general, these components are called 2D widgets and are laid out in the HUD in the screen coordinate system, where the *z* component is either zero or not at all used. This recipe will guide us to design and lay out 2D widgets on the screen coordinate system using OpenGL ES.

This recipe contains two recipes:

- The first recipe allows you to create the geometry of a simple button. Geometrical coordinates are specified in the local screen coordinate system, which is useful in designing the layout.

- The second recipe is implemented in the *There's more...* section of this recipe, where we used the ray-picking technique, making the button clickable. Selecting the button will change its color.

The next image shows the output of the first recipe. It contains six buttons of 32 x 32 dimensions. Each button is scaled by a factor of two, resulting in the final dimension of 64 x 64. The extreme left hand-side button (up button) is the parent of all the remaining buttons. This means any property applied to the parent will be propagated to all its children.

How to do it...

Here are the steps to implement this recipe:

1. Create `Button.h/.cpp` and define the `Button` class derived from the `Model` class:

```
class Button : public Model{
public:
    Button(Scene* parent,Model* model,ModelType type,vec3*
  vertices,vec2* textureCoordinates,char* texture);
    virtual ~Button();      // Destructor for Button class
    void InitModel();    // Initialize our Button class
    void Render();        // Render the Button class
private:
  char MVP, TEX; Image* image;  char* textureImage;
    vec3 vertices[4]; vec2 texCoordinates[4];
};
```

2. The `Button` class renders the geometry of the button. A button geometry has four vertices on which a texture is pasted, with the help of texture coordinates:

```
void Button::Render(){
    glBindBuffer(GL_ARRAY_BUFFER, 0);
    glUseProgram(program->ProgramID);

    glDisable(GL_CULL_FACE); // Disable culling
    glEnable(GL_BLEND);      // Enable blending
    glBlendFunc(GL_SRC_ALPHA,GL_ONE_MINUS_SRC_ALPHA);

    glActiveTexture (GL_TEXTURE0);
    glUniform1i(TEX, 0);
```

```
    if (image)
    {glBindTexture(GL_TEXTURE_2D,image->getTextureID());}

    TransformObj->TransformPushMatrix(); //Parent Level
    ApplyModelsParentsTransformation();

    if(isVisible){
        TransformObj->TransformPushMatrix(); // Local Level
        ApplyModelsLocalTransformation();

        glEnableVertexAttribArray(VERTEX_POSITION);
        glEnableVertexAttribArray(TEX_COORD);
        glVertexAttribPointer(TEX_COORD, 2, GL_FLOAT,
GL_FALSE, 0, &texCoordinates[0]);
        glVertexAttribPointer(VERTEX_POSITION, 3, GL_FLOAT,
            GL_FALSE, 0, &vertices[0]);
        glUniformMatrix4fv( MVP, 1, GL_FALSE,TransformObj->
TransformGetModelViewProjectionMatrix());
        glDrawArrays(GL_TRIANGLE_STRIP, 0, 4); // Draw
        TransformObj->TransformPopMatrix();//Local Level
    }

    Model::Render();
    TransformObj->TransformPopMatrix(); //Parent Level
}
```

3. Set up the heads up display using the orthographic projection system:

```
void Scene::setUpProjection(){
  TransformObj.TransformSetMatrixMode(PROJECTION_MATRIX );
  TransformObj.TransformLoadIdentity();
  int viewport_matrix[4];
  glGetIntegerv( GL_VIEWPORT, viewport_matrix );
  TransformObj.TransformOrtho( 0, viewport_matrix[2],
 viewport_matrix[3], 0 , -1, 1);
  TransformObj.TransformSetMatrixMode( VIEW_MATRIX );
  TransformObj.TransformLoadIdentity();
  TransformObj.TransformSetMatrixMode( MODEL_MATRIX );
  TransformObj.TransformLoadIdentity(); return;
}
```

4. In `NativeTemplate.cpp`, edit the `GraphicsInit()` function, as given in the following code. This function lays out buttons on the screen coordinate system. These buttons accept geometrical vertices and texture coordinates as an input, which are optional parameters. If these parameters are not supplied. The dimension of the button will be equal to the image size. The texture coordinate has default values (0.0, 0.0) and (1.0, 1.0) as the bottom-left and top-right respectively:

```
Renderer* graphicsEngine;
Scene* scene2;
Button* buttonUp, *buttonDown, *buttonLeft,
Button* buttonRight, *buttonForward, *buttonBackward;

bool GraphicsInit(){
    graphicsEngine = new Renderer();
vec2 texCoords[4]={
vec2(0.0, 0.0),
vec2(1.0,0.0),
vec2(0.0, 1.0),
vec2(1.0,1.0)
};

vec3 vertices[4]={
vec3(0.0,0.0,0.0),
vec3(400.0,0.,0.),
                        vec3(0.0,400.0,0.0),
vec3(400.0,400.0,0.0)
};

    scene2      = new Scene("ButtonScene");
    buttonUp    = new Button(scene2, NULL, None,
NULL, texCoords, "dir_up.png");
    buttonUp->SetName(std::string("Direction Up"));
    buttonUp->Translate(50.0, 100, 0.0);
    buttonUp->Scale(2.0, 2.0, 2.0);

    // MAKE THE buttonUp AS PARENT OF OTHER BUTTONS
    buttonBackward = new Button(scene2, buttonUp,
None, NULL, texCoords, "dir_down.png");
    buttonBackward->SetName(string("Direction Backward"));
    buttonBackward->Translate(250.0, 0.0, 0.0);
    buttonBackward->SetCenter(vec3(16, 16, 0));
    buttonBackward->Rotate(-135.0, 0.0, 0.0, 1.0);
    // SIMILARLY DEFINE OTHER BUTTONS. . . . .
```

```
// buttonDown, buttonLeft, buttonRight, buttonForward

   scene2->addModel(buttonUp); // ADD TO THE SCENE
   graphicsEngine->addScene(scene2);
   graphicsEngine->initializeScenes(); return true;
}
```

How it works...

The geometry of the 2D button widget is created using four vertices, which are specified in the screen coordinate system. This geometry is textured with the specified image with the help of texture coordinates on the geometry. OpenGL ES works in the Cartesian system, where the origin exists in the center of the viewport dimension in the logical coordinate system. Viewport also has the same coordinate system and works in the pixel coordinate system, but the origin in this case exists in the bottom-left corner as shown in the following image. In contrast, the 2D widget is designed in the device coordinate system, where the origin is considered as the top-left corner (see the following image).

Now, head-up-display is a mechanism in which we can formulate the device coordinate system by using the OpenGL ES coordinate system and the viewport. For this, we need to render the projection system of the scene with an orthographic view where the origin is shifted in the top-right corner in the setUpProjection function.

The button class objects are created in NativeTemplate.cpp in the GraphicsInit() function, where six buttons are created with different images on it. Each button is given a unique name so that it can be used later in the camera recipe. The following image shows these buttons on the right-hand side. In order to make the job simpler for placement of icons in the 2D HUD screen space, we made the first button (up direction) as the parent of other buttons. This way, we all buttons can be resized and moved by applying a single operation on the parent itself. Finally, render these buttons to the HUD using GraphicsRender():

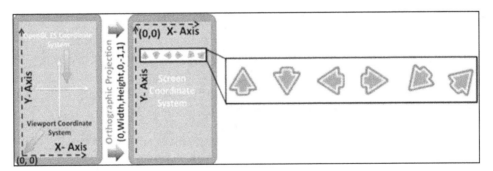

There's more...

Unlike how we implemented the picking technique in the last recipe, this time we will implement the picking technique in the button class, which will help us to know which button has been clicked on so that a user can perform the appropriate action in response to it. Refer to the next recipe in order to see how these buttons control the camera moved in a scene.

The Button class must be derived from the GestureEvent class and implemented to virtual gesture functions, such as TouchEventDown and TouchEventRelease in order to handle the gesture event and propagate them to child member objects:

```
class Button : public Model, public GestureEvent
    {//Multiple code skipped};
void Button::TouchEventDown(float x, float y){
    GLint viewport_matrix[4]   = { 0, 0, 0, 0 };
    glGetIntegerv( GL_VIEWPORT, viewport_matrix );
    glm::vec4 viewport(viewport_matrix[0],viewport_matrix[1],
                    viewport_matrix[2],viewport_matrix[3]);
    glm::vec3 win(x, viewport_matrix[3]-y, 0.0);
    mat4 matMV  = *TransformObj->TransformGetModelMatrix();
    mat4 matMVP = *TransformObj->TransformGetModelMatrix();
    glm::vec3 nearPoint = unProject(win, mat, matMVP, viewport);
    win.z = 1.0;
    glm::vec3 farPoint = unProject(win, matMV,matMVP, viewport);
    Ray ray0(nearPoint, farPoint-nearPoint);

    glm::vec3 intersectionPoint;
    if(IntersectWithRay( ray0, intersectionPoint)){
        printf("Intersect with %s", this->GetName().c_str());
        isPicked = !isPicked; clicked = true; return;
    }
    Model::TouchEventDown(x,y);
}

void Button::TouchEventRelease( float x, float y ){
    clicked = false; isPicked = false;
    Model::TouchEventRelease(x,y);
}
```

This class must override the `IntersectWithRay` function. In this, it performs a line and triangle intersection with two triangles that contains the button geometry. The following image shows the change in the color of the button when the touch down event occurs. The button gets restored to the original color when the touch release event fires:

Let's take a look at the following code:

```
bool Button::IntersectWithRay(Ray ray0, vec3& intersectionPoint){
    // CHECK INTERSECTION WITH FIRST TRIANGLE
    mat4 = *TransformObj->TransformGetModelMatrix();
    p0 = mat * GetEyeCoordinatesFromRoot() * vec4(vertices[0], 1.0);
    p1 = mat * GetEyeCoordinatesFromRoot() * vec4(vertices[1], 1.0);
    p2 = mat * GetEyeCoordinatesFromRoot() * vec4(vertices[2], 1.0);
    if ( intersectLineTriangle(ray0.destination, ray0.direction,
        vec3(p0.x,p0.y,p0.z), vec3(p1.x,p1.y,p1.z),
        vec3(p2.x,p2.y,p2.z), intersectionPoint)){
      return true;
    }

    // CHECK INTERSECTION WITH SECOND TRIANGLE
    p0 = mat * GetEyeCoordinatesFromRoot() * vec4(vertices[1], 1.0);;
    p1 = mat * GetEyeCoordinatesFromRoot() * vec4(vertices[3], 1.0);;
    p2 = mat * GetEyeCoordinatesFromRoot() * vec4(vertices[2], 1.0);;
    if ( intersectLineTriangle(ray0.destination, ray0.direction,
          vec3(p0.x,p0.y,p0.z), vec3(p1.x,p1.y,p1.z),
          vec3(p2.x,p2.y,p2.z), intersectionPoint)){
      return true;
    }
    return false;
}
```

See also

▶ Refer to the *Rendering text on Head Up Display* recipe in Chapter 8, *Font Rendering*

Navigating the scene with a camera system

In 3D graphics, a camera allows you to navigate through the 3D space; it can be used to perform the rotation and displacement on any arbitrary axis. In OpenGL ES, there is nothing such as a camera. This has to be implemented programmatically. Implementing a camera is extremely simple. In fact, we do not require any specific OpenGL ES APIs for this and it's all about manipulating matrices. In this recipe, we will simulate a first person camera.

How to do it...

Reuse the last implement recipe and perform the following steps to implement the camera system:

1. Create a `Camera.h/.cpp` file and define a `Camera` class derived from `Object`. This class contains three unit vectors: `Left`, `Up`, and `Forward`, which store directional unit vectors in the 3D space along the *x*, *y*, and *z* axis respectively. The `Position` specifies the location of the camera and Target specifies the location of the camera view:

```
struct ViewPort{ int x, y, width, height; };
struct CameraViewParams{ float left, right, bottom, top,
front, back; float fov, nearPlane, farPlane; };

class Camera : public Object{
vec3 Forward, Up, Right, Position, Target;
CameraType type; // Type of cameras

protected:
int viewport_matrix[4]; ViewPort viewPortParam;
CameraViewParams cameraViewParameters;

public:
Camera(string name, Scene* parent = NULL,
CameraType camType = perspective);

void Viewport (int x, int y, int width, int height);
virtual void Render ();
void Rotate(vec3 orientation, float angle);
void MoveForwards( GLfloat Distance );
// Similarly,define MoveBackwards, StrafeRightSide etc.

void SetLeft(float val) {cameraViewParameters.left=val;}
```

```
        // Similarly,define SetRight, SetBottom, SetTop Etc.

        float GetLeft(){ return
        cameraViewParameters.left; }
        //Similarly, define GetRight, GetBottom, GetTop etc Etc.
        vec3 PositionCamera(){return Position + Forward;}
    };
```

2. Define the rotation of the camera, as given in the following code:

```
#define DEGREE_TO_RADIAN   M_PI / 180.0f
#define RADIAN_TO_DEGREE   180.0f / M_PI
#define COS(Angle)  (float)cos(Angle*DEGREE_TO_RADIAN)
#define SIN(Angle)  (float)sin(Angle*DEGREE_TO_RADIAN)

void Camera::Rotate(vec3 orientation, float angle){
  if(orientation.x == 1.0){ //Rotate along X axis
    Forward=normalize(Forward*COS(angle)+Up*SIN(angle));
    Up      = -cross( Forward, Right ); }

  if(orientation.y == 1.0){ //Rotate along Y axis
     Forward=normalize(Forward*COS(angle)-Right*SIN(angle));
     Right  = cross( Forward, Up ); }

  if(orientation.z == 1.0){ //Rotate along Z axis
    Left = normalize(Right*COS(angle)+Up*SIN(angle));
    Up    = -cross(Forward, Right); }
}
```

3. Make the camera move along the three axes using the move function, as shown in the following code:

```
void Camera::MoveForwards(GLfloat d){
  Position += Forward*d;
}

void Camera::StrafeRightSide(GLfloat d){
  Position += Left*d;
}

void Camera::StrafeUpside(GLfloat d){
  Position += Up*d;
}

void Camera::MoveBackwards(GLfloat d){
```

```
    MoveForwards( -d );
  }

  void Camera::StrafeLeftSide(GLfloat d){
    StrafeRightSide(-d);
  }

  void Camera::StrafeDownside(GLfloat d){
    StrafeUpside(-d);
  }
```

4. The `Camera::Render()` sets up the projection matrix in the following code:

```
void Camera::Render(){
  Scene* scene = dynamic_cast<Scene*>(this->GetParent());
  Transform* TransformObj = scene->SceneTransform();
  glViewport( viewPortParam.x, viewPortParam.y,
  viewPortParam.width, viewPortParam.height );
  TransformObj->TransformSetMatrixMode(PROJECTION_MATRIX);
  TransformObj->TransformLoadIdentity();

  if ( type == perspective ){
    // Multiple code line skipped
    // Apply perspective view:TransformPerspective
  }else{
    // Multiple code line skipped
    // Apply Orthographic view: TransformOrtho
  }
}

TransformObj->TransformSetMatrixMode(VIEW_MATRIX);
TransformObj->TransformLoadIdentity();
vec3 viewPoint = Position + Forward;
TransformObj->TransformLookAt(&Position,&viewPoint,&Up);

TransformObj->TransformSetMatrixMode(MODEL_MATRIX);
TransformObj->TransformLoadIdentity();
}
```

5. Combine the two scenes that we created in previous recipes. The first scene contains the windmill. The second scene contains pick buttons. The former scene will be rendered to the perspective camera. However, the latter will make use of the HUD camera:

```
Camera *camera1, *camera2;
bool GraphicsInit(){
    graphicsEngine = new Renderer();
    scene1    = new Scene("MeshScene", graphicsEngine);
    camera1 = new Camera("Camera1", NULL);
    scene1->addCamera(camera1);
    // Multiple code lines skipped
    graphicsEngine->initializeScenes();

    scene2    = new Scene("ButtonScene");
    camera2 = new CameraHUD("Camera2", scene2);
    // Multiple code line skipped
    graphicsEngine->addScene(scene2);
    graphicsEngine->initializeScenes();}

bool GraphicsResize(int width, int height){
    graphicsEngine->resize(width, height);
    camera1->Viewport(0, 0, width, height);
    camera2->Viewport(0, 0, width, height);}
```

How it works...

A camera contains three orientation unit vectors: the forward (0.0, 0.0, and -1.0), right (1.0, 0.0, and 0.0), and up vector (0.0, 1.0, and 0.0). The first vector points to a direction where the camera is heading. For example, in the present case, the camera will move in the negative *z* axis direction. Similarly, the right vector specifies the direction of the movement in the *x* axis and the up vector in the *y* axis. The up vector can also be understood like a head, which specifies whether the camera is viewing a scene in the upside (0.0, 1.0, and 0.0) or upside down (0.0, -1.0, and 0.0) direction.

Using these vectors, the camera can be moved along any of the three axes. For example, if you want to move the camera five units ahead, then the product of |5| * forward will place your camera at (0.0, 0.0, or -5.0) looking in the same direction, whereas moving the camera right by four units places the camera at (4.0, 0.0, or -5.0). Again, the camera still looks in the negative *z* direction. In the present recipe, the camera's current position is translated using functions, such as `MoveForwards`, `StrafeRightSide`, `StrafeUpSide`, and so on. The orientation of the camera along *x*, *y*, or *z* axis can be changed using the `Rotate` function.

> The camera displacement on any arbitrary axis specified by the forward, right, and up unit vector does not affect the orientation of the camera. The orientation remains unchanged and the camera will continue to look in the same direction specified by the forward vector. The orientation of the camera can only be effected when the camera rotates along any of the arbitrary axis.

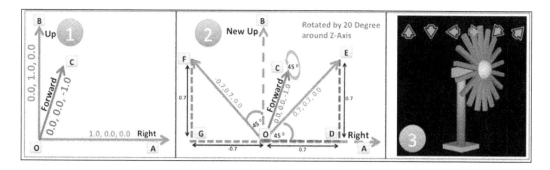

The preceding image (part **1**) shows the effect of rotation on the forward (**OC**), right (**OA**), and up (**OB**) vectors, when the rotation of 45 degree is performed along the z axis. This results (image part **2**) in the new right (**OE**) and new up (**OF**) vector. The forward vector has no changes as it rotates along the z axis:

$$x' = x \cos(\theta) + y \sin(\theta)$$
$$y' = -x \sin(\theta) + y \cos(\theta)$$
$$z' = z$$

$$OE = OD + DE$$
$$OE = OA*\cos(\theta) + OB*\sin(\theta)$$
$$OF = OG + GF$$
$$OF = -OA*\sin(\theta) + OB*\cos(\theta)$$

There's more...

The current recipe contains two cameras for each scene. The first camera renders the perspective projection system. The second camera renders the scene to the head-up-display in the orthographic projection view. The `Camera` class that we implemented in the last recipe cannot be programmed for HUD camera requirements. Therefore, we need a new `Camera` derivative class called `CameraHUD` to implement HUD.

The following code shows the implementation of the HUD camera. The `Render` function is overridden. This function queries the current viewport dimensions and maps it to the orthographic left-right and top-bottom parameters in such a way that the origin shifts from center to the top-left, same as the device screen coordinate system. For more information on HUD, refer to the *See also* subsection in this recipe:

```
class CameraHUD : public Camera{
public:
    CameraHUD(std::string name, Scene* parent = NULL);
    void Render();
    virtual ~CameraHUD();
};

    // Code skipped, see sample for CTOR and DTOR definition.
    void CameraHUD::Render(){ // Render HUD VIEW
    Scene* scene = dynamic_cast<Scene*>(this->GetParent());
    glViewport( viewPortParam.x, viewPortParam.y,
            viewPortParam.width, viewPortParam.height );

    Transform*  TransformObj = scene->SceneTransform();
    TransformObj->TransformSetMatrixMode(PROJECTION_MATRIX);
    TransformObj->TransformLoadIdentity();

    glGetIntegerv( GL_VIEWPORT, viewport_matrix );
    TransformObj->TransformOrtho( viewport_matrix[0],
        viewport_matrix[2], viewport_matrix[3],
         viewport_matrix[1] , -1, 1);
    // Code skipped, Load Model/View Matrix with Identity matrix.

}
```

See also

▶ Refer to the *Rendering text on Head Up Display* recipe in Chapter 8, *Font Rendering*

Implementing the scene with multiple views

One of the most common requirements for real time 3D applications is to render a scene to multiple view windows simultaneously. For example, a CAD/CAM-based application renders a scene to four types of views: perspective, orthographic front, side, and top view. In the scene graph architecture, multiple views are achieved with the help of rendering a scene to two or more cameras.

This recipe extends the last recipe to supporting multiple cameras, where each camera has different viewport region (which could be overlapped) and can have separate clear colors (depending on the requirement).

How to do it...

Here are the steps to implement this recipe:

1. Now on, the screen clear color and buffer clearing will be applied within the Camera view itself. Remove the clear code from `Renderer::render()`. Define a `vec4` type variable called `clearColor` to store the clear color information:

```
void Camera::SetClearColor(glm::vec4 color){
    clearColor = color;
}
```

2. Apply the clear color information and framebuffers in `Camera::render()`. In the same function, make sure that `glViewPort` and `glScissor` are passed on with exactly same dimensions. The `glScissor()` works if the scissor test is enabled. It defines a rectangular screen space region in the screen coordinate system beyond which nothing will be drawn:

```
void Camera::Render(){
    // Setup Viewport Info
    glViewport( viewPortParam.x, viewPortParam.y,
    viewPortParam.width, viewPortParam.height );
    // Apply scissoring
    glScissor ( viewPortParam.x, viewPortParam.y,
    viewPortParam.width, viewPortParam.height );

    glClearColor( clearColor.x, clearColor.y,
    clearColor.z, clearColor.w );
    glClear(GL_COLOR_BUFFER_BIT|GL_DEPTH_BUFFER_BIT);

    // Reuse code for Setting up Projection/Model/View
}
```

3. In `NativeTemplate.cpp`, edit the `GraphicsInit()` function as follows:

```
Camera *camera1, *camera2, *camera3, *camera4;
bool GraphicsInit(){
    graphicsEngine = new Renderer();
    scene1  = new Scene("MeshScene", graphicsEngine);
    camera1 = new Camera("Camera1", scene1);
    camera2 = new Camera("Camera2", scene1);
```

```
      camera3 = new Camera("Camera3", scene1);
      camera4 = new Camera("Camera4", scene1);
      // Multiple code line skipped
   }
```

4. Use `GraphicsResize()` and define the viewport size for all the four cameras defined in the preceding code. Specify the clear color information for each camera in order to paint the background of view:

```
bool GraphicsResize( int width, int height ){
    graphicsEngine->resize(width, height);
    // Third Quadrant
    camera1->Viewport(0, 0, width/2, height/2);
    camera1->SetClearColor(glm::vec4(0.0, 0.0, 0.0, 1.0));
    // Second Quadrant
    camera2->Viewport(0, height/2, width/2, height/2);
    camera2->SetClearColor(glm::vec4(1.0, 1.0, 1.0, 1.0));
    // Fourth Quadrant
    camera3->Viewport(width/2, 0, width/2, height/2);
    camera3->SetClearColor(glm::vec4(1.0, 0.0, 1.0, 1.0));
    // First Quadrant
    camera4->Viewport(width/2,height/2,width/2,height/2);
    camera4->SetClearColor(glm::vec4(1.0, 1.0, 0.0, 1.0));}
```

How it works...

A multiview scene has multiple cameras rendering the present scene to different parts of screen regions. Each different region is specified by the viewport dimension specified in the camera. In order to support multiple views in the scene graph, we need to:

1. Specify the viewport region. This will produce screen coordinates from the world coordinates of the scene with respect to the specified viewport dimension.

2. Clear the color. This is the color used to clear the color buffer each time framebuffer is drawn.

3. When a clear command is specified, it clears the complete framebuffer. As a consequence, you may not be able to see different views at all because the last camera's clear command has cleared the existing drawing in the framebuffer. This unexpected clearing of the color buffer can be avoided using the scissor test. In OpenGL ES 3.0, you can scissor a framebuffer region using the `glScissor` command, which defines a rectangular screen space region in the screen coordinate system beyond which nothing will be drawn.

The following command needs to the specified in order to achieve multiple cameras before using any model, view, and projection matrix:

```
glViewport ( viewPortParam.x, viewPortParam.y,
        viewPortParam.width, viewPortParam.height );
glScissor ( viewPortParam.x, viewPortParam.y,
        viewPortParam.width, viewPortParam.height );
glClearColor( clearColor.x, clearColor.y,
        clearColor.z, clearColor.w );
glClear(GL_COLOR_BUFFER_BIT|GL_DEPTH_BUFFER_BIT);
```

There's more...

The `glScissor()` will only work if the scissor test is enabled; `glScissor` defines a rectangle and calls the scissor box in window coordinates. The first two arguments: x and y specify the lower-left corner of the box. The width and height specifies the dimensions of the box.

To enable and disable the scissor test, call `https://www.khronos.org/opengles/sdk/docs/man/xhtml/glEnable.xml` and `https://www.khronos.org/opengles/sdk/docs/man/xhtml/glDisable.xml` with the `GL_SCISSOR_TEST` argument. This test is initially disabled. When the scissor test is enabled, only pixels that lie within the scissor box can be modified by drawing commands. Window coordinates have integer values at the shared corners of framebuffer pixels.

Syntax:

```
void glScissor(GLint x, GLint y, GLsizei width, GLsizei height);
```

Variables	Description
x, y	This specifies the lower-left corner of the scissor box. The initial value of x, y is (0, 0).
width, height	This specifies the width and height of the scissor box. When a GL context is first attached to a window, the width and height are set to the dimensions of that window.

See also

> ▶ Refer to the *Rendering text on Head Up Display recipe in Chapter 8, Font Rendering*

11
Anti-aliasing Techniques

In this chapter, we will cover the following recipes:

- ▸ Understanding the sampling rate technique
- ▸ Understanding the post processing technique
- ▸ Implementing fast approximate anti-aliasing
- ▸ Implementing adaptive anti-aliasing
- ▸ Implementing an antialiased circle geometry

Introduction

Anti-aliasing is a technique in computer graphics that improves the quality of the rendered image or video output displayed on the screen by minimizing jagged lines or the stair-step case effect. The raster screen is composed of hundreds of tiny square pixels arranged in a grid format. These pixels are sampled during the image rasterization process according to the shape of the geometry. Basically, the cause of anti-aliasing is the point sampling. These samples are represented by rectangular pixels, which are not sufficient to produce curved shapes. Edges in the image, which are round (not horizontal or vertical), are responsible for this stair-step case effect as it ends up coloring pixels like a stair arrangement. The aliasing problem is not much noticeable when an image or scene is still, but as soon as they are in motion, jagged edges are highly visible. The following image shows the rendering of an infinite detailed isosceles right triangle (**A**). The rasterization stage performs the sampling and displays it on the screen with limited sampling grid. Clearly, the stair-step case effect is easily visible on the hypotenuse (**B**). However, the edges of the base and perpendicular are aligned with horizontal and vertical grid pixels (**C**), thereby causing no jagged edges.

However, as soon as the triangle rotates, all edges will show the aliased effect:

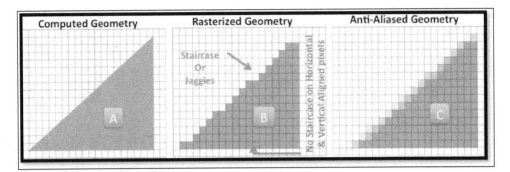

The anti-aliasing takes samples from nearby or background pixels and blends them with the color of the edge pixel to generate a smooth approximation such that it minimizes the stair-step case effect and makes the edges appear smooth.

Anti-aliasing can be caused from other various factors, such as specular highlights, shadows boundaries, geometry outlines, and so on, resulting in a rapid change in the color frequencies.

Anti-aliasing techniques can be categorized into two types: sampling rate and post processing techniques.

Understanding the sampling rate technique

In sampling rate technique, an increase in the amount of the sample rate in a pixel is used to decide the color of the pixel based on samples. This includes techniques, such as Super Sample Anti-aliasing (SSAA), Multi Sample Anti-aliasing (MSAA), Coverage Sampling Anti-aliasing (CSAA), which is usually driven on GPU hardware.

How to do it...

This section is a bit different from the rest of the *How to do it...* sections that we followed in the chapters. In this, we will discuss the various sampling rate techniques mentioned previously and the procedural difference between each of them. Let's discuss them in detail.

Super Sample Anti-aliasing (SSAA): This technique is also known as **Full-Scene Anti-Aliasing (FSAA)**. Here, the scene is first rendered to higher resolution and then downsampled to its original resolution by taking the average of its neighboring pixels. For example, if a given scene needs to be rendered to a resolution of 1920 x 1080, it's first rendered to a higher resolution of 3840 x 2160 on an off screen surface and downsampled. The off screen surface is four times bigger, resulting in 2 x 2 samples per pixels when downsized to its original resolution. The logic of FSAA is simple and results in fine quality, but it all comes at a very high computational cost because it requires all pixels to be available with the color and depth information per sample. This technique was available in early video cards and is no longer widely used in real time applications due to its tremendous computation cost.

Accumulation Buffer (**AA**): This technique is similar to the FSAA, but here the buffers are used with the same resolution and with more bits of color than the desired image. In order to produce the same 2 x 2 sample per pixel, four image buffers are created where each image view is moved half a pixel along the x or y axis as needed. These images are then summed up in the GPUs accumulation buffer and averaged to produce the anti-aliased output. The modern GPUs hardware does not have accumulation buffers. Instead, this can be performed using fragment shaders. The precision used in the pixel shader must be higher (10 to 16 bits per channel) to store the accumulated resultant color. The 8 bit precision may result in color banding artifact when blending is performed.

Multi-Sampling Anti-aliasing (**MSAA**): The large computational cost of SSAA results in the advent of MSAA. This technique produces lower acceptable quality, but it saves tremendous computation cost and has become the number one choice of GPU hardware vendors for a long time. Multisample takes more than one sample in the computation process for a given pixel in a single pass. There exists various pixel sampling schemes, as shown in the following image:

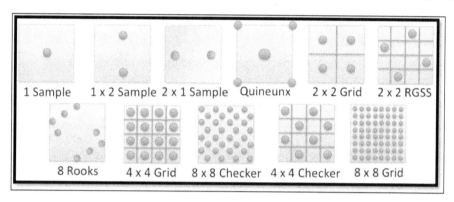

The sample rate may vary depending on the rate of the change in color frequencies. Cases such as shadows and geometry edges show a higher variation. Therefore, it requires more samples to process better results. The shading is computed from each fragment only once, which makes it faster than SSAA. For each sample, the corresponding color and depth information is stored separately.

The following image shows 1x and 4x sampling schemes. In the former case, the sampling position is not sufficient to overlap with the green triangle, thereby resulting in pixels that are colored in white. However, in the latter case, two out of four sampling locations are successfully in the geometry. Therefore, the interpolated resultant color falls in between these two colors, the extreme right-hand side image shows a shade bar of the 4x sampling scheme:

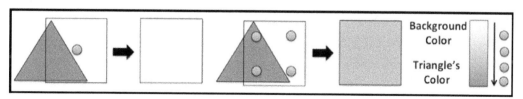

Coverage Sampling Anti-aliasing (CSAA): This technique is an improved version compared to MSAA. MSAA stores the color and depth information separately for each sample. However, this storage is unnecessary and can be completely avoided. The CSAA technique takes advantage of this drawback and avoids separate storages for the color and depth information; it uses an index-based approach. In this, each subpixel or sample stores an index to the fragment shader to which it's associated. All fragments are stored in a table format, which contains the color and depth information. Each fragment is identified by its unique index.

Understanding the post processing technique

In this type of technique, a scene is rendered to an off screen surface and processed with anti-aliasing algorithms. The process output is split up on the on screen surface. This type of anti-aliasing includes AMD's Morphological Filtering (MLAA), Fast Approximate Anti-aliasing (FXAA), Subpixel Morphological Anti-aliasing (SMAA), and so on.

How to do it...

In this, we will discuss the various post processing techniques mentioned earlier.

Fast Approximate Anti-aliasing (FXAA): FXAA is a post-processing filtering technique. This filter primarily does two things: it first detects edges and then applies the blurring algorithm to aliased edges. Like previous techniques, which are hardware dependent, FXAA can be highly useful for cases where anti-aliasing options are limited. FXAA gives very good performance. It's faster compared to MSAA and SSAA, making it a preferred choice for the gaming industry. This technique works in the image space. Therefore, it can be used in any case, such as the forward rendered image or the deferred rendered image:

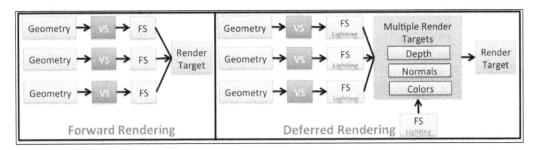

Forward rendering: This is the traditional path of the rendering execution model, where the geometry is first fed to the vertex shader followed by the fragment shader. Finally, the processed visual is rendered to the target. This whole procedure consists of four steps:

1. The geometry is computed.

2. Material characteristics, such as normals, bidirectional tangents, and so on, are defined.

3. The direction of the incident light is computed.

4. Object surfaces and light interactions are computed.

Deferred rendering: In the deferred rendering technique, the first two steps are separated from the last two steps, performing each of these in discrete stages of the rendering pipeline. Here, the scene is divided into two passes. The first pass is never used to perform any kind of shading. However, during this pass, the vital information required for shading is gathered (position, normals, material, and depth) in a set of textures and used in the second pass where the direct and indirect light information is computed to light the objects.

Implementing fast approximate anti-aliasing

There are two very important factors in anti-aliasing: performance and quality. A good anti-aliasing technique must be fast and should produce acceptable quality results. FXAA stands very positive on these aspects. It's faster compared to MSAA, which provides roughly 25 percent reduction in performance overhead compared to the SSAA technique. This works in the same resolution as the texture, which eliminates extra overhead similar to other techniques, where the texture has scaled to a higher resolution and then downsampled.

FXAA works on the specific details of an image; it systematically detects the stair-step case effect in the given image and blurs it out. Stair-steps are recognized with an edge detection algorithm. Therefore, the quality of edge detection and blurring algorithm are very important factors here. An incorrect algorithm may miss important edges or detect incorrect edges, which may produce an unpleasant quality after blurring.

Getting ready

In this recipe, we will implement the FXAA technique. Let's understand this implementation at a higher level.

The FXAA technique first renders a scene to an off screen surface using the **Frame Buffer Objects** (**FBO**). Like other screen space-based techniques, which operates a full scene, the FXAA technique can be run on selective areas that requires anti-aliasing. FXAA is implemented as a postprocessing shader. It detects edges in the rendered scene on the basis of the pixel luminosity. The detected edges are then smoothed out using their gradient. Both these processing are done under a single pass.

This recipe is like any other postprocessing recipe:

1. Create a FBO with the required dimensions.

2. Create a scene and render it to the FBO off screen surface.

3. Apply the FXAA technique in a single pass to the FBO-textured scene.

In this recipe, we will describe the third step, where we will implement the FXAA algorithm in the fragment shader. For more information on post screen techniques, refer to *Chapter 9, Postscreen Processing and Image Effects*.

How to do it...

The following code implements the FXAA technique algorithm in the fragment shader; this fragment shader operates on an off screen scene texture image:

```
#version 300 es
precision mediump float;

in vec2          TexCoord;       // Texture coordinates
uniform sampler2D   Tex1;        // FBO texture
uniform float       ScreenCoordX;  // X Screen Coordinate
uniform vec2        FBS;         // Frame Buffer Size
layout(location = 0) out vec4    outColor;

// Calculates the luminosity of a sample.
float FxaaLuma(vec3 rgb) {return rgb.y * (0.587/0.299) + rgb.x;}

void main() {
        float FXAA_SPAN_MAX    = 8.0;
    float FXAA_REDUCE_MUL   = 1.0/8.0;
    float FXAA_REDUCE_MIN   = 1.0/128.0;

    // Sample 4 texels including the middle one.
    // Since the texture is in UV coordinate system, the Y is
    // therefore, North direction is -ve and south is +ve.
    vec3 rgbNW = texture(Tex1,TexCoord+(vec2(-1.,-1.)/FBS)).xyz;
    vec3 rgbNE = texture(Tex1,TexCoord+(vec2(1.,-1.)/FBS)).xyz;
    vec3 rgbSW = texture(Tex1,TexCoord+(vec2(-1.,1.)/FBS)).xyz;
    vec3 rgbSE = texture(Tex1,TexCoord+(vec2(1.,1.)/FBS)).xyz;
    vec3 rgbM  = texture(Tex1,TexCoord).xyz;

    float lumaNW = FxaaLuma(rgbNW);    // Top-Left
    float lumaNE = FxaaLuma(rgbNE);    // Top-Right
    float lumaSW = FxaaLuma(rgbSW);    // Bottom-Left
    float lumaSE = FxaaLuma(rgbSE);    // Bottom-Right
```

```
    float lumaM   = FxaaLuma(rgbM);     // Middle

      // Get the edge direction, since the y components are inverted
      // be careful to invert the resultant x
       vec2 dir;
  dir.x = -((lumaNW + lumaNE) - (lumaSW + lumaSE));
  dir.y =  ((lumaNW + lumaSW) - (lumaNE + lumaSE));

      // Now, we know which direction to blur,
      // But far we need to blur in the direction?
      float dirReduce = max((lumaNW + lumaNE + lumaSW + lumaSE) *
      (0.25 * FXAA_REDUCE_MUL),FXAA_REDUCE_MIN);
      float rcpDirMin = 1.0/(min(abs(dir.x),abs(dir.y))+dirReduce);

      dir = min(vec2( FXAA_SPAN_MAX,  FXAA_SPAN_MAX), max(vec2(-
      FXAA_SPAN_MAX,-FXAA_SPAN_MAX), dir*rcpDirMin))/FBS;

      vec3 rgbA = (1.0/2.0)*(texture(Tex1, TexCoord.xy + dir *
      (1.0/3.0 - 0.5)).xyz + texture(Tex1, TexCoord.xy
      + dir * (2.0/3.0 - 0.5)).xyz);
      vec3 rgbB = rgbA * (1.0/2.0) + (1.0/4.0) * (texture(Tex1,
      TexCoord.xy + dir * (0.0/3.0 - 0.5)).xyz + texture
      (Tex1, TexCoord.xy + dir * (3.0/3.0 - 0.5)).xyz);

      float lumaB    = FxaaLuma(rgbB);
      float lumaMin   = min(lumaM, min(min(lumaNW, lumaNE),
      min(lumaSW, lumaSE)));
      float lumaMax    = max(lumaM, max(max(lumaNW, lumaNE),
      max(lumaSW, lumaSE)));

      if((lumaB < lumaMin) || (lumaB > lumaMax)){
        outColor = vec4(rgbA, 1.0);
      }else{
        outColor = vec4(rgbB, 1.0);
      }
  }
```

How it works...

The FXAA technique uses an interesting property of the human eye, which is luminosity or color brightness; our eyes are highly sensitive to it. Human eyes are very much capable of noticing the slightest change in luminosity. Detecting edges with color brightness works with almost all types of aliasing effect, such as specular or geometric aliasing. Luminosity or grayscale provides the brightness level in an image; it's helpful in detecting light and dark regions in the image space. The sharp transition in luminosity between two samples hints at the presence of an edge.

The FXAA filter implemented in this recipe takes five samplings around the current texel and analyzes these for the presence of an edge. The following image shows a triangle whose hypotenuse is suffering from the stair-step case effect (**A**). A certain section of its edge is processed with the FXAA filter to perform the anti-aliasing (**B**). This filter takes five samples and coverts them to luminous texels for edge-detection (**C**). This information is used by the blurring algorithm to blur the color intensity based on neighboring samples (**D**):

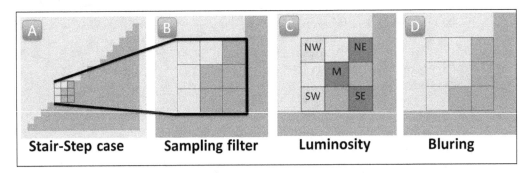

The `FBS` contains the size of the current off screen surface texture (FBO) and its reciprocal gives the dimension of a unit texel. This unit texel is added to the current texel (**M**) in various directions (top, bottom, left, and right) to produce new sampling texels **NW** (top-left), **NE** (top-right), **SW** (bottom-left), and SE (bottom-right) around the center texel (**M**). As the UV coordinate system has the inverted **Y** direction compared to the Cartesian coordinate system, we need to invert the North and South directions. As a result, you can see a negative sign for the north and south components:

```
vec3 rgbNW = texture(Tex1,TexCoord+(vec2(-1.,-1.)/FBS)).xyz;
vec3 rgbNE = texture(Tex1,TexCoord+(vec2( 1.,-1.)/FBS)).xyz;
vec3 rgbSW = texture(Tex1,TexCoord+(vec2(-1., 1.)/FBS)).xyz;
vec3 rgbSE = texture(Tex1,TexCoord+(vec2( 1., 1.)/FBS)).xyz;
vec3 rgbM  = texture(Tex1,TexCoord).xyz;
```

The FXAALuma function calculates the luminous weight for NW, NE, SW, SE and M samples as shown in the next image; these weights are used to find the direction of the blur.

```
float lumaNW = FxaaLuma(rgbNW);    // Top-Left
float lumaNE = FxaaLuma(rgbNE);    // Top-Right
float lumaSW = FxaaLuma(rgbSW);    // Bottom-Left
float lumaSE = FxaaLuma(rgbSE);    // Bottom-Right
float lumaM  = FxaaLuma(rgbM);     // Middle
```

The following image gives the formula to calculate the direction of the edge. If the result is a nonzero magnitude for the x and y component, an edge exists. As you can see, the directional formula determines the components of the edge direction along the x and y axis. Now, using this information, blurring can be performed in a specific direction:

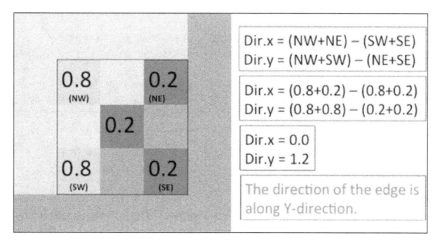

You may have noticed that the direction of x is inverted (negative). This is because the inverted signs used for north and south components are mentioned in the preceding code:

```
dir.x = -((lumaNW + lumaNE) - (lumaSW + lumaSE)); //Inverted
dir.y =  ((lumaNW + lumaSW) - (lumaNE + lumaSE));
```

We have got the direction. Now, we have to determine how far we should blur it in the given direction. In order to find the distance, we roughly normalized the direction vector in such a way that the smallest components become unity. For this, the magnitude of this direction vector (rcpDirMin) can be calculated taking the reciprocal of the smallest component directional vector. Now, the resultant is undefined if there occurs a divide by zero condition. For this, a delta component is added. We called this as reduced direction (dirReduce):

```
float rcpDirMin = 1.0/(min(abs(dir.x),abs(dir.y))+dirReduce);
```

The reduced direction calculation is pretty much easy; it's the maximum value of the product of the `FXAA_REDUCE_MUL` constant and the average value of all luminous intensities and the `FXAA_REDUCE_MIN` constant. These constants are very much dependent on the user observation. Therefore, it can be defined as uniforms to allow these experiments:

```
float dirReduce = max((lumaNW + lumaNE + lumaSW + lumaSE) *
                  (0.25 * FXAA_REDUCE_MUL),FXAA_REDUCE_MIN);
```

The unit directional vector can be calculated as `dir = dir * rcpDirMin`, but there is another problem here. What if the resultant product is very large. This will produce texels, which are far away from the current texel. We certainly don't want this because we are only interested in texels located nearby. So, we need to clamp the spanning of this resultant directional vector to some limited range using the following path. The `FXAA_SPAN_MAX` is a constant (8.0). The division of the result with FBS gives us the direction of the texture space for a unit texel in the UV direction:

```
dir = min(vec2( FXAA_SPAN_MAX,   FXAA_SPAN_MAX), max(vec2(-
              FXAA_SPAN_MAX,-FXAA_SPAN_MAX), dir*rcpDirMin))/FBS;
```

Now, we have the directional magnitude for blurring purposes. To perform the blur, take two samples along the same direction of the edge. The first sample, `rgbA` uses one-sixth of the forward (*dir * (2.0/3.0 - 0.5)*) and backward (*dir *(1.0/3.0 - 0.5)*) direction (*dir*) to calculate two samples from the `Tex1` texture. The resultant intensity is reduced by half:

```
vec3 rgbA = (1.0/2.0)*(texture(Tex1, TexCoord.xy + dir *
            (1.0/3.0 - 0.5)).xyz + texture(Tex1, TexCoord.xy
            + dir * (2.0/3.0 - 0.5)).xyz);
```

Similarly, the other sample, namely, `rgbB`, also comprises of two inner samples, which are half in the forward (*dir * (3.0/3.0 - 0.5)*) and backward (*dir * (0.0/3.0 - 0.5)*) direction from the current texel. Here, the resultant intensity is reduced by one-fourth and mixed with the resultant of `rgbA`. As the intensity of `rgbA` is already reduced by half, it's further reduced to one-fourth before mixing it with the resultant sampling vectors:

```
vec3 rgbB = rgbA * (1.0/2.0) + (1.0/4.0) * (texture(Tex1,
  TexCoord.xy + dir * (0.0/3.0 - 0.5)).xyz + texture
  (Tex1, TexCoord.xy + dir * (3.0/3.0 - 0.5)).xyz);
```

These two sample vectors (`rgbA` and `rgbB`) are used to perform a test to check if the sampled texture is too far. For this, we calculate the minimum and maximum luminosity from the given samples in `lumaMin` and `lumaMax`. Similarly, compute the luminosity for `lumaB` and store it in the `rgbB` variable:

```
float lumaB       = FxaaLuma(rgbB);
float lumaMin     = min(lumaM, min(min(lumaNW, lumaNE),
min(lumaSW, lumaSE)));
float lumaMax     = max(lumaM, max(max(lumaNW, lumaNE),
max(lumaSW, lumaSE)));
```

If the luminosity of `rgbB` is less than the minimum luminosity or greater than the maximum one, clearly, it's outside the expected range of the luminosity that we sampled. In this case, we will color the current fragment with `rgbA`, which is much closer to the sampled directed edge. On the other hand, if the luminosity range is within the expected range, use the `rgbB` color:

```
if((lumaB < lumaMin) || (lumaB > lumaMax)){
      outColor = vec4(rgbA, 1.0);
}else{
      outColor = vec4(rgbB, 1.0);
}
```

There's more...

In this section, we will discuss the advantages and disadvantage of using FXAA:

Advantages:

▸   FXAA is faster compared to MSAA and yet consumes less memory.

▸   This technique works in the image space as a filter. Therefore, it's easy to integrate it into the shader and does not require a highly computational cost.

▸   FXAA smoothens edges that are produced by alpha-blended textures and those resulted from fragment shader effects. It works on any technique, such as forward images or defer-rendered images.

▸   The cost of anti-aliasing is independent of the cost of rendering a scene. Therefore, the executional time for anti-aliasing a complex scene with millions of vertices and hundreds of texture is the same as a simple one, which contains a few hundred vertices with a handful of textures.

▸   The FXAA technique can be combined with other postprocessing filtering techniques. This will completely remove the extra cost of the anti-aliasing pass.

▸   If the information is available ahead of time to know which parts of the scene are going to be anti-aliased, using features, such as scissor testing, viewport information, the FXAA can be applied to selected regions.

Disadvantages:

- ▶ It requires a good quality edge detection algorithm; a poor quality algorithm may miss some of the edges that need to be aliased.

- ▶ Similarly, a good blurring algorithm needs to blur correct results.

- ▶ It does not handle the temporal anti-aliasing.

Temporal anti-aliasing causes the rendering objects to hop to appear to jump instead of giving an impression of smoothly moving objects towards them. The reason behind this kind of behavior is the rate at which the scene is sampled; the sampling rate is much lower compared to the transformation speed of objects in the scene. In order to avoid temporal anti-aliasing effects, the sampling rate of a scene must be at least twice as high as the fastest moving object.

See also

- ▶ Refer to the *Procedural texture shading with texture coordinates* recipe in *Chapter 6, Working with Shaders*

- ▶ Refer to the *Implementing render to texture with Frame Buffer Objects* recipe in *Chapter 7, Textures and Mapping Techniques*

Implementing adaptive anti-aliasing

The adaptive anti-aliasing mitigates the aliasing effects caused during the implementation of procedural shaders. As procedural shaders are programmed to produce dynamic textures, transition from the low to high frequency is very much known to the programmer, as they are the one to program it. For example, the polka dot recipe implementation generates dot patterns using a circle or sphere computational logic. It paints the fragment shader with one type of color if it falls inside the circle; otherwise, it uses the background color. In this case, the programmer knows very well that the transition from one color to another will be very sharp. This is where adaptive anti-aliasing is useful. It avoids such sharp color transitions by interpolating colors between two colors. These sharp transitions can be made smoother using many built-in shading language APIs, such as smooth, mix, and clamp.

In this recipe, we will produce an animated strip pattern and remove the aliasing effects on the strip edges by implementing an anti-aliasing procedural texture.

How to do it...

Use the following fragment shader to implement the adaptive anti-aliasing:

```
#version 300 es
precision mediump float;

// Reuse Phong shading light and material properties.
uniform float  Time;

// Flag to enable and disable Adaptive anti-aliasing
uniform int      EnableAdaptiveAA;

layout(location = 0) out vec4 FinalColor;

vec3 PhongShading{
    // Reuse Phong shading code.
}

in float objectY;
float Frequency = 6.0; // Controls number of stripes

// Reference: OpenGL Shading Language by Randi J Rost
void main() {
    if(gl_FragCoord.x < ScreenCoordX+1.0
            && gl_FragCoord.x > ScreenCoordX-1.0){
        FinalColor = vec4(1.0, 0.0, 0.0, 1.0);
        return;
    }

    float offset    = Time;

    // GENERATE fractional value 0.0, 0.1, ........, 0.9
    float sawtooth  = fract((objectY+offset) * Frequency);

    // Produce values in the range between [-1, 1]
    float triangle  = 2.0 * sawtooth - 1.0;

    // Produce continuous range from [ 1.0 ... 0.0 ... 1.0 ]
    triangle        = abs(triangle);
    float dp         = length(vec2 (dFdx(objectY+offset),
                                    dFdy(objectY+offset)));
```

```
float edge      = dp * Frequency * 4.0;
float square    = 0.0;

// Show the difference between aliased and anti-aliased.
if (gl_FragCoord.x < ScreenCoordX){
    square      = step(0.5, triangle);
}
else{
    square      = smoothstep(0.5-edge, 0.5 + edge, triangle);
}

FinalColor = vec4 (vec3 (square)*PhongShading(), 1.0);
}
```

How it works...

This recipe implements animated horizontal strip patterns. It uses the vertical component of object coordinates to produce this pattern. The object coordinates of the 3D mesh model on which the pattern is to be generated are passed on to the vertex shader, where it's shared with the fragment shader in the objectY variable. The vertical component of these object coordinates are added with the offset variable. The offset variable is a function of time. This animates the strip pattern by displacing it from its last position to some new position each time a new frame is rendered. These strip patterns will animate continuously from the top to bottom direction.

The Frequency variable controls the number of strips on an object. It is multiplied with object coordinates to scale its range. The fract() API of the shading language produces a decimal number ranging form 0.0 to 0.9, producing a pattern (**A**) that resembles a sawtooth. Multiplying these values with two and subtracting by one, we get a function that restricts the range between -1.0 and 1.0 (**B**). Finally, taking these absolute values produces a positive continuous range that varies from 1.0 to 1.0 (**C**), which are stored in the triangle variable:

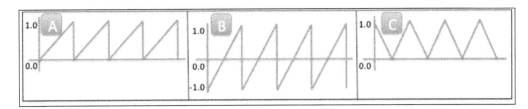

The strip pattern produces using the GLSL step API. This API returns 0.0 if the triangle is smaller than 0.5 and 1.0 if bigger, as show in the following figure (**D**):

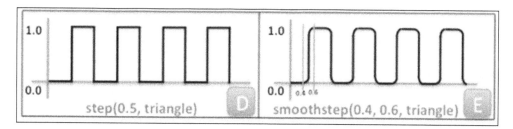

The output produced by the step API is shown in the following image (refer to the left-hand side of the red line). Clearly, aliased effects can be seen easily because output values switch from 0.0 to 1.0 and vice versa directly. This aliasing effect can be removed using an alternate API of GLSL called smoothstep. This API takes two parameters as an input value and performs the interpolation between the two. It avoids a sharp transition and interpolates a smooth range, as shown in the preceding image (**E**). Two input parameters in the smoothstep API are functions of the partial derivatives of the object coordinates along the x and y components:

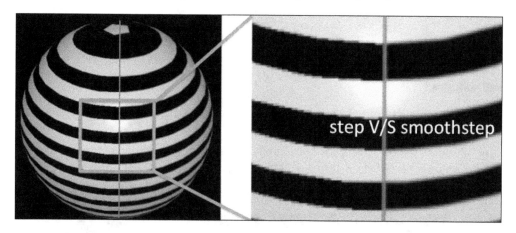

See also

▸ Refer to the *Procedural texture shading with texture coordinates* recipe in *Chapter 6, Working with Shaders*

▸ *Implementing an anti-aliased circle geometry*

Implementing an anti-aliased circle geometry

A circle is a very common geometric shape that is widely used across a variety of computer graphics application, such as rendering statistics with pie graphs, drawing sign boards, animating dot patterns, and so on. In this recipe, we will implement an antialiased circle geometry with the help of texture coordinates and make it smoother using the adaptive anti-aliasing technique from the previous recipe.

One way to implement the antialiased circle geometry is to generate a set of vertices along the circumference of the circle, where every two consecutive vertices are connected to the center vertex (origin), creating a triangular slice. Several such slices are required to create the skeleton of the circle, as shown in the following image. When these vertices are rendered with the triangle primitive, they produce a filled circle pattern. The smoothness of the produced circle shape is highly dependent on the number of vertices used along the circumference. The use of more vertices may degrade its performance as we try to achieve smoother edges along the circumference.

Advantages:

▸ As the circle geometry is represented with the vertices itself, the collision detection and pick test will be highly accurate.

Disadvantages:

▸ More and more vertices are required for smoother edges. Eventually, this comes at a cost of more performance overhead.

▸ By default, the edges of the circle are not anti-aliasing. Such geometric techniques may be very complex in terms of implementation.

▸ Changes in the dimension of the geometry may surface the aliased edges:

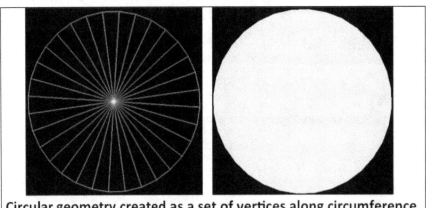

Circular geometry created as a set of vertices along circumference

In an alternate, we can use procedural shaders to produce circular geometries with the help of texture coordinates. One thing to note here is that the circle geometry produced in this technique is not a really a circle; it's a fake geometry that only comprises of four vertices. Irrespective of how big the circle is, it always uses the same number of vertices (4) to render a circle shape.

The basic principle of this technique is very simple. It uses four vertices to create a square and produces a perfect logical circle inscribed in it. Fragments that fall inside this circle are colored and the rest are masked by the alpha channel.

The circumference or edges of the circle are made smoother by processing it with the adaptive anti-aliasing technique. Here, a small portion along the circumference is interpolated from inside to outside to produce a smooth gradient.

Getting ready

Let's take a look at the high level implementation of this recipe:

1. Create a quad with vertices, as shown in the following image. The center of the quad must be at the origin (0.0, 0.0, 0.0).

2. Assign each vertex with a texture coordinate as follows. As per the texture coordinate convention, the origin always exists at the bottom-left part of the quad:

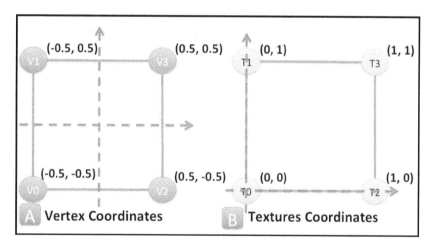

3. Specify the winding of vertices in an anticlockwise direction (**V0** > **V1** > **V2** > **V3**).

4. In the fragment shader, subtract each texture coordinate with a half vector along the UV direction. This will displace the origin from the bottom-left to the center of the quad.

5. Check each fragment distance from the displaced origin. If the current fragment is inside the outer radius range (say 0.5), then paint it with the required color; otherwise, alpha blend the fragment with the background color.

6. For anti-aliasing, take another radii called inner radius with a value smaller than the outer radii (say 0.4) and interpolate the color value based on the weight calculated from the position of the fragment texture coordinate inside the region between the inner and outer radii [0.4 0.5].

How to do it...

Here are the steps to understand the step-by-step implementation of this recipe:

1. Create a class called `Circle` in `Circle.h/.cpp`.

2. In the class constructor, define the vertex and texture coordinate in the vertices and `texCoords` variables respectively:

```
glm::vec2 texCoords[4] = {
    vec2(0.0f, 0.0f),vec2(0.0f, 1.0f),
    vec2(1.0f, 0.0f), vec2(1.0f, 1.0f)
};
memcpy(texCoordinates, texCoords, sizeof(glm::vec2)*4);

glm::vec3 tempVtx[4] = {
    vec3( -0.5f, -0.5f, 0.0f), vec3( -0.5f,  0.5f, 0.0f),
    vec3(  0.5f, -0.5f, 0.0f), vec3(  0.5f,  0.5f, 0.0f)
};
memcpy(vertices, tempVtx, sizeof(glm::vec3)*4);
```

3. Create the vertex shader file called `AACircleVertex.glsl`:

```
#version 300 es

// Vertex information
layout(location = 0) in vec3  VertexPosition;
layout(location = 1) in vec2  VertexTexCoord;

out vec2 TexCoord;

uniform mat4 ModelViewProjectMatrix;

void main( void ) {
    TexCoord = VertexTexCoord;
    gl_Position = ModelViewProjectMatrix *
                    vec4(VertexPosition,1.0);
}
```

4. Similarly, create `AACircleFragment.glsl` and add the following code:

```
#version 300 es
precision mediump float;
// Texture coordinates
in vec2 TexCoord;

uniform vec3        PaintColor;     // circle color
uniform float       InnerRadius;    // inside radius
uniform float       OuterRadius;    // outside radius
layout(location = 0) out vec4    outColor;

void main() {
    float weight = 0.0f;
    // Displace the texture coordinate wrt
    // hypothetical centered origin
    float dx      = TexCoord.x - 0.5;
    float dy      = TexCoord.y - 0.5;

    // Calculate the distance of this transformed
    // texture coordinate from Origin.
    float length = sqrt(dx * dx + dy * dy);

    // Calculate the weights
    weight = smoothstep(InnerRadius, OuterRadius, length );

    outColor = mix( vec4(PaintColor, 1.0),
                    vec4(PaintColor, 0.0), weight);
}
```

5. Define the scene in the `NativeTemplate.cpp`, as shown in the following code:

```
Renderer*        graphicsEngine; // Graphics Engine
Scene*           scene;          // Scene object
Circle*          circle;
Camera* camera;
bool GraphicsInit(){
    // Create rendering engine
    graphicsEngine  = new Renderer();

    // Create the scene
    scene = new Scene("MeshScene", graphicsEngine);

    // Create camera and added to the scene
```

```
        camera = new Camera("Camera1", scene);
        camera->SetClearBitFieldMask(GL_COLOR_BUFFER_BIT |
                                     GL_DEPTH_BUFFER_BIT);
        camera->SetPosition(glm::vec3 (0.00000, 0.0, 2.00000));
        camera->SetTarget(glm::vec3 (0.0, 0.0,0.0));

        // Create a new circle shape object
        circle = new Circle(scene, NULL, None);
        circle->SetName(std::string("My Circle"));

        scene->addModel(circle);
        graphicsEngine->initializeScenes();
        return true;
    }

    bool GraphicsResize( int width, int height ){
        // Create the view port
        camera->Viewport(0, 0, width, height);
        graphicsEngine->resize(width, height);
        return true;
    }

    bool GraphicsRender(){
        // Rotate the circle
        circle->Rotate(1.0, 1.0, 1.0, 1.0);
        graphicsEngine->render();
        return true;
    }
```

How it works...

This recipe mainly consists of two parts: the creation of the circle and smoothening the edges of the created circle. In the first part, the geometry is defined to create a base shape. The base shape is made up of four vertices to create a perfect square. These vertices are shared with the vertex shader to produce eye coordinates. Each of the vertex contains associated texture coordinates that are also passed on to the vertex shader and shared with the fragment shader. The fragment shader controls the shaded region of the perfect square in such a way that it appears as a perfect circle. All this is done using the texture coordinate manipulation. The following image shows the incoming texture coordinates mapped on the square geometry (**A**). As you can see, the origin in the first image appears in the bottom-left corner. This origin is logically moved to the center part of the square (**B**) by subtracting the texture coordinate with half the total dimension of the texture coordinate span in the UV direction.

This way, all texture coordinates get displaced with respect to the new origin in the center of the square:

```
float dx = TexCoord.x - 0.5;
float dy = TexCoord.y - 0.5;
```

The distance of the displaced texture coordinate is calculated and checked against the circle radii. If it's smaller than the given radii, it means that it's inside the circle and needs to be painted with `PaintColor`. The inner part will be colored with alpha 1.0 to appear solid. If the distance of the current fragment texture coordinate appears outside the given radius, then it's colored with alpha 0.0. This will make the outer part of the circle disappear:

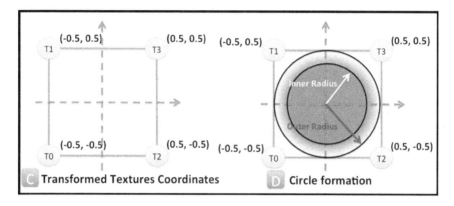

Transformed Textures Coordinates   **D** **Circle formation**

The second part of this technique makes the edges soft by processing it through adaptive anti-aliasing. For this, two radii (`InnerRadius` and `OuterRadius`) are used, as shown in the preceding image (**C**). Fragments that fall under the band of these two radii are interpolated for their color values on the basis of the weights obtained from the position of the texture coordinate in this band:

```
weight   = smoothstep( innerRadius, outerRadius, length );
outColor = mix( vec4(paintColor, 1.0),
                vec4(paintColor, 0.0), weight);
```

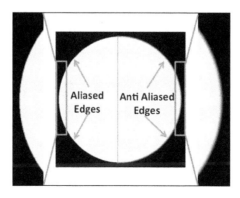

Aliased Edges   **Anti Aliased Edges**

This technique has some pros and cons:

Pros:

- ▶ This technique is highly performance efficient.
- ▶ This technique produces high quality circle shapes with smooth edges.
- ▶ Edge sharpness can be adjusted at runtime.
- ▶ The border of the circle can be rendered.
- ▶ Scaling does not effect the quality of the image. It can be adaptive.

Cons:

- ▶ This technique cannot perform the collision detection or pick test with high accuracy.
- ▶ This technique produces high quality shapes with smooth edges.

See also

- ▶ Refer to the *Creating a circular pattern and making them revolve* recipe in *Chapter 6, Working with Shaders*
- ▶ *Implementing adaptive anti-aliasing*

12
Real-time Shadows and Particle System

In this chapter, we will cover the following recipes:

- ▸ Creating shadows with shadow mapping
- ▸ Softening the shadow edges using PCF
- ▸ Using variance shadow mapping
- ▸ Simulating the particle system
- ▸ Transform feedback particle system with sync objects and fences

Introduction

Shadows play an important role in real-time rendering; they add depths to a rendering scene. The perceived light information on the 3D object looks much more realistic when rendered with shadows. Overall, shadows improve the realism of the rendering scene and provide a spatial relationship among objects. Rendering smooth and realistic shadows is a great topic of research in the field of computer graphics. The rendering process consumes a large performance. Therefore, the approach to render it must be a balanced trade-off between quality and performance. This even becomes more challenging on the embedded-side due to limited constraints on the memory and performance.

In this chapter, we will implement shadows using shadow mapping. This technique is relatively cheap as far as performance is considered and produces good results on embedded devices. We will make these shadows appear smoother using another technique called percentile closer filtering (PCF). In another technique called variance shadow mapping, we will improve the performance and quality of the generated real-time shadow.

This chapter will also help us understand the basics of particle rendering. We will implement two techniques to render the particle system. The first technique is bound to the CPU, whereas particles are updated and processed on the CPU-side and sent to the GPU only for rendering purposes. The second technique is implemented with a new feature of OpenGL ES 3.0 called transform feedback. This feature allows you to capture the vertex shader output to feedback again to the GPU for next frame rendering. The particle system is processed and rendered on the GPU-side. This way, it avoids the CPU intervention and makes the rendering process highly efficient.

Creating shadows with shadow mapping

In this recipe, we will bring more realism to scenes with shadows using a simple and widely accepted shadowing technique called shadow mapping to produce real-time shadows. This technique is called shadow mapping because it uses the depth information of the scene stored or mapped to a dynamically created depth buffer to produce real-time shadows.

This technique works in two passes:

- **First pass**: During the first pass, a scene is rendered from the perspective of light. Here, the scene is viewed from the position of light in the 3D space. In this way, it's clear to figure out what objects fall under the path of light. In other words, it provides the information of objects that are directly visible from the perspective of light. The scene's depth information is recorded in a FBO texture; this texture is called the shadow map. Certainly, if a light ray from the position of light passes through one or more objects, the object with the higher depth (behind the first object) from the perspective of light will be in the shadow. This technique heavily relies on the depth information captured in the shadow map; it stores the distance or depth of visible objects from the light position.

- **Second pass**: In the second pass, the scene is rendered from the intended camera position. Here, first the depth of each fragment is compared with the depth stored in the shadow map. This comparison checks whether or not the incoming fragment is under the light or not. If the fragment does not fall under the light, then fragment is colored with the ambient shadow color.

The following image shows the rendering of shadows as a result of the shadow mapping technique:

This section provides a high-level overview on how to implement shadow mapping:

- **Create cameras**: This creates two cameras, one is placed at the light source position called light camera and another is placed for normal scene rendering.

- **Shadow map**: This creates a FBO with depth texture, as we are only interested in recording the depth and do not require any color buffer here. The dimension of the depth texture is user-defined as per application requirements. In the current recipe, we have used dimensions similar to the render buffer, which is same as viewport dimensions.

- **Render from light's view**: This attaches the FBO as a current framebuffer and renders the scene from the perspective of light using the first pass and records the depth information in the shadow map. As we are only interested in the depth value, we can avoid the rasterization process in the first pass.

- **Render normal scene**: This again renders the scene, but this time from the normal camera view and shares the produced shadow map with the fragment shader during the second pass.

- **Vertex transformation**: During the second pass, vertex coordinates are transformed twice in the vertex shader to produce the following:

    - **Normal scene's eye coordinates**: The MVP matrix of the normal scene is used to produce eye coordinates to be used in `gl_position`.

    - **Eye coordinates from light's perspective**: Use the MVP matrix from the perspective of light (use light's camera) to produce eye coordinates, which is exactly the same as the one stored in the shadow map. These eye coordinates are called as shadow coordinates.

▶ **Homogeneous to texture coordinates**: Shadow coordinates are in the normalize coordinate system [-1, 1]. These are converted to the texture coordinate space [0, 1]. This is done by using premultiplied-based matrix in which a unit matrix is scaled by a factor of half and displaced by half-logical dimensions in the positive direction:

$$\begin{bmatrix} 0.5, 0.0, 0.0, 0.0, \\ 0.0, 0.5, 0.0, 0.0, \\ 0.0, 0.0, 0.5, 0.0, \\ 0.5, 0.5, 0.5, 1.0 \end{bmatrix}$$

▶ **Depth comparison**: This transformed shadow coordinate is shared with the fragment shader, where the current fragment determines whether it falls under the shadow or not using the `textureProj` API.

The following image on the left-hand side of the following image shows the rendering of the scene from the light's perspective, which produces the shadow map represented by the right-hand side image. The shadow map contains the depth information on a scale of 0.0 to 1.0. The values closer to 0.0 represents nearby objects. On the grayscale image, objects appearing darker are closer to the light camera:

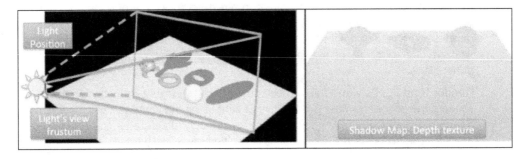

Getting ready

Unlike previous recipes, this recipe contains two custom classes for scene and model called `CustomScene` and `CustomModel`. The custom model contains other mesh models, which makes handling of model rendering very easy in the `NativeTemplate.cpp`. Similarly, the custom scene class simplifies the job of the scene, it's responsible for creating the shadow map, managing the light and normal view camera, and performing rendering in a two pass way.

This recipe uses Phong shading. There are two new uniform variables added: `LightCoordMatrix` and `ModelMatrix`. The former contains the product of the bias matrix, projection matrix and the view matrix from the perspective of light, whereas the latter contains model transformations. The product of these two variables are stored in `shadowCoord` and shared with the fragment shader. The `isLightPerspectivePass` uniform variable tells the fragment shader if it's in the first or second pass. The fragment shader contains the shadow map in `ShadowMap`.

How to do it...

Here are the steps to implement shadow mapping:

1. Make the following changes in the Phong vertex shader. Here, shadow coordinates are calculated in the `shadowCoord` variable:

```
// VERTEX SHADER - PhongVertex.glsl
// Reuse old code.. many lines skipped.
// Model View Project matrix
uniform mat4 LightCoordsMatrix, ModelViewMatrix,
NormalMatrix;
uniform mat4 ModelMatrix;

out vec3 normalCoord, eyeCoord;
out vec4 shadowCoord;

void main()
{
    normalCoord = NormalMatrix * Normal;
    eyeCoord    = vec3 ( ModelViewMatrix * VertexPosition );
    shadowCoord = LightCoordsMatrix
                       * ModelMatrix * VertexPosition;
    gl_Position = ModelViewProjectionMatrix *
    VertexPosition;
}
```

2. Similarly, implement the Phong fragment shader as follows. Here, fragments are colored based on their displace from the light and scene perspective:

```
// FRAGMENT SHADER - PhongFragment.glsl
// Many line skipped contain Material and light properties
in vec3  normalCoord, eyeCoord;
in vec4 shadowCoord;
uniform lowp sampler2DShadow ShadowMap;

layout(location = 0) out vec4 FinalColor;
```

```
    vec3 normalizeNormal, normalizeEyeCoord, normalizeLightVec,
    V, R, ambient, diffuse, specular;
    float sIntensity, cosAngle;
    uniform int isLightPerspectivePass;

    vec3 PhongShading(){ /* Reuse existing code */ }

    void main() {
        if(isLightPerspectivePass == 1){ return; }

        vec3 diffAndSpec = PhongShading();
        float shadow = textureProj(ShadowMap, shadowCoord);

        //If the fragment is in shadow, use ambient light
        FinalColor = vec4(diffAndSpec * shadow + ambient, 1.0);

        // Correct the Gamma configuration
        FinalColor = pow( FinalColor, vec4(1.0 / 2.2) );
        return;
    }
```

3. In the `CustomScene` function's constructor, create the shadow map buffer. For this, use the `FrameBufferObjectSurface` class to create an FBO with the depth texture. This is a high-level FBO class that encapsulates the creation of FBO:

```
CustomScene::CustomScene(std::string name, Object* parentObj)
            :Scene(name, parentObj){
    // Create the FBO
    fbo = new FrameBufferObjectSurface();

     // Generate the FBO ID
    fbo->GenerateFBO();

     depthTexture.generateTexture2D(GL_TEXTURE_2D, fbo->
       GetWidth(), fbo->GetHeight(), GL_DEPTH_COMPONENT32F,
       GL_FLOAT, GL_DEPTH_COMPONENT, 0, true, 0, 0,
       GL_CLAMP_TO_EDGE, GL_CLAMP_TO_EDGE,GL_NEAREST,
       GL_NEAREST );

    // Attached Depth Buffer
    fbo->AttachTexture(depthTexture, GL_DEPTH_ATTACHMENT);

    // Check the status of the FBO
```

```
    fbo->CheckFboStatus();
    lightPerspective = camera = NULL;
}
```

4. Initialize light and normal view cameras in the `initializeScene()` function:

```
void CustomScene::initializeScene(){
// Create camera view from lights perspective
lightPerspective = new Camera("lightPerspective", this);
    lightPerspective-
>SetClearBitFieldMask(GL_DEPTH_BUFFER_BIT);
    lightPerspective->SetPosition
                (vec3(this->lights.at(0)->position));
    lightPerspective->SetTarget(vec3 (0.0, 0.0,0.0));
    this->addCamera(lightPerspective);

    // Create scene's camera view.
    viewersPerspective = new Camera("Camera1", this);
    viewersPerspective->SetClearBitFieldMask
            (GL_COLOR_BUFFER_BIT | GL_DEPTH_BUFFER_BIT);
    viewersPerspective->SetPosition(vec3 (25.0, 25.0,25.0));
    viewersPerspective->SetTarget(vec3 (0.0, 0.0,0.0));
    this->addCamera(viewersPerspective);
    Scene::initializeScene(); // Call the base class.
}
```

5. Render the scene to the first pass using the perspective of light and the second pass as normal:

```
void CustomScene::render(){
    // Set Framebuffer to the FBO
    fbo->Push();

    // Render the scene from lights perspective
    lightPerspective->Render();

     // Cull the front faces to produce
    glEnable(GL_CULL_FACE);
    glCullFace(GL_FRONT);

    glEnable(GL_POLYGON_OFFSET_FILL);
    glPolygonOffset(2.5f, 20.0f);

    for( int i=0; i<models.size();  i++ ){
        currentModel = models.at(i);
```

```
            if(!currentModel){ continue; }

        // Set LIGHT PASS (PASS ONE) to True
        ((ObjLoader*)currentModel)->SetLightPass(true);
        currentModel->Render();
    }
    fbo->Pop();// Reset to previous framebuffer

    // Bind the texture unit 0 to depth texture of FBO
    glActiveTexture (GL_TEXTURE0);
    glBindTexture(GL_TEXTURE_2D, depthTexture.getTextureID());

    camera->Render();     // View the scene from camera
    glCullFace(GL_BACK); // Cull objects back face.
    glDisable(GL_POLYGON_OFFSET_FILL);

    for( int i=0; i<models.size();  i++ ){
        currentModel = models.at(i);
        if(!currentModel){ continue; }

        // PASS TWO => Normal scene rendering
        ((ObjLoader*)currentModel)->SetLightPass(!true);
        currentModel->Render();
    }
}
```

How it works...

In shadow mapping, a scene is constructed in the `CustomScene` class. This class creates an offscreen surface (FBO) to record the depth information of the scene. During the initialization (`InitializeScene`) phase, two camera objects are created (`lightPerspective` and `viewersPerspective`). The former camera is placed at the global light position from where the scene is lighted and the latter camera is placed at the viewer's position. The scene is rendered using two passes: one from the perspective of light and another from the perspective of a viewer. In order to let the rendering objects know about the current pass, the `ObjLoader::setLightPass` function is used; this function ensures that the object level states under these two passes.

The given scene is first rendered using the light's perspective pass, where it's bound to a FBO containing the depth buffer (depthTexture). The depth buffer captures the z-level or depth information of all rendering objects from the view generated by the camera placed in the light position. During this pass, front faces need to be culled and the polygon offset filling must be enabled in order to avoid the shadows acnes artefact. For more information, refer to *There's more...* section at the end of this recipe. In the vertex shader, eye coordinates positions are calculated in gl_position and captured in the depth buffer. This shader also contains calculations of shadow coordinates that are not necessary for the first pass and can be avoided. We consider this as an optimization and leave it to our reader to implement it. As the first pass only captures the depth information, any fragment shading operation will be unnecessary, therefore rasterization can be avoided here; we used a uniform variable (isLightPerspectivePass) to bypass rendering of the fragment shader. However, users can also use the glEnable (GL_RASTERIZER_DISCARD) API. This API turns off the rasterization process. For more information on the working of this API please refer to *Transform feedback particle system with sync objects and fences* recipe later in this chapter.

During the second pass, the viewer's camera is used to render the scene. This scene is rendered normally with back face culled and disabled polygon offset filling. The scene shares the captured depth information from the first pass to the fragment shader in the sampler2DShadow ShadowMap uniform variable.

> The sampler2DShadow is a special type of sampler. A sampler in a program represents a single texture of a specific type. The sampler2DShadow is used to represent the depth texture type, which contains the depth information of scene objects. It's very important to use the correct sampler; using a normal texture with the shadow map may give unpredictable results as the lookup function is different in this case. Each sampler has a different lookup function that is responsible for computing results based on input texture coordinates.

During this pass, normalize coordinates from the light (already contains projection and view info) are converted to the texture coordinate space using a premultiplied bias matrix, as mentioned in the introduction of this recipe. This coordinate is fed to the textureProj API, which performs a texture lookup with projection. Texture coordinates consumed from shadowCoord are in the texture coordinate form. In the textureProj API, these are converted to a homogenous form, where shadowCoord.xyz is divided by the last component, namely shadowCoord.w. The resulting third component (z) of shadowCoord in the shadow forms is used as the depth reference. After these values are computed, the texture lookup proceeds as in texture.

If the z value is greater than the value stored in the shadow map at a given position (x, y), the object is considered to be behind some surface. In this case, it renders to the shadow color (ambient); otherwise, it's rendered in the respective Phong shading.

There's more...

This section will describe some important aspects and limitations of shadow mapping.

The shadow map resolution

The quality of the shadow generated is highly dependent on the resolution of the texture to which the shadow map is constructed. The choice of the resolution depends on various factors. For example, a low-spec hardware may have limited memory or slow process power, choosing a high resolution shadow map may degrade the performance. In another case, the requirement is of higher quality in which only the high resolution shadow map makes sense. The following image shows the quality of shadows generated using various screen resolutions:

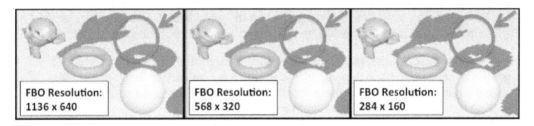

Aliasing affects

The shadow mapping technique suffers from an aliasing effect, which can be easily notified in various given images in this recipe. The reason for this aliasing is the sharp transition from the object color to ambient shadow color. There are various ways to reduce aliasing effects, such as increasing the resolution of the shadow map. See the preceding image. The quality of the shadow degrades as the resolution becomes low. The downside here is decrease in the performance as more samplings are taking place. The other effective and popular technique to fix aliasing artefacts is called **percentage closer filtering** (**PCF**). In this technique, edges soften by means of sampling. For more information, refer to the next recipe *Softening the shadow edges using PCF*.

Shadow acne

A very common problem that arises as a result of implementing the current technique is called shadow acne. The following image shows how the acne effect looks. This is caused when the first pass is executed with the back face culling enabled. The recorded depth texture stores the z value of the front face, which later when compared with the second pass produces large differences in depth values. These large differences are responsible for the shadow acne effect. This can be eliminated by rendering only back faces, which will result in more accurate depth comparison.

Therefore, the first pass must be performed using the front face culling. The depth texture formed using the front face culling in the first pass may still not be the same or close enough that are generated with the second pass. As a consequence of this, it results in rendering artefacts in which faces show the fade in and out effect. This visual unpleasantness can be eliminated by using the (glEnable(GL_POLYGON_OFFSET_FILL)) polygon offset. This polygon offset adds an appropriate offset (glPolygonOffset(2.5f, 20.0f)) to force resultant z values (in pass 1) to be closer enough (to pass 2) to mitigate the problem:

See also

▶ Refer to the *Phong shading – the per-vertex shading technique* recipe in *Chapter 5,
   Light and Materials*

▶ *Transform feedback particle system with sync objects and fences*

Softening the shadow edges using PCF

PCF stands for percentage-closer filtering. It is a well-known and simple technique to produce smooth shadow edges. The shadow mapping technique implemented in the previous recipe shows very sharp transitions among light and shadow pixels, thereby producing aliasing effects. The PCF technique averages these sharp transitions and results in smoother shadows. Unlike the other texture that provides the capability for texture filtering, which is basically a smoothening method to determine the color of a texture-mapped pixel, unfortunately, such filtering techniques cannot be applied to shadow mapping. Alternatively, multiple comparisons are made per pixels and averaged together.

As the PCF name depicts, it samples the shadow map using the current fragment and compares it with surrounding samples. The rule is to give more weightage to samples closer to the light source. In order words, it calculates the percentage of the area closer to the illuminated surface and not in the shadow. This is how the technique got its name.

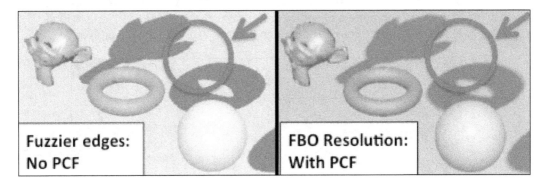

Fuzzier edges:
No PCF

FBO Resolution:
With PCF

Getting ready

For this recipe, we have reused the shadow mapping. The following steps provide a high-level overview on how to implement this recipe:

> **The prefiltered shadow map**: This shadow map needs to be prefiltered before using it in the PCF. Therefore, apply the linear texture filtering for texture minification and magnification. In the previous recipe, this corresponds to step two of the same section. This time, the 2D depth texture is created using the GL_LINEAR filter.

> **Depth comparison with PCF**: Shared transformed shadow coordinates in the fragment shader are used to produce multiple samples based on the filter size; multiple samples are always surrounded by the current fragment. Calculate the average result of all samples and use this value to scale the intensity of diffuse and specular components computed from Phong shading in the present recipe.

> **The filter size**: The choice of dimension of the kernel filter makes a great impact on the quality of the anti-aliased edge, but this comes at the cost of performance. Bigger the filter size, better the quality and slower will be the performance. For embedded platforms, the processing capability is a considerable factor. Therefore, based on our needs, the present recipe produces acceptable results with 2 x 2 filter (four samples).

How to do it...

As this technique is based on the shadow map, we will advise you to reuse previous recipes and add a few changes addressed in this section. Here are the steps to implement the shadow mapping source:

1. In the `CustomScene` constructor, create the depth texture with linear filtering this time; the last recipe uses the nearest option. This linear filtering samples depth values in an interpolated manner, which reduces the sharpness of the stored values based on the sampling of nearby depth samples:

```
// Inside CustomScene::CustomScene
fbo = new FrameBufferObjectSurface();
fbo->GenerateFBO();

// Generate the depth texture with linear filtering
depthTexture.generateTexture2D( GL_TEXTURE_2D,
    fbo->GetWidth(), fbo->GetHeight(),
    GL_DEPTH_COMPONENT32F, GL_FLOAT, GL_DEPTH_COMPONENT,
    0, true, 0, 0,GL_CLAMP_TO_EDGE, GL_CLAMP_TO_EDGE,
    GL_LINEAR, GL_LINEAR );

// Attached the Depth Buffer to FBO's depth attachment
fbo->AttachTexture(depthTexture, GL_DEPTH_ATTACHMENT);
```

2. Take the average of neighboring shadow coordinates. Make the following changes in the main function under `PhongFragment.glsl`:

```
// Many lines below skipped, please refer to the recipe code
void main() {
vec3 diff_Spec = PhongShading();

// APPLY the Percentage Closer filtering and use sum
// of the contributions from 4 texels around it
float sum = 0.0;
sum += textureProjOffset(ShadowMap, shadowCoord, ivec2(-1,-1));
sum += textureProjOffset(ShadowMap, shadowCoord, ivec2(-1,1));
sum += textureProjOffset(ShadowMap, shadowCoord, ivec2(1,1));
sum += textureProjOffset(ShadowMap, shadowCoord, ivec2(1,-1));

ambient    = MaterialAmbient  * LightAmbient;
```

```
// If the fragment is under shadow, use ambient light
FinalColor = vec4(diff_Spec * sum * 0.25+ ambient, 1.0);

// Correct the Gamma configuration
FinalColor = pow( FinalColor, vec4(1.0/2.2) );
}
```

How it works...

In the percentile close filtering technique for each incoming fragment, a set of samples are obtained from the filtering region. Each of these samples are projected to a shadow map with the reference depth to obtain binary depth results from the underlying lookup function. The shadow map texture contains the closest fragments from the light source. These depth comparisons are combined to compute the percentage of texels in the filtered region that are closer to the reference path. This percentage is used to attenuate the light.

See also

▸   *Using variance shadow mapping*

Using variance shadow mapping

In the previous recipe, we understood the implementation of PCF. It produces good quality soft shadows. The problem with PCF is that it requires more samples to produce better quality results. In addition, like standard textures, it's impossible to use prefiltered mipmapping to boost the process. Therefore, we must sample multiple texels to average out the resultant to compute the light attenuation on the current texel. The overall process to render the shadow can be slow.

Such drawbacks of PCF can be overcome by using variance shadow mapping. This technique relies on Chebyshev Probabilist Prediction, which makes use of mean and variation. The mean can be simply get from the shadow map texture and the (σ^2) variance can be calculated from the average value (**E(x)**) and the average square value (**E(x²)**):

Equation 1: $M_1 = E(x) = \int_{-\infty}^{x} xp(x)dx$ = average value over the filtered region

Equation 2: $M_2 = E(x^2) = \int_{-\infty}^{x} x^2 p(x)dx$ = average square value over filter region

Equation 3: $\sigma^2 = E(x^2) - E(x)^2$

Equation 4: $t = d - E(x)$, where d is depth of sample fragment

Equation 5: $P(x \geq t) \leq pmax(t) = \sigma^2 / (\sigma^2 + (t - E(x))^2)$, where x is random variable drawn from the distribution. P is the quantity which is exactly the same quantity we wish to compute in order to perform percentile close filtering.

Getting ready

To implement this recipe, we will reuse our first recipe on shadow mapping. The following guidelines will help you to understand the overall concept of variance shadow mapping:

1. Create the color buffer. In contrast to generic shadow mapping, this recipe uses the color buffer instead of the depth buffer. Therefore, the FBO now contains the color buffer instead of the depth buffer.

2. This is the pass one phase, where the depth of the scene will be recorded in the color buffer, which will store the **E(x)** and **E(x²)** values.

3. Compute variance and quantity. Use the preceding equation and calculate the variance and quantity for pass two.

How to do it...

In this recipe, we will create a new shader to record the depth information. Here are the steps to implement the shadow mapping source:

1. In the `CustomScene` class, define a new `Texture` variable called `colorTexture` for the color buffer. In the constructor, create a color buffer with a linear filtering of 16-bit floating precision. The format type must be in the RGB format:

```
// Inside CustomScene::CustomScene
fbo = new FrameBufferObjectSurface();
fbo->GenerateFBO();

// Generate the depth texture with linear filtering
colorTexture.generateTexture2D( GL_TEXTURE_2D,
    fbo->GetWidth(), fbo->GetHeight(),
    GL_RGB16F, GL_FLOAT, GL_RGB,
    0, true, 0, 0,GL_CLAMP_TO_EDGE, GL_CLAMP_TO_EDGE,
    GL_LINEAR, GL_LINEAR );

// Attached the Depth Buffer to FBO's depth attachment
fbo->AttachTexture(colorTexture, GL_COLOR_ATTACHMENT0);
```

2. Create a new vertex shader called `VSMDepthVertex.glsl` and share the computed vertex positions with the fragment shader:

```
#version 300 es
layout(location = 0) in vec4   VertexPosition;
uniform mat4    ModelViewProjectionMatrix;
```

```
out vec4    position;

void main(){
    gl_Position = ModelViewProjectionMatrix *
VertexPosition;
    position = gl_Position;
}
```

3. Similarly, create a fragment shader called `VSMDepthFragment.glsl` and store the depth square information in the first two coordinates of the output fragment:

```
#version 300 es
precision mediump float;
in vec4    position;
layout(location = 0) out vec4 FinalColor;

void main() {
    float depth = position.z / position.w ;
    //Homogenous to texture coordinate system ([-1,1]) to
[0,1]
    depth = depth * 0.5 + 0.5;

    float M1 = depth;           // Moment 1
    float M2 = depth * depth;   // Moment 2

    float dx = dFdx(depth);
    float dy = dFdy(depth);
    moment2 += 0.25*(dx*dx+dy*dy) ;


    FinalColor = vec4( moment1,moment2, 0.0, 0.0 );
}
```

4. Execute pass one and render the scene to FBO. This will use the preceding shaders and the depth value from the color buffer.

5. Modify the existing `PhongFragment.glsl` as follows. This time, instead of `sampler2DShadow`, we will use sample 2D as we will use the color buffer to store the depth information:

```
// Many line below skipped

in vec4    shadowCoord;

uniform sampler2D ShadowMap;
```

```
layout(location = 0) out vec4 FinalColor;


vec3 PhongShading(){ . . . }
vec4 homogenShadowCoords;

float chebyshevComputeQuantity( float distance){
    // Get the two moments M1 and M2 in moments.x
    // and moment.y respectively
    vec2 moments = texture(ShadowMap,
                    homogenShadowCoords.xy).rg;

    // Current fragment is ahead of the object surface,
    // therefore must be lighted
    if (distance <= moments.x)
        return 1.0 ;

    float E_x2 = moments.y;
    float Ex_2 = moments.x * moments.x;

    // Computer the variance
    float variance = E_x2 - (Ex_2);

    float t = distance - moments.x;
    float pMax = variance / (variance + t*t);

    return pMax;
}

void main() {
    vec3 diff_Spec = PhongShading();

    // Calculate the homogenous coordinates
    homogenShadowCoords = shadowCoord/shadowCoord.w;

    // Calculate the quantity
    float shadow = chebyshevComputeQuantity(
                        homogenShadowCoords.z);

    ambient     = MaterialAmbient  * LightAmbient;

    // If the fragment is in shadow, use ambient light
only.
```

```
        FinalColor = vec4(diff_Spec * shadow + ambient, 1.0);

        // Correct the Gamma configuration
        FinalColor = pow( FinalColor, vec4(1.0 / 2.2) );
        return;
    }
```

How it works...

The variance shadow mapping overcomes the limitation of PCF by providing the depth data in a form where it can be filtered linearly and can be used with algorithms and modern graphics hardware that support linear data. Like our first recipe, the overall algorithm is the same apart from the fact that now, we will use two component depth and its square to store it in the 16-bit precession color buffer. During the first pass, this color buffer stores the M1 and M2 moments sampled in the depth distribution of the filtered region. This computation takes place in the `VSMDepthFragment.glsl` fragment shader.

In the second pass, the color buffer is shared with the `phongFragment.glsl` fragment shader as a sample 2D uniform. Incoming shadow coordinates are converted to the homogenous form before performing any texture lookup. The z component of this transform coordinate gives the depth from the fragment from light's perspective. This depth value is used in the `chebyshevComputeQuantity` function to look up the texture. Lookup values are used to find the variance as per the previously mentioned equations, that is, equation 3. Finally, equation 5 is used to find the quantity that is exactly the same quantity we wish to compute in order to perform percentile close filtering. The returned quantity or weight value from this function is used to produce shadows as per the shadow mapping.

See also

- ▶ *Creating shadows with shadow mapping*
- ▶ *Softening the shadow edges using PCF*

Simulating the particle system

In computer graphics, the simulating particle system is a simulation of the natural phenomena, such as dust, smoke, rain, fireworks, and so on. This particle system contains large number of tiny particles, which can vary from few hundreds to millions in numbers. Each of the unit particles possess the same characteristics, such as velocity, color, lifespan, and so on. These particles are updated once every frame. During the update, the respective characteristics of particles are computed and updated. As a result, it makes them move or appear to change its color.

In this recipe, we will implement the particle systems. Each particle is made up of a quad and textured with translucent texture. Each particle possesses a specific color that changes with the update of time. Let's take an overview of this recipe to understand the implementation of the simulation of the particle system:

- ▶ **Define particle attributes**: This creates the data structure, which contains the important attributes of the vertex that includes particle position, color, and so on.

- ▶ **Particle geometry**: This defines the geometry of a single particle. It's represented by four vertices in the shape of a perfect square and contains respective texture coordinates. This particle object is used in conjunction with the view-projection matrix to produce several instances of particle in the 3D space.

- ▶ **Initialization**: This allocates the space for each particle's respective attribute and loads the texture. Compile the vertex and fragment shader.

- ▶ **Update**: This updates particles on each frame, calculates the new position of the particles and the remaining life of each, spawns new particle on each frame as the older particles dies

- ▶ **Render**: This renders the updated particles:

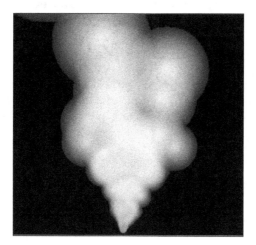

Getting ready...

This recipe uses the following data structures to manage particle properties and geometries:

- ▶ The Particle data structure:
    - ❏ pos: This represents the current particle position.
    - ❏ vel: This contains the current velocity of the particle.

        ❑   `life`: This represents the remaining life of the particle.

        ❑   `transform`: This contains the transformation information.

▸   The `Vertex` data structure:

        ❑   `pos`: This contains the vertex position in the 3D space.

        ❑   `texCoord`: This is the texture coordinate that corresponds to `pos`.

▸   The `MeshParticle` data structure:

        ❑   `vertices`: This contains the list of vertex objects.

        ❑   `vertexCount`: This represents the number of vertices in the list.

How to do it...

Here are the steps to implement the particle system:

1. Create a class called `ParticleSystem` derived from the `Model` class. In the constructor, load the texture image that needs to be textured on the particle quad surface. All the particles will share the same texture image:

    ```
    image = new PngImage();
    image->loadImage(fname);
    ```

2. Create the `ParticleVertex.glsl` vertex shader. This shader is responsible for updating vertice positions with the transformation information and sharing the remaining lifetime and texture coordinate information with the fragment shader:

    ```
    // ParticleVertex.glsl
    #version 300 es

    // Vertex information
    layout(location = 0) in vec3  position;
    layout(location = 1) in vec2  texcoord;

    uniform mat4 worldMatrix;
    uniform mat4 viewProjectionMatrix;
    uniform float lifeFactor;

    out vec2 texCoord;
    out float life;

    void main( void ) {
        texCoord          = texcoord;
    ```

```
    life              = lifeFactor;
    gl_Position       = viewProjectionMatrix*vec4(position,
1.0 );
}
```

3. Create the `ParticleFragment.glsl` fragment shader. This shader renders the textured quad. In addition, it uses a lifetime to control the opacity of the particle. The particle diminishes as it reaches its end:

```glsl
// ParticleFragment.glsl

#version 300 es
precision mediump float;

uniform sampler2D Tex1;
in vec2 texCoord;
in float life;

layout(location = 0) out vec4 outColor;

void main() {
    // directional light
    vec3 lightDir = normalize( vec3( 1.0, 1.0, 1.0 ) );
    // diffuse
    vec4 diffuseColor = vec4( 1, 1.0 - life, 0, 1 );
    vec4 texColor = texture( Tex1, texCoord );
    diffuseColor *= texColor;

    // final color
    vec4 color = vec4( 0.0, 0.0, 0.0, 1.0 );
    color.rgb = clamp( diffuseColor.rgb, 0.0, 1.0 );
    color.a = diffuseColor.a * life;

    // save it out
    outColor = vec4(texColor.xyz, 1.0);
    outColor = diffuseColor;
}
```

4. During the initialization of the particle system, compile and link the shader program using `DrawShader()`. Also, initialize particles with `InitParticles()`:

```
void ParticleSystem::InitModel(){
    DrawShader();       // Initialize the shader
    InitParticles();    // Initialize the particles
    Model::InitModel();// Call the base class
}
```

5. Implement the `DrawShader` function; this function compiles and links the shader. It loads necessary uniform variables from the vertex and fragment shader program:

```
void ParticleSystem::DrawShader(){

    // Load the shader file here, many lines skipped below
    . . . . . .

    // Use the compiled program
    glUseProgram( program->ProgramID );

    // Load the uniform variable from the shader files.
    TEX = GetUniform( program, (char *) "Tex1" );
    worldUniform = GetUniform(program,(char*)"worldMatrix");
    viewProjectionUniform = GetUniform( program,
    (char *) "viewProjectionMatrix" );
    life = GetUniform( program, (char *) "lifeFactor" );

    // Allocate the memory for Particle System. The
    // particle count are contained in the MAX_PARTICLES.
    particles = (Particle*)malloc(sizeof(Particle)*MAX_PARTICLES);

    // Start position of each particle (0.0, 0.0, 0.0)
    sourcePosition = glm::vec3(0.0, 0.0, 0.0);
}
```

6. The `InitParticles` function defines the geometry of particles. There is no need to create N number of geometries for N particles. We will create one and reuse it for all the particles. Additionally, this function also initializes all the particles. It provides random velocities to each particle, which varies from -2 to 2 units per microsecond in the horizontal direction and 4 to 8 in the vertical direction:

```
void ParticleSystem::InitParticles(){
    // define the type of mesh to use for the particles
    particleMesh        = CreateQuadrilateral();

    // define the type of mesh to use for the particles
    particleMesh        = CreateQuadrilateral();

    float lowestSpeed, highestSpeed, rangeSpeed;
    lowestSpeed = highestSpeed = rangeSpeed = 1.0f;

    for( ii = 0; ii < MAX_PARTICLES; ++ii ){
        Particle* p  = &particles[ ii ];
        p->transform = mat4();
        p->pos       = sourcePosition;
        p->life      = -1.0f;
        p->transform = translate(p->transform,p->pos);
        lowestSpeed  = -2.0;
        highestSpeed = 2.0f;
        rangeSpeed   = ( highestSpeed - lowestSpeed ) + 1;
        float f      = (float)(lowestSpeed + (rangeSpeed *
                            rand() / (RAND_MAX + 1.0f) ) );
        p->vel.x     = f;
        lowestSpeed  = 4.0;
        highestSpeed = 8.0f;
        rangeSpeed   = ( highestSpeed - lowestSpeed ) + 1;
        f            = (float)(lowestSpeed + (rangeSpeed *
                            rand() / (RAND_MAX + 1.0f) ) );
        p->vel.y     = f;
        p->vel.z     = 0;
    }
}
```

7. Define the geometry of the particle in the `CreateQuadrilateral` function:

```
MeshParticle* ParticleSystem::CreateQuadrilateral( void )
{
// Quadrilateral made of 2 triangle=>[0,1,2] & [0,2,3]
//   1-------0
//   |     / |
//   |   /   |
//   | /     |
//   2-------3

// Interleaved square vertices with position & tex
const Vertex quadVertices[] ={
// Triangle 1: Orientation [ 0, 1, 2 ]
{ {  1.0f,  1.0f,  0.0f }, { 1.0f, 1.0f } },
{ { -1.0f,  1.0f,  0.0f }, { 0.0f, 1.0f } },
{ { -1.0f, -1.0f,  0.0f }, { 0.0f, 0.0f } },

// Triangle 2: Orientation [ 0, 2, 3 ]
{ {  1.0f,  1.0f,  0.0f }, { 1.0f, 1.0f } },
{ { -1.0f, -1.0f,  0.0f }, { 0.0f, 0.0f } },
{ {  1.0f, -1.0f,  0.0f }, { 1.0f, 0.0f } },
};

// Allocate memory for particle geometry datastructure
const int Count    = 6;
MeshParticle* quad = ( MeshParticle* )malloc
( sizeof( MeshParticle ) );
quad->vertices     = (Vertex*)malloc(sizeof(Vertex) * Count);
memcpy( quad->vertices, quadVertices, Count*sizeof(Vertex) );
quad->vertexCount  = quadVertexCount;
return quad;
}
```

8. In the `Update()` function, calculate the relative difference between the current and last frame. This time, the difference is used by the `EmitParticles` function to update new position of a given particles based on its velocity:

```
void ParticleSystem::Update (){
    static clock_t lastTime = clock();
    clock_t currentTime     = clock();
    float deltaTime    = (currentTime - lastTime) /
```

```
                                (float)(CLOCKS_PER_SEC);
        lastTime            = currentTime;

        // update attribute for the particle emission
        EmitParticles( deltaTime );
        return;
    }
```

9. Implement the `EmitParticles()` function, as given in the following code. This function is responsible for updating particles. This function iterates each and every particle and updates its position and reduces the life span. As the life span of a particle becomes zero or less, it's considered to be dead. In the event of particles death, new particles are respawned:

```
void ParticleSystem::EmitParticles(float elapsedTime ){
    static float fRotation = 0.0f;
    if(fRotation>360.0){
        fRotation = 0.0;
    }

    int spawn    = 0;

    for(unsigned ii = 0; ii < MAX_PARTICLES; ++ii ){
        Particle* p = &particles[ ii ];

        // Living particles
        if(particle->life > 0.0f){
            unsigned int bIsEven = ( ( ii % 2 ) == 0 ) ? 1 : 0;
            particle->transform  = rotate( particle->transform,
            (bIsEven) ? fRotation : -fRotation, vec3(0.0,0.0,1.0));
            vec3 vel                = p->vel/100.0f * elapsedTime;
            p->pos                  = p->pos + vel;

            p->life             -= p->vel.y * elapsedTime;
            p->transform        = translate( p->transform, p->pos);
        }

        // Dead particles. Re-spawn more
        else{
            // Re-Spawn a max of 10 particles every frame
```

```
                    if( spawn++ > 10 ) { continue; }
                    particle->pos      = sourcePosition;
                    particle->life     = MAX_LIFE;
                    particle->transform = mat4();
                }

                float fScaleFactor = 1.0+(particle->pos.y * 0.25f);
                p->transform = scale(p->transform,
                    vec3( fScaleFactor, fScaleFactor, fScaleFactor ));
            }
        }
    }
```

10. Implement the `RenderParticles()`. This function first updates the particles before rendering:

```
void ParticleSystem::RenderParticles(){
    // Set the shader program
    glUseProgram( program->ProgramID );

    // All the particles are using the same texture, so it
    // only needs to be set once for all the particles
    glEnable(GL_BLEND);
    glBlendFunc(GL_SRC_ALPHA,GL_ONE_MINUS_SRC_ALPHA);
    glActiveTexture( GL_TEXTURE0 );
    if(image){
    glBindTexture( GL_TEXTURE_2D, image->getTextureID() );
    // Apply texture filter, below many lines are skipped...

    }

    glUniform1i( TEX, 0 );
    mat4 viewProj=*TransformObj->
                  TransformGetModelViewProjectionMatrix();

    // Loop through the particles
    unsigned int ii = 0;
    for( ii = 0; ii < MAX_PARTICLES; ++ii )
    {
        // Current particle
        Particle* p = &particles[ ii ];

        // Pointer to the particle mesh
```

```
MeshParticle* pMesh = particleMesh;

// Only draw the particle if it is alive
if( p->life > 0.0f ){
    // Set the particle transform uniform
    glUniformMatrix4fv( worldUniform, 1,
    GL_FALSE, ( const GLfloat* )&p->transform );

    // Set view and projection matrices
    glm::mat4 mvp = viewProj * p->transform ;
    glUniformMatrix4fv( viewProjectionUniform,
        1, GL_FALSE, ( const GLfloat* )&mvp );

    // Send the remaining life span.
    glUniform1f( life, p->life / MAX_LIFE );

    // Enable and Set the vertex attributes:-
    // position, texture coords
    glEnableVertexAttribArray( VERTEX_POSITION );
    glEnableVertexAttribArray( TEX_COORD );
    glVertexAttribPointer( VERTEX_POSITION, 3, GL_FLOAT,
    GL_FALSE, sizeof( Vertex ), &pMesh->vertices->pos );
    glVertexAttribPointer( TEX_COORD, 2, GL_FLOAT,
    GL_FALSE, sizeof( Vertex ),
    &pMesh->vertices->texCoord );

    glDrawArrays( GL_TRIANGLES, 0, pMesh->vertexCount );
    }
  }
}
```

How it works...

The `ParticleSystem` class manages the life cycle of the particle system. During the initialization of the program, each particle is given a specific position, velocity, life time, and color. The particles in the system are stored as an array format, forming a data pool. The CPU is responsible for updating the particle information and is sent across the updated information to the GPU to render them onscreen. This is not a very efficient mechanism because the CPU is very busy in processing particles and sending them to the GPU. In the next recipe, you will learn an efficient way of how to render the particle system with the transform feedback. Here, we will also implement particles using point sprites instead of treating them as textured quadrilaterals:

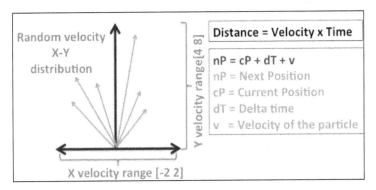

During the initialization process, all particles are distributed with random velocities along the X-Y direction in the range of [-2 2] and [4 8] respectively. The next position of the particle is updated by adding the current position with the product of the delta time (difference with respect to the last time the particle was updated) and its respective velocity. Blue arrows show the random distribution of velocity vectors in the 2D space.

Each particle's life span get condensed every time it's updated and finally reaches to its extinct point where the particles are no more active or visible onscreen. The dead particles still remains in the data pool and can be reinitiated again. This way, we reuse the same memory efficiently instead of allocating a new one. In this recipe, we respawn 10 particles in a go while rendering.

The size of particles are made to scale as they rise up in the Y direction. This information is gathered from the y component of the current position of the particle. We have used some adjustments in the code with some constants to control the scaling in a controlled manner mechanism. Finally, as the positions are updated and transformations are applied, particles can be sent to the GPU-side for rendering purposes.

See also

▶ Refer to *Applying texture with UV mapping* recipe *Chapter 7, Textures and Mapping Techniques*

Transform feedback particle system with sync objects and fences

The previous example of the particle system demonstrated that the animation of the particles with highly CPU bounded operations. Typically, the core parameters of the vertex, such as color, position, and velocity are always computed on the CPU-side. The vertex information flows in the forward direction. In this, the data information is always sent from the CPU to the GPU and is repeated for subsequent frames. This fashion incurs delays as one has to pay for the latency it takes from the CPU to the GPU.

However, it will be wonderful if the vertices got processed on the GPU and reused in the next frame. This is where the new OpenGL ES 3.0 feature called transform feedback comes into play. It's the process to capture the output from the vertex shader and feedback again to the GPU for the next frame. This way, it avoids the CPU intervention and makes the rendering efficient by vast GPU parallel processing. Typically, in this process, a VBO buffer acts as a special buffer and is connected to the vertex shader and collects the transformed primitives' vertices in it. In addition, we can also decide whether the primitives will continue their regular route to the rasterizer.

In this recipe, we will implement the particle system using the transform feedback feature where vertex parameters, such as velocity, life time, acceleration, and so on are computed on the vertex shader. The translated parameters are stored in the GPU memory and are fed to the next frame iteration. In addition, we will make it more efficient by using point sprites instead of quads.

This recipe also implements another new feature of OpenGL ES 3.0 called Sync Object and Fences. Fence is a mechanism by which an application informs the GPU to wait until a certain OpenGL ES specific operation is not completed. This way, the GPU can be prevented to pile up more operation into the command queues. A fence command can be inserted into the GL command stream like any other command. It needs to be associated with the sync object to be waited on. Sync objects are highly efficient as they allow you to wait on partial completion of GL commands.

Getting ready

This section provides a high-level overview on how to implement the particle system using the transform feedback:

1. There are two shaders required: Update and Draw. The former updates or processes the data for the particle emission and the latter uses the updated data to render particles.

2. At the initialization process, allocate two buffer objects to hold the particle data. It includes position, size, velocity, color, and life time. These buffers will be used in a ping-pong fashion, where one output of one buffer becomes the input of other in the next cycle or frame and vice versa.

3. While rendering, use one VBO as the input and the other as the output by bounding the former as `GL_ARRAY_BUFFER` and latter as `GL_TRANSFORM_FEEDBACK`.

4. Prohibits the drawing of fragments by disabling `GL_RASTERIZER_DISCARD`.

5. Executes the update shader with point primitives (`GL_POINTS`). Each particle is represented as a point. The vertex shader takes input from the first VBO and sends the processed data to the second VBO, which acts as a transform feedback output buffer.

6. This enables `GL_RASTERIZER_DISCARD` for fragments draw.

7. This uses the second VBO, which contains the processed data and sends it to draw shader by bounding as `GL_ARRAY_BUFFER`, render the particles.

8. Finally, once the frame is rendered, swap the two VBOs.

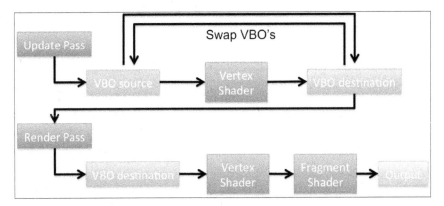

How to do it...

Here are the steps to implement the transform feedback recipe:

1. Create the update vertex shader called `TFUpdateVert.glsl` with the following code. This shader defines various attributes used for particle system; each attribute is given a specific location. This shader is responsible for receiving the attributes data and update them. The updated attributes are sent to the next stage using out variables:

```
#version 300 es
#define NUM_PARTICLES          200
#define ATTRIBUTE_POSITION     0
#define ATTRIBUTE_VELOCITY     1
#define ATTRIBUTE_SIZE         2
#define ATTRIBUTE_CURTIME      3
#define ATTRIBUTE_LIFETIME     4
```

```glsl
uniform float                time;
uniform float                emissionRate;
uniform mediump sampler3D    noiseTex;

layout(location = ATTRIBUTE_POSITION) in vec2    inPosition;
layout(location = ATTRIBUTE_VELOCITY) in vec2    inVelocity;
layout(location = ATTRIBUTE_SIZE) in float       inSize;
layout(location = ATTRIBUTE_CURTIME) in float    inCurrentTime;
layout(location = ATTRIBUTE_LIFETIME) in float   inLifeTime;

out vec2    position;
out vec2    velocity;
out float   size;
out float   currentTime;
out float   lifeTime;

float randomValue( inout float seed ){
    float vertexId    = float(gl_VertexID) /
float(NUM_PARTICLES);
    vec3 texCoord     = vec3( time, vertexId, seed );
    seed              += 0.41;//(.10/float( NUM_PARTICLES ));
    return texture( noiseTex, texCoord ).r;
}

void main(){
    float seed      = time;
    float lifetime  = (inCurrentTime - time)*10.0;
    if( lifetime <= 0.0 && randomValue(seed) < emissionRate )
    {
        position        = vec2( 0.0, -1.0 );
        velocity        = vec2( randomValue(seed) * 2.0 -
1.00,
                                randomValue(seed)  + 3.0 );
        size            = randomValue(seed) * 20.0;
        currentTime     = time;
        lifeTime        = 5.0;
    }
    else{
        position = inPosition; velocity   = inVelocity;
        size       = inSize;  currentTime = inCurrentTime;
        lifeTime = inLifeTime;
    }
    gl_Position = vec4( position, 0.0, 1.0 );
}
```

2. Create the update fragment shader called `TFUpdateFrag.glsl`. This shader is only a place holder for fragment shading so that the compilation of shader can be performed. This shader never comes into picture as the rasterization is turned off during the update:

```
#version 300 es
precision mediump float;
layout(location = 0) out vec4 fragColor;
void main(){
   fragColor = vec4(1.0);
}
```

3. Create a vertex shader called `TFDrawVert.glsl` for the render phase. This shader is responsible for rendering the updated data onscreen:

```
#version 300 es
#define ATTRIBUTE_POSITION        0
#define ATTRIBUTE_VELOCITY        1
#define ATTRIBUTE_SIZE            2
#define ATTRIBUTE_CURTIME         3
#define ATTRIBUTE_LIFETIME        4

layout(location = ATTRIBUTE_POSITION) in vec2    inPosition;
layout(location = ATTRIBUTE_VELOCITY) in vec2    inVelocity;
layout(location = ATTRIBUTE_SIZE) in float       inSize;
layout(location = ATTRIBUTE_CURTIME) in float    inCurrentTime;
layout(location = ATTRIBUTE_LIFETIME) in float   inLifeTime;

uniform float    time;
uniform vec2     acceleration;
uniform mat4     ModelViewProjectMatrix;

void main(){
   float deltaTime = (time - inCurrentTime)/10.0;
   if ( deltaTime <= inLifeTime ){
      vec2 velocity = inVelocity + deltaTime * acceleration;
      vec2 position = inPosition + deltaTime * velocity;
      gl_Position   = ModelViewProjectMatrix
                                  *vec4(position, 0.0, 1.0);
      gl_PointSize = inSize * ( 1.0 - deltaTime / inLifeTime );
   }
   else{
      gl_Position    = vec4( -1000, -1000, 0, 0 );
      gl_PointSize   = 0.0;
   }
}
}
```

4. Shade the fragment while rendering to `TFDrawFrag.glsl`:

```
#version 300 es
precision mediump float;
layout(location = 0) out vec4 fragColor;
uniform vec4 color;
uniform sampler2D tex;

void main(){
  vec4 texColor = texture( tex, gl_PointCoord );
  fragColor     = texColor * color;
}
```

5. Create `ParticleSystem.h/.cpp` derived from the `Model` base class and implement the `EmitShader()` function. This function will compile the `TFUpdateVert.glsl` and `TFUpdateFrag.glsl` shader files:

```
void ParticleSystem::EmitShader(){
program = ProgramManagerObj->ProgramLoad((char*) "TFEmit",
VERTEX_SHADER_PRG_EMIT, FRAGMENT_SHADER_PRG_EMIT);

glUseProgram( program->ProgramID );
emitProgramObject = program->ProgramID;

const char *feedbackVaryings[5] = { "position", "velocity",
"size", "currentTime", "lifeTime" };

// Set vertex shader outputs as transform feedback
glTransformFeedbackVaryings ( emitProgramObject, 5,
feedbackVaryings, GL_INTERLEAVED_ATTRIBS );

// Link program after calling glTransformFeedbackVaryings
glLinkProgram ( program );

emitTimeLoc = GetUniform(program,"time");
emitEmissionRateLoc = GetUniform( program, "emissionRate" );
emitNoiseSamplerLoc = GetUniform(program, "noiseTex" );
}
```

After the shader is compiled, specify the attribute that you want to capture in the transform feedback using the `glTransformFeedbackVaryings` API:

▶ **Syntax:**

```
void glTransformFeedbackVaryings(GLuint program,
GLsizei count, const char ** varyings, GLenum bufferMode);
```

Variable	Description
`program`	This is the handle of the program object.
`count`	This specifies the number of the vertex output variable used in the transform feedback process.
`varying`	This is an array of count zero-terminated strings that specifies the names of varying variables to be used for the transform feedback.
`bufferMode`	This specifies the mode under which vertex the output variable data is captured when the transform feedback is active. This variable can accept two enum: `GL_INTERLEAVED_ATTRIBS` or `GL_SEPARATE_ATTRIBS`. The former specifies how to capture the output variables in a single buffer. However, the latter captures each vertex variable output in its own buffer.

We are interested in capturing five vertex output variables: `position`, `velocity`, `size`, `currentTime`, and `lifeTime` in the transform feedback.

 The `glTransformFeedbackVarying` is always called before linking the program. Therefore, it's necessary to link the program object using `glLinkProgram`.

6. In the same file, implement the `DrawShader()` function. This function will compile `TFDrawVert.glsl` and `TFDrawFrag.glsl`:

```
void ParticleSystem::DrawShader(){
    program = ProgramManagerObj-
>ProgramLoad((char*)"TFDraw",
        VERTEX_SHADER_PRG_DRAW, FRAGMENT_SHADER_PRG_DRAW);
    glUseProgram( program->ProgramID );

    MVP = GetUniform( program, (char*)"ModelViewProjectMatrix");

    // Load the shaders and get a linked program object
    drawProgramObject = program->ProgramID;

    // Get the uniform locations
```

```
drawTimeLoc    = GetUniform(drawProgramObject,"time");
drawColorLoc   = GetUniform(drawProgramObject,"color");
drawAccelerationLoc = GetUniform(program, "acceleration");
samplerLoc = GetUniform (program, "tex");
}
```

7. Initialize the particle system in `ParticleSystem::InitParticles()`. This
   function initializes the array of particle object containing various particle properties.
   After initialization, these objects are stored in two different VBO buffer objects
   particle VBOs. These buffers are used by the transform feedback to update elements
   in VBOs in a ping-pong fashion, as mentioned in the preceding code:

```
void ParticleSystem::InitParticles(){

time        = 0.0f;
curSrcIndex = 0;
textureId   = image->getTextureID();

if(textureId <= 0){ return; }

// Create a 3D noise texture for random values
noiseTextureId = Create3DNoiseTexture ( 128, 50.0 );
Particle particleData[ NUM_PARTICLES ];

// Initialize particle data
for ( int i = 0; i < NUM_PARTICLES; i++ ){
   Particle *particle     = &particleData[i];
   particle->position[0]  = 0.0f;
   particle->position[1]  = 0.0f;
   particle->velocity[0]  = 0.0f;
   particle->velocity[1]  = 0.0f;
   particle->size         = 0.0f;
   particle->curtime      = 0.0f;
     particle->lifetime      = 0.0f;
}

// Create the particle VBOs
glGenBuffers ( 2, &particleVBOs[0] );

for ( int i = 0; i < 2; i++ ) {
glBindBuffer ( GL_ARRAY_BUFFER, particleVBOs[i] );
```

```
glBufferData ( GL_ARRAY_BUFFER, sizeof ( Particle ) *
NUM_PARTICLES, particleData, GL_DYNAMIC_COPY );
    }
  }
```

8. In `InitModel`, initialize the system as follows:

```
void ParticleSystem::InitModel(){
    UpdateShader();
    DrawShader();
    InitParticles();
    Model::InitModel();
    return;
}
```

9. Use the time and update the particle system in the `Emitparticles()` function:

```
void ParticleSystem::Update (){
static clock_t lastTime = clock();
clock_t currentTime      = clock();
float deltaTime          = (currentTime - lastTime)/
                           CLOCKS_PER_SEC*0.10;
lastTime                 = currentTime;
time                     += deltaTime;

EmitParticles ( deltaTime );
}
```

10. The `Emitparticles()` function flips the two VBO buffers each time the frame is rendered. This way, one VBO becomes the input (called source VBO) to the update shader. However, the other captures the processed output variables (called the destination VBO) and vice versa. Use the updated shader program and send the source VBO data and set up the destination VBO as the transform feedback buffer to capture results with the `glBindBuffer` API using `GL_TRANSFORM_FEEDBACK` and `glBindBufferBase` to bound to and index in the destination VBO.

During the update phase, we are only interested in computing the particle data. Therefore, we can disable the rasterization process:

```
void ParticleSystem::EmitParticles(float deltaTime ){
//UserData *userData = esContext->userData;
GLuint srcVBO = particleVBOs[ curSrcIndex ];
GLuint dstVBO = particleVBOs[ ( curSrcIndex + 1 ) % 2 ];

glUseProgram ( emitProgramObject );
```

```
    // transform feedback buffer
    SetupVertexAttributes ( srcVBO );

    // Set transform feedback buffer
    glBindBuffer(GL_TRANSFORM_FEEDBACK_BUFFER, dstVBO);
    glBindBufferBase (GL_TRANSFORM_FEEDBACK_BUFFER, 0, dstVBO);

    // Turn off rasterization - we are not drawing
    glEnable(GL_RASTERIZER_DISCARD);

    // Set uniforms
    glUniform1f(emitTimeLoc, time);
    glUniform1f(emitEmissionRateLoc, EMISSION_RATE);

    // Bind the 3D noise texture
    glActiveTexture(GL_TEXTURE0);
    glBindTexture(GL_TEXTURE_3D, noiseTextureId);
    glUniform1i(emitNoiseSamplerLoc, 0);

    // Emit particles using transform feedback
    glBeginTransformFeedback(GL_POINTS);
    glDrawArrays(GL_POINTS, 0, NUM_PARTICLES);
    glEndTransformFeedback();

    // Ensure transform feedback results are completed
    // before the draw that uses them.
    emitSync = glFenceSync(GL_SYNC_GPU_COMMANDS_COMPLETE, 0);

    //Allows fragment drawing
    glDisable ( GL_RASTERIZER_DISCARD );
    glUseProgram ( 0 );
    glBindBufferBase ( GL_TRANSFORM_FEEDBACK_BUFFER, 0, 0 );
    glBindBuffer ( GL_ARRAY_BUFFER, 0 );
    glBindTexture ( GL_TEXTURE_3D, 0 );

    // Ping pong the buffers
    curSrcIndex = ( curSrcIndex + 1 ) % 2;
}
```

The transform feedback can begin and end with the help of the following APIs syntax:

```
void glBeginTransformFeedback(GLenum primitiveMode);
void glEndTransformFeedback();
```

Variable	Description
`primitiveMode`	This specifies the type of the primitive that needs to be captured in the transform feedback attached buffer. The acceptable parameters are `GL_POINT`, `GL_LINES`, and `GL_TRIANGLES`.

It's very important to ensure that vertex output variables are written in the transform feedback attached buffers, so that the drawing command can use it safely. This requirement to ensure consistency between the update and drawing operation can be achieved by creating fences. A fence is created just after the transform feedback operation is activated. This fence is associated with a sync object, which waits in the rendering routine until the transform feedback operation is not completed.

11. The `RenderParticles()` function performs the drawing job. It waits for the sync object to ensure the successful completion of the transform feedback operation. Once done, the sync object is deleted and the drawing API are called to render the scene with the particle system:

```
void ParticleSystem::RenderParticles(){
    // Make sure that the GL server blocked until
    // transform feedback output is not captured.
    glWaitSync ( emitSync, 0, GL_TIMEOUT_IGNORED );
    glDeleteSync ( emitSync );
    glUseProgram(drawProgramObject);

    // Load the VBO and vertex attributes
    SetupVertexAttributes ( particleVBOs[ curSrcIndex ] );
    glUniformMatrix4fv( MVP, 1, GL_FALSE,(float*)
        TransformObj-
>TransformGetModelViewProjectionMatrix());

    glUniform1f ( drawTimeLoc, time );
    glUniform4f ( drawColorLoc, 1.0f, 1.0f, 1.0f, 1.0f );
    glUniform2f ( drawAccelerationLoc, 0.0f, ACCELERATION
);

    glEnable ( GL_BLEND );
    glBlendFunc ( GL_SRC_ALPHA, GL_ONE );
```

```
    // Bind the texture
    glActiveTexture ( GL_TEXTURE0 );
    glBindTexture ( GL_TEXTURE_2D, textureId );

    // Set the sampler texture unit to 0
    glUniform1i ( samplerLoc, 0 );
    glDrawArrays ( GL_POINTS, 0, NUM_PARTICLES );
}
```

How it works...

The transform feedback is a special stage in the OpenGL ES programmable pipeline. It exists right after the vertex shader, as shown in the following image. When the transform feedback is activated, it diverts the output from the vertex shader to the transform feedback. The transform feedback is registered with all the vertex output variables in which it needs to be captured. Data variables are captured in the special ping-pong VBO buffers:

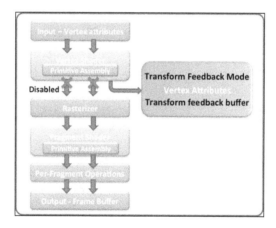

During the initialization process, two vertex buffer objects are created and set with the necessary particle data in it. These VBOs are attached to the transformed feedback and swapped with each frame. In this manner, one VBO contains the input data and captures processed variables and vice versa.

Each time the transform feedback is executed, a corresponding fence is created to acknowledge the completion of the transform feedback. This fence is associated with a sync object, which waits in the rendering function for the fence. When the fence is signaled, the wait is finished and the rendering commands are executed to render the particle system.

Particles are represented with GL_POINTS, where each point represents a tiny square. This command tells the GPU to draw each vertex as a square. The size of the point can be adjusted using gl_PointSize. Compared to the previous recipe, the sprite approach reduces the number of vertices required to represent a quad from four to one. A point sprite is a GPU built-in feature, where each point (representing a square) faces the camera. These can be textured with images without supplying texture coordinates explicitly, making it highly efficient for particle rendering.

See also

▸ Refer to the *Procedural texture shading with texture coordinates* recipe in *Chapter 6, Working with Shaders*

▸ Refer to the *Introduction* section in *Chapter 3, New features of OpenGL ES 3.0*

▸ Refer to the *Swizzling* recipe in *Appendix, Supplementary Information on OpenGL ES 3.0*

Supplementary Information on OpenGL ES 3.0

In this appendix, we will cover the following recipes:

- ▸ The fixed function and programmable pipeline architecture
- ▸ Software requirements for OpenGL ES 3.0 – Android ADT
- ▸ Developing Hello World Triangle application on Android Studio with OpenGL ES 3.0
- ▸ Software requirements for OpenGL ES 3.0 – iOS
- ▸ Opening a sample project in Android and iOS
- ▸ Application of the Lambert's cosine law
- ▸ Calculating cosine between two vectors
- ▸ Swizzling

The fixed function and programmable pipeline architecture

Before we dive into OpenGL ES programming, it's very important to understand how the underlying architecture is stacked. There are two types of OpenGL ES architectures: fixed and programmable pipelines. This section will provide you a simple overview of these architectures; this overview will also help us to grasp the technical jargon of computer graphics terminology.

Fixed pipeline architecture

The following image shows the OpenGL ES 1.1 fixed function pipeline architecture. It also provides the sequence of events from the moment input data is sent to the rendering engine to output an image generated on the screen.

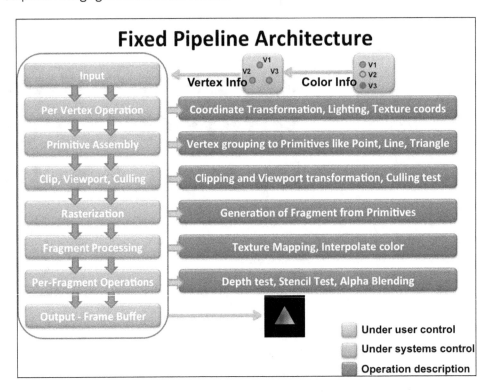

The **Input** refers to the supply of raw data and drawing information required by the rendering engine to draw an object on the screen. For example, the preceding image shows three vertices, and three color data are provided to the graphics engine as raw data. In addition, we specified the engine that will draw this raw data in the form of a triangle.

In **Per Vertex Operation**, transformations on input vertex coordinates are performed. Each geometrical input vertex is transformed on the basis of the camera view or object translation.

More specifically, at this stage, the modeling transformation is performed to convert object coordinates to world space coordinates. Further, these coordinates are converted to eye space coordinates by view transformation. Light information and texture coordinates are also calculated according to these transformations for all vertices. The second chapter, OpenGL ES 3.0 essentials, covers all the technical jargon that we have used for transformation in this section under *Transformation with the model, view, and projection analogies* recipe.

The **Primitive** assembly takes all the transformed coordinates from the previous stage and arranges them as per the specified draw or the primitive type (point, line, triangle) information provided at the input stage. For example, we supplied three vertices and instructed the engine to render them as a triangle. There are basically three types of primitives available in OpenGL ES: point, line, and triangle (also the variants of line and triangle). These basic three primitives can be used to render any complex geometry.

In the **Clip**, **Viewport**, and **Culling** stages, the projection transformation is applied to generate clip space coordinates. In this, vertices that are outside the camera viewing volume are discarded. The resultant vertex coordinates are treated with the perspective division where normalize device coordinates are generated. Finally, viewport transformation is applied to normalize device coordinates to form screen space pixel coordinates. Faces are culled on the basis of the direction of the face, as specified to the graphics engine.

Rasterization is the process of converting transformed screen space primitives (point, line, and triangle) to discrete elements called fragments. The output of each fragment are screen coordinates and related attributes, such as color, texture coordinates, depth, and stencil.

The fragment processing stage processes each fragment generated in the rasterization stage. This stage processes the fragment appearance information using the color or texture information.

The **per-fragment operations** stage performs some important tests before rendering images on screen. It consists of:

- **The pixel ownership test**: This is a test where pixel screen coordinates generated by the rasterization stage are tested to see whether they belong to the OpenGL ES context. For example, it may be possible that the rendering screen is overlaid with some text messages or obscured by other windows.

- **The scissor test**: This stage ensures that fragments that are present outside the rectangle formed by four values of the scissor rectangle region should not be considered in rendering.

- **The stencil and depth test**: This test checks the stencil and depth value to see whether the fragment needs to be discarded or not. For example, if two primitives are obscuring each other, the primitive fragment on top is kept by the OpenGL ES state. However, fragments belonging to the behind one will be discarded, irrespective of the rendering order.

- **Blending**: This is a process of generating new color information, using the previous color specified earlier in the same color buffer location.

- **Dithering**: This technique uses existing colors to create effects of other colors. For example, various shades of gray color can be produced using various patterns generated by white and black colors.

The programmable pipeline architecture

Unlike the fixed function pipeline, the programmable pipeline architecture provides the flexibility to modify some stages of the graphics pipeline. OpenGL ES 2.0 and 3.0 follows the programmable pipeline architecture. These stages are modified using special programs called shaders. The following image shows the programmable pipeline architecture for OpenGL ES 3.0. The architecture for 2.0 is also similar to the following image, except that it does not support a special stage called the Transform feedback. Transform feedback is a new stage introduced in OpenGL ES 3.0. This stage is responsible for capturing the processed vertex data buffer after the geometric shading stage. These programmable stages can be seen in the following figure with green boxes. Developers need to program the shader to render object using OpenGL ES 3.0.

The programmable pipeline architecture requires at least two shaders, namely, the vertex shader and the fragment shader to render geometry on screen. Without these shaders, rendering is not possible.

▶ The vertex shader is the first shader in the programmable pipeline architecture. Its responsibility is to perform processing on vertex coordinates to produce coordinate transformations. In most cases, it's used to calculate clipped coordinates from the model, view, and projection information. An example of the vertex shader is as follows:

```
#version 300 es
in vec4 VertexPosition;
void main() {
   gl_Position = VertexPosition;
};
```

▶ The fragment shader is the last shader that works on the pixel level; it uses the output data from the rasterization stage, which generates primitive fragments. This shader is responsible for calculating colors for each and every fragment rendering object on screen. The fragment shader is also capable of applying textures on the fragment shader. Here is an example of the fragment shader:

```
#version 300 es
precision mediump float;
out vec4 FragColor;
void main() {
   FragColor = vec4(0.0, 0.30, 0.60, 0.0);
};
```

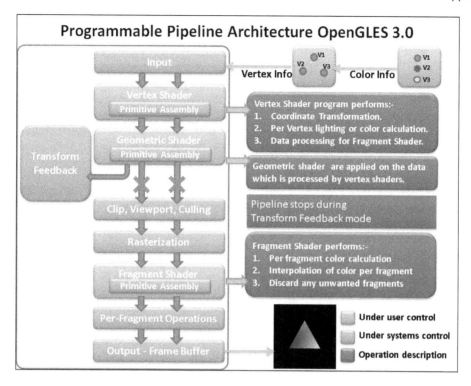

The programmable pipeline architecture needs a special type of language to program shaders. This language is called the OpenGL ES Shading Language. In this book, we will use specifications of OpenGL ES Shading Language 3.0.

Software requirements for OpenGL ES 3.0 – Android ADT

In the previous section, we have implemented the source code for our first simple program in OpenGL ES 3.0. We will use the same program to render the output on the Android and iOS platforms. This section will cover all the basic requirements that we need to develop OpenGL ES 3.0 applications on the Android platform.

Android is a Linux-based operating system; therefore, most of its development and configuration requires UNIX-based tools. This section discusses all the prerequisites for OpenGL ES 3.0's development on Android.

Android supports the OpenGL ES application development in two ways: the Java framework API and **Native Development Kit** (**NDK**). The Java framework APIs for OpenGL ES 3.0 focuses on the Java code style of development. Therefore, if you are developing an application purely in Java code, you can build the OpenGL ES 3.0 code within the Java-based application framework. In contrast, the NDK uses the C/C++ language to build the OpenGL ES 3.0 application. This is more suitable for developers who are interested to develop OpenGL ES applications in the C/C++ language. The additional benefit is that the same code can be used across different platforms, which support the C/C++ language, such as iOS, Blackberry, Windows, and so on. JNI works as an interface between the core Java application framework and the NDK C/C++ code.

This book focuses on the native development of the OpenGL ES application through NDK. We will also see the advantages of using NDK over Java framework APIs.

Getting ready

For Android development, you must ensure the following prerequisites are fulfilled on your machine (Window/Linux/Mac) before starting the development sessions. Download the following packages and proceed to the next section:

- **ADT bundle**: `https://developer.android.com/sdk/index.html`
- **Android NDK**: `http://developer.android.com/tools/sdk/ndk/index.html`
- **Cygwin**: `http://www.cygwin.com/install.html` (only for Windows users)

How to do it...

ADT bundle: Android Developer Tools (ADT) are a combo set of the Android software development kit. This provides us all necessary APIs, debugger, and test applications to build Android apps. It contains a variety of other tools that help us in profiling apps and provides an emulation support to run apps on an emulator.

Download the ADT bundle according to your operating system. The downloaded package will be in ZIP form; unzip it. This will extract a folder with the `adt-bundle-xxxxx` name. The name is dependent on the operating system and its version type: 32/64 bit.

This extracted ADT bundle contains the following important folders:

- **Eclipse folder**: This folder contains the Eclipse IDE, which is an integrated environment to develop Android applications. This special Eclipse lets users to quickly set up new Android projects, add framework packages, create UI, export `.apk`, and provide many more features.

- **SDK folder**: This folder contains tools to develop and debug your app; tools to support new features on the Android platform, sample apps, documentation, system images; and SDK dependent tools that are available when new platforms are released. For more information on the SDK, refer to `https://developer.android.com/sdk/exploring.html`.

 For the sake of better project management, keep your installation in the central location. We have created a folder called Android and extracted the ADT bundle within this folder. The folder name and location can be as per your personal choice.

- **JDK**: Depending on the ADT's requirements, you may need to update the Java Development kit. JDK contains tools to develop, debug, and monitor Java applications.

  Go to the previously mentioned URL and download the JDK. The minimum requirement is JDK 6.0. However, higher versions must be workable. Download the installer and install it on your machine. JDK automatically contains the **Java Runtime Environment** (**JRE**), which contains everything required to run Java applications on your system. Therefore, there is no need to install any other software package.

- **NDK**: The Native Development Kit is a toolset that helps to develop some parts of the Android application in the C/C++ language. It provides an interface between the Java and C++ code to communicate with each other. Download the latest NDK package and uncompress it into our Android folder.

- **Environment variables**: Make sure that you define the system environment variable path to locate your NDK, SDK, and platform tools. This will be helpful in running executables from command-line terminals. Additionally, we need to define `ANDROID_HOME` to locate the SDK folder in the ADT bundle. The following sample shows the definition of these environment variables in the `.bash_profile` file under the Mac operating system. Similarly, these need to be defined in other operating systems, according to their way of defining environment variables:

```
bash_profile
PATH=/usr/local/bin:/usr/local/sbin:$PATH

ANDROID_NDK=/Users/parmindersingh/Dev/Android/android-ndk-r9c
ANDROID_HOME=/Users/parmindersingh/Dev/Android/adt-bundle-mac/sdk

PATH=$ANDROID_NDK:$PATH
PATH=$ANDROID_HOME/tool:$ANDROID_HOME/platform-tools:$PATH
export ANDROID_HOME
```

▶ **Android SDK Manager**: In the ADT bundle folder, open Eclipse IDE and navigate to **Window | Android SDK Manager**. Install Android 4.3 and its related subcomponents, as shown in the following screenshot:

 For OpenGL ES 3.0, we need Android 4.3 (the Level 18 API) or higher versions.

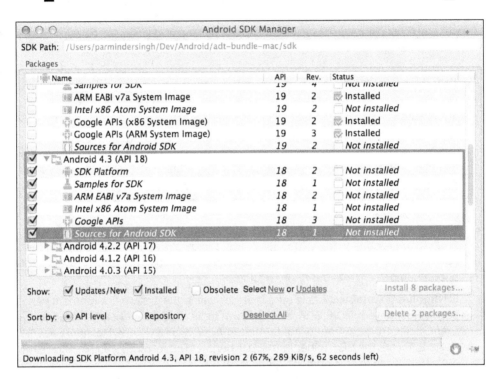

▶ **Cygwin**: Cygwin is a UNIX-based command-line terminal application that allows Windows users to compile and debug Unix-based applications.

1. Download the `setup.exe` from the URL mentioned in the previous section and execute it. This will open the installation interface for the app. Click on default selection on each window and click on the **Next** button until the list of packages needed to be installed does not appear.

2. Search for make and select **Devel/make**. Similarly, search shell, select Shells/bash, click on next and then click on **Finish**. This will install a Cygwin Terminal in your Windows program list. Make a shortcut on your desktop for quick launch. Refer to the following screenshot for assistance:

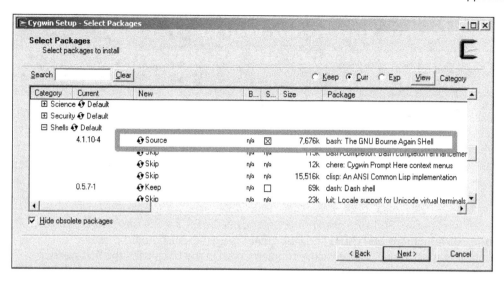

How it works...

The Android SDK provides a beautiful modular package that contains all required tools that are necessary to build an Android application. SDK and platform tools in conjunction with the SDK platform act as a backbone of the Android application development. These provide services to debug, manage, and deploy Android applications. They manage various Android platforms and related SDK APIs. This package also contains a customized eclipse for Android development; it helps to build the applications UI quickly. IDE provides special tools (such as the Android SDK Manager) that allow you to install new Android platforms and many other helper tools.

Android supports the development of some portions of its application in the C/C++ language. This kind of development is supported through the NDK tool; this tool offers an interface called Java Native Interface (JNI) that helps to set up communication between the Java framework and native code to communicate with each other. NDK needs a Unix-based command-line terminal to build C/C++ libraries. This command-line terminal is built in under UNIX-based operating systems. On Windows, it's provided by the Cygwin application. Developers build the code and export the native code functionality through libraries (.so/.dll/.a). The Android application uses these libraries in static or uses the shared form to integrate it into the application.

Developing the Hello World Triangle application on Android Studio with OpenGL ES 3.0

Android Studio is another new **Integrated Development Environment** (**IDE**) for the Android application development; the community is rapidly migrating to it. Unlike the other recipes in this book that are based on Android ADT, you can also use the Android studio to develop OpenGL ES 3.0 applications. It uses the Gradle build system to create scalable applications. The template-based wizard helps in designing common components and layouts quickly. This IDE has many other cool features to make the development quicker, robust, and reliable.

The previous recipe, *Software requirements for OpenGL ES 3.0 – Android ADT,* uses the **Android development tool** (**ADT**) and Eclipse ADT plugin to build Android-based OpenGL ES applications. All the recipes implemented in the book uses the ADT-based development system to program OpenGL ES 3.0 applications. However, we also want to provide an option to our readers to develop their recipes using Android Studio. Android Studio is very easy to use and set up. Unlike the ADT, it provides a rich interface and built-in support for NDK build. In this recipe, we will reuse the Android ADT-based first recipe: `HelloWorldTriangle` and create a new recipe using Android Studio.

Getting ready

Follow these steps to get and install Android Studio:

1. Go to `https://developer.android.com/sdk/installing/index.html?pkg=studio` to get the latest Android studio.

2. Download the latest SDK tools and platforms using the SDK Manager at `https://developer.android.com/tools/help/sdk-manager.html`.

3. You can learn to install the SDK package at `https://developer.android.com/sdk/installing/adding-packages.html`. For Android OpenGL ES 3.0, any API level greater than 18 will work completely fine.

4. Read the overview of the Android Studio at `https://developer.android.com/tools/studio/index.html` to know more about it.

5. Do not forget to set the Android SDK path; the setup will automatically ask you to provide the directory path for the Android SDK.

How to do it...

Follow the given steps to create the first Android Hello World application on Android Studio. I hope that after learning this, you can port the rest of the chapters recipe as per your need.

1. Create a new Android application project by navigating to **New | New Project**.

2. Set **Application name** as `HelloWorldTriangle` and **Company Domain** as `cookbook.gles`, as shown in the following screenshot:

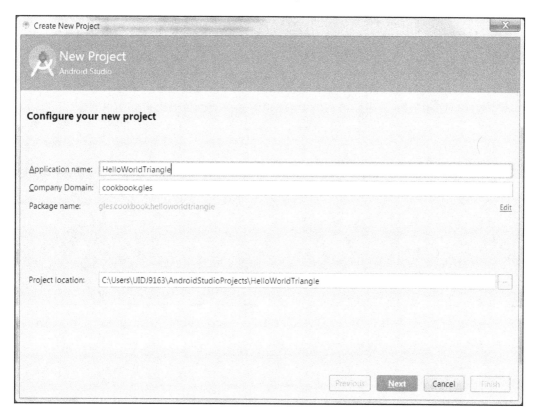

3. Select the target platform SDK's; we will use **API 18: Android 4.3 (Jelly Bean)**. Refer to the following screenshot for more information:

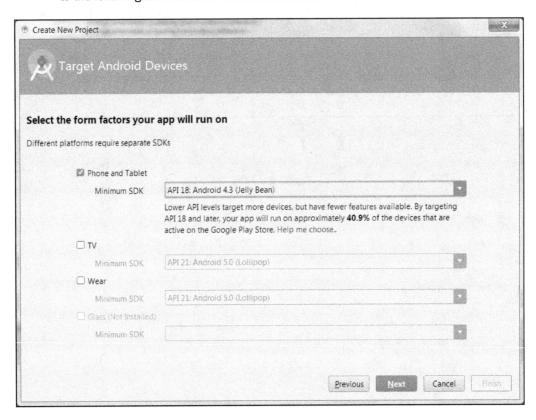

4. Create the **Blank Activity**, change **Activity Name** to GLESActivity, and click on **Finish**. This will create the project solution, as shown in the following screenshot:

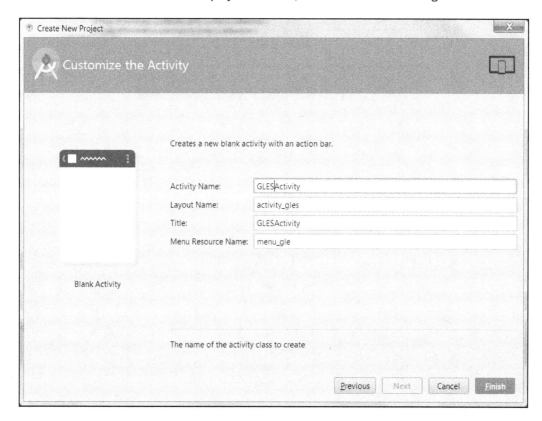

5. Select the current java folder or package name and select **File** | **New** | **Java Class**. Add two new classes called GLESView and GLESNativeLib.

6. Use the *Programming OpenGL ES 3.0 Hello World Triangle* recipe from *Chapter 1, OpenGL ES 3.0 on Android/iOS,* and copy its `JNI` folder to the `<ProjectLocation>\HelloWorldTriangle\app\src\main` location. This folder contains `Android.mk`, `Application.mk`, `NativeTemplate.h`, and `NativeTemplate.cpp`. The following screenshot shows the folder structure:

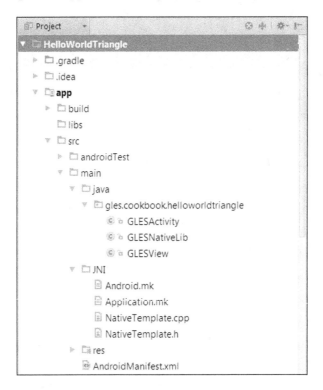

7. Similarly, use the *Programming OpenGL ES 3.0 Hello World Triangle* recipe from *Chapter 1, OpenGL ES 3.0 on Android/iOS,* and reuse the contents of `GLESActivity.java`, `GLESView.java`, and `GLESNativeLib.java` to the respective files of this project. Make sure that the package name should not be replaced because this project has different package name compared to the *Programming OpenGL ES 3.0 Hello World Triangle* recipe from *Chapter 1, OpenGL ES 3.0 in Android/iOS*. For more information, you can refer to the `HelloWorldTriangleAndroidStudio` example recipe provided with the sample code of this appendix.

8. Go to `NativeTemplate.h/.cpp` and correct the JNI interface declaration and definition. Replace the old package name with the new one. The following example shows the change we made in the `init()` function with respect to the new package name in the current recipe:

❑   The original declaration is as follows:

```
JNIEXPORT void JNICALL
Java_cookbook_gles_GLESNativeLib_init(JNIEnv * env, jobject
obj, jstring FilePath);
```

❑   The new declaration with the new package name is shown in the following
code:

```
JNIEXPORT void JNICALL
Java_gles_cookbook_helloworldtriangle_GLESNativeLib_init(JN
IEnv * env, jobject obj, jstring FilePath);
```

9.   Navigate to `Application.mk` and declare the build variant and version of the SDK
to be used for compilation. The `APP_ABI` tells the NDK compiler to build shared
libraries for every possible target. The `APP_PLATFORM` informs the compiler to use
a specified platform for compilation. For example, as we are using API level 18;
therefore, for OpenGL ES, the EGL and GLESv3 libraries will be referenced from the
platform API level 18:

```
//Application.mk
APP_ABI := all
APP_PLATFORM := android-18
```

10. Go to `build.gradle` present in the `<ProjectLocation>\HelloWorldTriangle
\app\build.gradle4` and make the following two changes:

❑   **The Module name**: This informs the native code module name to Gradle
system; this must be the same as the module name specified in the
`Android.mk`:

```
// Add the same module name present
// in the Android.mk file
ndk{
    moduleName "glNative"
}
```

❑   **The NDK external build**: This compiles the makefile manually using the
`ndk-build` command as we performed this for all other Android recipes. For
this, we need to inform the Gradle build system not to prebuild the NDK. The
`jni.srcDirs` tells the build system not to use the `ndk-build` command
from the Android Studio. The `jniLibs.srcDir` gives the location of the
build libraries for different targets using the external NDK compilation:

```
// Indicate the Android Studio not to use
// NDK from the IDE We will compile the
// project manually from Android.mk file.
sourceSets.main
        {
            jni.srcDirs = []
            jniLibs.srcDir 'src/main/libs'
        }
```

Refer to the following screenshot for the two changes we made in the
`build.gradle`:

```
apply plugin: 'com.android.application'

android {
    compileSdkVersion 22
    buildToolsVersion "22.0.1"

    defaultConfig {
        applicationId "gles.cookbook.helloworldtriangle"
        minSdkVersion 18
        targetSdkVersion 22
        versionCode 1
        versionName "1.0"

        // Add the same module name present in the Android.mk file
        ndk{
            moduleName "glNative"
        }
    }

    // Indicate the Android Studion not to use NDK from the IDE
    // We will compile the project manually from Android.mk file.
    sourceSets.main
        {
            jni.srcDirs = []
            jniLibs.srcDir 'src/main/libs'
        }

    buildTypes {...}
}
```

11. Open the command-line terminal. Navigate to the current `JNI` folder path and
    execute `ndk-build`. This command compiles source files and generates the shared
    library in the `<Project>\app\src\main\libs \<targetplatform>` folder path
    with the help of `Android.mk`.

12. After building the library, use Android Studio and click on the **Project Execute** button to view the output on the device or emulator. The following is the output of the Hello World Triangle:

How it works...

The working of this recipe is the same as we implemented in *Chapter 1, OpenGL ES 3.0 on Android/iOS* except the fact that we will now use Android Studio to build the project. Refer to the *Developing the Hello World Triangle application on Android Studio with OpenGL ES 3.0* recipe and look for the *How it works...* section. This section will provide the necessary details of the working of OpenGL ES along with Android Java and native interfaces for the OpenGL ES 3.0 application development.

See also

▸ Refer to the *Using JNI on Android to communicate with C/C++* and *Developing an Android OpenGL ES 3.0 application* recipes in *Chapter 1, OpenGL ES 3.0 on Android/iOS.*

Software requirements for OpenGL ES 3.0 – iOS

The specifications of OpenGL ES 3.0 are fully supported by iOS 7 and later versions. iPhone 5s, along with Apple's A7 GPU supports OpenGL ES 3.0 and the earlier version of OpenGL ES 2.0 and 1.1. Apple A7 GPU, provides the accessibility of all new features of OpenGL ES 3.0. It also has a larger pool of rendering resources. The shaders capability in 3.0 to access texture resource is twice as compared to OpenGL ES 2.0.

Getting ready

MAC provides the Xcode IDE for development of iOS applications, which targets iPhone, iPad, and iPod. The minimum requirements to support OpenGL ES 3.0 is version 5.0; all versions of Xcode beyond 5.0 supports iOS 7 build targets. This book will use the Xcode 5.2 version for its sample recipes.

How to do it...

OpenGL ES 3.0 is supported by the iOS 7 SDK on Xcode 5.0 and higher versions. The Xcode 5.0 version contains the iOS 7 SDK. If you are a new user, you can install it using your App store application. If you are using an older version of Xcode, you must update it to at least 5.0. The iOS 7 SDK and higher versions support OpenGL ES 3.0 through iOS 7 target devices.

How it works...

OpenGL ES 3.0 on the iOS7 with powerful GPU can perform sophisticated graphics rendering. The GPU is capable of high complex calculations in shaders for every pixel on the screen. OpenGL ES 3.0 is a C-based API seamlessly integrated into Object or C/C++. The OpenGL ES specification does not define the Windowing layer because the windowing mechanisms for all operating systems are very different from each other. Therefore, the underlying operating system is responsible for generating the rendering context to provide the windowing layer. In addition to this, the operating system must also provide a presentation layer where OpenGL ES can be rendered. iOS provides GLKit, which gives the presentation layer by providing the draw surface. GLKit was introduced in iOS 5 for the development of OpenGL ES. This is a 3D graphics development kit for OpenGL ES 2.0/3.0 using objective C/C++. This kit makes the programming job easier for the programmable pipeline architecture. For more information, refer to the Apple developer site at `https://developer.apple.com/library/ios/documentation/GLkit/Reference/GLKit_Collection/index.html`.

There's more...

GLKit is developed using the C/C++ objective language. This language is only supported in Mac and iOS-based applications. Therefore, if we want our code to be portable across platforms, we need to program it in C/C++. The Objective C language supports the C/C++ language seamlessly within its framework.

The game engines, which work beautifully across platforms, actually use their own platform-independent frameworks for OpenGL ES programming. These frameworks are similar to GLKit, or even more powerful. In our approach, we will develop our own engine from scratch in C/C++ in order to build an acceptable cross-platform 3D graphics framework for Android and iOS.

See also

Apple provides special references to develop OpenGL ES applications on iOS. These references cover various aspects of OpenGL ES with respect to iOS. For more information, visit `https://developer.apple.com/library/ios/documentation/3DDrawing/` `Conceptual/OpenGLES_ProgrammingGuide/Introduction/Introduction.html`.

Opening a sample project on Android ADT and iOS

Opening the sample source for the Android platform:

In the Eclipse ID, navigate to **New | Project | Android Project from Existing Code**. Click on **Next** and specify the path of the folder that contains `Android.xml`. Open the command-line terminal, change the directory path to the `JNI` folder, and execute the `ndk-build` command in the terminal. Launch application from Eclipse using **Run** or (*Ctrl + F11*) as the shortcut key.

 The path of the project should be the directory name that contains `Android.xml`.

Opening the sample source for the iOS platform:

Open the recipe folder and locate **<Project Name>.xcodeproj**, double-click on to open the project in the Xcode editor. Launch the application using **Product | Run** or (*Command + R*).

Application of the Lambert's cosine law

Let's understand how the cosine angle is calculated mathematically in order to implement Lambert's cosine law in our diffuse light shading recipe. The cosine angle between two vectors can be calculated using the dot product between them:

Dot product:

Dot product between the two vectors P (ai, bj, cz) and O (di, ej, fk) can be defined as the product of the magnitudes of the two vector and the cosine angle between them.

P.Q = |P| * |Q| *cos(θ)............Equation 1

Where |P| and |Q| are magnitude of P and Q, which can be calculated as:

$|P| = \sqrt{(a*a) + (b*b) + (c*c)}$ *and* $|Q| = \sqrt{(d*d) + (e*e) + (f*f)}$

Alternatively, it is the product of respective components along x, y and z components:

*P.Q = (ai, bj, cz) * (di, ej, fk) => (ai*di)+ (bi*ei) +(ci*fi)*

P.Q = (a*d)*(i*i) + (b*e)*(j*j) +(c*f)*(k*k) = ad + be + ef

P.Q = ad + be + ef............Equation 2

Equate Equation 1 and Equation 2:

ad + be + ef = |P|*|Q|*cos(θ)

If P and Q are units vectors, then Equation 1 can be deduced as:

P.Q = cos(θ)............Equation 3

We can also find the cosine angle by dividing |P|*|Q| both sides:

cos(θ) = (P.Q)/(|P|*|Q|)............Equation 4

Calculating cosine between two vectors

This is an illustration of how to calculate the cosine angle between two vectors formed by the **0**, **20**, and **0** points on a flat *x-z* plane surface and the light source situated at **20**, **20**, and **40**, as shown in the following figure:

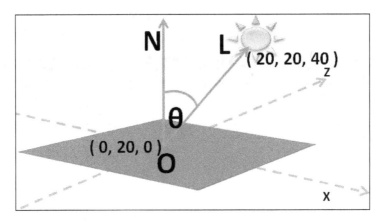

Calculate ON and OL vectors, as shown in the following code:

```
    OL = L - O = (20, 20, 40) - (0, 0, 0) => (20-0), (20-0), (40-0) =>
(20, 20, 40)
    ON = N - O = (0, 20, 0) - (0, 0, 0) => (0, 20, 0)
```

The dot product between OL and ON is as follows:

```
OL . ON = |OL| * |ON| * cos(θ)
```

Using *Equation 1*:

```
OL .ON = (20*0) + (20*20) + (40*0) = 400
```

Using *Equation 2*:

```
|OL|*|ON| = [√ (20*20) + (20*20) + (40*40)] * [ √ (0*0)
+(20*20)+(0*0)] = 979.79
```

Equating both equations, the result is shown in the following code:

```
400 = 979.79 * cos(θ);
```

Here, $\cos(\theta) = 0.40$ implies that the θ is 65.90 degrees.

Swizzling

Swizzling is a new GL shading language feature that allows you to rearrange components of a vector. For example:

```
vec4 A (1.0, 2.0, 3.0 , 4.0);
```

Here, vec4 is represented by the x, y, z, and w component. The result is as follows:

```
vec4 B = A.xxzz;
```

Now, B is equivalent to {1.0, 1.0, 2.0, 2.0}

Getting ready

The component access of the vec2/3/4s data type in the shading language can be considered either as vector, color, or texture coordinates or an array:

Form type	Components	Example: vec4(1.1, 2.2, 3.3, 4.4);
Vector	{x, y, z, w}	float a = v.x; float b= v.y;
Color	{r, g, b, a}	float a = v.r; float b= v.g;
Texture coordinates	{s, t, p, q}	float a = v.s; float b= v.t;
Array	[0, 1, 2, 3]	float a = v[0]; float b= v[1];

How to do it...

Swizzling is a mechanism of accessing a component directly using component names. For example:

```
vec4 v;
vec3 a = v.rgb;
vec3 a = vec3(v.r, v.g, v.b); // same thing as above
vec3 b = v.gbr;
vec4 c = v.wzxy;
vec2 d = v.ra;              // red,alpha
vec4 f = v.xxyy;           // ok to duplicate components
vec3 e = v.rgz;            // Incorrect. can't mix different component sets

vec2 u(1.0,2.0);
v = u.xyz;                 // Incorrect, vec2 doesn't have z
```

There's more...

In preceding cases, swizzling occurs on the right-hand side of assignments. However, swizzling may occur on the left-hand side of assignments as well:

```
vec4 u(1.0, 2.0, 3.0, 4.0);
u.xw = vec2(5.0, 6.0);     // u = (5.0, 2.0, 4.0, 6.0)
vec3 v(1.0, 2.0, 3.0);
v.xyz = v.yxz;             // v = (3.0, 2.0, 1.0)
v.xx = vec2(1.0, 2.0);     // Incorrect. Can't duplicate in l-value
v.rgb = vec2(1.0);         // Incorrect. Mismatch vec3,vec2
v.rgxy = vec4(...);        // Incorrect. mixing sets
```

Index

Thank you for buying
OpenGL ES 3.0 Cookbook

About Packt Publishing

Packt, pronounced 'packed', published its first book, *Mastering phpMyAdmin for Effective MySQL Management*, in April 2004, and subsequently continued to specialize in publishing highly focused books on specific technologies and solutions.

Our books and publications share the experiences of your fellow IT professionals in adapting and customizing today's systems, applications, and frameworks. Our solution-based books give you the knowledge and power to customize the software and technologies you're using to get the job done. Packt books are more specific and less general than the IT books you have seen in the past. Our unique business model allows us to bring you more focused information, giving you more of what you need to know, and less of what you don't.

Packt is a modern yet unique publishing company that focuses on producing quality, cutting-edge books for communities of developers, administrators, and newbies alike. For more information, please visit our website at www.packtpub.com.

Writing for Packt

We welcome all inquiries from people who are interested in authoring. Book proposals should be sent to author@packtpub.com. If your book idea is still at an early stage and you would like to discuss it first before writing a formal book proposal, then please contact us; one of our commissioning editors will get in touch with you.

We're not just looking for published authors; if you have strong technical skills but no writing experience, our experienced editors can help you develop a writing career, or simply get some additional reward for your expertise.

GLSL Essentials

ISBN: 978-1-84969-800-9   Paperback: 116 pages

Enrich your 3D scenes with the power of GLSL!

1. Learn about shaders in a step-by-step, interactive manner.

2. Create stunning visual effects using vertex and fragment shaders.

3. Simplify your CPU code and improve your overall performance with instanced drawing through the use of geometry shaders.

Less Web Development Essentials

ISBN: 978-1-78398-146-5   Paperback: 202 pages

Use CSS preprocessing to streamline the development and maintenance of your web applications

1. Produce clear, concise, and well-constructed code that compiles into standard compliant CSS.

2. Explore the core attributes of Less and learn how to integrate them into your site.

3. Optimize Twitter's Bootstrap to efficiently develop web apps and sites.

Please check **www.PacktPub.com** for information on our titles

OpenVZ Essentials

ISBN: 978-1-78216-732-7   Paperback: 110 pages

Create and administer virtualized containers on your server using the robust OpenVZ

1. Manage a multiple-server infrastructure with OpenVZ.

2. Explore OpenVZ Web Panel and utilize server templates.

3. Step-by-step guide that will help you to successfully install, configure, and manage virtualized containers using OpenVZ.

OpenCV Computer Vision Application Programming Cookbook

Second Edition

ISBN: 978-1-78216-148-6   Paperback: 374 pages

Over 50 recipes to help you build computer vision applications in C++ using the OpenCV library

1. Master OpenCV, the open source library of the computer vision community.

2. Master fundamental concepts in computer vision and image processing.

3. Learn the important classes and functions of OpenCV with complete working examples applied on real images.

Please check **www.PacktPub.com** for information on our titles